INTERMEDIAT
A GRAMMAR AND WORKBOOK

Intermediate Persian: A Grammar and Workbook comprises an accessible grammar and related exercises in a single volume. Each of the fourteen units deals with a particular grammatical point and provides associated exercises to help learners reinforce and consolidate their knowledge. There are additionally four appendices covering colloquial, polite, literary and journalistic styles.

Features include:

- a clear, accessible format
- many useful language examples
- clear, jargon-free explanations of grammar
- abundant exercises with full answer key
- units covering different levels of language
- a glossary of Persian–English terms that includes all Persian simple verbs and their roots
- a subject index

Intermediate Persian reviews many of the principal elements presented in its sister volume, *Basic Persian*, and introduces more advanced features and structures of the language. The two books form a compendium of the essentials of Persian grammar.

User-friendly and engaging, *Intermediate Persian* is suitable for both class use and independent study, making it an ideal grammar reference and practice resource for students and learners with some knowledge of the language.

Saeed Yousef is Senior Lecturer of Persian at the University of Chicago, USA. He is also a poet and has published books of literary criticism and translations.

Hayedeh Torabi was a Lecturer of Persian at the University of Chicago, USA. She is a published writer, essayist and translator.

Other titles available in the Grammar Workbooks series are:

Basic Cantonese
Intermediate Cantonese

Basic Chinese
Intermediate Chinese

Basic German
Intermediate German

Basic Irish
Intermediate Irish

Basic Italian

Basic Japanese
Intermediate Japanese

Basic Korean
Intermediate Korean

Basic Persian

Basic Polish
Intermediate Polish

Basic Russian
Intermediate Russian

Basic Spanish
Intermediate Spanish

Basic Welsh
Intermediate Welsh

Basic Yiddish

INTERMEDIATE PERSIAN: A GRAMMAR AND WORKBOOK

Saeed Yousef
Assisted by Hayedeh Torabi

Routledge
Taylor & Francis Group

LONDON AND NEW YORK

First published 2014 by Routledge

Published 2015 by Routledge
2 Park Square, Milton Park, Abingdon, Oxon OX14 4RN

Simultaneously published in the USA and Canada
by Routledge
711 Third Avenue, New York, NY 10017 USA

Routledge is an imprint of the Taylor & Francis Group, an informa business

British Library Cataloguing in Publication Data
A catalogue record for this book is available from the British Library

Library of Congress Cataloging in Publication Data
A catalog record for this book has been requested

ISBN: 978-0-415-61653-9 (hbk)
ISBN: 978-0-415-61655-3 (pbk)
ISBN: 978-0-203-75946-2 (ebk)

Typeset in Times Ten and B Lotus
by Graphicraft Limited, Hong Kong

Printed and bound in the United States of America
By Edwards Brothers Malloy on sustainably sourced paper.

CONTENTS

INTRODUCTION

This book is the follow-up to *Basic Persian*. While introducing some new categories and structures that have not been covered in the *Basic* volume, it expands on those already covered by giving new details and showing the usage nuances. The focus is standard modern Persian of Iran, although millions more use and understand Persian in different countries of Central Asia and beyond. With its abundant examples and exercises, *Intermediate Persian* is designed to assist learners of Persian at an intermediate or advanced level. Many of the subtleties and nuances of the language are being treated for the first time, especially having learners who are English speakers in mind. The book can be used independently (with answer keys supplied), but instructors of the language will also find it an indispensable complementary book for practicing grammar while using other texts for reading. Students can be asked to turn to this book (as well as to *Basic Persian*) as a source of reference and practice for each new grammatical subject, and each exercise is capable of being used in different ways to make it still more challenging. For instance, the students can be asked to translate the sentences back into the other language, change the tenses, and so on.

Units 1 to 14 are designed to bring the learners to a level beyond which only more work on vocabulary building and idioms will be necessary. The four appendices deal with different styles and levels of language (colloquial, polite, literary – and even 'journalistic' Persian). And throughout the book, whenever students need to be reminded of some basic rules (like tenses, etc.), they can always refer to the *Basic* volume. References to *Basic Persian* are given in the style '(see I/13.3)'. The glossary includes all the words used in the two volumes, but it has a bonus feature also: it includes all the Persian simple verbs (printed bold to be found more easily), whether used in the book or not.

As in the previous volume, in translations from Persian into English you might find *he* or *she* at random (when the antecedent is not specified), since there is no gender in Persian.

Vowels:

a	as *a* in *banner*	*ā*	as *a* in *bar*
e	as *e* in *belly*	*i*	as *i* in *machine*
o	as *o* in *border*	*u*	as *u* in *Lucy*

Diphthongs:

ow	as *ow* in *bowl*	*ey*	as *ey* in *prey*

Consonants:

b	as *b* in *boy*	*m*	as *m* in *mouse*
ch	as *ch* in *chair*	*n*	as *n* in *nose*
d	as *d* in *day*	*p*	as *p* in *pen*
f	as *f* in *fine*	*r*	like *r* in Italian *Roma*
g	as *g* in *goose*	*s*	as *s* in *sun*
gh	like *r* in French *Paris*	*sh*	as *sh* in *shy*
h	as *h* in *horse*	*t*	as *t* in *toy*
j	as *j* in *joy*	*v*	as *v* in *vase*
k	as *k* in *key*	*y*	as *y* in *yes*
kh	like *ch* in German *Achtung!*	*z*	as *z* in *zoo*
l	as *l* in *lamb*	*zh*	like *j* in French *jour*

Note: The glottal stop will be shown by an apostrophe (but is left out when in initial position).

Abbreviations (used mainly in the glossary):

adj. (adjective)	*intr.* (intransitive)	*prep.* (preposition)
adv. (adverb)	*lit.* (literary; literal)	*pres.* (present)
col. (colloquial)	*masc.* (masculine)	*sg.* (singular)
conj. (conjunction)	*n.* (noun)	*so.* (someone)
fem. (feminine)	*neg.* (negative)	*sth.* (something)
form. (formal)	*perf.* (perfect)	*subj.* (subjunctive)
gr. (grammar)	*pl.* (plural)	*temp.* (temporal)
imp. (imperative)	*poet.* (poetical)	*tr.* (transitive)
interj. (interjection)	*pr.* (pronoun)	*wrt.* (written)

All references to the first volume (*Basic Persian*) are preceded by: I/

UNIT ONE | ۱ فصل
Indirect speech | نقلِ قولِ غیرِ مستقیم

Indirect (or reported) speech

Indirect (or reported) speech in Persian has a golden rule that you should always remember: it is not how the sentence starts (i.e., the tense of the 'reporting verb') that determines what tense you should use – it is rather the tense of the verb in the *original* sentence, as you think it was *originally* said.

After the reporting verb you need که ('that'), which, as in English, can be dropped.

Similar to English, though not as strictly observed, there can be changes in adverbs – like the change from اینجا ('here') to آنجا ('there'), and the like.

1.1 Reporting present tense statements

When reporting some statement that was originally in the present tense, don't change the tense at all, even if the sentence starts with a past verb like 'she *said*....' What needs to be changed is the *person* (if you are not citing yourself) and, if necessary, some adverbs of time and place, and occasionally verbs like 'come/bring' to 'go/take.'

Examples:

Direct speech:

مینا (به من): 'فردا به خانه‌ات خواهم آمد.'

Reported speech (when cited by me):

مینا می‌گوید (که) فردا به خانه‌ام خواهد آمد.
مینا گفت/گفته بود (که) فردا به خانه‌ام خواهد آمد (we still use خواهد آمد)
(گفت or گفته بود despite the past)

1.2 Reporting past tense statements

When reporting statements that originally used the past tense, not a *backshift* of tenses (as in English), but a *change* of tenses would be necessary – and this again regardless of the tense of the reporting verb that starts the sentence. Persian has some straightforward and easy rules here; some of the tenses used have been developed specifically for this function and are used in indirect speech only.

1.2.1 Narrative or reporting tenses

The *present perfect* tense has traditionally been called ماضیِ نقلی ('narrative past') in Persian (see I/13.3), a fact that shows how closely this tense is related to reported or indirect speech. Apart from this tense and its progressive form, which are used independently also as tenses, there are one or two tenses used exclusively in reported speech: these are the narrative forms of past perfect (and past perfect progressive – a tense scarcely used), in which the past participle of the main verb is followed by the present perfect tense of the verb بودن (the auxiliary used to form perfect tenses). In Table 1.1 you see the tenses to be used in indirect speech when the original verb (in 'direct speech') is in one of the past tenses:

Table 1.1: Reporting a past statement

Direct Speech	→	Indirect Speech
SIMPLE PAST گذشتهٔ ساده (ماضی ساده) مینا: 'به آنجا رفتم.' Mina: 'I went there.'	→	PRESENT PERFECT (= 'NARRATIVE PAST') حال کامل (گذشته یا ماضی نقلی) مینا می‌گوید/گفت (که) به آنجا رفته (است) Mina says/said (that) she had gone there. (In Persian: 'has gone'!)
PAST PROGRESSIVE گذشتهٔ استمراری (ماضی استمراری) مینا: 'به آنجا می‌رفتم.' Mina: 'I was going/used to go there.' مینا: 'داشتم به آنجا می‌رفتم.' Mina: 'I was going there.'	→	PRESENT PERFECT PROGRESSIVE حال کامل استمراری (گذشته یا ماضی نقلی استمراری) مینا می‌گوید/گفت (که) به آنجا می‌رفته (است) Mina says/said (that) she had been going there. مینا می‌گوید/گفت (که) داشته (است) به آنجا می‌رفته (است) Mina says/said (that) she had been going there.[1]

[1] As you see here, داشتم, though part of the progressive structure, has been regarded as 'simple past' (for lack of می) and the tense has changed to present perfect (داشته است).

Table 1.1 (*cont'd*)

Direct Speech	→	Indirect Speech
PAST PERFECT گذشتهٔ کامل (ماضی بعید) مینا: ʼبه آنجا رفته بودم.ʼ Mina: 'I had gone there.'	→	NARRATIVE PAST PERFECT گذشتهٔ کامل نقلی (ماضی بعید نقلی) مینا می‌گوید/گفت (که) به آنجا رفته بوده است Mina says/said (that) she had gone there. (This tense is used in indirect speech only.)
PAST PERFECT PROGRESSIVE گذشتهٔ کامل استمراری (ماضی بعید استمراری) مینا: ʼمی‌توانسته بودم با کس دیگری ازدواج کنم.ʼ Mina: 'I could have married someone else.' (Not a very common tense; usually past progressive is used instead.)	→	NARRATIVE PAST PERFECT PROGRESSIVE گذشتهٔ کامل نقلی استمراری (ماضی بعید نقلی استمراری) مینا می‌گوید/گفت (که) می‌توانسته بوده (است) با کس دیگری ازدواج کند Mina says/said (that) she could have married someone else. (A tense possible in indirect speech only.)

And here again a table of all tenses, present and past, with short examples of reported speech:

Table 1.2: Reported speech in different tenses (+ subjunctive)

PRESENT	PAST	FUTURE	SUBJUNCTIVE
Simple			
ʼمی‌بینیʼ گفت می‌بینی	ʼدیدیʼ گفت دیده‌ای	ʼخواهی دیدʼ گفت خواهی دید	ʼشاید ببینیʼ گفت شاید ببینی
Progressive			
ʼ[داری] می‌بینیʼ گفت [داری] می‌بینی	ʼمی‌دیدیʼ گفت می‌دیده‌ای		
Perfect			
ʼدیده‌ایʼ گفت دیده‌ای	ʼدیده بودیʼ گفت دیده بوده‌ای		ʼشاید دیده باشیʼ گفت شاید دیده باشی
Perfect progressive			
ʼمی‌دیده‌ایʼ گفت می‌دیده‌ای	(not common!) ʼمی‌دیده بودیʼ گفت می‌دیده بوده‌ای		

Two observations here:

1) *All* the tense changes occur in the *past* column; absolutely no change of tense in other columns.
2) The *present perfect tense* and *present perfect progressive tense* are seen here on both the *present* column (as independent tenses; no change in reported speech because *present*) and on the *past* column as the reported forms of respectively *past tense* and *past progressive tense*.

1.3 An understandable exception

Sometimes Persian uses the past tense in subordinate clauses (mainly *time clauses* and conditional *if clauses*) in a present sense. (See *Basic Persian*, Units 16 and 18.) Example:

'وقتی فردا مادرم آمد، از او خواهم پرسید.'

Here آمد ('came') is not really functioning as the *past* tense but rather is the same as the present subjunctive بیاید, and for this same reason is treated as such: in indirect speech, the tense does not need to change to the *narrative past*, and you only change the person:

مینا گفت که وقتی فردا مادرش آمد، از او خواهد پرسید.

The same thing happens with past progressive or past perfect tenses when used in *conditional* (اگر) or *wish* (کاش) sentences. (See examples under 1.10 below.)

1.4 Questions

Reporting verbs for indirect questions are either پرسیدن and سؤال کردن (both meaning 'to ask') or simply verbs like گفتن ('to say'/'tell') and the like.

Be careful when translating 'if' in indirect questions: the word اگر (*agar*) in Persian is used only in the sense of conditional *if* and not for indirect questions. For *if* (= *whether*) in indirect questions use the word آیا (*āyā*), the universal word that can introduce all questions (less common, though, when a question word is present).

The word که ('that') can still be used in indirect questions after the reporting verb, as in indirect statements, with or without آیا, or can be dropped. Therefore, you might have که or آیا or (less commonly) both – or neither of them.

Examples:

مینا (به پرویز): ʼ(آیا) کجا می‌روی؟ʻ
← مینا از پرویز می‌پرسد/پرسید (که) (آیا) او کجا می‌رود.

مینا (به دارا): ʼ(آیا) به آنجا رفتی؟ʻ
← مینا از دارا می‌پرسد/پرسید (که) (آیا) به آنجا رفته (است).

1.5 Imperative and subjunctive, conditionals and wishes

- The *imperative* is only possible in *direct speech*; in reported speech it has to change to the subjunctive.
- The *subjunctive* has no tense to change (remember: like the *infinitive* in English); it remains unchanged.
- No change of tense required for *conditionals* and *wishes*.

Of course, other necessary changes (person, time adverb) have to be made. The reporting verb can be گفتن or verbs like خواستن (از کسی) ('to ask [*so.* to do *sth.*]'), خواهش کردن (*khāhesh kardan*, 'to request'), دستور دادن (*dastur dādan*, 'to order'), and the like.

You will see in the following examples that the tense of the reporting verb plays no role:

(Mina [to me]: 'Don't write مینا (به من): ʼروی این کاغذ ننویس!ʻ
on this paper!')
← مینا به من گفت/مینا از من خواست (که) روی آن کاغذ ننویسم.

(Mina [to the teacher]: 'Please repeat!') مینا (به معلم): ʼلطفاً تکرار کنید!ʻ
← مینا از معلم خواست/مینا از معلم خواهش کرد (که) تکرار کند.

(Mina [to Bābak]: 'You مینا (به بابک): ʼمی‌توانی امشب به اینجا بیائی.ʻ
can come here tonight.')
← مینا به بابک گفت که می‌تواند آن شب به آنجا برود.

(Mina [to her مینا (به پدرش): ʼکاش این را زودتر به من گفته بودی!ʻ
father]: 'I wish you had told me this sooner.')
← مینا به پدرش گفت کاش این را زودتر به او گفته بود.

1.6 Statements understood and treated as reported speech

Many verbs that deal with knowing, perceiving, realizing, assuming, claiming, and so on, are understood as verbs that introduce some reported speech and are treated as such; the above rules apply to all of them.

Consider a sentence like: 'When the car drew near, I noticed that there were four people inside.' Persian does not care about the verb *noticed* (past tense) and wants to know what passed your mind at the time of perception. At that time, you certainly said to yourself: 'There are four people inside the car.' Since that verb was originally in the present tense, Persian does not change it:

وقتی ماشین نزدیک شد، متوجّه شدم که چهار نفر در آن هستند.

Other examples:

در خیابان دیدم پلیس دارد یک نفر را دستگیر می‌کند.

او فکر می‌کرد من کمتر از هجده سال دارم.

ادّعا می‌کرد که هرگز به ایران نرفته است.

1.7 *Implied* reported speech

The 'narrative' tenses used in indirect speech are sometimes used in Persian merely for a distanced narration of a story ('as it is said . . . ,' 'as far as we know . . .'), or to show that you are not entirely certain about some past event. What you say then, using the narrative form, could carry a neutral to slightly 'disclaimerish' meaning:

- by saying 'مینا دیروز آمد' you are simply stating a fact;
- by saying 'مینا دیروز آمده است' you are saying the same thing with some distance, like something you just heard.

1.8 Subject: keep it or drop it?

If the subject of the reporting verb (the person who *says*) is the same as the subject of the sentence that immediately follows, the second one is usually dropped – especially in the third person. Keeping it would usually imply a change of subject (from one third person to another). Compare:

مینا گفت نخواهد آمد. ('Mina said she wouldn't come.' Here 'she' is usually understood as Mina herself.)

مینا گفت او نخواهد آمد. ('Mina said he/she wouldn't come.' Here او is more likely to be understood as not Mina, but someone else.)

1.9 How to translate certain tenses used in indirect speech

Consider this sentence in English: *Pari said that she had written the letter.* Based on the above sentence, Pari originally could have said:

a) *I wrote the letter*, or
b) *I have written the letter*, or
c) *I had written the letter*.

And based on what we learned earlier, the Persian translation for both (a) and (b) would be:

پری گفت که نامه را نوشته است.

and for (c) it would be:

پری گفت که نامه را نوشته بوده است.

Or consider this sentence: *We listened to his story, but we knew that he was lying.* You must have been saying to yourselves at the time: 'He is lying!' So the Persian translation should use a present tense:

به داستانش گوش کردیم، ولی می‌دانستیم که (دارد) دروغ می‌گوید.

1.10 Some examples of longer sentences with multiple verbs, or reporting reported speech

Only the translation for the sentence in direct speech will be given here.

علی: 'وقتی او را دیدم، خیلی مریض به نظر می‌آمد.' (Ali: 'She looked very ill when I saw her.')

علی گفت که وقتی او را دیده است، او خیلی مریض به نظر آمده است. →

اکبر: 'ناصر می‌گفت شما را اصلاً نمی‌شناسد.' :Akbar) اکبر: 'ناصر می‌گفت شما را اصلاً نمی‌شناسد.' (Akbar: 'Nāser said he doesn't know you at all.')

← اکبر گفت ناصر می‌گفته است مرا اصلاً نمی‌شناسد.

پرویز: 'به من گفتند کتابی را که دیروز گم کرده بودم پیدا کرده‌اند.' (Parviz: 'They told me that they had found the book that I had lost yesterday.')

← پرویز گفت به او گفته‌اند کتابی را که دیروز گم کرده بوده است پیدا کرده‌اند.

پویان: 'علی گفت کاش به مادرش نگفته بودیم که دیر می‌آید.' :Puyān) 'Ali said he wished we hadn't told his mother that he would be coming late.')

← پویان گفت علی گفته است کاش به مادرش نگفته بودیم که دیر می‌آید.

مریم: 'اگر به من خبر داده بودید که امروز می‌آئید خانه را تمیز می‌کردم.' (Maryam: 'If you had let me know that you were coming today, I would have cleaned the house.')

← مریم گفت اگر به او خبر داده بودیم که امروز می‌آئیم خانه را تمیز می‌کرد.

Exercises

Exercise 1.1

Simple statements
Change to indirect speech, using a past reporting verb.

Example:

مینا (به نیما): 'امروز خواهم آمد.'

Mina (to Nimā): 'I'll come today.'

← مینا به نیما گفت که امروز خواهد آمد.

Mina said to Nimā that she would come that day.

(In Persian, however: *will come today* in indirect speech also.)

۱. مینا (به من): 'فردا من و مادرم به بیمارستان خواهیم رفت.'
Mina (to me): 'Tomorrow my mother and I will go to the hospital.'

۲. مادرم (به دوستم): 'من خانواده‌تان را خیلی خوب می‌شناسم.'
My mother (to my friend): 'I know your family very well.'

۳. حسن (به معلم انگلیسی): 'خیلی تند حرف می‌زنید و من نمی‌فهمم.'
Hasan (to English teacher): 'You speak too fast and I don't understand.'

۴. برادر بابک (به بابک): 'می‌دانم که درسهایت را خوب نمی‌خوانی.'

Bābak's brother (to Bābak): 'I know that you don't study well.'

۵. پروین (به مادرش): 'دیروز وقت نداشتم که ظرفها را بشویم.'

Parvin (to her mother): 'Yesterday I had no time to wash the dishes.'

۶. ما (به پلیس): 'این مرد می‌خواست ماشینمان را بدزدد.'

We (to the police): 'This man wanted to steal our car.'

۷. پلیس (به همسایه‌مان): 'ماشین شما را در شهر دیگری پیدا کرده‌ایم.'

Police (to our neighbor): 'We have found your car in another city.'

۸. مادر (به دکتر): 'تمام روز داشت سرفه می‌کرد.'

Mother (to the doctor): 'He/she was coughing the whole day.'

۹. معلم (به پرویز): 'دیروز درست را بهتر یاد گرفته بودی.'

Teacher (to Parviz): 'You had studied/had learned your lesson better yesterday.'

۱۰. پرویز (به دارا): 'امروز ما داریم به مسافرت می‌رویم.'

Parviz (to Dārā): 'Today we are going on a trip.'

Exercise 1.2

Questions

Change to indirect speech, using a past reporting verb.

Example:

مینا (به نیما): 'خانه‌تان کجاست؟'

Mina (to Nimā): 'Where is your house?'

→ مینا از نیما پرسید که خانه‌شان کجاست.

Mina asked Nimā where his/their house was.

۱. مینا (به من): 'فردا با دوستتان به مسافرت نخواهید رفت؟'

Mina (to me): 'Won't you go on a trip tomorrow with your friend?'

۲. مادرم (به دوستم): 'آیا دیروز دیر به مدرسه نرسیدید؟'

My mother (to my friend): 'Didn't you get to school late yesterday?'

۳. حسن (به معلم انگلیسی): 'چرا آهسته‌تر حرف نمی‌زنید که ما بفهمیم؟'

Hasan (to English teacher): 'Why don't you speak more slowly so that we [can] understand?'

۴. پدر مینا (به مینا): 'از کدام مغازه این کفشها را خریدی؟'

Mina's father (to Mina): 'Which store did you buy these shoes from?'

۵. پروین (به مادرش): 'با کی داشتی دربارهٔ من حرف می‌زدی؟'

Parvin (to her mother): 'Who were you talking to about me?'

۶. ما (به پلیس): 'چرا قاتل را زودتر دستگیر نکرده بودید؟'

We (to the police): 'Why hadn't you arrested the murderer earlier?'

۷. پلیس (به همسایه‌مان): 'مطمئن هستید که او برنگشته است؟'

Police (to our neighbor): 'Are you sure that he/she has not
returned?'

۸. مادر (به دکتر): 'این قرص‌های زرد را هم قبل از غذا بخورد یا همراه با غذا؟'

Mother (to the doctor): 'Should he/she take these yellow pills also
before the meal or together with the meal?'

۹. معلم (به پرویز): 'می‌دانی چرا می‌خواهم پدر و مادرت را ببینم؟'

Teacher (to Parviz): 'Do you know why I want to see your parents?'

۱۰. پرویز (به دارا): 'نگفتند چرا به تو جایزه نمی‌دهند؟'

Parviz (to Dārā): 'Didn't they say why they're not giving you a
prize?'

Exercise 1.3

Orders and requests
Change to indirect speech, using a past reporting verb.

Example:

مینا (به نیما): 'به کسی نگو'

Mina (to Nimā): 'Don't tell anyone.'

← مینا از نیما خواست که به کسی نگوید.

Mina asked Nimā not to tell anyone.

۱. مینا (به من): 'لطفاً این لباسهای زشت را نپوش!'

Mina (to me): 'Don't put on these ugly clothes, please!'

۲. مادرم (به پدرم): 'لطفاً من را در خیابان نبوس!'

My mother (to my father): 'Please don't kiss me on the street!'

۳. حسن (به معلم انگلیسی): 'کمی دربارهٔ هوای لندن به ما بگوئید!'

Hasan (to English teacher): 'Tell us a little about London's weather!'

۴. معلم (به من): 'هیچوقت کیفت را آنجا نگذار!'

Teacher (to me): 'Don't ever put your bag there!'

۵. پروین (به مادرش): 'ببین آیا دامنی که خریده‌ام قشنگ است؟'

Parvin (to her mother): 'Look, is the skirt I [have] bought pretty?'

۶. ما (به پلیس): 'لطفاً بگوئید چقدر طول می‌کشد؟'

We (to the police): 'Please tell [us] how long it is going to take.'

۷. پلیس (به همسایه‌مان): 'نگران نباشید؛ همین‌جا (/همینجا) بمانید.'

Police (to our neighbor): 'Don't worry; stay right here!'

۸. مادر (به دکتر): 'خواهش میکنم آن قرصهای تلخ را دیگر به بچه ندهید!'

Mother (to the doctor): 'Please don't give the child those bitter pills again!'

۹. معلم (به پرویز): 'به پدر و مادرت بگو فردا به مدرسه بیایند!'

Teacher (to Parviz): 'Tell your parents to come to school tomorrow!'

۱۰. پرویز (به دارا): 'یک بار دیگر برای من توضیح بده!'

Parviz (to Dārā): 'Explain to me once more!'

Exercise 1.4

Conditionals and wishes

Change to indirect speech, using a past reporting verb.

Example:

مینا (به نیما): 'کاش دیروز نمی‌رفتی!'

Mina (to Nimā): 'I wish you hadn't gone yesterday!'

← مینا به نیما گفت کاش او دیروز نمی‌رفت.

Mina told Nimā she wished he hadn't gone yesterday.

۱. مینا (به من): 'اگر نمی‌توانی، بگذار من بکنم.'

Mina (to me): 'Let *me* do it if you can't.'

۲. مادرم (به دوستم): 'کاش موهایت را کوتاه نمی‌کردی!'

My mother (to my friend): 'I wish you hadn't cut your hair short!'

۳. حسن (به معلم انگلیسی): 'اگر آهسته‌تر حرف بزنید، می‌فهمم.'

Hasan (to English teacher): 'I'll understand if you speak more slowly.'

۴. پدر آذر (به آذر): 'اگر این را به مادرت بدهی خوشحال می‌شود.'

Āzar's father (to Āzar): 'Your mother will become happy if you give this to her.'

۵. پروین (به مادرش): 'کاش آن نامه را اصلاً نخوانده بودم!'

Parvin (to her mother): 'I wish I had not read that letter at all!'

۶. ما (به پلیس): 'اگر عجله نکنید، دیگر او را پیدا نخواهید کرد.'

We (to the police): 'If you don't hurry, you won't find him/her anymore.'

۷. پلیس (به همسایه‌مان): 'اگر فردا پول را به شما نداد، به ما خبر بدهید.'

Police (to our neighbor): 'Let us know if he/she doesn't give you the money tomorrow.'

۸. مادر (به دکتر): 'کاش این دوا را زودتر به او داده بودید.'

Mother (to the doctor): 'I wish you had given him/her this medicine sooner.'

۹. معلم (به پرویز): 'اگر این خط تو است، چرا نمی‌توانی بخوانی؟'

Teacher (to Parviz): 'If this is your handwriting, why can't you read [it]?'

۱۰. پرویز (به دارا): 'کاش من هم جرئت تو را می‌داشتم!'

Parviz (to Dārā): 'I wish I had your courage!'

Exercise 1.5

Time clauses and relative clauses
Change to indirect speech, using a past reporting verb.

Example:

مینا (به نیما): 'کتابی را که گفتی خریدم.' ('I bought the book you said.')
مینا به نیما گفت کتابی را که او گفته (است) خریده (است). →

1. مینا (به من): 'غذا که خوردیم، برویم سینما.' ('After we eat, let's go to the cinema.')

2. مادرم (به دوستم): 'وقتی آذر به دنیا آمد، قیافه‌اش عین فرشته بود.' ('When Āzar was born, she looked exactly like an angel [or: like *Fereshteh*].')

3. حسن (به معلم انگلیسی):
'معلمی که قبل از شما داشتیم نمی‌توانست اینها را توضیح بدهد.'
('The teacher we had before you could not explain these things.')

4. مادر نیما (به نیما): 'چرا همینکه عمویت آمد به اتاقت رفتی؟' ('Why did you go to your room as soon as your uncle came?')

5. پروین (به مادرش): 'داشتم تنم را می‌شستم که آب سرد شد.' ('I was washing my body when the water became cold.')

6. ما (به پلیس): 'مردی که ما دیدیم کمی قدّش بلندتر بود.' ('The man we saw was a bit taller.')

7. پلیس (به همسایه‌مان): 'آیا وقتی برگشتید تعجب نکردید که چرا در باز است؟' ('When you returned, weren't you surprised that the door was open?')

8. مادر (به دکتر): 'چشمی که درد می‌کند، چشم راست من است، نه چشم چپم.' ('The eye which aches [/has pain] is my right eye, not the left one.')

9. معلم (به پرویز): 'هرچه را که نمی‌فهمی، بپرس.' ('Ask whatever you don't understand.')

10. پرویز (به دارا): 'تا وقتی زنده بود، هروقت مرا می‌دید از تو می‌پرسید.' ('So long as he/she was alive, he/she asked about you whenever he/she saw me.')

Exercise 1.6

Mixed sentences
Translate the quoted statements, then change to indirect speech, using a past reporting verb.

Example:

آن پسر (به من): 'پدرم می‌خواهد با شما حرف بزند.'

→ 'My father wants to talk to you.'

آن پسر به من گفت (که) پدرش می‌خواهد با من حرف بزند.

١. خدا (به موسی): 'فقط شش روز در هفته کار کن، چون من دنیا را در شش روز خلق کردم.'

٢. فروغ: 'تمام روز در آئینه گریه می‌کردم.'

٣. حافظ: 'لطفِ خدا بیشتر از جُرمِ ما ست.'

٤. گوینده‌ٔ رادیو: 'می‌توانید این برنامه را در ساعت شش و نیم دوباره بشنوید.'

٥. بچه (به مادرش): 'من توی شکم تو بیدار بودم یا خواب؟'

٦. دکتر (به من): 'فکر می‌کنم دیروز غذای بدی خورده بودید.'

٧. مینا (به دوستش): 'قبول کن که تو معنی این شعر را نفهمیده‌ای.'

٨. دوست مینا (به مینا): 'اگر تو معنی‌اش را می‌دانی، به من بگو.'

٩. پلیس (به من و دوستم): 'ماشینتان را اینجا بگذارید و با من بیائید.'

١٠. بابک (به پرویز): 'اگر من کمک نکرده بودم، چطور اینها را تنهائی می‌بردی؟'

به شُتُرمُرغ گفتند بِپَر، گفت شترم، گفتند بار بِبَر، گفت مُرغم!

They told the ostrich ['camel-bird']: Fly! It said: I'm a camel!
They said to him: Carry loads! It said: I'm a bird!

(Used for people who can always find some excuse.)

UNIT TWO | فصل ۲

'Self': emphatic, reflexive and possessive usages of khod
Objective pronouns

خود، خویش، خویشتن: کاربُردهای تأکیدی، انعکاسی و مِلکی
ضمیرهای مفعولی

2.1 خود [khod, 'self' or 'one's own']

In less formal, casual Persian, خود [khod] is used with *pronominal suffixes* attached to it (the same set of suffixes you learned as *possessive pronouns* in I/4.2.2).

Table 2.1: خود ('self') for different persons

myself	خودم [kho.dam]
yourself	خودت [kho.dat]
himself/herself (itself)	خودش [kho.dash]
ourselves	خودمان [kho.de.mān]
yourselves	خودتان [kho.de.tān]
themselves	خودشان [kho.de.shān]

خود **has three different functions:**

A. *To emphasize some fact, or to show that someone does something alone and on his/her own.*

Examples:

(من) خودم بهتر از تو او را می‌شناسم. (I myself know him better than you do.)

(تو) خودت آن را به من دادی. (You yourself gave it to me.)

14

دخترم می‌خواهد خودش دربارهٔ آن به شما بگوید. (My daughter wants to tell you about it herself.)

بچه دوست دارد خودش غذایش را بخورد. (The child likes/prefers to eat [its food] [by] itself.)

In this *emphatic* function, instead of using the suffixes, sometimes the personal pronouns are used – or even nouns and names – all preceded, of course, by the connector *ezāfe*.

Thus, instead of خودم [kho.dam], you can say خودِ من [kho.de man], or, similarly, خودِ تو [kho.de to] instead of خودت [kho.dat], or you can say خودِ شَهر ('the city itself'), etc. (See Table 2.2 below.)

Examples:

خودِ تو از همه دیرتر آمدی. (You yourself came later than everybody else.)

چرا از خودِ ما نپرسیدند؟ (Why didn't they ask us [ourselves]?)

فیلمش را دیده‌ام، ولی خودِ کتاب را نخوانده‌ام. (I've seen its movie, but I haven't read the book itself.)

B. *Reflexive*: when the subject of the verb ('initiator') is the same as the object ('target').

Examples:

بعد از سه روز خودم را در آینه دیدم.

چرا تصمیم گرفتید خودتان را بکشید؟

این پیرمرد همیشه با خودش حرف می‌زند.

C. *Possessive* (= *one's own*): to show possession with more emphasis, sometimes with more clarity.

Examples:

من هنوز قلمم را لازم دارم؛ قلم خودت را بردار.

حتّی به برادر خودش هم اطمینان ندارد.

مادر تو را بیشتر از مادر خودم دوست دارم.

In this *possessive* function, it can sometimes help avoid the ambiguity in third person possessive cases, already mentioned in I/4.6. (See also 2.2 below.) Compare:

i) مینا کتابش را آورد (Mina brought her book. – This *could* be her own book, but could also be someone else's, maybe even 'his'?)

ii) مینا کتاب او را آورد (Mina brought his/her book. – This time we know that it was certainly someone else's book.)

iii) مینا کتاب خودش را آورد (Mina brought her [own] book. – Here also no ambiguity.)

2.2 خود in formal and colloquial Persian

In formal, written Persian (never spoken), خود [khod] is usually used alone (more often post-positioned, no *ezāfe*).

Table 2.2: خود ('self') – formal vs. informal

	LESS FORMAL/SPOKEN	FORMAL/WRITTEN
myself	خودم [khodam] or خودِ من [khod-e man]	من خود [man khod]
yourself	خودت [khodat] or خودِ تو [khod-e to]	تو خود [to khod]
himself/herself (itself)	خودش [khodash] (general) or خودِ او [khod-e 'u] (for humans)/ خودِ آن [khod-e ān] (for non-humans)	او خود ['u khod] آن خود [ān khod]
ourselves	خودمان [khodemān] or خودِ ما [khod-e mā]	ما خود [mā khod]
yourselves	خودتان [khodetān] or خودِ شما [khod-e shomā]	شما خود [shomā khod]
themselves	خودشان [khodeshān] or خودِ آنها [khod-e ānhā]/ خودِ ایشان [khod-e ishān] (for more respect)	آنها خود [ānhā khod] ایشان خود [ishān khod]

Two notes about خود when used alone in this formal way:

* When خود is preceded by pronouns or by nouns/names, it can only be used for the subject, not for the object: من خود [man khod] is always *I myself* and never *me myself*.

    Correct: من خود مینا را دیدم [man khod minā rā didam = I myself saw Mina.]

Wrong: You can't say من مینا خود را دیدم when you want to say 'I saw Mina herself.'
(Here خود مینا [*khod-e minā*] with *ezāfe* would be correct, but not مینا خود [*minā khod*].)

- When خود is used alone, usually the subject of the verb or the context shows which person is the antecedent. When you say به اتاقِ خود رفتم , this means 'I went to *my* [own] room.'

In written, more literary (or poetical) Persian, خویش [*khish*] and خویشتن [*khish.tan*] can be used as synonyms of خود [*khod*]:
A line by the poet حافظ [*Hāfez*, Hafiz]:

ما آزموده‌ایم در این شهر بختِ خویش (We have tried our (own) luck in this town.)

Compare:

دوستم/دوستِ من (my friend)
دوستِ خودم (my [own] friend)
دوستم خودش (my friend him/herself) (formal: دوستم خود)
خودِ دوستم (my friend him/herself) (formal: دوستم خود)

(Note that دوستِ خود by itself wouldn't show *whose* own friend we are talking about.)
More examples of خود with its different functions:

او خود کتاب را آورد. (He himself brought the book. – Here *khod* without *ezāfe*; *form.*)

او خودِ کتاب را آورد. (He brought the book itself. – Here *khod-e* with *ezāfe*.)

او کتاب خود را آورد. (He brought his [own] book. – *form.*)

او کتاب خَودش را آورد. (He brought his [own] book.)

او خودَش کتاب را آورد. (He himself brought the book.)

از خودت خجالت بکش! (Shame on you! – *lit.* 'Be ashamed of yourself!')

از سایهٔ خودش هم می‌ترسد. (He's even afraid of his own shadow.)

در آن شهر زیاد نماند و به سفر خود ادامه داد. (He didn't stay long in that city and continued his own trip [*safar-e khod*].)

شاید شما از خود بپرسید که چرا زندگی بهتری ندارید. (You may ask yourself why you don't have a better life.)

او هیچوقت سؤالهای خودش را فراموش نمی‌کرد. (He never forgot his own questions.)

2

'Self':
emphatic,
reflexive and
possessive
usages of
khod

Objective
pronouns

2.3 Objective pronouns

The same pronouns you have learned as *possessive pronouns* (here used as suffixes after *khod-*; see Table 2.1 above) can be used as *objective pronouns*, usually replacing the direct object, but sometimes the indirect object too, and sometimes used as the object of certain prepositions. This is common in both colloquial and formal Persian.

Important similarity: we remember that when used as possessive pronouns, suffixed pronouns cannot be used when some emphasis is needed. کتاب من and کتابَم are both *my book* but only من in the first version can be used with emphasis, not ـَم in the second version. The same is true when these are used as objective pronouns: they are unstressed and without emphasis.

2.3.1 As direct object

The DDO-marker (= Definite Direct Object Marker) را is dropped and the objective suffix is added to the verb, usually written joined:

Table 2.3: Examples for objective pronouns

OBJECTIVE SUFFIXES	SENTENCES WITH NOUNS AND PRONOUNS AS OBJECTS	OBJECTIVE SUFFIXES USED
ـ م [-*am*, me]	من را می‌شناسد *man rā mi-shenāsad* He/she knows me.	می‌شناسدم *mi.she.nā.sa.dam* He/she knows me.
ـ ت [-*at*, you (*sg.*)]	تو را می‌بینم *to rā mi-binam* I see you [*sg.*].	می‌بینمت *mi.bi.na.mat* I see you [*sg.*].
ـ ش [-*ash*, him/her/it]	او را دید/مینا را دید/آن را دید *ān rā did/minā rā did/'u rā did* He/she saw him or her/Mina/it.	دیدش *di.dash* He/she saw him/her/it.
ـ مان [-*emān*, us]	ما را می‌بَرَند *mā rā mi-barand* They (will) take us.	می‌بَرندمان *mi.ba.ran.de.mān* They (will) take us.
ـ تان [-*etān*, you (*pl.*)]	شما را نمی‌کشیم *shomā rā nemi-koshim* We won't kill you [*pl.*].	نمی‌کشیمتان *ne.mi.ko.shi.me.tān* We won't kill you [*pl.*].
ـ شان [-*eshān*, them]	آنها را بخر/کتابها را بخر *ketābhā rā bekhar/ānhā rā bekhar* Buy the books./Buy those/them.	بخرشان *be.kha.re.shān* Buy them.

Possible confusions

دیدم [*didam*] means 'I saw' – with '-*am*' being the conjugational ending
for 1*sg*. But it can also mean 'He/she saw me' – this time '-*am*' being the
objective pronoun and the verb being just دید for 3*sg*. Or consider these:

می‌بینیم [*mi-binim*, we see], and

می‌بینیم [*mi-bini-am*, you see me] – this one should preferably be
written as می‌بینی‌ام (same pronunciation) to avoid this confusion.

Compound verbs

The objective suffixes can be attached to either the verbal or non-verbal
part of the compound verb.

Examples:

آن را باز کردم. (I opened it.) → باز کردَمش or بازَش کردم

تو را پیدا کردیم. (We found you.) → پیدا کردیمَت or پیدایَت کردیم

آنها را برداشتند. (They picked them up.) → برداشتندِشان or برِشان داشتند

این را قبول کن. (Accept this.) → قبول کنش or قبولش کن

دیگر تو را دوست ندارم. (I don't like you any more.)
→ دیگر دوست ندارَمَت or دیگر دوستَت ندارم

This is common in both colloquial and formal; attaching the suffixes to the
non-verbal part is slightly more common in colloquial than in formal
Persian.

2.3.2 As indirect object

Not as common, and not used for all indirect objects. Some of the
occurrences involve verbs which are now used with indirect objects but in
earlier times were used with direct objects and no preposition. For instance,
the verb گفتن would normally use the preposition به as in: به او گفتم ('I
said *to* him.'/'I told him.') In early modern Persian, however, this verb
often used a direct object, i.e.: او را گفتم – a form still used in poetical
language. Example:

به پویا گفتم. (I said to Puya.) → گفتمش

Some verbs can have their object either direct or indirect:

(پروین را نگاه کرد or به پروین نگاه کرد) (He looked at Parvin.)
→ نگاهش کرد (less common: نگاه کردش)

2

'Self':
emphatic,
reflexive and
possessive
usages of
khod

Objective
pronouns

آن را گوش کردم (or به آن گوش کردم) (I listened to it.)

← گوشش کردم (less common: گوش کردمش)

آن را ادامه دادیم (or به آن ادامه دادیم) (We continued it.)

← ادامه‌اش دادیم (or: ادامه دادیمش)

With verbs that can have two objects (direct and indirect), using only these objective pronouns can lead to some ambiguity: گفتمش could be both 'I said *it*' and 'I told *him/her*.' Other examples:

دادمش. (= I gave *it* [to him] or I gave *him* [*sth.*])

نشان دادمش/نشانش دادم. (= I showed *it* [to him] or I showed *him* [*sth.*])

2.3.3 As object of prepositions

Though not possible with all prepositions and in all prepositional idioms, this is very common in Persian. Examples with برایِ ('for') and دربارهٔ ('about'):

برایَم، برایَت، برایَش، برایِمان، برایِتان، برایِشان

دربارهام، دربارهات، دربارهاش، دربارهمان، دربارهتان، دربارهشان

Examples with some other prepositions:

نزدیکَم است ← نزدیکِ من است

نزدیکَش است ← نزدیکِ اتاقِ من است

پیشِشان رفتیم ← پیشِ پدر و مادرِ تو رفتیم

پیشِتان می‌مانم ← پیشِ تو و پدرت می‌مانم

رویَش نشست ← رویِ آن نشست

تویَش چه داری؟ ← [here *tu-ye* = inside] تویِ جیبت چه داری؟

پُشتَش یک باغ است ← پُشتِ خانهٔ ما یک باغ است

کی کنارِتان نشسته بود؟ ← کی کِنارِ شما نشسته بود؟

جلوِشان یک دیوار بود ← جلوِ آنها یک دیوار بود

زیرش بود ← زیرِ کیفِ تو بود

In formal Persian, objective pronouns are not usually attached directly to prepositions like به, با, از and several others. We shall see later (in Appendix II) how these are treated in colloquial/Tehrani Persian.

Exercises

Exercise 2.1

Which words in each of the following sentences would require *ezāfe*? Write these words and then translate the sentence into English. (If different readings – with or without *ezāfe* – are possible, mention both.)

Example:

مینا خود بابک را دید

→ a) *khod-e*, 'Mina saw Babak himself';
   b) *khod*, 'Mina herself saw Babak.'

۱. با گوش خودم شنیدم که می‌گفت نخواهد آمد.

۲. اوّل به حمّام رفتم و خودم را شستم.

۳. پدرش را دیدم ولی خود ناصر را ندیدم.

۴. ناصر خود به شهری نزدیک تهران رفته بود.

۵. در آن شهر ناصر خانه‌ای برای خود خرید.

۶. پنجره‌ها کوچک بودند ولی خود خانه بزرگ بود.

۷. در خانه خود همیشه غذا می‌پخت و به کارخانه می‌برد.

۸. اگر خودتان را در آینه ببینید از خنده می‌میرید.

۹. من فقط عکسش را دیده‌ام ولی تو خود مینا را دیده‌ای.

۱۰. مادر خود بابک در سال ۱۳۲۴ (= 1945) به دنیا آمده بود.

Exercise 2.2

Translate the following into Persian, using *khod*. When different forms are possible for *khod*, write all of them, starting with the less formal version(s). (Some of the words you can use have been given at the end of the exercise.)

Example:

They saw their own father. → a) آنها پدرِ خودشان را دیدند,

b) آنها پدرِ خود را دیدند

1. My own brother's house was sold.
2. They knew nothing about the house itself.
3. Don't show yourselves to those young men.
4. I can't hide myself under this small table.
5. Dogs never forget their own owners.
6. I only want the shoelace, not the shoe itself.

7. The man himself was not much better than his neighbor.
8. I used to buy my clothes myself when in high school.
9. She found the book but couldn't find her own glasses.
10. He killed himself two days after his son's suicide.

فروختن/دربارهٔ/هیچ/دانستن/جوان/نشان دادن/پنهان کردن/سگ/صاحب/فراموش کردن/فقط/بندِ کفش/همسایه/دبیرستان/لباس/عینک/پیدا کردن/خودکشی/کشتن

Exercise 2.3

Add the appropriate form(s) of *khod* to the sentence, starting with the less formal version if there are two or more options.

Example:

چشمم را بستم. (my own eyes)

a) چشم خودم را بستم, (b چشم خود را بستم ←

1. (Mina herself) من مینا را خیلی خوب می‌شناختم.
2. (we ourselves) ما چند روز در آن شهر ماندیم و بعد برگشتیم.
3. (that city itself) ما چند روز در آن شهر ماندیم و بعد برگشتیم.
4. (my little brother himself) برادر کوچک من آن پرنده را دید.
5. (my own little brother) برادر کوچک من آن پرنده را دید.
6. (the bird itself) برادر کوچک من آن پرنده را دید.
7. (Ali himself) علی به من نگفته بود که پدرش مرده است.
8. (me myself) علی به من نگفته بود که پدرش مرده است.
9. (his own father) علی به من نگفته بود که پدرش مرده است.
10. (his father himself) علی به من نگفته بود که پدرش مرده است.

Exercise 2.4

Rewrite the following sentences by using objective suffixes for the words specified, then translate. (Write different versions if necessary.)

Example:

دیروز شما را ندیدم. (شما)

→ دیروز ندیدمتان. (I didn't see you yesterday.)

١. چرا آن را برای من نیاوردی؟ (من)

٢. فیلم طولانی بود و نمی‌توانستم آن را ببینم. (آن)

٣. بعد از دو هفته کتاب را به همین کتابخانه پس دادم. (کتاب)

۴. اگر گرسنه نیستی، آن غذا را نخور. (آن غذا)

۵. خیلی زود ما را پیدا کردی. (ما)

۶. قبل از آنکه به پلیس بگوید او را کشتند. (او)

۷. همینکه شما را می‌بیند از خوشحالی می‌رقصد. (شما)

۸. اگر ماشینتان را تعمیر کنید، آن را بهتر می‌خرند. (ماشینتان/آن)

۹. می‌توانی آن را نگاه کنی، ولی به آن دست نزن. (آن/آن)

۱۰. کاش اسمِ او را فراموش نکرده بودم و به شما می‌گفتم. (اسمِ او/شما)

Exercise 2.5

Change the objective suffixes to nouns and pronouns by using the clues
given. If there are two objective suffixes for the same person, use a noun
for the first one and a pronoun for the second one.

Example:

برداشتمش و به مریم دادمش (قلم)

← قلم را برداشتم و آن را به مریم دادم

۱. پاره‌اش نکن، لازمش دارم. (نامه)

۲. قبل از آنکه بخوابی، خاموشش کن. (چراغ)

۳. دوستم ندارد و دروغ می‌گوید. (من)

۴. در کتابخانه ندیدمشان و به خانه برگشتم. (دوستانم)

۵. غذایش دادم و صبر کردم تا بخوابد. (بچّه)

۶. کمکمان کنید تا این کار را زودتر تمام کنیم. (ما)

۷. می‌خواستیم دعوتتان کنیم ولی شماره تلفنتان را نداشتیم. (شما)

۸. آن روز در خانۀ برادرت تو را دیدم ولی بعد از آن دیگر ندیدمت. (تو)

۹. همانجا گذاشتمش تا علی راحت‌تر پیدایش کند. (کلید)

۱۰. ممکن است مالِ همسایه باشد، بازش نکن. (بسته)

Exercise 2.6

Translate your answers to the previous exercise.

کارد دستۀ خودش را نمی‌بُرَد.

A knife wouldn't cut its own haft.

(= A will always support B.)

UNIT THREE | فصل ۳

Definite and indefinite, singular and plural: review and expansion

Vocative case

معرفه و نکره، مفرد و جمع: مرور و تکمیل

شکل ندائی

3.1 A review of definite and indefinite

Units 6 and 7 in *Basic Persian* cover *definite* and *indefinite* in detail.

When nouns are used in a general or generic sense, Persian uses the noun in its absolute form (i.e., without any determiners for definite/indefinite or plural):

هوا مهمّ است. (Air is important.)

اتاق هوا ندارد. (The room has no air.)

اسب حیوانِ نجیبی است. (Horses are noble animals./A horse is a noble animal.)

ما اسب نمی‌خوریم. (We don't eat horses.)

Question: In the sentence اتاق هوا ندارد (The room has no air), how do we know that اتاق [room] is definite?

Answer: Through context. Do *all* rooms have no air? No. It is not 'room' in its general/generic sense.

Moving from *indefinite* (things encountered or mentioned for the first time) **to** *definite*:

روی یک درخت پرنده‌ای دیدم؛ پرنده از میوه‌های درخت می‌خورد.
   (I saw a bird on [/in] a tree; the bird was eating from the fruit[s] of the tree.)

روی یک نیمکت مردی نشسته بود؛ کنار مرد روی نیمکت نشستم.
   (A man was sitting on a bench; I sat beside the man on the bench.)

24

کتابی خریدم ولی نویسندهٔ کتاب را نمی‌شناختم. (I bought a book,
but I didn't know the author of the book.)

It is the context that in many cases determines the use of the DDO-marker
rā (see I/7.3). This is what we know for sure:

- we don't use *rā* if the verb is intransitive;
- we don't use *rā* for an *indirect* object (our clue: *preposition*);
- we *normally* don't use *rā* for an *indefinite* object, though *occasionally* we do.

On the other hand,

- we *have to* use *rā* for a *definite direct object* (= DDO).

Distinguishing a *direct object* is not very difficult (= an object for which
we are not using a preposition), but how do we know that it is *definite*
also? Some clues:

- it is a pronoun (like من or تو);
- it is a proper noun or name (like مینا or ایران);
- it is a noun modified by demonstrative or superlative adjectives (like
  بهترین کتاب or آن کتاب);
- it is a noun in the possessive case (like کتابم);
- also: *most* modified or plural nouns in the absence of indefinite determiners (like کتابها or کتابِ ارزان).

There certainly remain some gaps here, some in-between cases where you
are not quite sure whether to use *rā* or not; the good news is: in most of
such cases using *rā* is optional.

Some examples of sentences both with and without definite/indefinite
determiners:

a) Uncountable nouns (here آب):

آب مهمّ است. (Water is important.)

آب گرم است. (The water is warm.)

آب یک عنصر حیاتی است. (Water is a vital element.)

آب رودخانه‌ها شیرین است. (The water of the rivers/river water is sweet.)

بسیاری از ماهیها در آبهای شور زندگی می‌کنند. (Many fish live in salty waters.)

این دستگاه آب شور را شیرین می‌کند. (This apparatus makes salty water sweet.)

با غذای گرم نباید آب سرد بنوشیم. (We shouldn't drink cold water with
warm food.)

3

Definite and
indefinite,
singular
and plural:
review and
expansion

Vocative case

آب را باید قبل از نوشیدن بجوشانیم یا تصفیه کنیم. (We must boil or purify water before drinking.)

من قبل از غذا آب می‌خورم. (I drink water before eating.)

من آب را قبل از غذا می‌خورم. (I drink the water before eating.)

در قابلمه آب ریختم. (I poured water into the pot.)

آب را در قابلمه ریختم. (I poured the water into the pot.)

از این لیوان آب نخور. (Don't drink [water] from this glass.)

آب این لیوان را نخور. (Don't drink the water of this glass.)

در آبِ کثیف شنا نکن. (Don't swim in dirty/unclean water.)

آب را کثیف نکن. (Don't dirty the water.)

به بچه آب کثیف نده. (Don't give the child dirty/unclean water.)

آن آب کثیف را دور بریز. (Pour out/empty that dirty/unclean water.)

دوستم یک بطری آب به من داد. (My friend gave me a bottle of water.)

خواهرم آب خودش را به من داد. (My sister gave me her [own] water.)

b) Countable nouns:

اسبی دیدم. (I saw a horse.)

اسب سفیدی دیدم./یک اسب سفید(ی) دیدم. (I saw a white horse.)

اسب سفید را دیدم. (I saw the white horse.)

اینجا اسب زیاد دارد. (There are a lot of horses here.)

اینجا اسبهای سفید زیاد می‌بینم. (I see white horses here a lot.)

اسبهای سفید را دیگر نمی‌بینم. (I don't see the white horses any more.)

در تهران ماندم و کتاب ترجمه کردم. (I stayed in Tehran and translated books.)

در تهران ماندم و کتاب را ترجمه کردم. (I stayed in Tehran and translated the book.)

در تهران ماندم و کتابها را ترجمه کردم. (I stayed in Tehran and translated the books.)

ترجمهٔ کتاب را تمام کردم. (I finished translating the book.)

دو سیب خوردم. (I ate two apples.)

یک سیبِ ترش خوردم. (I ate a sour apple.)

سیبِ تویِ یخچال را خوردم. (I ate the apple in the fridge.)

از سیبهای درخت خوردم. (I ate from the apples of the tree.)

سیبهای درخت را خوردم. (I ate the apples of the tree.)

سیبهای یک درخت را خوردم. (I ate the apples of a tree.)

As the last two examples show, the possessive case makes the *apples* definite, regardless of the *tree*, which can be definite or indefinite. Another example would be عکسی دیدم (I saw a picture) vs. عکس مردی را دیدم (I saw a man's picture = I saw <u>the</u> picture of a man).

One more tip about *rā* (when using *rā* for an indefinite object is optional): you are much more likely to use it if the object is a person. Compare 'a book' and 'a man' in the following sentences:

روی زمین کتابی دیدم و آن را برداشتم. (I saw a book on the ground [/floor] and picked it up.)

روی زمین مردی را دیدم ولی نزدیکش نرفتم. (I saw a man on the ground [/floor] but did not go near him.)

In the latter sentence, using *rā* after *mardi* is optional and you can drop it, but then you would be treating that man like some bag of potatoes (which is okay if that is really how you want to sound).

3.1.1 Position of indefinite -i: some more limitations

When the noun is modified by an adjective, colloquial Persian would *always* add the indefinite -*i* to the adjective (e.g., کتاب خوبی), whereas in more formal Persian the -*i* can be added to the noun as well (e.g., کتابی خوب; see I/6.2). In certain cases, however, this latter option would not be possible even in formal Persian.

With certain quantifiers that precede the noun, the indefinite -*i* (if needed) is added to the adjective (if present) and not to the noun. Some examples of such words are *har*, *chenin*, *hich* and *che* in the following sentences, all requiring -*i* to be added to the adjective:

هر کتابی قیمتی دارد. (Every book has a price.)
But: هر کتاب خوبی قیمتی دارد (Every good book has a price.)

هرگز چنین کتابی نخوانده بودم. (I had never read such a book.)
But: هرگز چنین کتاب خوبی نخوانده بودم (I had never read such a good book.)

هیچ کتابی ندیدم. (I didn't see any book.)
But: هیچ کتاب جالبی ندیدم (I didn't see any interesting book.)

چه کتابی نوشته‌اید؟ (What book have you written?)
But: چه کتاب دیگری نوشته‌اید؟ (What other book have you written?)

3

Definite and
indefinite,
singular
and plural:
review and
expansion

Vocative case

3.1.2 Using rā with certain verbs

Apart from all other factors, the nature of the action expressed by the verb plays a great role in making an object appear definite or not. Consider the verb کشتن (*koshtan*, to kill). A butcher can say:

گوسفندی (را) کشتم و گوشتش را فروختم. (I killed/slaughtered a sheep and sold its meat.)

For the butcher, using *rā* after 'sheep' is optional, because he is only doing what he usually does. Not so for you if for some reason you have to kill/slaughter a sheep: you would certainly need *rā* then, even if you are using the indefinite determiner as well. Killing a human being, fortunately, is never treated as something commonplace, even if it happens in battle, and you always use *rā*:

در جنگ سربازی را کشت و هرگز این را فراموش نکرد. (He killed a soldier in the war and never forgot it.)

خرسی از جنگل بیرون آمد و سگی را کشت. (A bear came out of the woods and killed a dog.)

Certain verbs seem to need a definite object in all cases: due to the intensity of the action, an indefinite object without *rā* (which could sound 'casual') is hardly thinkable. Examples:

پسری را کتک زدند و فرار کردند. (They beat up a boy and ran away.)

در خیابانِ ما دارند ساختمانی را تعمیر می‌کنند. (They are repairing a building on our street.)

کتابی را فراموش کرده بودم و مجبور شدم به خانه برگردم. (I had forgotten a book and had to go back home.)

آن مرد سگی را از رودخانه نجات داد. (That man rescued a dog from the river.)

معمولاً چای را به قهوه ترجیح می‌دهم. (I usually prefer tea to coffee.)

یک آپارتمان نو را به یک خانهٔ قدیمی ترجیح می‌داد. (He preferred a new apartment to an old house.)

3.1.3 Other uses of indefinite -i

a) The unstressed, indefinite suffix *-i* can be used to refer to some small or insignificant amount or number; this is a meaning which is absent in یک (*yek*) when used alone for indefinite (not *yek* + *-i*). Very often

– though not always – it is the non-verbal part of a compound verb to
which this suffix is added. Examples:

به دخترم پول دادم که لباس بخرد. (I gave [some] money to my
daughter to buy clothes.)

به دخترم **پولی** دادم و به اداره رفتم. (I gave some [small amount of]
money to my daughter and went to the office.)

بعد از شنا نیم ساعت استراحت کردم. (I rested for half an hour after
swimming.)

در آنجا **استراحتی** کردیم و نزدیکِ غروب برگشتیم. (We took a short
rest there and returned close to sunset.)

از پنجره نگاه کردم. (I looked from the window.)

از پنجره **نگاهی** کردم. (I threw a glance from the window.)

It can also be used to show indifference or carelessness, as when you
do something in a slapdash fashion:

کفشی پوشیدم و از خانه بیرون دویدم. (I put on some shoes and ran
out of the house.)

b) Unstressed *-i* is also used in the sense of *every*, *each* or *per* (similar to
هر, *har*):

روزی دو بار (twice a day) = هر روز دو بار or دو بار در روز
(twice each day)

متری هزار تومان (1,000 Tumāns per meter) = هر متر هزار تومان
(each meter 1,000 Tumāns)

3.2 More on singular/plural

a) *Compound nouns*
When two or several words are treated as a single concept, the plural
suffix is usually added to the last word; a different position can sometimes
change the meaning:

تخته سیاهها در این مدرسه خیلی کهنهاند. (The blackboards in this
school are very old.) – Here تخته سیاه is treated as a single concept.

تختههای سیاه را برای سقف میخواهم. (I want the black boards
[/planks] for the roof.)

29

3

Definite and
indefinite,
singular
and plural:
review and
expansion

Vocative case

تمام آدم بزرگها اوّل بچّه بودهاند. (All grown-ups have once been
[= were once] children.) [From *The Little Prince*.]

بیشتر آدمهای بزرگ در اوّل زندگی سختی داشتهاند. (Most of the great
people have had a difficult life in the beginning.)

قد درازها باید در ردیفِ آخر بنشینند. (Tall guys should sit in the
last row.)

شما با این قدهای درازتان نمیتوانید در ردیف اوّل بنشینید. (With these
tall statures [of yours] [= as you are so tall] you cannot sit in the
first row.)

With a number of compound nouns made from Arabic loan words, it is
common in official and administrative language to use the Arabic broken
plural for the first noun, something of which not all writers approve:

Table 3.1: Plural of compounds – some examples

SINGULAR	BROKEN PLURAL	Persian PLURAL
وکیل مدافع (*vakil modāfe'*, attorney)	وکلای مدافع (*vokalā-ye modāfe'*)	وکیلهای مدافع (*vakil-hā-ye modāfe'*), or وکیل مدافعها (*vakil modāfe'-hā*)
رئیس جمهور (*ra'is[-e] jomhur*, president [of a country])	رؤسای جمهور (*ro'asā-ye jomhur*)	رئیس جمهورها (*ra'is[-e] jomhur-hā*)
وسیلهٔ نقلیّه (*vasile-ye naghliyye*, vehicle)	وسایل نقلیّه (*vasāyel-e naghliyye*)	وسیلههای نقلیّه (*vasile-hā-ye naghliyye*)

b) *Some unavoidable Arabic broken plurals, the case of double plurals,
and more*

In official and administrative Persian, some Arabic broken plurals are as
common as Persian ones; some of them are very common in colloquial
Persian also. And with a few of the borrowings from Arabic you always
use the broken Arabic plural even in colloquial Persian.

Examples of words almost always using the Arabic plural:

شخص (*shakhs*, person), *pl.* اشخاص (*ashkhās*, persons, people)

فرد (*fard*, individual), *pl.* افراد (*afrād*, individuals, people)

مال (*māl*, property), *pl.* اموال (*amvāl*, properties, belongings)

اهل (*ahl*, native [of a place]), *pl.* اهالی (*ahāli*, residents or inhabitants)

ادبی (*adabi*) means *literary* and ادبیات (*adabiyyāt*, originally *pl.* of
ادبیّه) means *literature*.

Sometimes the Arabic plural is used in a specific sense for which the
Persian plural cannot be used. Examples:

- حقّ (*hagh*, right [*n.*]). In socio-political contexts, حقوق (*hoghugh*) is the
  common plural and not حق‌ها (*hagh-hā*), as in *human rights* (حقوق
  بشر, *hoghugh-e bashar*). Additionally, *hoghugh* means 'salary'.
- انتخاب (*entekhāb*, selection or choice). انتخابات (*entekhābāt*) is the
  word used for *elections* and not انتخاب‌ها (*entekhāb-hā*), which means
  selections or *choices*.
- اصلاح (*eslāh*, correction, improvement). Here also, although the
  Persian -*hā* is possible, it is only *eslāhāt* which can be used in the
  sense of [political] *reforms*.
- دوا (*davā*, drug, medicine), دواها (*davā-hā*) means *drugs* and the
  broken plural ادویه (*adviye*) means *spice[s]*.
- مطبوع (*matbu'*) is common only as an adjective ('*pleasant*') while
  مطبوعات (*matbu'āt*) means *the press*.
- طرف (*taraf*) means *side*, طرفها means *sides* or *parties* while اطراف
  (*atrāf*) means *around* or *surroundings*.
- مرسوم (*marsum*) is *custom* or *customary*, while the plural مراسم
  (*marāsem*) means *ceremony* and is usually treated as singular,
  allowing the use of the double plural مراسم‌ها (*marāsem-hā*,
  ceremonies).

The double plural is possible with some other plurals also, like ادویه‌ها
('spices'), etc. And occasionally an Arabic singular is hardly known or
only seldom used in Persian, while the plural is a common word. Some
examples:

ارباب (*arbāb*, boss, master); والدین (*vāledeyn*, parents); اولاد (*owlād*,
children [in relation to parents]); اراجیف (*arājif*, balderdash,
baloney); نجوم (*nojum*, astrology).

3

Definite and
indefinite,
singular
and plural:
review and
expansion

Vocative case

c) *Firstly, secondly, etc. – and some more ordinal numbers and fractions*
To say *firstly, secondly*, etc., add *tanvin* to Persian ordinal numbers (which
would then change the *-om* to *-oman*). Understandably, this is common for
only the first few numbers. Both Arabic and Persian versions are common
for numbers 1–5:

Table 3.2: Firstly, secondly, etc.

	COMMON WORD	LITERARY
firstly	اوّلاً (*av.va.lan*)	نخست (*no.khost*)
secondly	دوّماً (*dov.vo.man*) or ثانياً (*sā.ni.yan*)	دو دیگر (*do di.gar*)
thirdly	سوّماً (*sev.vo.man*) or ثالثاً (*sā.le.san*)	سه دیگر (*se di.gar*)
fourthly	چهارماً (*cha.hā.ro.man*) or رابعاً (*rā.be.'an*)	
fifthly	پنجماً (*pan.jo.man*) or خامساً (*khā.me.san*)	

Some of the Arabic fractions that are common in Persian (sometimes pre-
ceded by the Persian یک, one):

نصف (*nesf*, half = نیم) – very common, but use نیم for half-hours.

ثلث (*sols*, one-third = یک سوّم) – used especially for quarters/terms in
academic year (excluding summer).

ربع (*rob'*, one-fourth = یک چهارم) – used especially for a quarter of
an hour.

خمس (*khoms*, one-fifth = یک پنجم) – used mostly in an Islamic
context for religious taxes.

عشر (*oshr*, one-tenth = یک دهم).

3.3 The stressed *-e* (or *-i*) suffix with quantities and time expressions

You must be familiar with the stressed *-e* added to سال ('year') for giving
an age:

یک پسر دو ساله [*yek pesar-e do sāle*, 'a two-year-old boy'] (I/8.5/3)

This *-e* can be added to many *number + noun* combinations, especially those
about time and age. (Another word you already know is دوباره [again, for
the second time] made from دو بار [twice].)

Other examples:

The stressed
-e (or -i)
suffix with
quantities
and time
expressions

یک بچّهٔ ده روزه (a ten-day old child)

یک سفرِ شش ماهه (a six-month journey)

یک هواپیمای دو موتوره (a two-engine plane/a twin-engine aircraft)

یک دوچرخه (a bicycle)

یک مردِ دو زنه (a man with two wives)

If the word already ends in *-e*, then usually a stressed *-i* is added instead of another *-e* (written as ای with *alef*). Occasionally *-i* is added to some words ending in consonants and is written joined. This stressed *-i* should not be confused with the unstressed one discussed earlier in this unit (3.1.3). Examples:

یک صحبت پنج دقیقه‌ای (a five-minute conversation)

یک سفرِ سه هفته‌ای (a three-week journey)

To say *by ones* or *by twos*, etc., say:

یکی یکی (by ones; one by one)

تَک تَک (*tak tak*, singly, one by one); more *form.*: یک به یک or

یکایک (*yekāyek*, each one, singly, every single one)

دو به دو or دوتا دوتا (by twos, two by two)

دوتائی (by twos; also: the two of [us/you/them])

سه به سه or سه تا سه تا (by threes, three by three)

سه تائی (by threes; also: the three of [us/you/them])

Also compare the following:

یک بار/یکبار (once)

یکباره (all at once, suddenly)

برای بارِ اوّل/برای اوّلین بار (for the first time)

دو بار (twice)

دوباره (again)

برای بارِ دوّم/برای دوّمین بار (for the second time)

سه بار (three times)

سه باره (threefold, thrice)

برای بارِ سوّم/برای سوّمین بار (for the third time)

33

3

Definite and
indefinite,
singular
and plural:
review and
expansion

Vocative case

3.4 The vocative case

The vocative is nothing but *direct address*, and the only thing which is required here is a shift of the stress: in direct address the stress, normally on the last syllable, has to shift to the first syllable. The names and titles مینا, علی, پروانه and آقای ایرانی (Mr. Irani) are normally pronounced with stress on the last syllable as *Minā́*, *Alí*, *Parvāné* and *āghāye Irāní*, but when you are calling/addressing them, the stress is on the first syllable: *Mínā!*, *Áli!*, *Párvāne!* and *ā́ghāye Irāni!* In what now sounds either archaic or poetical, the nouns in the vocative case used to be preceded by the particle ای [*ey*, 'O'] or occasionally suffixed by an unstressed -*ā* (and no change of stress). It can still be encountered in contemporary Persian when address-ing God: ای خدا! [*ey khódā*] or خدایا! [*khodā́yā*, with the glide -*y*- added here between the two vowels], both meaning *O God!*

Exercises

Exercise 3.1

In which of the following sentences could you consider *rā* optional? Put that *rā* in brackets after the word preceding it. Example:

روزنامه‌ای را خریدم و خبرهایش را خواندم

← روزنامه‌ای (را) (The second *rā* in this sentence is not optional!)

۱. کمی بعد لباس مناسبی را انتخاب کردم و آن را خریدم.

۲. امروز لباس گرمتری بپوش چون باید برف را پارو کنی.

۳. آیا ممکن است شخصی یک شخص دیگر را بکشد و آن را فراموش کند؟

۴. استاد دانشجوئی را برای آن کار انتخاب کرد.

۵. نامه‌ای برای استادم نوشتم و مقاله را برایش فرستادم.

۶. نکته‌ای را درست نفهمیدم و بعداً از او پرسیدم.

۷. با خواندن آن کتاب چیزهائی را فهمیدم که قبلاً نمی‌دانستم.

۸. معنیِ کلمه‌ای را نمی‌دانستم و آن جمله را نفهمیدم.

۹. دخترها را نمی‌شناختم ولی پسری را شناختم و به طرفش رفتم.

۱۰. پلیس زنها را فوراً آزاد کرد ولی مردی را تا روز بعد در زندان نگه داشت.

Exercise 3.2

Translate the sentences from Exercise 3.1 into English.

Exercise 3.3

Give the plural of the following compound nouns (treated as single concepts with no *ezāfe*) by using *-hā*; then separate the words and change the first noun to plural. Translate each version into English. Example:

کتابخانه

a) کتابخانه‌ها [*libraries*], b) کتابهای خانه [*books of the house*] ←

۱. خمیر دندان. ۲. توپ بازی. ۳. آشپزخانه. ۴. دندانپزشک. ۵. شاگرد اوّل.
۶. پدر بزرگ. ۷. سیب زمینی. ۸. خواهر برادر. ۹. روزنامه. ۱۰. دکتر بازی.

Exercise 3.4

In which of the following sentences is the unstressed *-i* suffix used not just as indefinite determiner but to demonstrate the insignificance of some amount or careless/hasty treatment of something? Mention the words using such a suffix.

۱. غروب زیبائی بود و ما نیم ساعتی در ساحلِ دریا غروب را تماشا کردیم.

۲. اراجیفی را که او گفته است به کس دیگری نگو.

۳. قبل از آنکه دیر شود باید سفری به آن شهر بکنیم.

۴. ای‌کاش قبل از امتحان توضیحی کوتاه می‌داد تا بدانیم از ما چه می‌خواهد.

۵. آقای دکتر توضیحی دربارهٔ آن دوا داد ولی من حرفهایش را فراموش کرده‌ام.

۶. گریه‌ای کرد و از ما خواست که او را ببخشیم.

۷. با دوستش آشتی کرد و او را به مهمانی دعوت کرد.

۸. هر روز چند دانشجوئی را در کلاس می‌بینیم و صحبتی می‌کنیم.

۹. به ایران نرفته‌ام ولی چند کتابی دربارهٔ این کشور خوانده‌ام.

۱۰. مردی مسلمان از یک خانم آمریکائی آدرس نزدیکترین کتابخانه را
می‌پرسید.

Exercise 3.5

Translate the sentences from Exercise 3.4 into English.

3

Definite and
indefinite,
singular
and plural:
review and
expansion

Vocative case

Exercise 3.6

Write these in Persian.

1. A tricycle. 2. A six-finger hand. 3. A bilingual book. 4. A two-hour program. 5. A two-horse carriage. 6. A ten-second farewell. 7. A three-bed room. 8. A seven-room house. 9. A two-way (Persian: 'two-direction') street. 10. A two-day celebration.

Some words that could help:

چرخ /برنامه /کالسکه /جشن /خیابان /خداحافظی /تخت /اتاق /انگشت /زبان /ثانیه /
اسب /ساعت

کوه به کوه نمی‌رسد، آدم به آدم می‌رسد.

A mountain wouldn't reach another mountain,
a man reaches another.

(Used when you unexpectedly encounter someone you know.)

UNIT FOUR | ۴ فصل

Persian equivalents of English modal verbs | معادلهای فارسی برای افعال ناقصِ انگلیسی

More on subjunctive | بازهم دربارهٔ التزامی

4.1 English modal verbs (or some semi-modals) and their Persian equivalents

In Persian, it is only باید [*bāyad*, must] which is comparable to English modals in defectiveness: it has only one form and is not conjugated. (Some other forms like می‌باید [*mi-bāyad*], بایست [*bāyest*], می‌بایست [*mi-bāyest*] or the rather archaic بایستی/می‌بایستی [*bāyesti/mi-bāyesti*] are treated in contemporary Persian as synonyms for باید with no distinction.) Another potential modal, شاید [*shāyad*], is used more like an adverb ('maybe') rather than the modal 'may/might.' The rest are adverbs or multi-word constructions with verbs that are conjugated in the normal way.

Table 4.1 will show where Persian would use the *subjunctive* and where *perfect (or past) subjunctive* for English modals and their perfect forms.

Shall, will and would
For *shall* and *will* you can usually use the Persian *future tense*, and you know that there is no 'future perfect' tense in Persian: you should use *present perfect* for *shall have* and *will have*.

Would is a different story. There being no *future in the past* in Persian, you would need to check the units on conditionals and reported speech. *Would have* appears usually in *irrealis* or *counterfactual* statements, which is again covered in units on conditionals and wishes.

For *would* used in polite requests, see *could* in Table 4.1.

For *would rather* you should simply use the verb ترجیح دادن (*to prefer*) and conjugate it as a normal verb, or use some expression like بیشتر دوست داشتن (*to like better ['more']*). In both cases use تا (not از) for *than* and place the verb before تا (and use تا آنکه or تا اینکه if a second verb is needed):

Table 4.1: English modals or some semi-modals and their Persian equivalents

Modals	Present	Past
must/have to/ must have/ had to	OBLIGATION: They must go. بروند (که) بروند/مجبور هستند (که) بروند NO OBLIGATION: They don't have to go. نیست بروند (که) بروند/مجبور نیستند/اجباری ندارند بروند / لازم نیست بروند PROHIBITION: They mustn't go. بروند (که) نباید بروند/(آنها) اجازه ندارند بروند CONJECTURE/GUESSWORK: That must be Mina. باشد مینا اینجا باید (آنها)/نباید بروند آن باید مینا باشد	PAST OBLIGATION: They had to go. بروند (که) بروند/مجبور بودند بروند/(آنها) باید می‌رفتند/مجبور بودند NO OBLIGATION IN PAST: They didn't have to go. بروند/لازم نبود بروند (آنها) مجبور نبودند (که) بروند/اجباری نداشتند (آنها) PAST PROHIBITION: They weren't [allowed] to go. اجازه نداشتند بروند (آنها) نباید می‌رفتند/(آنها) CONJECTURE/GUESSWORK FOR PAST: That must have been Mina. آن باید مینا بوده باشد
should/ought to/should have	OBLIGATION/PROPRIETY/RECOMMENDATION: We should go. باید برویم یمانی اینجا بمانی/باید اینجا بمانی/لازم است اینجا بمانی	UNREALIZED PAST OBLIGATION OR PROPRIETY: We should have gone by now. را بگیریم تا حالا باید می‌رفتیم/لازم بود آن رفتیم/لازم بود آن
need/need have	NECESSITY: You need to stay here. اینجا بمانی/باید اینجا بمانی/لازم است اینجا بمانی NO NECESSITY: You needn't stay here. اینجا بمانی لازم نیست/نبایستی اینجا بمانی	PAST NECESSITY: I needed to say that. آن را بگویم NO NECESSITY IN PAST: You didn't need to say that./You needn't have said that. آن را نگویی لازم نبود آن را بگویی/مجبور نبودی
had better	PROPRIETY/RECOMMENDATION: You had better see him. او را ببینی بهتر است	PAST PROPRIETY (→ SEE 'SHOULD HAVE'): [You should have seen him.] او را می‌دیدی بهتر بود

may/may have/might have	POSSIBILITY: He may/might come. شاید بیاید/ممکن است بیاید/امکان دارد بیاید	PAST POSSIBILITY: He may/might have come. شاید آمده باشد/ممکن است آمده باشد/امکان دارد آمده باشد
	ASKING FOR PERMISSION: May I go? اجازه می‌دهید بروم؟/می‌توانم بروم؟/می‌شود بروم؟/ممکن است بروم؟	—
	GIVING PERMISSION: You may go now. حالا می‌توانید بروید	—
can/could/ could have/ be able to	ABILITY/INABILITY: I can [/I am able to] write./I can't [/I'm not able to] write. می‌توانم بنویسم/نمی‌توانم بنویسم	PAST ABILITY/INABILITY: I could [/couldn't] write. می‌توانستم بنویسم/نمی‌توانستم بنویسم
		PAST ACCOMPLISHMENT/FAILURE TO ACCOMPLISH: I was able to [= managed to] write./I wasn't able to [= failed to] write. توانستم بنویسم/نتوانستم بنویسم (موفق شدم)/نوشتم
	POSSIBILITY/IMPOSSIBILITY: It can [/can't]/could [/couldn't] get worse. می‌تواند (/نمی‌تواند) بدتر شود/ممکن است (/نیست) بدتر شود	PAST POSSIBILITY/IMPOSSIBILITY: It can [/can't]/could [/couldn't] have gotten worse. می‌توانست (/نمی‌توانست) بدتر شده باشد/ممکن است (/نیست) بدتر شده باشد
	SUGGESTION: We could pick another color. می‌توانیم رنگ دیگری انتخاب کنیم (۱)	SUGGESTION FOR PAST: We could have picked another color. می‌توانستیم رنگ دیگری انتخاب کنیم
	ASKING FOR PERMISSION/REQUEST: Could I leave? اجازه می‌دهید بروم؟/می‌توانم بروم؟/می‌شود بروم؟/ممکن است بروم؟	

[1] In this usage می‌شود has the same meaning as ممکن است ('it is possible'), always conjugated for third person. (See also *impersonal* constructions in Unit 7.)

4

Persian
equivalents of
English modal
verbs

More on
subjunctive

I'd rather be a cat:

بیشتر دوست دارم (/ترجیح می‌دهم) یک گربه باشم.

I'd rather be a cat than a mouse:

بیشتر دوست دارم (/ترجیح می‌دهم) یک گربه باشم **تا** یک موش.

I'd rather be on a trip than stay at home:

بیشتر دوست دارم (/ترجیح می‌دهم) سفر کنم **تا اینکه** در خانه بمانم.

However, if you want to use the above verbs with nouns and not a second verb, you would need the prepositions به and از for respectively ترجیح دادن and بیشتر دوست داشتن:

گربه را **به** موش ترجیح می‌دهم.

سفر (کردن) را بیشتر **از** ماندن در خانه (/در خانه ماندن) دوست دارم.

And how about *would* in a sense close to *used to* (repeated actions in the past)? In Persian you simply use the *past progressive*:

پارسال هر هفته به خانهٔ ما می‌آمد تا از مادرم فارسی یاد بگیرد. (Last year

he would come/used to come to our house every day to learn
Persian from my mother.)

او تندتر و تندتر پارو می‌زد، ولی قایق به ساحل نزدیک نمی‌شد.

(He paddled/would paddle faster and faster, but the boat wouldn't
get close to the shore.)

Could have also needs some attention:

• Sometimes it is closer to 'probability' (*may/might*), as when you say,
'Any student could have written that on the board.' The Persian translation would be:

هر شاگردی می‌تواند (/ می‌توانست/ می‌توانسته است) آن را روی تخته نوشته باشد.

• Sometimes it is about some very real possibility which was not realized,
as when you say, 'Why did you talk to the officer like that? He could
have arrested you.' Here you wouldn't use the past subjunctive, and
'He could have arrested you' should be translated as:

می‌توانست تو را دستگیر کند ,or

ممکن بود تو را دستگیر کند

Finally, *let's*: For *let's* simply use 1*pl., subj.* – although this can also be
preceded by the imperative بگذار/بگذارید or بیا/بیائید (here گذاشتن in the
sense of 'to allow'). Examples:

برویم شهر. (Let's go to the city.)

دیگر آنجا غذا نخوریم. (Let's not eat there any more.)

بیا/بیائید این فیلم را با هم نگاه کنیم. ([Come] let's watch this movie together.)

بگذار/بگذارید از او هم بپرسیم. (Let's ask him also.)

4.2 شاید (shāyad) – with and without subjunctive

Since شاید can function as both an adverb (*maybe/perhaps*) and a modal (*may/might*), using the subjunctive after it is optional. The present tense would be almost the same as the subjunctive, and the perfect subjunctive would be pretty much the same as the present perfect tense; in both cases, however, using the subjunctive would slightly increase the uncertainty. Compare:

شاید نمی‌داند. (Maybe she doesn't know.)

شاید نداند. (She may not know.)

شاید رفته است. (Maybe she has gone.)

شاید رفته باشد. (She may have gone.)

4.3 باید (bāyad) – different usages

This is what we know so far about *bāyad*:

A. *bāyad + subjunctive* = must/have to
B. *bāyad + perfect subjunctive* = must have
C. *bāyad + past progressive* = had to
D. *bāyad + past progressive* = should have
E. See 7.2 for باید in *impersonal* constructions.

(Note that C and D have the same form.)

Examples for the above usages:

a) باید صورتش را ببینی تا شباهتها را بهتر تشخیص بدهی (You must see his face to better recognize/distinguish the similarities.)

b) باید صورتش را دیده باشی چون درست جلو تو ایستاده بود (You must have seen his face, because he was standing right in front of you.)

c) حتماً خوشحال نبودی از اینکه باید هرروز صورتش را می‌دیدی (You certainly weren't happy [with the fact] that you had to see his face every day.)

d) وقتی که خبر را شنید باید صورتش را می‌دیدی! (You should have seen his face when he heard the news!)

4

Persian
equivalents of
English modal
verbs

More on
subjunctive

a) (He has to call the police and بايد به پليس زنگ بزند و موضوع را بگويد
tell/report the matter.)

b) (He must بايد به پليس زنگ زده باشد؛ الآن يک ماشين پليس جلوِ در است
have called the police; a police car is in front of the door now.)

c) (For a few weeks he had براى چند هفته بايد هرروز به پليس زنگ مى‌زد
to call the police every day.)

d) (You should have called بايد به پليس زنگ مى‌زدى، چون تو مسئول بودى
the police, because you were responsible.)

4.4 Some verbs after which you need the subjunctive

With only a few exceptions, almost all of these are verbs after which the
infinitive (with or without *to*) is used in English. The most common of
these verbs can be grouped in the following categories:

1. *Verbs of needing, wanting, liking, preferring, being ready [to . . .]:*

احتياج داشتن، خواستن، دوست داشتن، ترجيح دادن، حاضر بودن

نمى‌دانستم که مى‌خواهد به ايران برود.

احتياج دارد [به اينکه] اقلاً هفته‌اى يک بار پدرش را ببيند.

حاضر بود بميرد امّا زنِ آن مرد نشود.

2. *Verbs of wishing, hoping, expecting, praying:*

آرزو/اميد/انتظار/توقّع داشتن، دعا/آرزو کردن، اميدوار/منتظر بودن

آرزو مى‌کنم هرگز در زندگى طعم خوشبختى را نچشند.

دعا کنيد که او زودتر از زندان آزاد شود.

اميدوار بودم شما را هم در آن برنامه ببينم.

آيا توقع دارى همهٔ اين حرفها را بشنود و هيچ چيزى نگويد؟

The expression خدا کند (*lit.,* 'may God grant it that . . .') is practically the
same (in meaning and usage) as *I hope*:

(I hope he hasn't forgotten.) خدا کند فراموش نکرده باشد

(I hope he won't find out.) خدا نکند بفهمد (= خدا کند نفهمد)

3. *Verbs of trying, attempting:*

سعى/تلاش/کوشش کردن، کوشيدن

راديوى دشمن تلاش مى‌کند با اخبارِ نادُرُست مردمِ را فريب بدهد.

دويست سال قبل مردى در آلمان کوشيد مثل پرندگان پرواز کند.

چرا همهٔ مردم کوشش نمى‌کنند که شهر را تميز نگه دارند؟

4. *Verbs of planning, deciding, intending:*

قصد/خیال/در نظر داشتن، تصمیم گرفتن

در نظر دارند اینجا یک مدرسهٔ خیلی بزرگتر بسازند.
آیا قصد ندارید به نامه‌اش جواب بدهید؟
دولت تصمیم گرفت یاد گرفتنِ فارسی را برای اقلیّتها اجباری کند.

5. *Verbs of arranging, being supposed to, being about to:*

قرار گذاشتن/بودن، ترتیبی دادن، نزدیک بودن

در قرن گذشته چند بار نزدیک بود که جنگِ جهانیِ سوّم شروع شود.
آیا قرار نبود مادرتان هم در این سفر با شما باشد؟
ترتیبی دادیم که مادرش او را در فرودگاه ببیند.

6. *Verbs of succeeding, managing, having the capability:*

توانستن (see also 4.1 above)، موفق شدن، توفیق یافتن، قادر بودن/کردن

وقتیکه عکس را دید، توانست همه چیز را به یاد بیاورد.
هرگز این توفیق را نیافتم که پدرتان را قبل از مرگش ببینم.
او قادر بود با هر دو دستش بنویسد.

7. *Verbs of asking, requesting, pleading, demanding, commanding:*

خواستن، خواهش کردن/داشتن، تقاضا کردن/داشتن، دستور دادن، التماس کردن

باید از او بخواهید که جلو خانمها حرفهای زشت نزند.
خواهش می‌کنم دربارهٔ گذشته‌ام چیزی از من نپرسید.
دولت نمی‌تواند به مردم دستور بدهد که خوشبخت باشند.

8. *Verbs of suggesting, recommending, advising:*

توصیه/پیشنهاد/نصیحت کردن

گربه توصیه کرد که موشها غذاهای سالم بخورند.
پدرم پیشنهاد کرد بجای ادبیات، پزشکی بخوانم.
خیلی نصیحتش کردیم که سیگار نکشد، ولی گوش نمی‌کرد.

9. *Verbs of insisting, emphasizing:*

اصرار کردن/داشتن، تأکید کردن

آنها اصرار دارند که او در آمریکا به دنیا نیامده است.
اصرار نکن که حتماً شب به خانهٔ ما بیایند.
خیلی تأکید کردم که دیرتر از ساعتِ دَه برنگردد.

4

Persian
equivalents of
English modal
verbs

More on
subjunctive

10. *Verbs of encouraging, allowing, letting:*

تشویق کردن، اجازه دادن/داشتن، مجاز کردن، گذاشتن

تو اجازه نداری با من اینطور حرف بزنی.
شنیدنِ این خبر آنها را تشویق کرد که چند نامهٔ دیگر بفرستند.
بگذار ببینیم دیگر چه دروغهائی دارد که بگوید.

11. *Verbs of forbidding, banning, depriving:*

منع/ممنوع کردن، محروم کردن (از)

The first three are the different ways you can say 'The mayor banned
smoking in restaurants':

شهردار (این را) ممنوع کرد که کسی در رستورانها سیگار بکشد.
شهردار این را که کسی در رستورانها سیگار بکشد ممنوع کرد.
شهردار سیگار کشیدن در رستورانها را ممنوع کرد.
معلم شاگردها را از نوشتن روی میز منع کرد.
او را از تحصیل محروم کردند.

12. *Verbs of convincing or being convinced, accepting, agreeing, approving,
promising, swearing:*

قانع کردن/شدن، تصویب کردن/شدن، موافقت کردن، قبول کردن،
رضایت دادن، پذیرفتن، قسم خوردن

Note: with some of these verbs, the use of the subjunctive is not
necessary if they are about some *fact* – and not *something that is to
happen.*

قبول کرد/پذیرفت که غذا خوشمزه است.
موافقت کردند که تا پنجشنبه بمانند.
همسایه‌مان رضایت داد که دیوار را درست کند.

13. *Verbs of deserving, being qualified, having the right:*

شایسته/سزاوار/لایق بودن، شایستگی/لیاقت داشتن، حق داشتن

او لیاقتِ آن را ندارد که دوست من باشد.
شما حق دارید که این حرف را بگوئید.
آیا سزاوار است که ما غذا برای خوردن نداشته باشیم؟

14. *Verbs of doubting, assuming, supposing, guessing:*

شک کردن، شک/تردید داشتن، مطمئن نبودن، اطمینان نداشتن، تصور/گمان
[نَـ] کردن، حدس زدن

Note:

شک wouldn't need *subj.* when negative. And when شک is followed
by شاید, it is شاید that determines whether *subj.* is needed or not
(see شاید above, under 4.2).

گمان and تصور, on the contrary, would always need *subj.* when negative,
but sometimes when affirmative also.

حدس can be followed by *subj.* or not, depending on the degree of
uncertainty.

شک دارم/مطمئن نیستم/اطمینان ندارم که او مرده باشد.
حدس نمی‌زدم که بخواهد آن کتاب را از من بگیرد.
تصور/گمان می‌کنم که او این را گفته است (/گفته باشد).

15. *Verbs of possibility and likelihood:*

ممکن/غیرِ ممکن بودن، امکان/احتمال داشتن، بعید بودن

خیلی بعید است که او هنوز تو را به یاد داشته باشد.
احتمال دارد که باز ازدواج کرده باشد.
ممکن نیست تا این ساعت بیدار باشند.

16. *Verbs of obligation, urgency and necessity:*

مجبور کردن/شدن، اجبار/الزام/لزوم/ضرورت داشتن، لازم/ضروری بودن

او را مجبور کردند که همهٔ کارها را با دست راستش بکند.
شما اجباری ندارید که تا این ساعت بیدار بمانید.
آیا واقعاً لازم/ضروری بود رنگ مویتان را تغییر بدهید؟

17. *Verbs of remembering, forgetting, knowing/learning/teaching + how or
other question words (the second verb subj. if English uses the infinitive;
see Unit 14 for more details, see also Table 8.2):*

به یاد آوردن، فراموش کردن، دانستن (که چطور/کجا/...)، یاد دادن/گرفتن،
آموختن

به یاد آوردم که کتابش را به او بدهم.
فراموش کردم گوشت بخرم.
بچه‌ها از او یاد گرفتند/آموختند که با دست غذا نخورند.

4

Persian
equivalents of
English modal
verbs

More on
subjunctive

18. *Verbs of beginning, starting:*

شروع کردن، آغاز کردن

Note: using *subj.* is only one of the possible structures here; see below the different ways of saying 'The professor started to speak,' with *subj.* being the last choice:

استاد شروع به صحبت کرد.

استاد صحبت را شروع کرد.

استاد شروع کرد (به این) که صحبت کند.

19. *Verbs of causing, leading to:*

باعث/موجب/سبب (باعثِ... /موجبِ... /سببِ...)، (به...) شدن، (به...) انجامیدن/ منجر شدن

اطلاعاتِ غلطِ او باعث/موجب/سبب شد که راه را گم کنیم.

شکستِ این کشور در جنگ منجر به آن شد که رئیس جمهورش تغییر کند.

20. *Verbs of daring, having the courage, or fearing, worrying, being too shy or feeling embarrassed:*

ترسیدن، ترس داشتن، نگران بودن، خجالت کشیدن، جرئت کردن، جرئت داشتن

خجالت می‌کشد دربارهٔ آن موضوع صحبت کند.

دانشجویان جرئت نکردند به استاد بگویند که زیپش باز است.

نمی‌ترسی (که/از اینکه) او دوباره برگردد؟

21. *Verbs of hastening, being in a hurry:*

عجله کردن/داشتن

هیچ عجله‌ای ندارم که همین امروز او را ببینم.

عجله کردیم که او را زودتر به بیمارستان ببریم.

22. *Verbs of getting used to, being easy or difficult:*

(به...) عادت کردن/داشتن، سخت/آسان بودن

عادت دارد روزی چند ساعت با دوستش تلفنی صحبت کند.

کار آسانی نیست که کسی در زمستان در این دریاچه شنا کند.

4.5 Subjunctive in certain adjectival clauses

In the last examples above (*being easy/difficult to ...*) we have in fact adjectival clauses, and using the subjunctive in adjectival clauses is very common, especially with interrogative or negative general statements. Compare the following:

همهٔ بچّه‌ها شیطانند. (All children are naughty.)

آیا بچّه‌ای هست که شیطان نباشد؟ (Is there any child who isn't naughty?)

هیچ بچّه‌ای نیست که شیطان نباشد. (There's no child who isn't naughty.)

دارم کتاب می‌خوانم. (I'm reading a book.)

کتابی دارم که بخوانم. (I have a book to read.)

کتابی دارم که خیلی جالب است. (I have a book which is very interesting.)

کتابی به من بدهید که جالبتر باشد. (Give me a book which is more interesting.)

4.6 *Too ... to* and *enough to*

a) For '*too ... to*' in Persian you need:
a *comparative adj./adv.* + که ... از آن + *subj.*

Examples:

او جوانتر از آن است که این چیزها را بفهمد. (He is too young to understand these things.)

او زرنگتر از آن است که چنین اشتباهی بکند. (He is too smart to make such a mistake.)

او بهتر از آن من را می‌شناسد که دربارهٔ من چنین فکری بکند. (He knows me too well to think of me in such a way [/to have such thoughts about me].)

او بیش/بیشتر از آن دربارهٔ موضوع می‌داند که به پلیس نگوید. (He knows too much about that matter not to tell the police.)

این پرنده تندتر از آن پرواز می‌کند که بتوانم عکسش را بگیرم. (This bird flies too fast for me to be able to take its picture.)

Note: in this structure, if you don't use *subj.*, the meaning would totally change: in the English translation you would simply use a comparative adjective and no infinitive. Compare the following with the first two examples above:

او جوانتر از آن است که مادرش می‌گوید. (He is younger than [what] his mother says.)

او زرنگتر از آن است که شما فکر می‌کنید. (He is smarter than [what] you think.)

4

Persian
equivalents of
English modal
verbs

More on
subjunctive

b) For '*enough to . . .*' in Persian you need:

آنقدر + *adj./adv.* + a verb + که.

Instead of آنقدر it is possible to use به اندازهٔ کافی or آن اندازه ('to the sufficient extent or amount').

In this structure, the verb takes the main stress, and that is why if you
are using the verb *to be*, you would need its longer, '*hast*' version (for
emphasis). Without the stress on the verb, the meaning would change to
'so much that' or 'to the extent that' – and no subjunctive would then be
necessary (nor the longer version of *to be*). Compare:

او آنقدر زرنگ است که همه چیز را می‌فهمد. (He is so smart that he
understands everything.)

او آنقدر زرنگ هست که این چیزها را بفهمد. (He is smart enough to
understand these things.)

او آنقدر عاقل است که چنین اشتباهی نمی‌کند. (He is so wise that he
wouldn't make such a mistake.)

او آنقدر عاقل هست که چنین اشتباهی نکند. (He is wise enough not to
make such a mistake.)

شما آنقدر پول دارید که هر سال تابستان به سفر می‌روید. (You have so
much money that you travel in summer every year.)

شما آنقدر پول دارید که تابستان امسال به سفر بروید. (You have enough
money to travel this summer.)

4.7 Conjunctions that need the subjunctive

Some conjunctions – like the conditional *if* (I/16) and some of the conjunctions used in time clauses (I/18) – *can* be followed by the subjunctive; but
there are some that *always* require the use of the subjunctive, like those
meaning *before* (قبل از/پیش از; see I/18.2), or those meaning *in order to*
(see Unit 12 for different usages of تا). Here are a few more examples.

a) The prepositions بدون and بی (both meaning 'without') as well as بجای
('instead of') can all be used as conjunctions by adding آنکه (see I/17.2 for
the rule) – and then they would always need the subjunctive. Examples:

او دو هفته بی غذا/بدونِ غذا زنده ماند.

او دو هفته بی آنکه/بدونِ آنکه غذا بخورد زنده ماند.

ما بجایِ تماشای فیلم جنگ و صلح، کتابش را خواندیم.

ما بجایِ آنکه فیلم جنگ و صلح را تماشا کنیم، کتابش را خواندیم.

b) The correlative conjunctions خواه...خواه... [*khāh...khāh...*] and
چه...چه... [*che...che...*], both meaning 'whether...or...,' would
always need the subjunctive:

خواه شما بیائید خواه نیائید، ما فردا به مشهد خواهیم رفت.

چه بخواهد چه نخواهد، باید با آن مردِ پیر ازدواج کند.

c) The same applies to هر چقدر/هر قدر (که)... or هرچه (که) (and the
more formal versions هر آنچه که or هر اندازه که, all meaning 'whatever'/
'no matter what/how' or 'however much that') when used for what is
to happen next. Compare:

هر چه گفت، هیچ جوابی ندادم. – no *subj.* here!

هرچه بگوئی به او خواهم گفت. – here *subj.*!

هرقدر بخواهی، دارم.

Exercises

Exercise 4.1

Start the following sentences with دیروز and make the necessary changes
in the verbs, then translate the sentence. Example:

او را تشویق می‌کنم که به ایران برگردد.

→ دیروز او را تشویق کردم که به ایران برگردد. (Yesterday I encouraged
him to go back to Iran.)

١.   پیشنهاد می‌کنم نامه را تمام کند.

٢.   شاید با دوستش به کتابخانه برود.

٣.   سعی می‌کنیم غذای خوشمزه‌تری درست کنیم.

۴.   باید چهار صفحهٔ دیگر از آن کتاب را ترجمه کند.

۵.   ترجیح می‌دهم در خانه بمانم و درس بخوانم.

۶.   دوست دارم چند ساعت در هوای آزاد راه بروم.

٧.   لازم است از دکترت دربارهٔ قرصها سؤال کنی.

٨.   قرار است دوستم را به فرودگاه ببرم.

٩.   می‌ترسم پدرم بگوید که پول دانشگاهم را نخواهد داد.

١٠. رئیسم قصد دارد ما را دو ساعت زودتر به خانه بفرستد.

4

Persian
equivalents of
English modal
verbs

More on
subjunctive

Exercise 4.2

In the following sentences change the first verb to negative (and make
other changes if necessary); then translate. Example:

اطمینان دارم که خودش خبر دارد

اطمینان ندارم که خودش خبر داشته باشد ← (I'm not sure if he himself
knows [about it].)

١. در هفتهٔ اول ممکن است در شهر دیگری باشم.

٢. آیا از تو خواسته‌اند نامه را فقط بیاوری و خودت نخوانی؟

٣. آیا می‌دانید دخترم چطور فارسی یاد گرفته است؟

۴. فکر می‌کنم روزِ شنبه از ایران برمی‌گردند.

۵. فکر می‌کرد من هنوز با زنِ اوّلم زندگی می‌کنم.

۶. شک داشتیم که بخواهند فقط دو روز بمانند.

٧. آیا قبول دارید که کارتان اشتباه بوده است؟

٨ خیلی سعی کردیم او را قانع کنیم که خودش را نکشد.

٩. تردید دارم که هنوز در آن شهر باشد.

١٠. پدرش اوّل اجازه می‌داد آن دوستش را ببیند.

Exercise 4.3

Fill out the blanks by using the correct form of the verb in the question,
then translate the answers only. Example:

– ‘آن مقاله را نوشتی؟’ – ‘نه، قصد دارم مقالهٔ دیگری ....
بنویسم ← (No, I intend to write another article.)

١. – ‘دخترتان گربه دارد؟’ – ‘نه، و امیدوارم هرگز ....‘

٢. – ‘غذا خورده‌ای؟’ – ‘نه، ولی قرار است با مینا ....‘

٣. – ‘کتاب را خواندی؟’ – ‘هنوز نه، ولی هفتهٔ آینده آن را ....‘

۴. – ‘پرویز را دیدی؟’ – ‘هنوز نه، ولی تصمیم دارم فردا او را ....‘

۵. – ‘با بابک حرف زده‌ای؟’ – ‘امروز نه، ولی دیروز داشتم با او ....‘

۶. – ‘پروین ماشینت را خرید؟’ – ‘نه، ولی شاید مینا آن را ....‘

٧. – ‘امکان دارد خانه نباشد؟’ – ‘نه، حتماً امروز خانه ....‘

٨ – ‘با این اتوبوس می‌روی؟’ – ‘همیشه نه، صبح‌ها باید با اتوبوس دیگری ....‘

٩. – ‘نمی‌ترسی که پدرت فهمیده است؟’ – ‘نه، ولی می‌ترسم مادرم ....‘

١٠. – ‘دوستت فارسی یاد گرفت؟’ – ‘نه، ولی باید تشویقش کنم که ....‘

Exercise 4.4

Write the correct form of the verb based on the English translation. Example:

باید زودتر .... (آمدن)، الآن خیلی دیر است (You should have come earlier; it's too late now.)

می‌آمدی ←

1. می‌بینم را ماشینش (آمدن)، .... ما از زودتر باید (She must have come earlier than us; I see her car.)

2. (آمدن) .... اداره به زودتر خیلی صبح‌ها باید جدید، شغل این در (In this new job, he had to come to the office much earlier in the morning.)

3. (تمام کردن) .... امسال را درست باید (You have to finish your studies this year.)

4. می‌کنی فکر ازدواج به که (تمام کردن) .... را درست باید (You must have finished your studies as you're thinking about marriage.)

5. باشی راحت حالا تا (تمام کردن) .... را درست باید (You should have finished your studies so that you could be at ease now.)

6. (تمام کردن) .... را درست باید امسال همین آیا؟ (Did you have to finish your studies this same year?)

7. شوید گرسنه تا (شنا کردن) .... ساعت یک باید (You must swim for one hour to get hungry.)

8. می‌خواندیم درس بعد و (شنا کردن) .... باید اوّل آنجا (There we had to swim first and then study.)

9. (شنا کردن) .... رودخانه طرفِ آن تا باید (She must have swum as far as the other side [/bank] of the river.)

10. شود تاریک هوا تا (صبر کردن) .... باید (You [sg.] have to wait until it gets dark.)

11. برویم هم با همه که (صبر کردن) .... باید رفتی، زودتر که کردی بدی کار (It was a bad thing you did that you left earlier; you should have waited for us all to go together.)

12. بزنند؟ تلفن تو به تا (صبر کردن) .... باید همیشه آیا (Did you always have to wait until they called you?)

13. (صبر کردن) .... خیلی باید می‌رسی، نظر به خسته (You look tired; you must have waited a lot.)

14. بوده دروغ حرفها آن که (فهمیدن) .... باید دیگر حالا (You [pl.] must have understood by now that those words had been lies.)

15. می‌کند را کار این چرا (فهمیدن) .... باید هستی برادرش که تو (You who are his brother should have understood why he was doing this.)

4

Persian
equivalents of
English modal
verbs

More on
subjunctive

Exercise 4.5

Translate these sentences into English.

۱. آنقدر زرنگ هست که زنِ خوبی پیدا کند.

۲. هوا آنقدر سرد هست که پالتو بپوشی.

۳. آنقدر نزدیک هستند که حرفهای ما را بشنوند.

۴. آنقدر گرسنه هستم که غذا بخورم.

۵. آنقدر احمق هستی که این اشتباه را باز هم تکرار کنی.

۶. آنقدر ضعیف هست که نتواند راه برود.

۷. بچّه آنقدر خسته هست که بخوابد.

۸. من آن قدر پول دارم که برای دخترم یک ماشین بخرم.

۹. آنقدر حرف زد که منظورش را بفهمیم.

۱۰. آنقدر این خانه را دوست دارم که آن را نفروشم.

۱۱. آنقدر بچهاش را دوست دارد که برایش لباس نو بخرد.

۱۲. آنقدر خودخواه هست که آن را باور کند.

Exercise 4.6

In the sentences from Exercise 4.5, change *ānghadr ... ke* ('enough') to
bish az ān ... ke ('too') without changing the meaning (this will require
changes in the affirmative/negative also). Then translate into English.
Example:

آنقدر خوب درس خوانده است که در امتحان قبول شود. (He has studied
well enough to pass the test.)

بیش از آن درس خوانده است که در امتحان قبول نشود. (He has →
studied too well to fail [/not to pass] the test.)

ماهی را هر وقت از آب بگیری تازه است.

Whenever you catch the fish, it's fresh.

(= It's not too late yet; don't give up/let's do it.)

UNIT FIVE | فصل ۵

More on conditionals | باز هم دربارهٔ شرطی‌ها

If, unless; otherwise, | اگر، مگر، وگرنه، انگار
as if

5.1 Some substitutes for اگر [*ágar, if*]

While اگر often appears to be little different from وقتیکه in time clauses, we can have a stronger, more emphatic 'condition' by using conjunctions that mean *provided that*, namely:

به شرطِ آنکه/به شرطی که/مشروط به آنکه

They are not very common in the past ('irrealis') conditions – especially never placed at the beginning of the sentence – and they would always need the subjunctive.

The conjunction در صورتی که (in case, in the event that) is also very close to this group, though not as strong (and, therefore, the use of the subjunctive is not obligatory).

To say 'I'll buy you that shirt provided that you study well,' you can use one of the following forms:

به شرطی که خوب درس بخوانی، آن پیرهن را برایت می‌خرم.
آن پیرهن را به شرطی که خوب درس بخوانی برایت می‌خرم.
آن پیرهن را به شرطی برایت می‌خرم که خوب درس بخوانی.
آن پیرهن را برایت می‌خرم، به شرطی که خوب درس بخوانی.

در صورتی که can also be used in a similar way:

در صورتی که زودتر برسند، برای تماشای آن فیلم هم وقت خواهیم داشت.

or it can be used as a synonym of در حالی که meaning *whereas/while* (see I/18.5) – and always at the beginning of the second clause in this sense:

او را دستگیر کردند، در صورتی که او مغازه را آتش نزده بود.

5.2 مگر [mágar, if not; unless]

اگر (or just مگر) مگر که or مگر اینکه/آنکه (or just مگر) can be used as the negative of اگر ('if') in conditional sentences. It has, however, one major difference from the English *unless*: it always introduces the second clause and is never at the beginning of a sentence when used in the sense of *unless*. Compare:

اگر تو بروی، من هم می‌روم.
اگر تو نروی، من هم نمی‌روم.
من نمی‌روم مگر اینکه تو هم بروی.

5.2.1 Other uses of مگر

a) مگر is used in questions to show disbelief or surprise (or protest, indignation) – this means that you normally expect to hear the opposite of what you are saying (regarding affirmative/negative).

او آنجا بود؟ means 'Was he there?'

مگر او آنجا بود؟ still means 'Was he there?' although it is more like 'But was he really there?' and shows that you expect to hear: نه، نبود (No, he wasn't).

مگر او آنجا نبود؟ (Wasn't he there?) would have the opposite effect; it is closer to 'But he was there, wasn't he?' and you expect to hear: چرا، بود (Yes, he was). (For چرا used to give an affirmative answer to a negative question see I/4.8). Examples:

چرا جواب نمی‌دهی؟ مگر زبانت را گربه خورده است؟
چرا به پلیس نگفتی؟ مگر این شهر پلیس ندارد؟
چرا عصبانی می‌شوی؟ مگر من از چه گفتم؟
همه دارند می‌دوند، مگر چه اتفاقی افتاده؟

This usage of مگر is similar to a usage of که, and sometimes they are used for emphasis in two consecutive sentences which only differ in using affirmative and negative – the affirmative form of one has the effect of the negative form of the other, and vice versa:

مگر نیامد؟ او که آمد!
(But didn't he come? He did come, alright?)
او که نمی‌داند! مگر می‌داند؟
(But he doesn't know – or does he?)

The adverb آخر (ākhar) is also close in certain ways to مگر/که when used as a filler to justify a situation. Examples:

آخِر چرا از من نپرسیدی؟ (But why didn't you ask me?)

نرفتم، آخِر دیگر تاریک شده بود. (I didn't go; it was already dark.)

b) The interrogative phrase مگر نه؟ [*magar na*] is used in colloquial Persian in a way similar to the English question tags.

او را می‌شناسی، مگر نه؟ (– بله، می‌شناسم./– نه، نمی‌شناسم.)
You know him, don't you? (– Yes, I do./– No, I don't.)

این مقاله را نخوانده بودی، مگر نه؟ (– چرا، خوانده بودم./– نه، نخوانده بودم.)
You hadn't read this article, had you? (– Yes, I had./– No, I hadn't.)

c) Sometimes مگر is simply a preposition meaning *except* or *other than* – its synonyms being غیر از, جُز/بِجُز and الّا – as in these examples:

همه آمدند مگر (/بجز/غیر از/الّا) پرویز.
هیچ کاری نمی‌کند مگر (/بجز/غیر از/الّا) خوردن و خوابیدن.

It would be wrong to conclude from the equation 'مگر = *except*' that 'مگر اینکه' can always be used for *except that*: if you are using *except that* to show a *difference* (= *with the difference that/but for the fact that*), then the appropriate Persian equivalent would be: با این فرق که or با این تفاوت که. Examples:

دُرُست مثلِ مادرش است، با این تفاوت که قدّش بلندتر است.
هوای اینجا مثلِ تهران است، با این فرق که خیلی تمیزتر است.

In most of the other cases, *except that* can be translated into Persian as بجز اینکه/غیر از اینکه/الّا اینکه (as in these examples):

آنجا هیچ کاری نکردیم بجز اینکه (/غیر از اینکه/الّا اینکه) خوردیم و خوابیدیم.
چیزی از او نخواستم بجز اینکه (/غیر از اینکه/الّا اینکه) درسهایش را بهتر بخواند.

And sometimes you can just use the word فقط (or تنها in more formal language, both meaning *only*) as in these examples:

مقالهٔ خوبی نوشته‌ای، فقط کمی طولانی است.
قصد داشتم به شما بگویم، فقط پیدایتان نکردم.

Using مگر اینکه in the above examples would not be possible.

5.3 وگرنه [*va gar na*, otherwise; if not so; or else]

As in English, وگرنه [or نه اگر, *otherwise*] is usually not used at the beginning of a sentence. Two common synonyms are الّا و [*va el.lā*] and صورتِ این غیرِ در [*dar gheyr-e in surat*]. Examples:

باید دستهایت را بشوئی، وگرنه اجازه نمی‌دهم غذا بخوری.

بگو بچّه‌ها با کبریت بازی نکنند، وگرنه تمام خانه آتش می‌گیرد.

باید کار را تمام کنی؛ در غیر این صورت، بَه تو پول نخواهند داد.

باید صبح تا شب درس بخوانی، و الّا قبول نمی‌شوی.

5.4 انگار [*engār*, as if]

انگار – and the more formal or literary. گوئی – do not need the subjunctive, because what is expressed after them is treated as some pseudo-fact:

طوری با من حرف می‌زنی انگار (که) من احمقم.

آنقدر لاغر شده‌ای که انگار یک هفته است غذا نخورده‌ای.

انگار حرفهای یک هفته پیشِ خودت را فراموش کرده‌ای.

بعد از جنگ همه چیز را از نو ساختند، گوئی هیچ اتّفاقی نیفتاده است.

5.4.1 To look as if

The verbs رسیدن/آمدن نظر به and (in *form./lit.* Persian) نمودن (all meaning 'to look, to seem, to appear') need the subjunctive when negative, but normally no subjunctive when affirmative, unless you want to decrease the likelihood when talking about what is going to happen next. (See also I/14.2.4.) Compare:

به نظر می‌رسد که حالت خوب نیست.

به نظر نمی‌رسد که امشب غذای خوشمزه‌ای داشته باشیم.

5.5 More on tenses in counterfactual conditionals

We know that there are only two tenses that can be used in counterfactual conditionals: *past progressive* and *past perfect*. (See I/16.2.) We also learned that the *past progressive* is the more common of the two tenses, especially in the main clause. Here we can add that the *past perfect* is usually not used in the main clause if

- it has the nature of some general statement (whether true or false);
- some frequency adverb (always, every day, etc.) is mentioned; or
- the tense of the first verb (in the if-clause) is *past progressive* and the action of the verb in the main clause could not have happened *before* that.

In the following examples of counterfactual conditionals, the tense of the verb in the main clause cannot be *past perfect*:

اگر خدائی می‌بود، اینهمه مردم در بدبختی زندگی نمی‌کردند.

اگر می‌دانستم از ایران رفته (است)، هر روز به خانه‌اش تلفن نمی‌زدم.

اگر درِ سفارتخانه را باز می‌کردند، مردم از دیوار بالا نمی‌رفتند.

Exercises

Exercise 5.1

Combine the two sentences by using مگر اینکه ('unless'); then translate. Example:

آن را می‌آورم. خیلی سنگین نیست.

← آن را می‌آورم، مگر اینکه خیلی سنگین باشد. (I'll bring it unless it's too heavy.)

١. فردا بر می‌گردد. مادرش اجازه می‌دهد.

٢. مادر بزرگ گفت به تو نخواهم گفت. نمی‌گذاری تو را ببوسم.

٣. او انتخاب می‌شود. مردم عقل ندارند.

۴. این غذا را نمی‌خورم. خیلی گرسنه نیستم.

۵. برای او کار نمی‌کنم. خودش نمی‌خواهد.

۶. امروز در رستوران غذا می‌خورم. شوهرم آشپزی نکرده است.

٧. تو را دوست نخواهد داشت. هرچیزی که می‌گوید قبول نمی‌کنی.

٨. در آن خانه زندگی نخواهیم کرد. مجبور نیستیم.

٩. دیگر با او حرف نخواهم زد. از من عذرخواهی نمی‌کند.

١٠. به تو احترام خواهند گذاشت. نمی‌دانند که شغلت چیست.

Exercise 5.2

Translate the following into English.

١. به تو اعتماد دارم، وگرنه این را به تو نمی‌گفتم.

٢. بچّه‌هایم کوچک هستند، وگرنه می‌توانستم کار کنم.

۳. دیروز خبر نداشت، وگرنه آنقدر نمی‌خندید.

۴. باید پنجره را باز بگذاری، وگرنه اتاق خیلی گرم می‌شود.

۵. باید میوه و سبزی بیشتر بخوری، وگرنه حالت بهتر نمی‌شود.

۶. ایرانیها آدمهای تنبلی هستند، وگرنه اینقدر شاعر نداشتند.

۷. می‌خواهم به ایران بروم، وگرنه فارسی یاد نمی‌گرفتم.

۸. آن مصاحبه را بخوان، وگرنه او را خوب نخواهی شناخت.

۹. به ما دروغ گفته است، وگرنه خودش هم می‌آمد.

۱۰. مردم او را دوست دارند، وگرنه به او رأی نمی‌دادند.

Exercise 5.3

In the sentences from the previous exercise (5.2), begin the first clause
with اگر ('if') and delete وگرنه ('otherwise'); other changes might also be
necessary. Then translate. Example:

باید آن کار را به تو بدهد، وگرنه آدم احمقی است

← (If he doesn't give you اگر آن کار را به تو ندهد، آدم احَمقی است

that job, he is a stupid person.)

Exercise 5.4

Choose one of the words/conjunctions:

اگر – مگر اینکه – وگرنه – انگار – فقط – با این تفاوت که

to fill in the blanks in the following sentences, then translate the sentence.
Example:

.... فردا روز خیلی سردی خواهد بود

(It seems that tomorrow is going to be a very cold day.) انگار ←

۱. .... وقت داری می‌گویم.

۲. ماشینم خراب بود، .... می‌آمدم.

۳. خیلی عصبانی بود، .... فهمیده بود.

۴. من هم او را خواهم دید، .... اصلاً نیاید.

۵. می‌خواستم بگویم، .... جرئت نکردم.

۶. .... نمی‌دانست چرا گفت می‌داند؟

۷. من هم همان حرف شما را گفتم، .... توهین نکردم.

۸. امروز هم خواهم آمد، .... کمی دیرتر.

۹. باید به او کمک کنم .... تمام نخواهد کرد.

۱۰. .... نمی‌دانستی که او ازدواج کرده؟

Exercise 5.5

Provide the correct form of the verb, then translate. Example:

دیگر او را هرگز نخواهم دید، مگر اینکه او به خوابِ من .... (آمدن)
بیاید ← (I'll never see him again unless he comes/appears in my dream.)

۱. اگر آن کتاب را .... (نـ + خواندن، 2sg.) بهتر است امروز به کلاس نروی.

۲. امیدوارم به او زنگ بزند، وگرنه برادرش هرگز .... (نـ + فهمیدن).

۳. می‌توانم در حیاط سیگار بکشم، مگر اینکه برایت فرقی .... (نـ + کردن).

۴. این هیچ شباهتی به پارتی ندارد، مگر اینکه شما صدای موسیقی را بلندتر .... (کردن).

۵. اگر .... (نـ + خواستن، 3sg.) کتاب را بخرد، باید از کتابخانهٔ عمومی قرض می‌گرفت.

۶. اگر تو را ندیده بودم، .... (فکر کردن، 1sg.) اتفاق بدی افتاده است.

۷. اگر خانه آتش می‌گرفت، .... (دانستن) چطور آن را خاموش کنید؟

۸. اگر .... (در نظر داشتن، 2pl.) با او ازدواج کنید، این کار را همین امسال بکنید.

۹. با او ازدواج نخواهم کرد، مگر اینکه خیلی .... (اصرار کردن، 3sg.).

۱۰. اگر فردا شما طلاق .... (گرفتن)، آیا بچّه از داشتنِ پدر یا مادر محروم نمی‌شود؟

Exercise 5.6

Translate the following into Persian; some of the words you can use have
been given at the end of the exercise.

1. Don't call me again if you hate me so much.
2. I won't write that letter unless he earnestly begs.
3. Unless you succeed in finding the mouse, I wouldn't dare sleep in
   this room.
4. They shouldn't drink this water if they haven't boiled it first.
5. He is a good person; otherwise he wouldn't have given you your money.
6. Is it bad if the color of one eye differs from that of the other?
7. My parents are not much different, except that they are younger.
8. How did you tell them what you wanted if you didn't know the language?
9. Don't tell her about it if you don't want everybody to know.
10. It looks as if they are encouraging him to go back to Iran.

اینقدر/بد آمدن/زنگ زدن/التماس کردن/موفّق شدن/موش/پیدا کردن/جرئت
کردن/جوشاندن/نوشیدن/آدم/پول/دادن/رنگ/چشم/فرق داشتن/جوان/
زبان/دانستن/فهمیدن/همه/دربارهٔ/به نظر رسیدن/تشویق کردن

در خانه اگر کس است، یک حرف بَس است.

If there's someone home, one word is enough.

(= I don't care if you don't follow my advice.)

UNIT SIX	۶ فصل
Causative form	شکلِ سببی
Optative mood	شکلَ دعائی
Past participle as verb	اسم مفعول در مقام فعل
Deleting a similar verb	حذفِ فعل مَشابه
Regulars on the march!	پیشرَویِ افعالَ باقاعده

6.1 Causative form

This is a very common form used to make causative/transitive verbs from intransitive verbs (or occasionally to give a causative sense to an already transitive verb).

The formation is quite regular: you add the suffix ـاندن (*-āndan*) to the present stem (sometimes these verbs have a more formal or literary version also with the suffix ـانیدن [*-ānidan*]). The resulting verb is also always regular. To get the present stem, you only drop *-dan* (or *-idan*) from the end of the new infinitive.

Note 1: Not all the verbs have this causative form.

Note 2: Not all the infinitives ending in *-āndan* are the causative form of another infinitive – which means that some can even be intransitive (like ماندن [*māndan*], to stay). But the great majority of them are.

Note 3: The verb نشستن (*neshastan*, to sit, *pres.* stem *neshin*) uses the shortened causative form نشاندن (*neshāndan*, to cause to sit). Also, in colloquial Persian you hear the causative/transitive form شکاندن (*shekāndan*) for the verb شکستن (*shekastan*, to break, both *tr.* and *intr.*).

Examples:

سلام مرا (= من را) به خانواده‌تان برسانید. (Say hello from me./Give my greetings to your family.)

دیروز برگشت ولی کتابم را برنگرداند. (He returned yesterday but did not return my book.)

می‌توانی این غذا را به بچّه بخورانی؟ (Can you feed this food to the child?)

6

Causative form

Optative mood

Past participle
as verb

Deleting a
similar verb

Regulars on
the march!

Table 6.1: How causative verbs are formed (from left to right)

Simple Infinitive (often intransitive)		+ -ĀNDAN (-ĀNIDAN)	Causative Infinitive (always transitive)	
INFINITIVE	PRES. STEM		INFINITIVE	PRES. STEM
خوردن to eat	خور *khor*		خوراندن (خورانیدن) *khorāndan (khorānidan)*, to feed; to cause to eat	خوران *khorān*
خوابیدن to sleep	خواب *khāb*		خواباندن (خوابانیدن) *khābāndan (khābānidan)*, to put to bed; to cause to sleep	خوابان *khābān*
رسیدن to reach	رس *res*		رساندن (رسانیدن) *resāndan (resānidan)*, to cause to reach; to deliver	رسان *resān*
برگشتن to return (*intr.*)	برگرد *bargard*		برگرداندن *bargardāndan*, to [cause to] return (*tr.*)	برگردان *bargardān*
ایستادن to stand	ایست *ist*		ایستاندن *istāndan*, to cause to stand	ایستان *istān*
دویدن to run	دو *dow/dav*		دواندن *davāndan*, to cause to run	دوان *davān*
پریدن to fly	پر *par*		پراندن *parāndan*, to cause to fly	پران *parān*
پوشیدن to wear	پوش *push*		پوشاندن *pushāndan*, to cause to wear; to cover	پوشان *pushān*
ترسیدن to fear	ترس *tars*		ترساندن *tarsāndan*, to scare	ترسان *tarsān*

6.2 Optative mood

An outmoded mood now, it was used in early modern Persian as a form of prayer, for wishing and cursing. In poetical/archaic language you can still encounter examples of this, which mostly consist of changing the third person -ad ending to -ād. Thus, دهاد (dahād) and کناد (konād) would be the optative forms of respectively dādan and kardan.

The only verb whose *optative* mood is still widely used is the verb بودن (to be), its irregular optative form being باد (bād, sometimes بادا [bādā] in poetry, meaning 'May [it] be . . .'), especially common in the expression 'Long live . . . :'

زنده باد آزادی! (Long live freedom!)

هرچه بادا باد! ([proverb:] Come what may!/Whatever will be, will be!)

6.3 Past participle as verb

Sometimes a past participle alone – without being part of a perfect tense or structure – is used as a verb.

6.3.1 When است is deleted

In the third person singular of the present perfect tense, colloquial Persian always drops است – this happens often enough in more formal, written Persian as well – thus leaving the past participle behind: پدرم آمده instead of پدرم آمده است (My father has come). This is probably the only case where using a single past participle as verb is acceptable in all levels of language and is not considered 'bad' or careless Persian.

6.3.2 'Having not yet . . .'

Another 'acceptable' case is one in which the past participle is negative and is used in the sense of 'having not yet . . .' (which can also be seen as a shortened version of a Persian equivalent for *had hardly/scarcely . . . when . . .*; see 12.4).

In this usage, regardless of the negative *na-* that usually takes the main stress, the stress is on the last syllable of the past participle, and no وَ (and) follows it. Examples:

هنوز در را باز نکرده، فریاد زد که گرسنه است. (Having barely opened the door, he shouted that he was hungry. Or: Scarcely had he opened the door when . . .)

هنوز الفبای کار را یاد نگرفته، می‌خواست به اندازهٔ تو حقوق بگیرد. (Having barely learned the ABCs of the job, he wanted to get a salary as high as yours.)

The following examples (still negative, with final stress, and no *va*) are very close to the ones above:

6

Causative form

Optative mood

Past participle
as verb

Deleting a
similar verb

Regulars on
the march!

غذا نخورده کجا داری می‌روی؟ (Where are you going without having eaten?)

نمی‌گذارم پولِ من را نداده از اینجا برود. (I won't let him leave this place before he gives me [/not having given me] my money.)

6.3.3 *To be avoided:* participial absolute

In written Persian, especially in official/administrative language, you often come across another usage of past participle (or *participial absolute*) as verb, a practice hated and avoided by writers of 'good' Persian.

In its most acceptable (or least hated) version, the rule is to change one or more verbs (of the same tense) in a longer sentence to past participles and only keep the verb at the end of the sentence in its finite form – which will also determine the tense and person of the past participles. It is recommended to drop the conjunction 'and' when a finite verb changes to a past participle, but this is often neglected, to make things worse. Example:

Normal sentence:

به خانه برگشتیم و غذا خوردیم. (We returned home and ate.)

After the change (not recommended!):

به خانه برگشته غذا خوردیم. (Same meaning; here خوردیم is what shows the tense and person of برگشته.)

Still worse would be keeping the conjunction:

به خانه برگشته و غذا خوردیم.

And still worse would be using this form when verbs are not of the same tense and/or person, which can be confusing as well.

6.4 Deleting a similar verb

Here also you usually keep the finite verb at the end of the sentence and somehow 'shorten' or delete the verb(s) before it in longer sentences, which is done in two ways: deleting similar auxiliary verbs and deleting similar verbal parts of compound verbs. Deleting other verbs, or the verb at the end of the sentence, is much less common, and deleting verbs that are not similar is considered a grammatical mistake.

This is also a feature common in written Persian only – and not much loved even there.

Examples (with deleted verbs in brackets):

او خیلی زودتر از ما آمده (بود) و غذا خورده بود.

آن نامه نوشته (شده است) و برای آنها فرستاده شده است.

آنها با همه صحبت (کردند) و دربارهٔ مشکلات تحقیق کردند.

بعداً پنجره‌ها باز (شدند) و اتاقها تمیز شدند.

پدرم به اصفهان (رفت) و از آنجا به شیراز رفت.

او به جنوبِ فرانسه رفت و از آنجا به ایتالیا (رفت).

6.5 Regulars on the march!

In the course of its simplification, modern Persian has been moving away
from simple, irregular verbs. The two main strategies have been:

a) using compound verbs with only a few verbs – mainly کردن and شدن ;
b) making regular verbs out of the irregular ones.

The latter strategy requires adding *-idan* to the present stem of the verb.
The irregular verb is then usually used in written/literary language only,
and the present stem for both versions of the verb would be the same.

Examples for a):

آلودن [*āludan*, to pollute, to dirty] → آلوده کردن/شدن [*ālude kardan/
shodan*, to make or get dirty and polluted]

خستن [*khastan*, to wound (obsolete)] → خسته کردن/شدن [*khaste
kardan/shodan*, to make or get tired]

Examples for b):

خفتن [*khoftan*, to sleep] → خوابیدن [*khābidan*, to sleep]

کوفتن [*kuftan*, to pound, to hammer] → کوبیدن [*kubidan*, to pound,
to mash]

رُستن [*rostan*, to grow] → روئیدن [*ru'idan*, to grow]

رَستن [*rastan*, to escape or be saved] → رهیدن [*rahidan*] → رها شدن
[*rahā shodan*]

In the case of *kuftan/kubidan*, their past participles give the names of two
famous Persian dishes: کوفته [*kufte*, ball of ground meat mixed with other
ingredients, in other countries known as *kufta*, *kofta* or *köfte*] and کوبیده
[*kubide*, skewer of ground meat kebab].

6

Causative form

Optative mood

Past participle
as verb

Deleting a
similar verb

Regulars on
the march!

Exercises

Exercise 6.1

Provide the causative form of the same verb used in the first part of each
sentence (all simple past tense, except one imperative and one subjunctive);
then translate. Example:

موضوع را نمی‌فهمید، ولی من به او ....

→ فهماندم (He didn't understand the subject, but I made him understand.)

۱. نمی‌خواستم برگردم، ولی او به زور مرا ....

۲. از همان غذائی که خودش می‌خورد به بچّه ....

۳. من معمولاً از سگ نمی‌ترسم، ولی این سگ خیلی مرا ....

۴. قبل از اینکه خودش بخوابد، همهٔ بچّه‌ها را ....

۵. خیلی دیر رسیدند و بالاخره آن نامه را به من ....

۶. این سگ باید خیلی بدود تا تو را هم کمی ....

۷. لباس گرمی بپوش و شب هم خودت را خوب ....

۸. پدرم نشست و برادر کوچکم را روی پایش ....

۹. هفتهٔ اوّل خیلی سخت گذشت ولی (ما) هفتهٔ دوّم را راحت‌تر ....

۱۰. خیلی می‌خندید و همه را ....

Exercise 6.2

Translate the following and say

a) would you read the verb as ending in *-ānd* or *-ānad*?
b) Which of the verbs are causative?

Example: او می‌داند
→ He knows. (*-ānad*, not causative)

۱. دیروز کتاب می‌خواند.

۲. فردا در آن برنامه یک ترانه می‌خواند.

۳. چرا بچّه را روی میز خواباند؟

۴. ممکن است با صدای بلندش همه را بترساند.

۵. آیا بیشتر از پنج ساعت ماند؟

۶. برای آنکه زود برسد، خیلی سریع راند.

۷. اگر او معلم باشد درس را خوب به شاگردان می‌فهماند.

۸. می‌گوید که خواهد توانست ولی نمی‌تواند.

۹. خوشحالم که آمد و پیغام را به شما رساند.

۱۰. واقعاً حرفهایم شما را ترساند؟

Exercise 6.3

Re-write the following sentences by replacing the past participles with complete verbs (+ conjunctions if necessary), then translate. Example:

پروین به خانه رفته دوش می‌گیرد

پروین به خانه می‌رود و دوش می‌گیرد (Parvin goes home and takes → a shower.)

۱. بشقاب را برداشته به آشپزخانه بردم.

۲. کتاب را باز کرده تا صفحهٔ صد و هفده خواندم.

۳. آن خانم کیست که آنجا نشسته هیچ نمی‌گوید؟

۴. پدر و مادرش به مدرسه رفته با معلم صحبت کرده‌اند.

۵. دیگر او را هرگز ندیده با او حرف نخواهیم زد.

۶. آن ماشین را فروخته ماشین بهتری بخرید.

۷. می‌خواهد زبان فارسی را یاد گرفته به ایران سفر کند.

۸. او هرگز به مدرسه نرفته حتّی نمی‌تواند اسمش را بنویسد.

۹. قبلاً به خانهٔ ما آمده با برادرم حرف زده بود.

۱۰. باید آب را جوشانده چای درست کنید.

Exercise 6.4

Translate the following sentences.

۱. از ماشین پیاده شده به بیمارستان رفتند.

۲. ظرفها را نشسته نباید جلو تلویزیون بنشینی.

۳. چند بار گربه‌اش را گم کرده و دوباره پیدا کرده بود.

۴. غذایش را تمام کرده ولی هنوز نخوابیده.

۵. در روزهای گذشته او را چند بار دیده با او به سینما رفته‌ام.

6

Causative form

Optative mood

Past participle
as verb

Deleting a
similar verb

Regulars on
the march!

۶. از چند خیابان گذشته به آن ساختمان بزرگ رسیدیم.

۷. هنوز به تهران نرسیده ماشینمان خراب شد.

۸. این سیب کاملاً رسیده نیست، یک سیب دیگر بده.

۹. سوارِ تاکسی شده به خانه‌ام برگشتم.

۱۰. بالاخره آن پرنده از روی شاخه پریده از ما دور شد.

Exercise 6.5

In which of the sentences from the previous exercise are we using a *past participle* in a way that colloquial/spoken Persian usually avoids? Mention the numbers and the past participle.

جوجه را آخرِ پائیز می‌شمرند.

They count the chicks at the end of autumn.

(= Don't rejoice too early!)

UNIT SEVEN | فصل ۷

Impersonal forms | شکلهای غیر شخصی

7.1 Impersonal with آدم [*ādam*]

The only equivalent in Persian to the English impersonal *one* is آدم [*ādam*, in literary Persian آدمی, *ādami* with stressed final -*i*], but Persian can get even more impersonal than this (see 7.2) – or much less (see 7.3). *Ādam* is used as a singular noun, functioning as the subject or object of verbs. (When used as object, English might prefer to translate this آدم as *you* or *people* or use other pronouns.) Examples:

آدم باید خیلی مواظب باشد. (One must be very careful.)

آدم نمی‌داند چه بگوید. (One doesn't know what to say.)

آدم را می‌ترسانی. (You scare one [/me/people].)

به آدم نمی‌گویند کجا برود. (They don't tell one [/you/people] where to go.)

However, sometimes آدم is used simply in the sense of *a person/a human*, especially when accompanied by indefinite markers (*yek* or unstressed -*i*). If آدم is used in a plural sense, it simply means *people*. Examples:

اتاق پر از آدم بود. (The room was full of/filled with people.)

آیا هیچ آدم مطلعی پیدا نکردی؟ (Didn't you find any well-informed person?)

مثل آدم غذا بخور! (Eat like a human!/Watch how you eat!)

آدمها باید یاد بگیرند چطور مواظبِ طبیعت باشند. (People must learn how to protect/care for nature.)

7.2 Entirely impersonal constructions

There are a few entirely impersonal constructions in Persian, all of which use the *past stem* (also called *short infinitive*):

a) باید [bāyad] + *past stem* = 'one must . . .'/'one has to . . .'
b) می‌توان [mi-tavān] + *past stem* = 'one can . . .'
c) می‌شود [mi-shavad] + *past stem* = 'one can/may . . .'/'it is possible to . . .'
d) می‌شد [mi-shod] + *past stem* = 'one could [have] . . .'/'it was possible to . . .'

باید (a) and می‌توان (b) have no past tense in contemporary Persian, but می‌شود (c) changes to می‌شد (d) for past, which can even be used as the past tense substitute of می‌توان (b).

The once past versions of باید – namely, بایست [bāyest], بایستی [bāyesti], or می‌بایست [mi-bāyest] and می‌بایستی [mi-bāyesti] – are now used loosely as less common synonyms of *bāyad* in the present tense and can all be followed by the *past stem* like باید (a), with the same function and meaning.

If می‌شود and می‌توان (b and c) are preceded by something that requires the subjunctive, they change to بتوان [be-tavān] and بشود [be-shavad], but this doesn't affect the past stem:

شاید بتوان گفت که این سردترین شهر ایران است. (Perhaps one can say that this is the coldest city in Iran.)

شاید نشود امروز به آنجا رفت. (One might not be able to go there today.)

Now that you have learned the last possible construction with باید in Persian (see 4.3), let us see them all together: four constructions with five different usages.

Table 7.1: All constructions possible with *bāyad* (from left to right)

bāyad	+	past stem	=	impersonal ('one')	باید رفت One must go.
bāyad	+	subjunctive	=	must *or* have to	باید برود He must go.
bāyad	+	perfect subjunctive	=	must have	باید رفته باشد He must have gone.
bāyad	+	past progressive	=	should have	باید می‌رفت He should have gone.
			=	had to	باید می‌رفت He had to go.

Examples:

بايد به آدمها آموزش داد که چطور طبيعت را حفظ کنند.) (One must educate/teach people how to preserve/protect nature.)

می‌توان گفت که بزرگترين کشتارهای تاريخ در قرن بيستم اتفاق افتاده است. (One can say that the biggest massacres of history took place in the twentieth century.)

بايد بتوان با او صحبت کرد. (One must be able to talk to him.)

اين قرصها را نمی‌شود با هم خورد. (One cannot take these pills together.)

چطور می‌شد آن اراجيف را باور کرد؟ (How could one believe that garbage?)

For more examples with می‌شود see also Unit 4 (Table 4.1).

7.3 Some quasi-impersonal idioms

There are a variety of idioms in Persian using a construction that can hardly be called *impersonal*, because the *person* is clearly there – only not where you normally expect it to be: not as the conjugational ending of the verb. In these constructions, the tense of the verb can change, but not its person: the verb always remains third person singular for all persons, and the 'person' – the real *subject* – is attached as a possessive/dative suffix to the word that can be said to be the 'grammatical' subject of the verb.

We are already familiar with this construction from earlier discussions of speaking about age (I/8.5.1). One option for giving an age was:

X years + possessive suffixes + verb *to be* (3sg.)

In the sentence من بيست سالم است (*man bist sāl-am ast*, I am 20), the grammatical subject is *sāl* (year), which is always third person singular, and the real subject is shown by the suffix -*am* attached to *sāl*. To better understand an idiom like سردم است (*sard-am ast*, I feel cold), we should analyze it like this: '[For] *me* [it] *is cold.*' (Compare this with the German dative version: *Mir ist kalt.*) To make it still easier to understand, it can be said that the *grammatical subject* here is سرد – always third person singular – and the *real subject* (to be used in translation) is the personal suffix added to *sard*. Instead of changing the conjugational endings of the verb, this -*am* should change: to say 'they feel cold' you say سردشان است (*sard-eshān ast*), and so on.

Similarly, بَسَم است (*bas-am ast*; Tehrani: بسّمه, *bassame*) means '[For] *me* [it] *is enough.*' (German: *Mir reicht's.*)

The contemporary, colloquial phrase ‏چه ات است؟‏ (*che-at ast?*; Tehrani: ‏چته؟‏ *che-te?*) has its older, dative version (now used in literary language only) as: ‏تو را چه می‌شود؟‏, all meaning 'What's wrong with you?' (German: *Was ist mit dir?*) To say 'What's wrong with them?' you simply change ‏ات‏ to ‏شان‏ and say: ‏چه شان است؟‏ (Tehrani: ‏چشونه؟‏ *cheshune?*), while the verb remains the same.

See below for some examples of the most common impersonal idioms, most of which deal with sensations, feelings and emotions. (An asterisk is used to show where you add the suffixes.)

‏از ... خوش* آمدن‏ (to like):

> ‏از فیلم خوشت خواهد آمد.‏ (You're going to like the movie.)
>
> ‏از این کارش خوشم نیامد.‏ (I didn't like what he did [lit., 'this deed of his'].)

‏از ... بد* آمدن‏ (to dislike or hate):

> ‏از این رنگ خیلی بدم می‌آید.‏ (I really hate this color.)
>
> ‏ظاهراً از تو بدش نمی‌آید.‏ (Apparently he likes you/has fallen for you.)

‏خواب* آمدن‏ (to feel/get sleepy):

> ‏هنوز هوا تاریک نشده، چطور خوابت می‌آید؟‏ (It's not dark yet, how can you feel sleepy?)

‏خواب* بُردن‏ (to fall asleep):

> ‏ما هنوز داشتیم حرف می‌زدیم که او خوابش بُرد.‏ (We were still talking when he fell asleep.)

‏دیر* شدن‏ (to be late):

> ‏نمی‌توانم بیشتر از این صبر کنم، دیرم شده.‏ (I can't wait more/longer than this; I'm late.)

‏خنده*/گریه* گرفتن‏ (to have to or to start to laugh/cry):

> ‏سریع از اتاق بیرون رفتم چون خنده‌ام گرفته بود.‏ (I left the room quickly because I had to laugh.)
>
> ‏وقتی درباره مادرش پرسیدیم، گریه‌اش گرفت.‏ (When we asked about her mother, she started to cry.)

‏دل* خواستن‏ (to wish/want):

> ‏بچه‌ها دلشان می‌خواهد این فیلم را ببینند.‏ (The children want to watch this movie.)

For similar idioms about remembering/forgetting see also Unit 14.

For idioms about putting on or wearing clothes see Unit 8.

In some cases, it is also possible in such idioms to use a noun or an independent pronoun (instead of using the suffixed possessive pronoun), as with these verbs:

دل* تنگ شدن (برای) (to miss):

خیلی دلم برای آن روزها تنگ شده. (I really miss those days.) – here *del-am* can change to *del-e man*.

دل* سوختن (برای/به حالِ) (to feel pity for or take pity on):

دلت به حالِ سگ و گربه می‌سوزد ولی به حالِ این بچّه نه. (You feel pity [/show compassion] for dogs and cats but not for this child.)

خوش گذشتن (به*) (to have a good time; to enjoy one's time):

تازه دوستش مرده، چطور انتظار داری به او (/به مریم) خوش بگذرد؟

بد گذشتن (به*) (to have a bad time)

در آن دو سال خیلی به ما (/به من و همسرم) بد گذشت.

The last two (بد گذشتن and خوش گذشتن) become totally impersonal when no pronoun/noun is mentioned for the person who has a good or bad time:

دیشب خیلی خوش گذشت. (Last night it was hilarious.)

با پروین خیلی خوش می‌گذرد. (It's a lot of fun with Parvin.)

Note: Some verbs may belong to this group in one of their senses only. Example:

بر خوردن (به) (to encounter, to come across) = a normal verb, conjugated for all persons:

در خیابان به مینا برخوردم. (I bumped into Mina on the street.)

به مقالۀ جدیدی برخوردند. (They came across a new article.)

بر خوردن (به*) (to be offended) = *quasi-impersonal*, conjugated always for 3*sg.*:

خیلی به من برخوْرد. (I was really offended.)

امیدوارم به شما برنخورَد. (I hope you won't take offense.)

Exercises

Exercise 7.1

Make impersonal, present tense sentences with the words given (some might also require a preposition); then translate. (You wouldn't need to change the order.) Example:

پدر بزرگم – نَوَد و پنج – سال* بودن

پدر بزرگم نَوَد و پنج سالش است (My grandfather is 95 years old.) ←

۱. گربه‌ها – موش‌ها – دل* نـ+ سوختن

۲. اگر شب – قهوه بخوری – دیر – خواب* بردن

۳. اگر تاکسی – نگیریم – دیر* شدن

۴. آیا شما – دانشگاه قبلی‌تان – دل* تنگ شدن؟

۵. چرا تو اینقدر – غذای ایرانی – بد* آمدن؟

۶. هر وقت – شراب می‌خورم – گرم* شدن

۷. چراغ را – خاموش کن – من – خواب* آمدن

۸. آدم – این بچّه‌های گرسنه – دل* سوختن

۹. وقتیکه – لباسش را – دیدیم – ما همه – خنده* گرفتن

۱۰. اگر هزار بار – این فیلم را – ببینم – باز هم – گریه* گرفتن

Exercise 7.2

Translate the following into English.

۱. در ایران نمی‌توان شراب خورد، مگر نه؟

۲. با یک خانم نمی‌توان اینطور حرف زد.

۳. باید نامهٔ دیگری برای دانشگاه نوشت.

۴. اینجا نمی‌شود زیاد سروصدا کرد.

۵. تا پارسال می‌شد بدونِ ویزا به آنجا رفت.

۶. نمی‌توان این فیلم را دید و نخندید.

۷. نباید بچّه را هر سال به یک مدرسهٔ جدید فرستاد.

۸. کاش می‌شد دوباره جوان شد.

۹. در این کشور می‌توان با یک دخترِ دَه ساله ازدواج کرد.

۱۰. آیا می‌شود یک قورباغه را به اندازهٔ یک گربه دوست داشت؟

Exercise 7.3

Change the structure of the sentences in the previous exercise from impersonal to personal (or quasi-impersonal: آدم), using the pronoun or noun given below as subject; then translate.

These are the nouns/pronouns you should use (or just have in mind) for each of the sentences in the previous exercise:

۱. مردم ۲. تو ۳. ما ۴. شما ۵. تو ۶. آدم ۷. ما ۸. من ۹. من ۱۰. مردها ۱۱ آدم

Example:

اصلاً نمی‌شود به او اعتماد کرد (من)

← اصلاً نمی‌توانم به او اعتماد کنم (I cannot trust him at all.)

Exercise 7.4

Translate the following and write in brackets those words which constitute the impersonal structure. (There is only one sentence without any impersonal structure.) Example:

جلوِ بچّه نباید حرفهای زشت گفت

→ One should not utter ugly words before children. (نباید ... گفت)

۱. از اینجا نمی‌شود دید.

۲. اوّل باید دربارهٔ خانواده‌شان تحقیق کرد.

۳. آیا حتماً باید این زبان را یاد گرفت؟

۴. نباید دربارهٔ شغلِ جدیدش زیاد نگران بود.

۵. ممکن است دیدنِ شوهرش لازم نباشد ولی خودش را حتماً باید دید.

۶. می‌توان از خودش پرسید که چرا ما را تعقیب می‌کرده.

۷. پلیس به همسایه‌مان گفته است که نباید به هیچ چیزی دست زد.

۸. دکتر، من باید بدانم که می‌توان امیدی داشت یا نه؟

۹. نمی‌شد از اوّل راستش را به من بگوئی؟

۱۰. کاش بتوان روزی معنیِ این حرف را فهمید!

۱۱. شهر شیکاگو باید یک بار در آتش می‌سوخت تا از نو ساخته شود.

۱۲. باید دانست که قبلاً در اروپا می‌شد دانشمندان را به‌عنوانِ کافر در آتش سوزاند.

Exercise 7.5

Which of the following sentences is using an impersonal (or quasi-impersonal) structure?

۱. این کتاب را فقط در کتابخانه باید خواند.

۲. باید از دو هفته قبل به رئیسش خبر می‌داد.

۳. بابک را امروز می‌توان در خانهٔ مادرش دید.

۴. آیا همین امروز باید آن نامه را برگرداند؟

۵. آیا می‌شود آن مقاله را در اینترنت هم پیدا کرد؟

۶. خوب است که اینجا می‌شود بدون صدای موسیقی صحبت کنیم.

۷. از گوشتِ نپخته اصلاً خوشم نمی‌آید.

۸. نمی‌توان فقط نگاه کرد و هیچ کاری نکرد.

۹. از بیکاری خسته شد و به خانه‌اش برگشت.

۱۰. چرا نمی‌شد کمی زودتر رفت؟

با یک دست نمی‌شود دو هندوانه برداشت.

One cannot hold two watermelons in one hand.

(= Do things one at a time!)

UNIT EIGHT	فصل ۸
Position of verbs in the sentence	جای فعل در جمله
Verbs of state	فعلهای حالت
Putting on and taking off clothes	پوشیدن و درآوردنِ لباس
To want, to be able to, to know	خواستن، توانستن، دانستن

8.1 Position of verbs in the sentence

In a standard Persian sentence the verb is usually placed at the end of the sentence or clause. Colloquial Persian, however, leaves room for some flexibility in this regard. In particular, after a *verb of movement*, words denoting a location or destination can be placed after the verb. In such cases, we are more likely to drop the preposition in the adverbial phrase that follows the verb. Examples:

بعد از دو هفته همسرش برگشت (به) مشهد. (After two weeks his/her
   spouse returned to Mashhad.)

رفتیم (به) آلمان به امیدِ آنکه علی را ببینیم ولی آنجا نبود. (We went to
   Germany in the hope of seeing Ali, but he was not there.)

شیر را ریخت توی لیوان (و) گذاشت جلو بچّه. (She poured the milk
   into the mug and put [it] in front of the child.)

شوهرش را انداختند (به/توی) زندان و حتّی اجازهٔ ملاقات هم ندادند.
   (They threw her husband in jail and didn't even give [her]
   a visiting permit.)

In colloquial Persian you can find examples with no 'movement' in the verb, or with no 'location/destination' mentioned:

8

Position of
verbs in the
sentence

Verbs of state

Putting on
and taking
off clothes

To want,
to be able to,
to know

چند روز بمان (در) تهران تا با شهر آشنا شوی (Stay in Tehran for
a few days to get to know the city.)

تلاش زیادی کردم برای پنهان کردن اضطرابم (I tried hard to hide
my anxiety.)

زنش را معرفی کرد به همکارش و رفت بلیط بخرد (He introduced his
wife to his colleague and went to buy tickets.)

خیلی می‌ترسید از عواقبِ آن، ولی چاره‌ای نبود (He was very much afraid
of its consequences, but there was no way out/he had no other choice.)

8.2 Verbs of state

Persian verbs of *state* use a *perfect* tense where English would use a *progressive* tense. These verbs – a small group – are treated as normal verbs when their focus is on the *action*, but as *state verbs* when their focus is only showing the *state* in which the subject of the verb is. You already know four important verbs of this group: خوابیدن ('to sleep') ('to stand'), ایستادن ('to sit'), نشستن ('to sleep') and پوشیدن ('to wear') (see I/13.3/b). Here are a few more verbs:

دراز کشیدن، چمباتمه زدن، تکیه کردن، در آغوش گرفتن، خیره شدن

And here are some pairs of examples showing them as both state verbs and normal verbs:

وقتیکه دیدم روی تخت دراز کشیده است، فکر کردم خواب است. (When
I saw her lying/saw that she was lying on the bed, I thought she
was asleep.)

در حدودِ نیم ساعت می‌شود که غذایش را خورده است و دراز کشیده است.
(It is about half an hour since she has eaten and has lain down.)

مینا آن دختری است که به آن درخت تکیه کرده است و دارد با دوستش
حرف می‌زند. (Mina is the girl [who is] leaning against that tree and
talking to her friend.)

ظاهراً سرش گیج رفته (است) و به دیوار تکیه کرده (است) که نیفتد.
(Apparently she has felt dizzy and has leaned against the wall in
order not to fall [down].)

ببین چطور عروسکش را در آغوش گرفته (است) و خوابش برده (است)!
(See how she is holding her doll in her arms and has fallen asleep!)

جلو همهٔ آن مرد را در آغوش گرفته (است) و بوسیده است. (She has
embraced that man in front of everybody and has kissed him.)

چند ساعت بود که آنجا چمباتمه زده بود و از جایش تکان نمی‌خورد
(It was a few hours that he was squatting there and did not move/
budge from his place.)

همینکه آنجا چمباتمه زده بود، ماری نیشش زده بود (As soon as he had
squatted there, a snake had bitten him.)

8.2.1 To put on, to be wearing and to take off clothes

As already mentioned, پوشیدن belongs to these state verbs. There are some
other compound verbs and idioms that can be used as synonyms, some
used for only certain articles of clothing – and some of them use a quasi-
impersonal construction (see Table 8.1 below).

8.3 Past and past progressive of certain verbs

With certain verbs like خواستن (to want), توانستن (to be able to) and دانستن
(to know), the past progressive, which is the tense more commonly used,
shows some *PASSIVE* state of *wanting*, *knowing* or *being able* in general
(with the *mi-* prefix used in its durative function), while the simple past
tense shows the more *ACTIVE* side of these verbs at some particular moment
in the past. They might need different verbs in English translation.

8.3.1 خواستن

In the past progressive tense, خواستن with *mi-* is the passive *state* of wanting, while without *mi-* (simple past) it is more an *act* and indicates some
immediate or sudden decision or intention (similar to 'being just about
to'). Compare the following examples with and without *mi-*:

وقتی جوان بود می‌خواست هنرپیشه بشود. (When she was young, she
wanted to become an actress.)

خواست/می‌خواست به او سلام کند، ولی خجالت کشید. (He wanted to
say 'hello' to her, but was [too] timid/bashful.) – The version without
mi- (simple past) has more of an act: he was just about to do so.

– 'چرا نخواستی با او حرف بزنی؟' – 'نخواستم/می‌خواستم، ولی او وقت
نداشت.' (– 'Why didn't you want to talk to him?' – 'I wanted to,
but he had no time.')

همینکه خواستم اسمش را بپرسم، مادرش صدایش کرد و فهمیدم اسمش
چیست. (Just as I wanted to ask her name, her mother called her
and I found out what her name was.)

آیا پلیس از تو خواست که از ماشین پیاده شوی؟ (Did the police want/
ask you to get off the car?)

Table 8.1: Most common expressions for putting on, taking off and wearing

ARTICLE	TO PUT ON	TO BE WEARING	TO TAKE OFF
general (excluding head, hands, feet), e.g. clothes, shirt, jacket, pullover, suit, skirt, etc.	I am putting on a shirt: پیرهن می‌پوشم (col.) پیرهن به تن می‌کنم (form.)	I am wearing a shirt: پیرهن پوشیده‌ام (col.) پیرهن به تن دارم (form.)	I am taking off my shirt: پیرهنم را در می‌آورم (col.) پیرهن را از تن بیرون می‌آورم (form.)
hat	I am putting on a hat: کلاه سرم می‌گذارم (col.) کلاه به سر می‌گذارم (form.)	I am wearing a hat: کلاه دارم (col.) کلاه سرم است (col.) کلاه بر سر دارم (form.)	I am taking off my hat: کلاهم را برمی‌دارم (col.) کلاه از سر برمی‌دارم (form.)
glasses	I am putting on my glasses: عینک می‌زنم (col.) عینک (به) چشمم می‌گذارم (col.) عینک به چشم می‌گذارم (form.)	I am wearing glasses: عینک دارم (col.) عینک زده‌ام (col.) عینک به چشم دارم (form.)	I am taking off my glasses: عینک را برمی‌دارم (col.) عینک برمی‌دارم (col.) عینک از چشم برمی‌دارم (form.)
gloves	I am putting on my gloves: دستکش دستم می‌کنم (col.) دستکش به دست می‌کنم (form.)	I am wearing gloves: دستکش دارم (col.) دستکش دستم است (col.) دستکش به دست دارم (form.)	I am taking off my gloves: دستکشم را درمی‌آورم (col.) دستکش از دست درمی‌آورم (form.)
pants/trousers, shoes and socks (example given for pants only)	I am putting on my pants: شلوارم را می‌پوشم (col.) شلوار پایم می‌کنم (col.) شلوار به پا می‌کنم (form.)	I am wearing pants: شلوار دارم (col.) شلوار پوشیده‌ام (col.) شلوار پایم است (col.) شلوار به پا دارم (form.)	I am taking off my pants: شلوارم را درمی‌آورم (col.) شلوار از پا درمی‌آورم (form.)
walking stick	I take my walking stick in my hand: عصایم را دستم می‌گیرم (col.) عصا به دست دستم می‌گیرم (form.)	I have my walking stick in my hand: عصا دستم است (col.) عصا به دست دارم (form.)	

همیشه می‌خواستم سوار آن ماشین بشوم. (I always wanted to ride in that car.)

از او خواستیم (که) سوار شود، ولی ترسید. (We asked him to get in [the car], but he was afraid.)

8.3.2 توانستن

The past progressive tense of توانستن (with *mi-*) shows a general *state* of capability (or, if negative, inability), while its simple past (with no *mi-*) shows more the *act* of *managing to do* something (or, if negative, *failing to do* something) – again at some particular point of time in the past. Examples:

از یکی از پنجره‌ها **می‌توانستیم** دریاچه را ببینیم. (From one of the windows we could see the lake.)

وقتی پنجره باز شد، **توانستیم** دریاچه را ببینیم. (When the window was opened, we were able to see the lake.)

خوشبختانه **می‌توانستم** شنا کنم و **توانستم** خودم را با شنا به ساحل برسانم. (Luckily I could swim and was able to/managed to reach [/bring myself to] the shore by swimming.)

8.3.3 دانستن *and related verbs*

The object of دانستن is often a statement (= *to know that* . . .) and, when used in this way, we have a similar difference between its *simple past* and *past progressive* tenses, the latter being by far the more common. *I knew* is usually می‌دانستم, and you use it without می‌ only when by *I knew* you mean *I realized*, as in these examples:

وقتی به آنجا می‌رفتم، **می‌دانستم** که ممکن است خانه نباشد. (When [/As] I was going there, I knew that he might not be home.)

همینکه صورتش را دیدم، **دانستم** که همه چیز را به او گفته‌اند. (As soon as I saw his face, I knew that they had told him everything.)

Even when used in this sense, the form without *mi-* is not usually used for negative or interrogative. There are other verbs that are much more common in Persian for the *act* of realization, a fact that contributes to making دانستم (without *mi-*) such a rare occurrence: instead of دانستم, you are much more likely to say فهمیدم/متوجّه شدم (or, in more formal Persian, دریافتم). Examples:

آیا همینکه او را دیدی، فهمیدی (/متوجّه شدی) که آبستن است؟ (Here دانستی would sound awkward.)

صورتم را دید، ولی نفهمید (/متوجّه نشد) که من مینا نیستم. (Here ندانست would be wrong.)

8

Position of
verbs in the
sentence

Verbs of state

Putting on
and taking
off clothes

To want,
to be able to,
to know

دانستن is not used for *knowing a person*, where شناختن is usually used, and again we will witness the same difference between شناختم (*act* = 'I recognized') and می‌شناختم (*state* = 'I knew'), as in these examples:

برادرت را تا همین دیروز **نمی‌شناختم.** (I didn't know your brother until [just] yesterday.)

همینکه پدرت را دیدم، او را **شناختم.** (As soon as I saw your father, I recognized him.)

To know how to do something is more often expressed by بلد بودن in colloquial Persian.

Considering the different meanings of the verb *to know* in English and its different usages, it would be helpful to have some examples of this verb used in different senses and see how it has been translated into Persian:

Table 8.2: *To know* and its Persian equivalents

Who knows!	کسی چه می‌داند!
How should I know?	از کجا بدانم؟
I know/knew his name.	اسمش را می‌دانم/می‌دانستم.
I know/knew him well.	او را خوب می‌شناسم/می‌شناختم.
I know/don't know [how to play] chess.	شطرنج بلدم/بلد نیستم.
I know that street.	آن خیابان را می‌شناسم.
I know that he will come.	می‌دانم که می‌آید.
I know how to go there.	می‌دانم چطور آنجا بروم.
He doesn't know how to drive.	بلد نیست (= نمی‌داند چطور) رانندگی کند.
I know him to be a good man.	او را آدم خوبی می‌دانم.
I knew that he was Iranian.	می‌دانستم که ایرانی است.
He spoke only a few words, and I knew [= I realized] that he was Iranian.	فقط چند کلمه حرف زد، و من فهمیدم (/متوجّه شدم) که ایرانی است.
I know about his past.	از گذشتهٔ او باخبرم (/خبر دارم/اطّلاع دارم/ مُطّلِعم)./دربارهٔ گذشته‌اش می‌دانم.
I will let you know.	به تو خبر خواهم داد.
Let us know about the time of your arrival.	از زمانِ وُرودتان ما را باخبر (/مُطّلع) کنید./ زمانِ وُرودتان را به ما اِطلاع بدهید.

Exercises

Exercise 8.1

Write the correct form of the verb, then translate.

١. یک ساعت اینجا ایستاده بود ولی الآن رفت که روی آن نیمکت .... (نشستن).

٢. دختری که در این عکس کنار تو .... (نشستن) کیست؟

٣. مادر بچّه را .... (در آغوش گرفتن) و سعی کرد او را آرام کند.

۴. خیلی خسته بود و فوراً روی تخت .... (دراز کشیدن).

۵. چرا آنجا .... (چمباتمه زدن) و هیچ کاری نمی‌کنی؟

۶. مرد قدبلندی در ردیف اوّل .... (ایستاده) و نمی‌توانم خواننده را خوب ببینم.

٧. پیرهنت کثیف شده است چون به آن دیوار .... (تکیه کردن).

٨. از این زنی که به ما .... (خیره شدن) می‌ترسم.

٩. آن پسری را که دارد کنار پرویز .... (نشستن) می‌شناسی؟

١٠. سروصدا نکنید، بچّه دارد .... (خوابیدن).

Exercise 8.2

Provide the correct verb for *wearing*, *putting on* and *taking off*, then translate. Example:

در ایران مردم در داخلِ خانه کفش ....

← نمی‌پوشند (In Iran people don't wear shoes inside the house.)

١. در ایران وقتیکه وارد خانه می‌شوی، باید کفشت را از پایت ....

٢. کتاب را ببست و عینک را از ....

٣. اگر خوب نمی‌بینی، چرا عینکت را ....

۴. لطفاً شلوارت را .... تا دکتر زانویت را ببیند.

۵. جورابم خیس شده بود و باید آن را ....

۶. از لباسی که تو الآن به .... خوشم می‌آید.

٧. می‌دانی چرا من دیروز لباس سیاه به .... ؟

٨. من کلاههائی را که تو .... خیلی دوست دارم.

٩. این کفش کهنه را نمی‌توانی در یک مهمانی ....

١٠. نمی‌دانم چرا مردها باید تصمیم بگیرند که زنها چه لباسی ....

8

Position of
verbs in the
sentence

Verbs of state

Putting on
and taking
off clothes

To want,
to be able to,
to know

Exercise 8.3

Provide the correct form of the verb خواستن ('to want'), then translate.
Example:

دیروز آمده بود چون (او) .... با تو حرف بزند

(She had come yesterday because she wanted to talk to you.) می‌خواست ←

۱. دیروز منتظرت بودیم و .... با تو یک فیلم ببینیم.

۲. هفتهٔ قبل شما باید از ناصر .... برایتان یک خانه پیدا کند.

۳. چرا تو هر وقت .... با من حرف بزنی، چشمهایت را می‌بندی؟

۴. این را فعلاً می‌برم ولی هر وقت تو .... برایت می‌آورم.

۵. (من) چند بار .... جوابش را بدهم، ولی باز پشیمان شدم.

۶. شوهر قبلی‌ام همیشه .... به من شنا یاد بدهد، ولی خودش در دریاچه غرق شد.

۷. همینکه بچّه مادرش را دید، .... به طرفِ او بدود، ولی افتاد.

۸. می‌توانستی بهترین خواننده باشی، به شرطِ آنکه خودت واقعاً ....

۹. اگر شما از او .... بعید است که قبول نکند.

۱۰. از کسی مثلِ او می‌توان .... که با رئیس جمهور صحبت کند.

Exercise 8.4

Provide the correct form of the verb توانستن ('to be able to'), then translate. Example:

به او نخواهم گفت چون .... گریه‌اش را ببینم

(I won't tell him because I can't see him/his crying.) نمی‌توانم ←

۱. بعد از چند هفته انتظار دیروز .... او را ببینم.

۲. آیا .... تفاوتها را از دور تشخیص داد؟

۳. اگر او را ببینید .... به او پیشنهاد کنید مقاله را کوتاهتر کند.

۴. بالاخره روز دوشنبهٔ قبل.............. در خانه‌اش با او صحبت کنیم.

۵. در قدیم فقط پولدارها.............. با کالسکه سفر کنند.

۶. آیا .... امیدوار بود که آن قانون تصویب شود؟

۷. می‌دانی ادیسون [Edison] چطور .... برق را اختراع کند؟

۸. بله، .... بالای درخت بروی، ولی سرت گیج خواهد رفت.

۹. چه کسی .... آن شیر را روی میز ریخته باشد؟

۱۰. ممکن نیست او .... این کار را دیروز انجام بدهد.

Exercise 8.5

Use either دانستن or بلد بودن to translate the following sentences; write both versions wherever possible. (Some of the words you might need have been given at the end of the exercise.) Example:

I knew the meaning of that word.
معنی آن کلمه را بلد بودم/می‌دانستم ←

1. I know why he doesn't like you.
2. It was a new lesson, but I knew all the words.
3. It was then that I realized where he was going.
4. Do you want to know the truth?
5. I know where to go.
6. I knew where he was going.
7. I know that he has not returned yet.
8. I don't know how many pictures he has taken of us.
9. I don't know how many pictures to take.
10. I know that taking these pictures has been a difficult job.

دوست نداشتن/جدید/کلمه/حقیقت/برگشتن/عکس (گرفتن)/سخت

Exercise 8.6

Translate into English.

۱. بلدید عکس بگیرید؟

۲. فوراً او را شناختم.

۳. ماشینش را دیدم، و فهمیدم که دارد برمی‌گردد.

۴. به او خبر بدهید که منتظرش هستیم.

۵. خبر داری چه اتفاقی افتاده؟

۶. خیلی وقت است از حال او خبری نداریم.

۷. اطلاع ندارم آن خانه را کی خریده است.

۸. باید خبرش کنیم که پدر دوستش فوت کرده.

۹. خوب نیست او را در بی‌خبری نگه دارید.

۱۰. عکس را به من نشان داد، و من پدرش را شناختم.

خدا خر را شناخت که شاخش نداد.

God knew the donkey, therefore gave him no horns.

(Used for a person who is a failure but potentially dangerous.)

UNIT NINE

More on compound verbs

Ways to avoid passive

فصل ۹

دربارهٔ فعلهای مرکب

راههائی برای پرهیز از مجهول

9.1 Separability of compound verbs

The verbal part of compound verbs can often be separated from non-verbal parts in different ways – we saw earlier how an objective suffix can be placed between the two parts of a compound verb (see 2.3 to 2.3.2):

برداشتن: برش داشتم. (= آن را برداشتم.)

نگه داشتن: نگهمان داشتند. (= ما را نگه داشتند.)

9.1.1 If the first part is a prefix (as in برداشتن بر)

An objective suffix can come between the two parts of some of the most common verbs of this group:

برشان گرداندیم. (We returned them.) → آنها را برگرداندیم.

درش نیاور. (Don't take it out/off.) → آن را در نیاور.

9.1.2 If the first part is an adjective (as in تمیز کردن)

Apart from objective suffixes, some modifiers/intensifiers can be added to the adjective, or sometimes comparative suffixes:

خانه را **تمیز کردیم**.

خانه را **تمیزتر کردیم**. (= خانه را بیشتر تمیز کردیم.)

خانه را **تمیزتر از همیشه کردیم**. (= خانه را بیشتر از همیشه تمیز کردیم.)

9.1.3 If the first part is a noun (as in صحبت کردن)

The two parts can be separated by different words, even by whole adverbial or relative clauses:

صحبت کردیم.

صحبت‌هائی کردیم.

صحبت‌های خیلی جالب و مفیدی کردیم.

صحبت‌هائی که با رئیس جدیدمان کردیم خیلی مفید بودند.

صحبت‌هائی که قبل از آنکه شما بیائید با رئیس جدیدمان کردیم خیلی مفید بودند.

9.2 Transitive compound verbs turned intransitive

There are a few compound verbs that have embraced or rather absorbed their objects in such a way that they are treated as intransitive – and may cause confusion when compared with their English equivalents. You already know the most common of these:

- خوردن is *to eat* – and *transitive*: you always need an object.
- غذا خوردن is also *to eat* – but *intransitive*: no object needed, because you already have غذا as the unspecified, general object.

Thus, you can't just say می‌خورم if you want to say *I'm eating*.

And, on the contrary, you can't say کباب غذا می‌خورم if you want to say *I'm eating kabāb* – here غذا would be redundant and you should just say کباب می‌خورم.

It is the same with غذا پختن (to cook; *intr.*) vs. پختن (*tr.*), or the compound verb درس خواندن (to study; *intr.*) vs. خواندن (*tr.*):

دارد در اتاقش درس می‌خواند. (He is studying [lit.: 'reading his lessons'] in his room.)

او می‌خواهد تاریخ بخواند. (He wants to study history.) – Here you shouldn't repeat درس before the verb.

او دارد کتاب می‌خواند. (He's reading a book.)

9.3 More ways to avoid passive

That Persian is not very fond of the passive we already know (see I/20.1). Here we learn one or two expressions that can give a statement a quasi-passive meaning without using the real passive. One common expression is مورد (*mowred-e*) + some noun (usually the non-verbal part of a compound verb) + the verbs قرار گرفتن (which is the intransitive version of قرار دادن) or sometimes واقع شدن. This would draw the focus from the *subject* to the *object*, which is thus *being subjected to* the action described by the noun that follows it. Examples:

ما آن موضوع را بررسی کردیم. (We looked into that matter.)

= ما آن موضوع را موردِ بررسی قرار دادیم. (We subjected that matter to our investigation.)

→ آن موضوع موردِ بررسی قرار گرفت. (That matter was looked into.)

= آن موضوع بررسی شد.

استعدادش را تحسین کردند. (They admired her talent.)

= استعدادش را موردِ تحسین قرار دادند. (Her talent was the object of admiration.)

→ استعدادش موردِ تحسین قرار گرفت./استعدادش موردِ تحسین واقع شد. (Her talent was admired.)

= استعدادش تحسین شد.

هیچ توجّهی به حرفهای من نمی‌کنند. (They pay no attention to my words.)

= حرفهای مرا هیچ موردِ توجّه قرار نمی‌دهند. (They subject my words to no attention.)

→ حرفهای من اصلاً موردِ توجّه قرار نمی‌گیرد. (My words are not heeded at all.)

= به حرفهای من هیچ توجّهی نمی‌شود.

Sometimes the verb changes to بودن or شدن after the مورد construction, occasionally with other changes in the phrasing – often when a 'real passive' is grammatically not possible or not common. Examples:

پدرم خیلی به اشعارِ حافظ علاقه دارد (My father likes the poems of Hāfez a lot.)

→ اشعارِ حافظ موردِ علاقۀ پدرم هستند (The poems of Hāfez are the object of my father's great affection.) – or, better still:

شاعرِ موردِ علاقۀ پدرم حافظ است (My father's favorite poet is Hāfez.)

(No 'real passive' version possible here.)

کدام پیشنهاد را قبول می‌کنید؟ (Which proposal would you go for?)

← پیشنهادِ موردِ قبولِ شما کدام است؟ (Which is the proposal you would accept?)

= کدام پیشنهاد (از سوی شما) قبول می‌شود؟ (Which proposal would be accepted [by you]?)

The word تحتِ [*taht-e*] means *under*. It is not always interchangeable with the much more common word زیرِ [*zir-e*], but it comes closer to the English *under* in certain constructions similar to موردِ (where زیرِ cannot be used), as in تحتِ بررسی [*taht-e bar-rasi*, 'under investigation'] or تحتِ اشغال [*taht-e eshghāl*, 'under occupation']. Examples in sentences:

او را در بیمارستان معالجه کردند (They treated him in the hospital.)

← او در بیمارستان تحتِ معالجه قرار گرفت (He underwent treatment in the hospital.)

سبکِ کوبیسم بر نقاشیهای او اثر (/تأثیر) گذاشته است (Cubism has influenced her paintings.)

← نقاشیهای او تحتِ تأثیر سبکِ کوبیسم است (Her paintings are under the influence of [/are influenced by] Cubism.)

= نقاشیهای او از سبکِ کوبیسم تأثیر گرفته است)

Exercises

Exercise 9.1

If you detect a compound verb in the following sentences, write its infinitive. (Tip: There are two sentences with no compound verbs.) Example:

با رئیس جدیدمان صحبتهای خیلی مفیدی کردیم

صحبت کردن ←

١. برای کمک به مادرم یک روز بیشتر در اصفهان ماندم.

٢. بعد از صحبت با رئیس جدیدش نمی‌دانست چه باید بکند.

٣. این دوای جدید خیلی بچّه را آرامتر از قبل کرده.

۴. این بخشی از کمکی است که صلیب سرخ به مردم کرده است.

۵. چرا اینقدر زود می‌خواهی پسش بگیری؟

۶. باید سعیِ بیشتری برای ویرایشِ آن مقاله بکنم.

۷. گفتند دیگر دیر است و پسمان فرستادند.

۸. این هوا او را مریض‌تر می‌کند.

۹. تمام اصرارِ من به خاطرِ علاقه‌ای است که به تو دارم.

۱۰. آمدنِ او به خاطرِ اصراری بود که من کردم.

Exercise 9.2

Translate the sentences from Exercise 9.1 into English.

Exercise 9.3

Change the *mowred-e* or *taht-e* constructions back to constructions using compound verbs. (Find the corresponding verbs in the glossary.) Example:

برخوردِ او موردِ اعتراض واقع شد

← به برخوردِ او اعتراض شد or به برخوردِ او اعتراض کردند

۱. می‌دانید چرا او را موردِ شکنجه قرار داده بودند؟

۲. در آن سه روزی که تحتِ شکنجه بود، اجازه نداشت بخوابد.

۳. او را تحتِ فشار گذاشتند که بگوید کجا بوده است.

۴. موضوع موردِ بررسی احتیاج به دقت زیادی داشت.

۵. می‌دانم که این موضوع موردِ علاقهٔ شما هم هست.

۶. او تحتِ هیچ شرایطی موردِ عفو قرار نخواهد گرفت.

۷. او یکی از آدمهای موردِ اعتمادِ من است.

۸. در موردِ قرارداد باید بگویم که هنوز تحتِ بررسی است.

۹. شاگردان کلاسِ دوّم موردِ تشویق قرار گرفتند.

۱۰. پیشنهادش موردِ موافقتِ ما قرار نگرفت.

Exercise 9.4

Translate the sentences from Exercise 9.3 into English.

Exercise 9.5

Translate the following into Persian. (Some of the words you can use have been given at the end of the exercise.)

1. I don't see Parvin; is she still cooking?
2. No, she's reading a story to [Persian: *for*] her daughter.
3. You love cooking, but you don't always eat what you've cooked.

4. If you want to study the contemporary history of Iran, you should go to another university.
5. I know that she goes to college [Persian: *university*], but I don't know what she's studying.
6. Had you studied better, you could have had better grades.
7. One cannot eat Persian food and not fall in love with it.
8. Iranians usually eat with spoons and forks.
9. Knives are used in the kitchen or for eating certain fruits.
10. How can you study with this loud music?

آشپزی/آشپزخانه/داستان/خواندن/همیشه/پختن/خوردن/تاریخ/معاصر/رشته
/درس/دانشگاه/نمره/عاشق شدن/معمولاً/قاشق/چنگال/کارد/بعضی/میوه/استفاده/
موسیقی/بلند

دیوار موش دارد، موش گوش دارد.

The wall has mice, the mice have ears.

(= We can be overheard.)

UNIT TEN	۱۰ فصل
Nouns and adjectives made from verbs	ساختن اسم و صفت از فعل
Some prefixes and suffixes	چند پیشوند و پسوند

Nouns and adjectives made from verbs

Here we learn some of the most common ways of making nouns and adjectives from verbs (usually by adding certain suffixes). It must be known, however, that the words must be common in the language and you can't usually create new words on your own.

10.1 Infinitive + stressed -i

We know that we can add stressed -i to adjectives to make nouns and to nouns to make adjectives or other related nouns (see I/6.3). When added to infinitives, it usually works in a similar way to the English -able/-ible suffix: it is about some (usually passive) potential and means 'worthy of' or 'fit for' or occasionally (with intransitive verbs) something bound to happen.

Examples of participles of potential (passive): infinitive + stressed -i

پذیرفتنی *paziroftani*, acceptable

خواستنی *khāstani*, desirable

دوست داشتنی *dust-dāshtani*, amiable

سُتودنی *sotudani*, admirable

شدنی *shodani*, doable; possible

خواندنی *khāndani*, readable; worth reading

خوردنی *khordani*, edible; fit to eat; food

مردنی *mordani*, feeble, about to die

ماندنی *māndani*, lasting

دیدنی *didani*, worth seeing

گفتنی *goftani*, worth saying

شنیدنی *shenidani*, worth listening

بافتنی *bāftani*, product of hand-knitting

نوشیدنی *nushidani*, drink

آبِ آشامیدنی *āb-e āshāmidani*, drinking water

بهِ یاد ماندنی *be yād māndani*, memorable

Note 1: There are certain words that have this meaning of potentiality or fitness and can be placed before an infinitive instead of adding this -*i*. Often interchangeable, all of them mean *worthy of* or *fit for*, and all would need *ezāfe*. The most common one is قابل [*ghābel-e*], and the more formal ones include درخور [*darkhor-e*], سزاوار [*sezāvār-e*], شایستة [*shāyeste-ye*] and شایان [*shāyān-e*]. Examples:

قابلِ خوردن = خوردنی (fit to eat)

شایستة بهِ یاد ماندن = بهِ یاد ماندنی (worth remembering)

شایانِ ستایش or شایانِ ستودن = سُتودنی (admirable, praiseworthy)

درخورِ گفتن = گفتنی (worth mentioning)

سزاوارِ دیدن = دیدنی (worth seeing)

For negative (= '*un—able*'), add نـ/نا [*na-/nā-*] to the infinitive + -*i*, or change قابل [*ghābel-e*] to غیرِقابل [*gheyr-e-ghābel-e*]:

باورکردنی (*bāvar-kardani*, believable) → باورنکردنی (*bāvar-na-kardani*, unbelievable); or consider از یاد نرفتنی (*az yād na-raftani*, unforgettable)

قابلِ گفتن (*ghābel-e-goftan*, speakable, sayable) → غیرِقابلِ گفتن (*gheyr-e-ghābel-e-goftan*, unspeakable)

(Sometimes ـپذیر [*-pazir*] (from the verb پذیرفتن) and its negative ناپذیر [*-nā-pazir*] are added to nouns to give a similar meaning, like چاره پذیر [*chāre-pazir*, remediable] or شکست ناپذیر [*shekast-nā-pazir*, invincible], but these can be said to be 'agent participles' of compound verbs, to be covered below, in 10.2/A.)

Note 2: With the verbs رفتن, آمدن and برگشتن, this added -*i* in colloquial Persian can also give the meaning of *while on the way to some place*, as in these examples:

برگشتنی، کمی نان هم بخر. (On your way back, buy some bread too.)

آمدنی، علی را توی راه دیدم. (While coming, I saw Ali on the way.)

رفتنی، توقفی هم در شیراز کردند. (On their way [going], they also made a stop in Shirāz.)

10

Nouns and
adjectives
made from
verbs

Some
prefixes and
suffixes

10.2 Present stem

A. Present stem + -ande = agent participle

This usually gives the *agent*, similar to the English *-er/-or* suffix:

خواننده ← خوان ← خواندن
= to sing → sing → singer

This is especially common for professions and tools. With compound verbs, however, the present stem alone often assumes this meaning without adding *-ande*. This participle can be a noun, an adjective, or both. Examples:

خواندن (to read, to sing) → خواننده (reader, singer)
　　but: کتابخوان (a bookworm, one who loves reading) – and not
　　'کتاب خواننده' !
گرفتن (to take, to receive) → گیرنده (receiver)
　　but: سختگیر (unyielding, inflexible, serious)
تراشیدن (to carve, to whittle) → تراشنده (carver)
　　but: مداد تراش (pencil-sharpener)
کشتن (to kill) → کشنده (fatal, lethal)
　　but: آدمکش (murderer)
فروختن (to sell) → فروشنده (seller)
　　but: وطن‌فروش (traitor [to one's country])
شکستن (to break) → شکننده (fragile)
　　but: عهد شکن (promise breaker; disloyal)
راندن (to drive) → راننده (driver)
پریدن (to fly) → پرنده (bird; 'flyer')
بُردن (to take [away]; to win) → بَرنده (winner)
باختن (to lose; to play or gamble) → بازنده (loser)
بازی کردن (to play) → بازیکن (player [in sports])
خسته کردن (to tire, to bore) → خسته کننده (boring, tiring)
سرگرم کردن (to amuse) → سرگرم کننده (amusing)

Notes:

- As the last two examples show, even with compound verbs sometimes the *-ande* suffix is used (especially with کردن).

- If needed, the glide -*y*- should be added before -*ande*, as in گوینده [*guyande*, speaker; from گفتن, present stem گو] and آینده [*āyande*, coming; future; from آمدن, present stem آ].
- You can add stressed -*i* to these words to make abstract nouns (not very common with compounds ending in کننده); if it is the form ending in -*ande*, then the glide -*g*- (گ) would be required and the *silent hé* (ه) is dropped:

راننده (*rānande*, driver) → رانندگی (*rānandegi*, driving)

and very often you form new compound verbs with these:

راندن ← راننده ← رانندگی ← رانندگی کردن
سخت گرفتن ← سختگیر ← سختگیری ← سختگیری کردن
کتاب فروختن ← کتابفروش [bookseller] → کتابفروش [to sell books]
[bookstore, or selling books] → کتابفروشی کردن [to sell books]

- In translating western scientific or political terms into Persian, the verbs شناختن [*shenākhtan*, to know, to discern] and گرویدن/گرائیدن [*geravidan/gerā'idan*, to incline] have proven to be very helpful, the former for sciences and the latter for schools of thought or literary trends. Examples:

زمین‌شناس [*zamin-shenās*, geologist], زمین‌شناسی [*zamin-shenāsi*, geology]

جامعه‌شناس [*jāme'e-shenās*, sociologist], جامعه‌شناسی [*jāme'e-shenāsi*, sociology]

واقع‌گرا [*vāghe'-gerā*, realist], واقع‌گرائی [*vāghe'-gerā'i*, realism]

عقل‌گرا [*aghl-gerā*, rationalist], عقل‌گرائی [*aghl-gerā'i*, rationalism]

B. Present stem + -ān = present participle

This is very close to the English *present participle* and is used as a verbal adjective or an adverb/adjective of manner, but sometimes as a noun also.

خندیدن (to laugh) → خندان (laughing; cheerful)
خندیدن (to laugh) → خنده کنان ([while] laughing)
گریستن (to cry, to weep) → گریان (crying, weeping)
گریستن (to cry, to weep) → گریه کنان (crying, weeping)
رقصیدن (to dance) → رقصان (dancing)
رفتن (to go) → روان (going; flowing; running; fluent; soul)
نگریستن (to look) → نگران (concerned; anxious, worried)

10

Nouns and
adjectives
made from
verbs

Some
prefixes and
suffixes

سوختن (to burn) → سوزان (ablaze; burning; hot; scorching)

ارزیدن (to be worth; to cost) → ارزان (cheap ['worth the price'])

نمودن (to show; to represent; to appear) → نمایان (apparent; appearing)

پائیدن (to last; to watch or guard) → پایان (end [*n.*])

Notes:

- As the last two examples show, here also the glide -*y*- is added when needed.
- Sometimes a present participle is repeated and the meaning intensified:

پُرسان پُرسان [*porsān-porsān*]: after or while asking many times (for directions);

دَوان دَوان [*davān-davān*]: running fast.

Partial repetition:

لنگ لنگان [*lang-langān*]: limping.

- Sometimes two present participles form a bond and are said together:

افتان و خیزان [*oftān-o-khizān*]: falling and rising; walking with difficulty;

ترسان و لرزان [*tarsān-o-larzān*]: fearing and trembling.

- The present stem of causative verbs (see 6.1) already ends in -*ān*; these verbs don't usually form a present participle by adding another -*ān*. Interestingly, the present participle of simple verbs from which causative ones are made is the same as the present stem of this latter group. Examples:

سوزان [*suzān*] is the present participle of سوختن (to burn) but the present stem of its causative form سوزاندن (cause to burn);

خندان [*khandān*] is the present participle of خندیدن (to laugh) but the present stem of its causative form خنداندن (cause to laugh).

C. Present stem + -ā = participle of potential (active)

This participle is similar to *infinitive* + -*i* (see 10.1 above) in that it is about some potential, but this time it is usually an *active* potential, not *passive*. And it differs from the -*ande* participle (section *A* above) in that it is often about the *state* of having this potential rather than the *act* of putting it to use. شنیدنی [*shenidani*] is what is worth hearing, شنونده [*shenavande*] is a listener, and شنوا [*shenavā*] is a person capable of hearing. More examples:

توانستن (to be able) → توانا (capable; mighty)

دانستن (to know) → دانا (wise)

دیدن (to see) → بینا (capable of seeing; not blind)

داشتن (to have) → دارا (wealthy)

خواندن (to read) → خوانا (legible)

زیبیدن (to befit, to become) → زیبا (beautiful)

فریفتن (to charm) → فریبا (charming)

گرفتن (to take, to catch) → گیرا (attractive; catching)

رسیدن (to reach) → رسا (far reaching and loud)

گذشتن (to pass) → گذرا (fleeting; transient)

رَهیدن or رَستن (to escape; to become free) → رَها (free)

D. Present stem + -esh = verbal noun

Present stem + *-esh* will give an active and abstract verbal noun and is very common. When you need the noun form of a verb (as after prepositions), you can often use this form instead of the Persian infinitive (provided that it does exist and has the same meaning!).

It is also very common to make compound verbs with these verbal nouns – which are increasingly replacing the simple verbs.

گشتن (to turn, to stroll)

   → گردش (stroll)

   → گردش کردن (to stroll)

سُتودن (to admire, to praise)

   → ستایش (admiration, praise)

   → ستایش کردن (to admire, to praise)

نکوهیدن (to blame, to reproach)

   → نکوهش (blame, reproach)

   → نکوهش کردن (to blame or reproach)

خواستن (to want)

   → خواهش (request)

   → خواهش کردن (to request)

10

Nouns and
adjectives
made from
verbs

Some
prefixes and
suffixes

نُمودن (to show, to appear)

→ نمایش (a play; showing)

→ نمایش دادن (to show; to present)

افزودن (to increase)

→ افزایش (increase)

→ افزایش دادن/یافتن (to increase)

کاستن (to decrease)

→ کاهش (decrease)

→ کاهش دادن/یافتن (to decrease)

گرویدن/گرائیدن (to incline)

→ گرایش (inclination)

→ گرایش داشتن/یافتن (to be inclined)

This suffix is usually not added to compound verbs, which would just add
-*i* to the 'agent participle' instead (and the agent participle, as we saw
above, uses the present stem alone when it comes to compound verbs):

بینش (insight) → دیدن

but: خوش‌بینی (optimism) or پیش‌بینی (foresight);

گزینش (selection) → گزیدن

but: کارگزینی (recruitment office) or همسرگزینی (spouse selection);

رَوش (method, way) → رفتن

but: پیشرَوی (moving forward, advancing) or کجرَوی (deviation,
aberration);

سوزش (burning sensation or twinge) → سوختن

but: آتش‌سوزی (fire accident or incineration) or دلسوزی (pity).

One rare example of adding -*esh* to a compound is سرزنش (blaming), from
the compound بر سر زدن (to slap on the head with the hand) – while we
say سینه زنی (chest-beating [a Shiite ritual]) or پاروزنی (rowing).

10.3 Past stem

A. Past participle

The most common of the nouns/adjectives made from the past stem we
already know: the *past participle* (= past stem + -*e* or *silent hé* – see I/13.1),
sometimes hardly recognizable as past participles: like the common adjective خسته (*khaste*, tired) made from the now archaic verb خستن (*khastan*,
to wound); even a noun like بسته (*baste*, package) doesn't always remind
us of the equally common verb بستن (*bastan*, to tie, to close).

B. Short infinitive (past stem) as noun

Some of the words we have learned so far as *nouns* were in fact *short infinitives*, like خرید (shopping) and شکست (defeat), past stems of respectively خریدن (to buy) and شکستن (to break).

In the following sentences short infinitives have been used as nouns, and you know that in each case by just adding ـَن (-an) you will have the full infinitive.

بلیطِ رفت بخرم یا بلیطِ رفت و برگشت؟ (Should I buy a one-way ticket or a return ticket?) → رفتن and برگشتن

بعد از بازگشتِ دخترش حالش بهتر شد. (After the return of her daughter her health improved.) → بازگشتن (= برگشتن) = to return

از دیدِ این فیلسوف انسان هیچ مسئولیتی ندارد. (In the view of this philosopher, man has no responsibility.) → دیدن

از دریافتِ نامه‌تان خیلی خوشحال شدم. (I was very pleased to receive [/'from receiving'] your letter.) → دریافت کردن = to receive

شناختِ این مسائل آسان نیست. (Understanding these problems is not easy.) → شناختن

پرداختِ کرایه را فراموش نکنید. (Don't forget the payment of rent.) → پرداختن

چرا نمی‌گوئی خواستِ واقعی‌ات چیست؟ (Why don't you say what you really want [/what your real desire is]?) → خواستن

نشستِ بعدی سه هفته بعد خواهد بود. (Next session will be in three weeks.) → نشستن

رسیدِ این خرید را گم کرده است. (He has lost the receipt of this purchase.) → خریدن and رسیدن

پیشرفتِ او در ریاضی خیلی خوب بود. (His progress in math was very good.) → پیش رفتن = to advance

Sometimes you have a compound verb, a second compound with a short infinitive, and a third one made from the agent participle, with the same or slightly different meanings. Compare:

پیش رفتن = to go forward, to advance

پیشرفت کردن = to make progress (as in studies)

پیشرَوی کردن = to advance (as armies in warfare) – Here پیشرَوی is made from the agent participle پیشرو (*pish-row*, forerunner, pioneer, progressive).

99

10

Nouns and
adjectives
made from
verbs

Some
prefixes and
suffixes

C. Past and present stems together

Occasionally you might see a past stem followed by the present stem of either the same verb or another verb. The two stems (connected through وَ, here pronounced *o*) make a new word or concept; they are sometimes written together as one word and و is dropped in writing (not in pronunciation). Some examples:

گفتگو or گفت و گو (*goft-o-gu*, from گفتن *goftan*, to say) – it means 'conversation' and we have the compound verb گفتگو کردن also ('to engage in conversation').

جُستُجو or جُست و جو (*jost-o-ju*, from جستن *jostan*, to seek/find) – it means 'searching' and there is the compound verb جستجو کردن also ('to search or look for').

شُستُشو or شُست و شو (*shost-o-shu*, from شستن *shostan*, to wash) – it means 'washing' and can be used to make other compound verbs.

پُرس و جو (*pors-o-ju*, from the two verbs پُرسیدن *porsidan*, to ask, and جستن *jostan*, to seek) – it means 'inquiry' and we have the compound verb پُرس و جو کردن also ('to make a search or inquiry').

In بَندوبَست (*band-o-bast*, the two stems of بستن = 'collusion' or a secret deal), however, the present stem precedes the past one. (And, of course, we sometimes have compounds using two present stems or even two imperatives, similar to 'hide-and-seek' in English.)

D. Past stem + -ār

The nouns using this suffix sometimes are similar to those using the *-ande* suffix (the 'agent' – see 10.2/A) and sometimes are little different from the infinitive used as noun, but can also make words with different meanings. Examples of these with some related words:

خریدار (*kharidār*, from خریدن): purchaser – for this concept there is no خرنده with the *-ande* ending!

خریداری (*kharidāri*, purchase)

خواستار (*khāstār*, from خواستن): one who wants; desirous (similar in meaning to the present participle خواهان *khāhān* used as noun)

گرفتار (*gereftār*, from گرفتن): captive, occupied, busy

گرفتار کردن (*gereftār kardan*, to catch or arrest, to entangle, to preoccupy)

گرفتاری (*gereftāri*, captivity, entanglement, trouble)

رفتار (*raftār*, from رفتن): behavior

   رفتار کردن (*raftār kardan*, to behave or act)

کُشتار (*koshtār*, from کشتن): butchery; slaughter; massacre

مُردار (*mordār*, from مُردن): cadaver, corpse

گفتار (*goftār*, from گفتن): saying; speech

دیدار (*didār*, from دیدن): visit

   دیدار کردن (*didār kardan*, to visit)

10.4 '-*āne*' suffix

This suffix, which is originally a suffix of manner, is used to make

a) adjectives from nouns;
b) adjectives (for non-humans) from other adjectives (that should be used for humans only); and
c) adverbs from adjectives.

Examples for a):

– (yearly) سالانه, (monthly) ماهانه, (daily) روزانه ← روز، ماه، سال

  the last two sometimes add -*iyāne* and become ماهیانه/سالیانه

مردانه ← مرد (manly, masculine, of men or men's)

زنانه ← زن (womanly, feminine, of women or women's)

کودکانه/بچّگانه ← کودک/بچّه (childish, childlike, of children or children's)

دوستانه ← دوست (friendly)

عاشقانه ← عاشق (romantic, amorous; amorously).

Examples for b):
Some adjectives that are about specifically human qualities add this -*āne* suffix when used for inanimates or abstract nouns and activities:

مینا عاقل است. [Minā is wise.] → این کار مینا عاقلانه نبود. [This deed of Minā's/What Minā did was not wise.]

تو احمق نیستی. [You are not stupid.] → تصمیم تو احمقانه بود. [Your decision was stupid.]

Examples for c):
Although adjectives can generally be used as adverbs in Persian without any change, most of those describing human qualities (mentioned above) usually add the -*āne* suffix when used as adverbs.

10

Nouns and
adjectives
made from
verbs

Some
prefixes and
suffixes

او عاقل است. (He is wise.)

حرفهای او عاقلانه است. → (His words are wise.)

او عاقلانه حرف می‌زند. → (He speaks wisely.)

او عاشق است. (He is in love.)

این یک نامهٔ عاشقانه است. → (This is a romantic letter.)

او عاشقانه به همسرش نگاه می‌کرد. → (He looked amorously at his spouse.)

شما زیرکید. (You are smart.)

جوابتان زیرکانه بود. → (Your response was smart.)

خیلی زیرکانه عمل کردید. → (You acted very smartly.)

If the *-āne* version of an adjective is not common, other solutions should be found – like changing the adjective to an abstract noun (by adding stressed *-i*) and using با (with) or از روی (from): زیرک [*zirak*] and زرنگ [*zerang*] both mean *smart*, but there is no زرنگانه, and the last example above would look like this if we were to use زرنگ:

شما زرنگید. (You are smart.)

جوابتان از روی زرنگی بود. → (Your response was smart.)

خیلی با زرنگیِ عمل کردید. → (You acted very smartly.)

Also, certain adverbs (like those modifying the whole sentence) usually need *-āne*:

خوشبخت (lucky, fortunate, happy) → خوشبختانه (luckily, fortunately)

بدبخت (unlucky, unfortunate) → بدبختانه (unluckily, unfortunately)

متأسّف (sorry, regretful) → متأسفانه (regrettably, unfortunately)

(See also Unit 11 for more on adverbs.)

10.5 Some prefixes and suffixes

A. Having vs. not having, negation and opposition

HAVING: با- (*bā-*, 'with') is a very common prefix; پُر- (*por*, '-ful') is a stronger prefix meaning 'full of' (or 'having lots of'); common suffixes used in this group are ـدار (*-dār*, from the verb داشتن), ـمند (*-mand*), and ـناک (*-nāk*).

NOT HAVING: If there is too little of something or some quality, کم- (*kam-*) may be used as prefix; the total absence is shown by بی- (*bi-*).

While the above prefixes and suffixes are usually added to nouns, ـَ (na-) and -نا (nā-) are often added to adjectives, present stems and participles for negation, and only seldom to nouns.

A common way of expressing the progression from *absence* to *having lots of* is:

bi- → kam- → ba- → por-.

Examples with the words حوصله (*howsele*, patience), فایده (*fāyede*, benefit, use), and ارزش (*arzesh*, value):

بی‌حوصله impatient; bored	کم حوصله irritable; not very patient	با حوصله patient	پر حوصله very patient
بی‌فایده useless	کم فایده of little use	با فایده (= مُفید) useful	پر فایده very useful
بی ارزش worthless	کم ارزش of little value	با ارزش (= ارزشمند) valuable	پر ارزش highly valuable

Examples with other prefixes/suffixes:

- ـدار (-*dār*): بچه‌دار (*bachche-dār*, having child/children), پولدار (*pul-dār*, rich), خانه‌دار (*khāne-dār*, housewife), دیندار (*din-dār*, believer)
- ـناک (-*nāk*): ترسناک (*tars-nāk*, frightening), دردناک (*dard-nāk*, painful), خطرناک (*khatar-nāk*, dangerous), شرمناک (*sharm-nāk*, ashamed)
- ـمند (-*mand*): علاقمند/علاقه‌مند، ارزشمند (*arzesh-mand*, valuable), علاقه‌مند (*alāghe-mand*, interested), نیرومند (*niru-mand*, powerful), ثروتمند (*servat-mand*, wealthy)
- ـنا/نـ (*na-/nā*): نترس (*na-tars*, fearless), نفهم (*na-fahm*, stupid, uncomprehending), ناچیز (*nā-chiz*, insignificant, worthless), نامعلوم (*nā-ma'lum*, unclear, unknown)

The prefix *bā-* can often be substituted by دارای (*dārā-ye*, having) and *bi-* by بدونِ (*bedun-e*, without) or فاقدِ (*faghed-e*, lacking)

The word غیرِ (*gheyr-e*, with *gheyr* originally meaning 'other') is often used as a prefix to make antonyms:

ممکن (*momken*, possible) → غیرِ ممکن (*gheyr-e-momken*, impossible) – also ناممکن (*nā-momken*) in more formal or literary language.

103

10

Nouns and
adjectives
made from
verbs

Some
prefixes and
suffixes

واقعی (vāghe'i, real) → غیرِ واقعی (gheyr-e-vāghe'i, unreal)

انسانی (ensāni, human, humane) → غیرِ انسانی (gheyr-e-ensāni,
  inhuman, inhumane)

مسئولانه (mas'ulāne, responsible, responsibly) → غیرِ مسئولانه (gheyr-e-
  mas'ulāne, irresponsible, irresponsibly)

Another useful word, usually functioning as the *anti-* prefix, is ضِدِّ (zed-de):

ضدِّ انقلابی (zed-de-enghelābi, counter-revolutionary)

B. Activities, professions

Some common prefixes of this category are کار (-kār) سگار /سگر (-gar/-gār),
and the originally Turkish چی (-chi). Examples:

کارگر (kār-gar, worker), آهنگر (āhan-gar, ironsmith)

خواستگار (āmuz[e]gār, teacher of elementary school),
  (khāst[e]gār, suitor)

معدنکار (ma'dan-kār, miner, mine worker), شبکار (shab-kār, night
  shift worker)

شکارچی (shekār-chi, hunter), پستچی (post-chi, mailperson)

C. Causing and provoking

Two common suffixes here are انگیز (-angiz, from انگیختن, to stir, to provoke) and آور (-āvar, from آوردن, to bring), usually added to abstract nouns
to make adjectives. These could have been covered under 10.2/A (*agent
participle*) also, because they are in fact nothing but the present stems of
the verbs آوردن and انگیختن; thus, حیرت‌انگیز (heyrat-angiz, astonishing)
and دردآور (dard-āvar, causing pain) can be said to be the agent participles
of the compound verbs درد آوردن and حیرت انگیختن. Other examples:

بحث‌انگیز (bahs-angiz, controversial), نفرت‌انگیز (nefrat-angiz, hateful,
  revolting)

خجالت‌آور (khejālat-āvar, embarrassing), خواب‌آور (khāb-āvar, sedative)

D. Resemblance

Suffixes used to show resemblance are مانند- (-mānand), ـوار (-vār), ـسان
(-sān) and سگونه /سگون (-gun/-gune). Examples:

اسب‌مانند (asb-mānand, horse-like), تَپّه‌مانند (tappe-mānand, hill-like)
دیوانه‌وار (divāne-vār, madly, like crazy), بیگانه‌وار (bigāne-vār, like strangers)
گربه‌سان (gorbe-sān, feline, cat-like), برق‌سان (bargh-sān, fast, like lightning)
گلگون (gol-gun, rosy, rose-like), دُعاگونه (do'ā-gune, prayer-like)

Some independent words (+ *ezāfe*) that mean 'like' are usually placed before the noun that they modify and (similar to *like* in English) function like prepositions. The most common of them are مثل (*mesl-e*, like) and شبیه/شبیه به (*shabih-e/shabih be*, similar to); in formal/written Persian the words مانند (*mānand-e*) and بگونهٔ (*be-gune-ye*) are used in a similar sense; بسان (*be-sān-e*) and چون (*chon*) or همچون (*ham-chon*) are used in poetical language. Compare the usage:

اسب‌مانند = مانندِ اسب، مثلِ اسب

دیوانه‌وار = مثلِ دیوانه‌ها

گربه‌سان = بسانِ گربه، شبیه به گربه

گلگون = به گونهٔ گل، به رنگِ گل، مانندِ گل

To learn more about the structures used for resembling/comparing see Unit 11.

E. Time and location

Quite a few of the words you have learned so far are using suffixes that denote time or location; some of the more common ones are: گاه (-gāh, as in دانشگاه), (دانشگاه), (-estān, as in کودکستان), کده (-kade, as in دانشکده), اَباد (-ābād, as in اسلام‌آباد [Islamabad]), زار (-zār, as in گلزار [golzār, rose garden]).

Exercises

Exercise 10.1

Define the following words in Persian by using short and simple relative clauses, then translate. Examples:

کتابفروش کسی است که کتاب می‌فروشد ← کتابفروش
(A bookseller is someone who sells books.)
ساعت‌ساز کسی است که ساعت می‌سازد ← ساعت‌ساز
(A watchmaker is someone who makes watches.)

۱. باربَر ۲. راننده ۳. سنگتراش ۴. نامه‌رسان ۵. فرمانده ۶. گیرنده ۷. فرستنده
۸. بازنده ۹. سیاهپوش ۱۰. ماهیگیر.

10

Nouns and
adjectives
made from
verbs

Some
prefixes and
suffixes

Exercise 10.2

Find the different nouns and adjectives made from verbs in each sentence
and write the verb on which they are based. Example:

صدای این خواننده خیلی غم‌انگیز است (This singer's voice is very sad.)

خواننده (خواندن), غم‌انگیز (غم انگیختن) ←

1. او دروغگوی ماهری است و آیندهٔ خوبی در سیاست خواهد داشت (He is
a skilled liar and will have a good future in politics.)

2. کمی بعد از رأی‌گیری، شمارش آراء را شروع کردند (Shortly after the
voting, they started the counting of the votes.)

3. تعدادی از سربازان هم به شورشیان پیوستند (A number of the soldiers
also joined the rebels.)

4. ‏'رانندهٔ تاکسی' از مهمترین فیلمهای این کارگردان است (*Taxi Driver* is one
of the most important films by this director.)

5. آن ثروتِ بادآورده خیلی زود بر باد رفت (That easily gained wealth
['brought with the wind'] was very soon gone with the wind.)

6. دستگیری او از اتفاقات خبرساز آن سال بود (His arrest was one of the
newsmaking events of that year.)

7. سخنران بعدی نتوانست بموقع بیاید و جلسه تعطیل شد (The next speaker
wasn't able to come on time and the session was ended.)

8. حرفهای آن آدم نادان مشکل‌آفرین شد (The words of that stupid person
created problems [/'became problem-creating'].)

9. یک پشهٔ خونخوار را شکار کردم (I hunted/trapped a bloodsucking
mosquito.)

10. با کم شدنِ کتابخوانها، کتابفروشها بیکار می‌شوند (With the decrease of
readers [of books], booksellers lose their jobs ['become jobless'].)

Exercise 10.3

Change the '-*ān*' present participle to a clause with در حالیکه ... ('as/
while . . .'), then translate. Example:

خندان وارد اتاق شد

در حالیکه می‌خندید وارد اتاق شد ← (He entered the room [while he
was] laughing.)

١. بچهٔ همسایه گریان به خانه‌شان رفت.

٢. اشک‌ریزان از آنجا دور شد و هنوز فریاد زنان را می‌شنید.

۳. فریادزنان وارد خانه شدند و به دنبالِ مردهای خانه گشتند.

۴. خودش را لنگ لنگان به من رساند و از حال مادرم پرسید.

۵. بچه‌ها شادی کنان به هدایا حمله کردند.

۶. گردش کنان تا کنارِ آن دریاچهٔ کوچک رفتیم.

۷. چند نفر نزدیک شدند و تبریک گویان او را بوسیدند.

۸. شناکنان خودش را به قایق نزدیک کرد.

۹. لبخندزنان گفت: 'در عفو لذّتی است که در انتقام نیست.'

۱۰. دوان دوان تا خانهٔ عمویم رفتم و خبر را گفتم.

Exercise 10.4

Fill in the blanks by using one of the words given below (don't use any word twice), then translate. Words from which to choose:

محترم/محترمانه، احمق/احمقانه، استاد/استادانه، ناامید/ناامیدانه، شجاع/شجاعانه

۱. کیفت حتماً پیدا خواهد شد، خیلی .... نباش.

۲. هنوز جوان است ولی خیلی .... پیانو می‌زند.

۳. با این حرفهای .... نشان داد که از کسی نمی‌ترسد.

۴. چطور ممکن است یک مردِ .... چنین حرف زشتی بزند؟

۵. این سگِ .... نگذاشت آن مرد دخترم را بدزدد.

۶. من از کارهای .... خودم خجالت می‌کشم.

۷. عصبانی شدم چون با من .... حرف نزد.

۸. در کارِ خودش .... است و در این شهر خیلی معروف است.

۹. حدس می‌زدم که او ناصر نباشد، ولی باز هم .... اسمش را پرسیدم.

۱۰. ممکن است او همه چیز را نداند ولی .... نیست.

Exercise 10.5

Try to guess the meaning and translate:

۱. بی‌پایان ۲. ضدّ آمریکائی ۳. نادرست ۴. بی‌جواب ۵. فاقد حمّام ۶. بی‌فکر ۷. غیرِلازم ۸. پُرلذّت ۹. نامهربان ۱۰. ناتوان

10

Nouns and
adjectives
made from
verbs

Some
prefixes and
suffixes

Exercise 10.6

Use a word with one of the prefixes *bi-*, *kam-* or *por-* to complete the
sentences, then translate. Example:

کسی که هیچ پولی ندارد، .... است

بی‌پول ← (One who has no money is penniless.)

۱. کسی که کار ندارد، .... است.

۲. کاری که خیلی خطر دارد، .... است.

۳. کاری که خیلی دردِسر داشته باشد، .... است.

۴. کتابی که زیاد غلط ندارد، .... است.

۵. کاری که نتیجه‌ای ندارد، .... است.

۶. کسی که سواد کافی ندارد، .... است.

۷. کسی که خیلی کار می‌کند، .... است.

۸ کاری که بموقع نباشد، .... است.

۹. آدمی که زیاد حرف می‌زند، .... است.

۱۰. کسی که زیاد عقل ندارد، .... است.

دشمنِ دانا بُلندت میکند   بَر زَمینت میزند نادانِ دوست

(سعدی)

The wise enemy lifts you, the foolish friend throws you down.

(= Foolish friends are worse than wise enemies.)

UNIT ELEVEN	فصل ۱۱
Exclamative form	شکل بیانِ تعجّب
More on adjectives/adverbs	باز هم صفت و قید
Comparison of adjectives	مقایسهٔ صفات
Ezāfe	اضافه

11.1 Exclamative form

Persian uses the word چه [*che*] with both nouns and adjectives in exclamative phrases and sentences. When used with nouns, the indefinite -*i* is also added to the noun or to the (last) adjective if the noun is modified by adjective(s).

Unlike the interrogative *che*, which changes to چی [*chi*] in spoken/ Tehrani Persian, this چه always remains the same and does not change.

The word عجب [*ajab*, usually an interjection: 'how strange'] can also be used in such structures; in colloquial Persian you can also use چقدر ('how much') instead of چه, but mainly with adjectives (not nouns) or to modify the verb, in which case the verb will take the main stress.

Examples:

a) *With nouns:*

چه روزی!/عجب روزی! (What a day!)
چه پرنده‌هائی!/عجب پرنده‌هائی! (What birds!)

b) *With adjectives:*

چه دیر!/عجب دیر!/چقدر دیر! (How late!)
چه قشنگ!/عجب قشنگ!/چقدر قشنگ! (How beautiful!)

c) *Nouns and adjectives together:*

چه روز سردی!/عجب روز سردی! (What a cold day!)
چه پرنده‌های کوچک و قشنگی!/عجب پرنده‌های کوچک و قشنگی!
    (What small beautiful birds!)

11

Exclamative
form

More on
adjectives/
adverbs

Comparison
of adjectives

Ezāfe

d) *In a sentence:*

دیروز چه (/عجب) روز سردی بود! (What a cold day it was yesterday!)

چه (/عجب) دخترهای قشنگ و باهوشی دارید! (What pretty and smart daughters you have!)

چقدر می‌خوری! (How much you eat! [= you eat a lot!]) – Here the verb (in this case *mí-*) takes the main stress; compare with a normal question in which the stress is on *ché-ghadr*:

چقدر می‌خوری؟ (How much do you eat?)

11.2 Some idiomatic usages of exclamative *che*

- *Che + noun + ke + negative verb*:
  This usually has a meaning similar to خیلی + *an affirmative verb*, and the English translation would probably require an affirmative verb. Examples:

  چه رشوه‌ها که نداد تا پسرش آزاد شود! (= خیلی رشوه داد تا پسرش آزاد شود)

  (What bribes he gave to have his son freed!)

  چه حرفها که پشت سرش نمی‌زنند! (= خیلی پشت سرش حرف می‌زنند)

  (What things they say behind his back!)

- چه بسیار [*che besyār*] is used to emphasize the high frequency of the occurrence; a more colloquial synonym would be چقدر زیاد ('how much'):

  چه بسیار او را نصیحت کردند. (How much/How often they advised/warned him!)

  آن روزها چه بسیار او را می‌دیدم. (How often I saw him those days!)

- چه بسا [*che basā*] is used for conjecture and speculation, when you are wondering: it is similar to 'maybe' (شاید, *shāyad*) or 'could it be that ... ?':

  چه بسا نمی‌داند؟ (Maybe he doesn't know?)

  چه بسا آمده و ما را پیدا نکرده. (It's possible that he has come and has not found us.)

- چه رسد به (تا) (with رسد or برسد being *subj.*) means 'let alone/not to mention/much less'; often preceded by هم (in the sense of 'even') for more emphasis:

بچه هم ندارم، چه رسد به نوه. (I don't even have children, let alone grandchildren.)

حتی سلام هم نگفت، تا چه برسد به اینکه دست بدهد. (He didn't even say hello, let alone shake hands.)

- به ... چه! (*be ... che!*) – in its more complete form used with مربوط (است) (*marbut [ast]*) or ربطی دارد (*rabti dārad*, both meaning 'is related') – is a common but rather rude way of saying that something does not concern someone, and it is originally an interrogative phrase turned exclamative. (You can use a question mark or an exclamation mark.)

به من چه! (I don't care!/Why should I care?)

به من چه مربوط (است)؟ (Why should it concern me?/Why should I care?)

به تو چه! (None of your business!/It doesn't concern you!)

به پدرت چه ربطی دارد؟ (It's none of your father's business.)

(See also 4.7 for چه...چه... or هرچه که, and see 11.6 below for هرچه + comparative.)

11.3 Forms of adverbs – reviewing and expanding

a) *Adjectives*

Most of the time, adjectives can be used as adverbs:

این قلم خوب است./این قلم خوب می‌نویسد. (This pen is good./This pen writes well.)

عصبانی بود./عصبانی حرف می‌زد. (He was angry./He talked angrily.)

b) به/با + *abstract noun*

This is similar to saying *with anger* instead of *angrily*. The به which is used to make adverbs is often written joined as بـ (and ـه is dropped), while به as preposition is written separately. Sometimes either به or با can be used, sometimes only one of them. Examples:

این قلم بخوبی می‌نویسد./این قلم خوب می‌نویسد. (This pen writes well.) – Note that we don't have ببدی and بد should also be used as adverb.

11

Exclamative
form

More on
adjectives/
adverbs

Comparison
of adjectives

Ezāfe

در را بآسانی باز کردم./در را آسان باز کردم. (I opened the door easily.)

البته! با خوشحالی گفتم: ('Of course!' I said happily.)

با تعجب به من نگاه می‌کرد. (He was looking at me with astonishment.)

Some examples of adverbs with *be-* for which you cannot use *bā-*:

بتدریج [*be-tadrij*, gradually], بموقع [*be-mowghe'*, on time],
بزودی [*be-zudi*, soon], بتنهائی [*be-tanhā'i*, alone],
بتازگی [*be-tāzegi*, recently].

For more emphasis, sometimes instead of به or با, expressions like در/با
کمال [*dar/bā kamāl-e*] or در/با نهایت [*dar/bā nahāyat-e*] are used, in this
usage both meaning 'with utmost'/'at the height of'/'extremely':

در نهایتِ بی‌سلیقگی لباس می‌پوشید. (He wore clothes very tastelessly.)
با نهایت احترام به او سلام کرد. (He greeted her most respectfully.)

c) *-āne suffix*

We learned about the *-āne* suffix (that produces both adjectives and adverbs) in 10.4:

بی‌صبرانه منتظرِ جوابش بودم. (I waited for her response impatiently.)
هزاران زندانی را وحشیانه قتل عام کردند. (They brutally massacred thousands of prisoners.)

d) *Adjective + tanvin*

This is mostly for adjectives borrowed from Arabic, and in contemporary Persian the *tanvin* sign (pronounced as a final *-an*; see I/1.2.6) is usually placed on an *alef*, regardless of the original Arabic spelling. Adjectives borrowed from Arabic usually have a different form for the abstract noun: سریع [*sari'*] is *fast* and سرعت [*sor'at*] is *speed*. Compare in the following examples the different adverb forms:

'He answered quickly.' =
سریع جواب داد.
به سرعتِ جواب داد.
سریعاً جواب داد. (pronounce *sari'an*)

'He strongly objected.' =
او به شدّتِ مخالفت کرد.
او شدیداً مخالفت کرد. (pronounce *shadidan*)

You can't usually find adjectives that have both -*āne* (c) and *tanvin* (d) forms; it is either one or the other.

For numerative adverbs made from ordinal numbers, see 3.2/c. Some useful adverbs with *tanvin*:

فوراً [*fowran*, immediately], نسبتاً [*nesbatan*, relatively], بعداً [*ba'dan*, afterwards], مخصوصاً [*makhsusan*, especially], تقریباً [*taghriban*, approximately, almost], معمولاً [*ma'mulan*, usually], غالباً [*ghāleban*, often], اتّفاقاً [*ettefāghan*, incidentally, by chance].

11.4 Much/many/a lot (of)

The words خیلی [*kheyli*] and زیاد [*ziyād*] in colloquial/less formal Persian, بسیار [*besyār*] or فراوان [*farāvān*] in more formal and بسی [*basi*] in literary/ poetical language are all used to mean *much, many* or *a lot of*.

Table 11.1: A lot (of)

	COLLOQUIAL/INFORMAL	FORMAL/WRITTEN	LITERARY/POETICAL
He has a lot of pain.	خیلی درد دارد زیاد درد دارد دردِ زیادی دارد	بسیار درد دارد دردِ بسیار دارد دردِ بسیاری دارد دردِ فراوان دارد دردِ فراوانی دارد	فراوان درد دارد بسی درد دارد
He has a lot of books.	خیلی کتاب دارد زیاد کتاب دارد کتابهای زیادی دارد	بسیار کتاب دارد کتابهای بسیار دارد کتابهای بسیاری دارد کتابهای فراوان دارد کتابهای فراوانی دارد	فراوان کتاب دارد بسی کتاب دارد
He writes a lot.	خیلی می‌نویسد زیاد می‌نویسد	بسیار می‌نویسد فراوان می‌نویسد	بسی می‌نویسد

زیاد .vs خیلی – some differences

- Don't use زیاد adverbially to modify an adjective in affirmative sentences, though it is common in the negative:

هوا خیلی سرد است (do not use زیاد here), but:
هوا زیاد سرد نیست/ هوا خیلی سرد نیست

11

Exclamative
form

More on
adjectives/
adverbs

Comparison
of adjectives

Ezāfe

- Use خیلی with comparative adjectives and adverbs, not زیاد:

خیلی زودتر or خیلی زیباتر

In this case, even when negative, خیلی (or چندان, *chandān*; see 12.3) are the preferred adverbs.

Much too/too much: If you use زیادی [*ziyādí*] with stressed -*i*, the meaning is *much too* or *too much*. (In Table 11.1, *ziyādi* ended in unstressed, indefinite -*i*.) Expressions like زیاده از حد [*ziyāde az hadd*], بیش از حد [*bish az hadd*] or بیش از اندازه [*bish az andāze*] can also be used. Examples:

این درس زیادی سخت است. (This lesson is [much] too difficult.)

شما بیش از حد به خودتان مطمئن هستید. (You trust yourself too much.)

کار نمی‌کند و بیش از اندازه حرف می‌زند. (He doesn't work and talks too much.)

11.5 Little/a little and few/a few

کم [*kam*] can be used for both *little* and *few*.

کمی with -*i* can also be used in this sense but only after (and not before) a *plural noun (or uncountable noun) + ezāfe*. If used before, it would mean *a little* or *a few*:

کمی پول = some/a little money

پولِ کمی = little money

A little or *a few* can be expressed in the following ways:

- کمی [*kami*, a little] or قدری/مقداری [*ghadri/meghdāri*, both meaning 'some amount of'] for uncountables
  (Note: when these are followed by از [*az*, of], thus becoming definite, Persian allows the use of the plural even for uncountables);
- چند (تا) [*chand (tā)*, some] or تعدادی [*te'dādi*, a number of] for countables.

چند and تعدادی are followed by singular nouns,

چند تا از and تعدادی از by plural nouns.

کم and کمتر can be used as adverbs also in the sense of *hardly* or *less frequently*.

Table 11.2: Few, little, etc.

a few	چند/چند تا سیب خریدم. (I bought some/a few apples.) چند تا از سیبها را خوردم. (I ate some/a few of the apples.) تعدادی دانشجو دیدم. (I saw a number of students.) با تعدادی از دانشجوها حرف زدم. (I talked to a number of the students.)
a little	کمی شکر خریدم. (I bought some/a little sugar.) کمی از شکر(/شکرها) را در آب ریختم. (I poured some/a little of the sugar into the water.) کمی/قدری/مقداری پول به من داد. (He gave me some/a little money.) مقداری از پول (پولها) را به من داد. (He gave me some of the money.)
few/little	کم سیب خریدم./سیب کم خریدم./سیبهای کمی خریدم. (I bought few apples.) کم پول به من داد./پول کم به من داد./پولِ کمی به من داد. (He gave me little money.)
adverbial usage	او را خیلی کم می‌شناسم. (I hardly know him./I know him very little.) کمتر کسی این را می‌داند. (Hardly anyone knows/Few people know this.) او را کم می‌بینم./کمتر او را می‌بینم. (I hardly see him [at all].)

As you may have noticed, *kam-tar* + an indefinite noun = *hardly any*; as in:

کمتر کسی می‌داند که او کجاست. (Hardly anyone knows where he is.)

کمتر کسی هست که بداند او کجاست. (There is hardly anyone who knows where he is.)

کمتر روزی هست که او را نبینم. (There is hardly any day when I don't see him.)

کمتر مردی را می‌بینی که اینقدر در خانه کار کند. (You hardly see a man who works so much at home.)

11

Exclamative
form

More on
adjectives/
adverbs

Comparison
of adjectives

Ezāfe

11.6 More on comparison of adjectives/adverbs

a) بیشتر *(more) and* کمتر *(less) – a different usage*

You know that بیشتر with *ezāfe* means 'most of', e.g. بیشترِ روزها = *most of the days*; and sometimes بیشتر is used as an adverb meaning *mostly*:

این کتاب بیشتر دربارهٔ تاریخ آفریقا است. (This book is mostly about the history of Africa.)

Examples of بیشتر and کمتر without the second part of the comparison being mentioned:

باید بیشتر بخوابی. (You should sleep more.)

او را کمتر می‌بینم. (I see him less often.)

Occasionally different meanings can be possible, especially when some amount/quantity is mentioned.
For instance, the sentence این کتابخانه پنجاه هزار کتاب بیشتر دارد can mean:

i. This library has more than 50,000 books.
ii. This library has 50,000 books more [than some other library, not mentioned here].

The same ambiguity can happen with کمتر, for instance
پرویز سی سال کمتر دارد can mean:

i. Parviz is below 30.
ii. Parvis is 30 years younger.

b) هرچه + *comparative*

- هرچه **followed by two comparatives** is similar to two English comparatives preceded by *the*:

  هرچه زودتر، بهتر (The sooner, the better.)
  هرچه زودتر بروید بهتر خواهد بود. (The sooner you go, the better it will be.)

- هرچه **followed by only one comparative** has the meaning of 'as ... as possible':

  هرچه زودتر (As soon as possible.)
  نامه را هرچه سریعتر تمام کن. (Finish the letter as fast as possible.)
  توفیقِ هرچه بیشترِ شما را آرزو می‌کنم. (I wish you the utmost success/as much success as possible.)

The latter version (with one comparative) would be close in meaning to:

superlative + noun + ezāfe + ممکن *(momken, possible),*

or using expressions like در نهایتِ *(dar nahāyat-e,* with the utmost), as in these examples:

با احترام هرچه بیشتر جواب دادم. (I responded with as much respect [/as respectfully] as póssible.)

= با بیشترین احترام ممکن جواب دادم. (I responded with the most respect possible [/as respectfully as possible].)

= در نهایتِ احترام جواب دادم. (I responded with the utmost respect.)

The expression بیش از پیش (more than before, more than ever) is also very close to هرچه بیشتر and they are sometimes interchangeable.

c) *Comparative with* تا *[tā] instead of* از *[az]*

The preposition used for the comparative is از (see I/8.1.1). However, if the second part (or 'standard') of comparison is mentioned after the main verb, then تا is used instead of از – and this can occasionally reduce ambiguities:

The sentence (من) مینا را بیشتر از تو می‌بینم can have two meanings:

i) I see Mina more than [I see] you, *or*
ii) I see Mina more than you [do].

By changing (من) مینا را بیشتر از تو می‌بینم to the version with تا, we would have two different versions for (i) and (ii):

i) (من) مینا را بیشتر می‌بینم تا تو را
ii) من مینا را بیشتر می‌بینم تا تو

As you notice, in (i) it is the final را that brings clarity, and in (ii) we can't drop the subject because it needs emphasis.

Similarly, the sentence به من کمتر از تو پول داد can have two meanings, and we will give here the version with تا for each of those meanings:

i) He gave me less money than you [did].
او به من کمتر پول داد تا تو. (note that او cannot be dropped here);
ii) He gave less money to me than to you.
(او) به من کمتر پول داد تا به تو. (Note the clarifying presence of the second به here.)

11

Exclamative
form

More on
adjectives/
adverbs

Comparison
of adjectives

Ezāfe

The comparative with *tā* is usually used in affirmative sentences; it would sound a little awkward with the negative.

d) *Superlative with* ezāfé

So far you have learned to say

- یک سیبِ بزرگتر (*yek sib-e bozorgtar*, a bigger apple), and
- بزرگترین سیب (*bozorgtarin sib*, the biggest apple) (see I/8.1.2) – which means: superlative precedes the noun and needs no *ezāfe*.

However, when used before plural nouns, an *ezāfe* can be added to the superlative – if needed – to function like *of* after an English superlative. 'The biggest *of* the apples', then, would be بزرگترین سیبها (*bozorgtarin-e sib-hā*) while بزرگترین سیبها (*bozorgtarin sib-hā*) without *ezāfe* would simply mean 'the biggest apples'.

Other examples:

بهترین میوه (*behtarin mive*, the best fruit)

→ بهترین میوه‌ها (*behtarin mive-hā*, the best fruits)

→ بهترینِ میوه‌ها (*behtarin-e mive-hā*, the best of the fruits)

خوشگلترین دختر (*khoshgeltarin dokhtar*, the prettiest girl)

→ خوشگلترین دخترها (*khoshgeltarin dokhtar-hā*, the prettiest girls)

→ خوشگلترینِ دخترها (*khoshgeltarin-e dokhtar-hā*, the prettiest of the girls)

11.7 Equal comparison; resemblance and sameness

The most common structure used in Persian for equal comparison ('*as . . . as . . .*') is:

$$be\text{-}/b\bar{a} + abstract\ noun + ez\bar{a}fe$$

به زیبائیِ [*be zibā'i-ye*] = as beautiful as

You know how you can make adverbs by using an abstract noun after به or با (see 11.3/b) – here you only need to add an *ezāfe* to that structure. به is more common here than با and is usually written separately. (To make abstract nouns from adjectives, add stressed -*i*, as in زیبا → زیبائی; see I/6.3). See comparisons with adverbial use in the following examples:

با دقّت/به دقّت به حرفهایم گوش کرد. (He carefully listened to my words.)

او با دقّتِ یک ماشین کار میکند. (He works with the precision of [as precisely as] a machine.)

بسرعت کتش را پوشید و رفت. (He quickly put on his jacket and left.)

به سرعتِ برق از خانه بیرون دوید. (He ran out of the house as fast as lightning.)

دستهایش به سردیِ یخ بود. (His hands were as cold as ice.)

موهایش به سفیدیِ برف است. (Her hair is as white as snow.)

شیراز به بزرگیِ اصفهان نیست. (Shiraz is not as large as Isfahan.)

When the second part of the comparison is a singular demonstrative pronoun (این or آن), it is more common to place it before the abstract noun (with no *ezāfe*):

گلی به این قشنگی (a flower as beautiful as this) is more common than

گلی به قشنگیِ این.

Expressions like به اندازۀ/بقدر (meaning 'to the size/extent/amount of') can also be used to convey this kind of equal comparison:

من به زرنگیِ تو نیستم. (I'm not as smart as you.)

= من به اندازۀ تو زرنگ نیستم.

این کتاب به سادگیِ کتابِ قبلی نیست. (This book is not as simple as the previous one.)

= این کتاب بقدرِ کتابِ قبلی ساده نیست.

Using به اندازۀ/بقدر is especially common in cases where the basis of comparison is not an 'abstract' noun, or with longer compound adjectives:

به قدرِ دهنت حرف بزن. (Talk as big as your mouth.)

هرچقدر هم که درس خوانده باشد، به اندازۀ یک الاغ نمیفهمد. (However much he may have studied, he doesn't understand so much as a donkey.)

این فیلم به اندازۀ فیلمِ قبلی خسته کننده نبود. (This film was not so boring as the previous one.)

Using همان (*hamān*, the same, that same) or the more colloquial همین (*hamin*, the same, this same) before اندازه and قدر is also very common, giving them the meaning of *as much/to the same amount or extent*, while

11

Exclamative
form

More on
adjectives/
adverbs

Comparison
of adjectives

Ezāfe

using که before the second part of the comparison (which can then turn into a clause by adding a verb):

برادرش هم همانقدر پُرحرف بود. (His brother was also as [much] talkative.)

برادرش هم همانقدر پُرحرف بود که خودش. (His brother was also as talkative as him[self].)

تا جائی که or تا آنجا که is used in the sense of 'as much as/so far as':

تا آنجا که من می‌دانم ... (So far as I know ...)

تا جائی که به شما مربوط می‌شود ... (As much as it concerns you ...)

We learned a few prefixes earlier that are used to show resemblance (see 10.5/D). Some more words now:

Words that mean *like* (used as *prep.*):

- colloquial + formal: مثل (*mesl-e*), شبیهِ (*shabih-e*)
- formal/written: مانندِ (*mānand-e*)
- poetical: همانندِ (*hamānand-e*), چون (*chon*), همچون (*ham-chon*), به سانِ (*be sān-e*)

Words that mean *alike* (*adj.*):

- colloquial + formal: مثل هم (*mesl-e ham*), شبیه (*shabih*), مشابه (*moshābeh*)
- formal/written: همانند (*hamānand*), همسان (*ham-sān*), یکسان (*yek-sān*)

Verbs that mean *to resemble* (all of them with به):

- مشابهت داشتن (*moshābehat dāshtan*), شباهت داشتن (*shebāhat dāshtan*), شبیه بودن (*shabih budan*), مانستن (*mānestan*)

For *exactly like* use درست مثلِ (*dorost mesl-e*) or عینِ (*eyn-e*) before the noun, and for *the same as* use همان (*hamān*) predicatively.

Examples:

This is how you say 'a dog is like/resembles a wolf' (or they are alike) in Persian (ignoring the more literary/poetical versions):

- سگ مثلِ گرگ است.
- سگ و گرگ مثلِ هم هستند.

- سگ شبیهِ گرگ است.
- سگ و گرگ شبیه (/شبیهِ یکدیگر) هستند.
- سگ مانندِ گرگ است.
- سگ به گَرگ می‌ماند.
- سگ و گرگ به یکدیگر می‌مانند.
- سگ به گرگ شباهت دارد.
- سگ و گرگ به یکدیگر شباهت دارند.
- سگ و گرگ مشابه (/مشابهِ یکدیگر) هستند.
- سگ و گرگ به یکدیگر مشابهت دارند.

11.8 Adjective placed before noun. More on *ezāfe*

Adjectives are usually placed after the noun, and they are connected
through an *ezāfe*, as in مردِ خوب (*mard-e khub*, the good man). In poetical
language, however, the adjective can be placed before the noun, the two
words making some sort of compound, and there is no *ezāfe*.

You might ask now: Can I say خوبمرد (*khub-mard*) instead of مردِ خوب?
Answer: No, you can't – because:

a) you are not writing a poem, are you? and
b) even if you were, then you should substitute the word خوب with the
more literary/poetical sounding word نیک and say نیکمرد (*nik-mard*, a
good and benevolent man).

Some very common compound words, however, use this form:

پیرزن (*pir-zan*, old woman, used in a generic sense) = زنِ پیر (*zan-e pir*)

پیرمرد (*pir-mard*, old man, used in a generic sense) = مردِ پیر (*mard-e pir*)

سفیدپوست (*sefid-pust*, white-skinned, belonging to the white race)

سیاهپوست (*siyāh-pust*, black-skinned, belonging to the black race)

خوشبخت (*khosh-bakht*, fortunate)

بدبخت (*bad-bakht*, unfortunate)

The omission of *ezāfe* does not happen only when the adjective precedes the
noun. Even where the adjective follows the noun (as in standard usage),
the connecting *ezāfe* can occasionally be omitted if the two words form a
fixed (or 'lexicalized') compound, a lexical unit with an independent meaning. One such example is تخته سیاه (*takhte-siyāh*, blackboard), which differs
from تختهٔ سیاه (*takhte-ye siyāh*, a black plank or board). Other words that
you already know are پدربزرگ and مادربزرگ.

121

11

Exclamative
form

More on
adjectives/
adverbs

Comparison
of adjectives

Ezāfe

Exercises

Exercise 11.1

Choose one of the following to fill in the blanks, then translate:

a) چه (b هرچه (c چه بسا (d چه بسیار (e چه رسد به (f چه رسد به اینکه

Example:

مینا نیامد، .... نمی‌دانست که باید بیاید.

→ چه بسا (Mina didn't come; maybe she didn't know that she had to come.)

۱. بالاخره او را خواهم دید، .... در خانهٔ خودش در تهران چه در اصفهان.

۲. فکر می‌کردم او این حرف را گفته است، ولی .... اشتباه کرده باشم.

۳. خیلی کم گردش کردیم، ولی نمی‌دانی .... هوای خوبی بود!

۴. این باغ وحش حتّی یک خرس هم ندارد، .... فیل.

۵. باید برای شام .... سریع‌تر به خانه برگردیم.

۶. حالا عجله نکن، بعداً در ایران .... برای این کار وقت خواهی داشت.

۷. چیز بیشتری نمی‌دانم و .... می‌دانستم به شما گفتم.

۸. دیگر نمی‌خواهم اسمش را بشنوم، .... از او کتاب قرض بگیرم.

۹. ممکن است من درسم را خوب نخوانده باشم، ولی این به شما...............؟

۱۰. در تمام این سالها .... خواسته است برایش خریده‌ام.

Exercise 11.2

Choose the correct answer. Example:

او می‌تواند (خوب/خوبی/کمال خوبی) بنویسد.

→ خوب

۱. من می‌توانم آن را از اینجا (راحتی/براحتی/در کمال راحت) ببینم.

۲. نامه‌ای را که از من خواسته‌اند باید (به سریع/سرعت/سریعاً) بنویسم.

۳. خودت عاقل هستی ولی این (برادرت/کارت/سگت) عاقلانه نبود.

۴. ما زیاد وقت نداریم و احتیاج به یک جوابِ (سریع/سرعت/سریعا) داریم.

۵. مثل حیوانهای (وحشی/وحشیانه/وحشیانه‌ای) به ما حمله کردند و کتکمان زدند.

۶. به شکل (وحشی/وحشیانه/وحشیانه‌ای) به او حمله کردند و کتکش زدند.

۷. شهر (فوراً/نسبتاً/قبلاً) آرام است و می‌توانید خانه را ترک کنید.

۸. داروی این دکتر هم نتوانست بچّه را (آرام/آرامی/به آرامی) کند.

۹. صدای بدی ندارد ولی امروز در برنامه خیلی (بد/بدی/به بدی) خواند.

۱۰. لازم نیست خیلی (دوست/دوستی/دوستانه) با او حرف بزنید.

Exercise 11.3

Choose one of the following to fill in the blanks; the translations will help you to make the right choice:

a) کم b) کمی c) کمتر d) زیاد e) زیادی f) بیشتر

Example:

(I didn't stay longer بیشتر نماندم چون خیلی .... وقت داشتم because I had very little time.)

کم ←

۱. او حتماً خواهد آمد ولی باید .... بیشتر صبر کنید.
(She will certainly come, but you have to wait a little longer.)

۲. باید یک جفت کفش نو بخرم ولی پول .... دارم.
(I must buy a pair of shoes, but I have too little money.)

۳. .... استادی به اندازهٔ او دانشجوها را می‌خنداند.
(Hardly any professors make the students laugh as much as he does.)

۴. این کفش فقط کمی تنگ است، ولی آن یکی .... تنگ بود.
(These shoes are only a little small ['tight'], but those were too small.)

۵. .... روزها او را در خیابان جلو آن مغازه می‌بینم.
(Most of the days I see him on the street in front of that store.)

۶. از وقتی که آبستن شده .... او را در کتابخانه می‌بینم.
(Since she got pregnant I have hardly seen her at all in the library.)

۷. اگر کمی .... حرف می‌زد، همه خوابشان می‌برد.
(If he had talked a little longer, everybody would have fallen asleep.)

۸. باید .... درس بخوانی تا نتیجهٔ خوب بگیری.
(You must study a lot to get good results.)

۹. اصلاً کار نمی‌کرد چون .... تنبل بود.
(He never worked because he was too lazy.)

۱۰. این تمرین برای من .... آسان بود.
(This exercise was too easy for me.)

123

11

Exclamative
form

More on
adjectives/
adverbs

Comparison
of adjectives

Ezāfe

Exercise 11.4

Change the comparatives with *az* to comparatives with *tā*. Example:

او از من دیرتر رسید

او دیرتر رسید تا من ←

۱. پدرم خیلی بهتر از من شطرنج بازی می‌کند.

۲. درس دوّم را خیلی زودتر از درس اوّل تمام کردیم.

۳. خربزه‌های ایران خیلی بزرگتر و شیرینتر از خربزه‌های آمریکا بودند.

۴. در مدارس ایران بیشتر از مدارس آمریکا به ریاضیات توجه می‌کنند.

۵. او خیلی سریعتر از من کار می‌کند.

۶. تو بیشتر از خواهرت در خانه می‌مانی.

۷. شما این مقاله را دقیقتر از او ترجمه کرده‌اید.

۸ این چیزها را بچّه‌ها بهتر از آدم‌بزرگها می‌فهمند.

۹. ما خانه‌مان را زودتر از شما خریدیم.

۱۰. درس تاریخ جالبتر از فلسفه است.

Exercise 11.5

Translate into English.

۱. نگاه کن، درست عینِ مادرش می‌خندد!

۲. اوضاع کشور به همان خرابیِ قبل است.

۳. سخنران به بزرگیِ مشکلات کشور اشاره کرد.

۴. کمتر شاعری به بزرگیِ حافظ می‌توان یافت.

۵. من به اندازهٔ شما به موسیقیِ سنّتی علاقه ندارم.

۶. باید برای این بچّه‌تان هم همانقدر وقت صرف کنید که برای قبلی می‌کردید.

۷. تا به حال موئی به این قرمزی دیده بودی؟

۸ مگر دیوانه بود که با مردی به این بدی ازدواج کرد؟

۹. روزهای من به تاریکیِ شبهای شما شده‌اند.

۱۰. من بقدر تو بدبین نیستم ولی خیلی هم خوشبین نیستم.

Exercise 11.6

Translate into Persian. You don't need to mention all possible synonyms, but if two structurally different renderings are possible mention both. (Some of the words you can use have been given at the end of the exercise.)

1. This dog is as large as a horse.
2. This parrot talks exactly like people. [Use آدم/آدمها for *people*.]
3. Believe me, I'm as tired as you are.
4. Are days in summer as long as nights in winter?
5. She resembles a flower in this dress.
6. I'll die if I run as fast as you do.
7. Onion is almost as useful as garlic.
8. Will garlic smell as bad by any other name? (Use 'with' for 'by.')
9. This exercise was as boring as the previous one.
10. I hope he doesn't act as stupidly as he talks.

سگ/اسب/بزرگ/طوطی/آدم/درست مثلِ/باور کردن/خسته/خسته

کننده/روز/شب/تابستان/زمستان/دراز/لباس/گل/تند/دویدن/مردن/پیاز/

سیر/مفید/تقریباً/بو/بدبو/تمرین/قبلی/امیدوار/رفتار/احمقانه

ملّا شدن چه آسان، آدم شدن چه مشکل!

How easy to become a mullah, how hard to become a human!

(= It's not some education that makes you a good person.)

UNIT TWELVE | فصل ۱۲

Correlative conjunctions | حرفِ ربط‌هایِ پیوسته

More on subordinate clauses | باز هم جملاتِ تبعی

A review of *tā* | مرورِ 'تا'

12.1 Correlative conjunctions

Correlative (or *reciprocating*) conjunctions work in pairs, usually joining words (or groups of words) that are of equal weight. If the sentence has only one main verb, it is usually placed before the second part of these conjunctions; using a comma to separate the two parts is optional.

In the following list, you already know the first two (see 4.7).

- خواه ... خواه ... [*khāh ... khāh ...*] and ... چه ... چه [*che ... che ...*] both mean 'whether ... or ...':

  من خواهم رفت، چه تو بیائی چه نیائی. (I'll go, whether you come or you don't.)

  باید آن را بخوانی، خواه خوشت بیاید خواه نه. (You must read it, whether you like it or not.)

Based on this '*khāh ... khāh ...*' conjunction (from the verb خواستن), Persian has the very common adverbs خواه ناخواه (*khāh-nā-khāh*, willy-nilly, whether desired or not, no matter what) or خواهی‌نخواهی (*khāhi-nakhāhi*, same meaning):

  خواهی نخواهی یک روز می‌فهمد. (One day he will find out, whether you like it or not.)

- یا ... یا ... [*yā ... yā ...*] means 'either ... or ...':

  یا امروز می‌آید یا فردا. (She comes either today or tomorrow.)

  یا درس بخوان یا به مادرت کمک کن. (Either study or help your Mom.)

126

- ... نه ... نه [na ... na ...] means 'neither ... nor ...':

  نه خیلی سخت است نه آسان. (It's neither very difficult nor easy.)

  نه نامه‌ای نوشت، نه تلفنی زد. (He neither wrote a letter nor
  telephoned.)

Note that if you have words like هیچ or هرگز (that normally require a
negative verb) in sentences with 'neither ... nor ...,' you don't need a
negative verb any more:

  نه هیچوقت او را می‌بینم نه دوستش را. (Neither do I ever see her
  nor her friend.)

- ... هم ... هم [ham ... ham ...] means 'both ... and ...':

  هم خواهرت را می‌شناسم، هم برادرت را. (I know both your brother
  and your sister.)

  هم خانه را تمیز کرد، هم غذا پخت. (He both cleaned the house and
  cooked.)

Note: with all of the above correlative conjunctions, in colloquial/
less careful Persian you might see a redundant و [va, and] before the
second part, especially if the relation between the two parts is not that
strong:

  هم مادرم مرد و هم در امتحان رد شدم. (Both my mother died and
  I failed in the exam.)

- ... هم ... بلکه ... نه تنها [na tanhā ... balke ... ham ...] means 'not only ... but
  also ...;' sometimes the word بلکه in this construction is omitted, and
  it is possible to say نه فقط [na faghat] instead of نه تنها:

  نه تنها به تو دروغ گفته، بلکه به من هم. (He has not only lied to you
  but to me as well.)

  نه فقط خوب می‌خواند، (بلکه) خوب هم می‌رقصد. (She not only
  sings well but also dances well.)

  نه تنها درسش را تمام کرد، (بلکه) کارِ خوبی هم پیدا کرد. (She not
  only finished her studies but found a good job too.)

12

Correlative
conjunctions

More on
subordinate
clauses

A review of *tā*

12.2 More on subordinate clauses and matching adverbial phrases

Several types of subordinate clauses have already been covered, like *relative clauses* (I/19), *if-clauses* in conditionals (I/16) and *time clauses* (I/18).

Subordinate clauses usually need conjunctions which are often a preposition + آنکه/اینکه (see I/17). Here we learn more about conjunctions used in clauses of purpose ('so that'), cause ('because'/'therefore'), result ('so/such ... that'), contrast/concession ('although') – and also certain temporal idioms (like *had hardly* and *no sooner*; see 12.4).

12.2.1 Clauses of purpose, cause and effect

A. To say 'He came here (in order) to see you,' you normally say in Persian:

به اینجا آمد **که** تو را ببیند.

The conjunction که in the above sentence can also be dropped, or can be replaced by any of the following conjunctions:

تا/برایِ آنکه/به قصدِ آنکه (/به این قصد که)/به منظورِ آنکه (/به این منظور که)/به نیّتِ آنکه (/به این نیّت که)/به خاطرِ آنکه (/به این خاطر که)/با هدفِ آنکه (/با این هدف که)

Here you can switch the two clauses but you can't use که or تا (in this sense) at the beginning of the first clause:

برای آنکه تو را ببیند به اینجا آمد.

Another possibility would be using a preposition:

برایِ دیدنِ تو به اینجا آمد. (He came here for [/with the purpose of] seeing you.)

Instead of برایِ in the above sentence, you can use any of the following:

به قصدِ/به منظورِ/به نیّتِ/به خاطرِ/با هدفِ

B. To say 'He came here because he wanted to see you,' you normally say in Persian:

به اینجا آمد **چون** می‌خواست تو را ببیند.

Instead of the conjunction چون in the above sentence you can use any of the following:

چونکه/زیرا/چرا که/برای اینکه/به خاطرِ آنکه/به دلیلِ آنکه/به جهتِ آنکه/ به سببِ آنکه

You can switch the two clauses again, only you can't use زیرا or چراکه at the beginning of the sentence – and you can additionally use ازآنجاکه instead:

چون می‌خواست تو را ببیند به اینجا آمد.

C. To say 'He wanted to see you; therefore, he came here,' you normally say in Persian:

می‌خواست تو را ببیند، **به همین دلیل** به اینجا آمد.

Instead of به همین دلیل in the above sentence you can use any of the following:

پس/بنا بر این/برایِ همین/به همین قصد/به همین منظور/به همین نیّت/به همینِ خاطر/به خاطرِ همین/به همین جهت/به همین سبب/در نتیجه

Two notes:

- As you noticed, به خاطرِ can both mean *for the purpose of* (which is about the future) and *because of* (which is about the past).
- It is good to be reminded again that اینکه is more common than آنکه in less formal Persian – while some expressions like به سبب and به جهتِ are more formal and for these آنکه would be a better fit.

12.2.2 Clauses of contrast/concession

In *concessive* statements you have words like اگرچه meaning *although*.

A. To say 'Although it was raining, we waited,' you normally say in Persian:

اگرچه باران می‌آمد، منتظر شدیم.

Instead of اگرچه ('although') in the above sentence you can use any of the following:

هرچند/با اینکه (/با آنکه)/با وُجودِ اینکه/علیرغمِ آنکه/به رغمِ آنکه

12

Correlative
conjunctions

More on
subordinate
clauses

A review of *tā*

You can switch the two clauses, using the same conjunctions.

Sometimes in clauses of concession, two conjunctions are used for emphasis, each introducing one of the clauses. Though an obvious redundancy, this is not a rarity in Persian:

اگرچه بارانِ خیلی تندی می‌آمد، ولی باز هم منتظر شدیم.

به رغمِ and علی‌رغمِ, با وُجودِ can be used as prepositions also:

با وُجودِ باران، منتظر شدیم.

B. To say 'It was raining; nevertheless, we waited,' you normally say in Persian:

باران می‌آمد، **با اینهمه** منتظر شدیم.

Instead of با اینهمه ('however') in the above sentence you can use one of the following:

با وجودِ این/با این وجود/معهذا/معذلک/علیرغم آن/به رغم آن

12.2.3 Clauses of result (or consequence)

In *clauses of result* (or *consequence*), Persian usually uses different words in the first clause and begins the second clause with که [ke]. The words used include:

- آنقدر/اینقدر/بقدری/به‌اندازه‌ای all meaning 'so, so much, so many, to such an extent':

آنقدر خسته بود که فوراً خوابش بُرد. (She was so tired that she immediately fell asleep.)

آنقدر پول دارد که نمی‌داند با آن چکار کند.

آنقدر کتاب خواند که کور شد.

بقدری سریع رفت که کیفش را فراموش کرد.

See 4.6/b for more examples with آنقدر in a different sense.

Also note that '...آنقدر...که' differs from '...آنقدر...تا', the latter usually meaning 'keep doing something until ...:'

آنقدر تلفن زدم تا بالاخره کسی جواب داد. (I kept calling until someone finally answered.)

- به) طوری) (*col.*), جوری (still more *col.*), به گونه‌ای (*form./lit.*), all meaning 'in such a way':

  طوری راه می‌رفت که معلوم بود خسته است. (He walked in such a way that it was obvious that he was tired.)

  به گونه‌ای بیمار بود که باید به بیمارستان برده می‌شد.

  For '...طوری...که انگار' (in such a way as if...) see 5.4.

- چنان (*form./lit.*):

  چنان زیباست که همه را می‌فریبد (She is so beautiful that she spellbinds everybody.)

  چنان زیبا می‌خواند که چندین بار جایزهٔ اوّل را بُرد.

  چنان کار سختی را در یک هفته نمی‌توان تمام کرد.

  Note that '...چنان...که گوئی' (in such a way as if...) is a formal or literary version of '...طوری...که انگار' (see 5.4):

  form.: چنان سخن می‌گفت که گوئی ما کودکیم (He talked in such a way as if we were children.)

  col.: طوری حرف می‌زد (که) انگار ما بچّه‌ایم (Same meaning.)

- چندان (so, so much, so many) (*poet.*)

  چندان دیر بود که همگان خفته بودند. (It was so late that everybody had gone to bed.)

Compare this with the colloquial version:

آنقدر دیر بود که همه خوابیده بودند.

Another example:

چندان کتاب در آن خانه یافت که حیرت کرد. (He found so many books in that house that he was astounded.)

12.3 Other usages of چنان and چندان. More conjunctions

A. چندان *[chandān]*

In its usage as *consecutive conjunction*, the word چندان was labeled above as *poetical*, which limited its usage. However, چندان can be used in colloquial Persian as 'much/that much' in negative sentences:

12

Correlative
conjunctions

More on
subordinate
clauses

A review of *tā*

او را چندان نمی‌شناسم. (I don't know him much.)

این درس چندان سخت هم نبود. (This lesson was not that difficult.)

نه چندان = نه زیاد = 'not much':

'نه چندان؛ اشتها نداشت.' – '؟غذا خورد' – (–) (– 'Did he eat?' – 'Not much;
he had no appetite.')

B. چنان‌که *[chenān-ke]*

چنان‌که (also written چنانکه) is different from 'چنان ... که ...' (*so ... that ...*)
and means *as* or *the way that*:

... چنانکه می‌دانید (As you know ...)

... چنانکه می‌بینید (As you see ...)

... چنانکه به ما گفته‌اند (As we have been told ...)

چنانکه is formal (like چنان itself); a very common colloquial synonym is
همانطورکه (*hamān-towr-ke*, written also همان‌طورکه):

... همانطورکه به شما گفته بودم (As I had told you ...)

C. همچنان‌که *[ham-chenān-ke]*

همچنان‌که [*ham-chenān-ke*, in the same way that] has two meanings and
functions:

1) It can have the same meaning as چنانکه (see above), maybe even more
   formal:

   ... همچنانکه اعلام شده است (As it has been announced ...)

2) It means در حالیکه (the temporal 'while/as' or 'at the same time that'):

   همچنانکه غذایش را می‌خورد، به اخبار رادیو گوش می‌کرد. (At the
   same time that he was eating, he was listening to the news
   on the radio.)

Note 1:
Used as adverb (and not conjunction), همچنان [*ham-chenān*] means *still*
(*form.*; its colloquial synonym being هنوز, *hanuz*), while همچنین [*ham-
chenin*] means *also* or, in the negative, *neither/nor* (= نیز, *niz*, both of them
form.; their colloquial synonym being همینطور, *hamin-towr*):

او همچنان (= هنوز) در مشهد کار می‌کند. (He still works in Mashhad.)

ما همچنین (= همینطور) به یک ماشین بزرگتر احتیاج داریم. (We also need a larger car.)

تو نخوابیدی، من هم همینطور. (You didn't sleep, and neither did I.) – In more formal/literary language, the last part should have been من نیز همچنین. (See also 13.2.1.)

Note 2:
There is no همچنین که (*ham-chenin-ke*) in contemporary Persian, although in the colloquial/Tehrāni accent you hear همچین که/همچیکه (*hamchin-ke/ hamchi-ke*) used as a synonym for همینکه (*hamin-ke*, as soon as) – which is a temporal conjunction used in time clauses (see I/18.3).

12.4 Temporal idioms: *had hardly/scarcely* and *no sooner*

For the idiomatic 'had hardly [/scarcely/barely] ... when ...' what you need in Persian is:

hanuz (هنوز) + negative past perfect + *ke* (که)

This can also have shorter versions: sometimes no *hanuz*, and sometimes just a negative past participle instead of the past perfect (as mentioned earlier; see 6.3.2). But it works best when all ingredients are there:

هنوز تنم را نشسته بودم که آب سرد شد. (I had scarcely washed my body when the water became cold.)

هنوز قصه را شروع نکرده بودم که خوابش برد. (I had hardly started the story when he fell asleep.)

For 'no sooner ... than ...' you need no negative, and you use تازه instead of هنوز:

tāze (تازه) + past perfect + *ke* (که)

تازه قصه را شروع کرده بودم که خوابش برد. (No sooner had I started the story than he fell asleep.)

تازه در را باز کرده بودم که گربه بیرون دوید. (I had no sooner opened the door than the cat ran out.)

12

Correlative
conjunctions
More on
subordinate
clauses
A review of *tā*

Compare with همینکه or with تا:

همینکه در را باز کردم، گربه بیرون دوید. (As soon as I opened the door,
the cat ran out.)

= تا در را باز کردم، گربه بیرون دوید.

And this seems to be a good point to turn our attention to تا.

12.5 A review of the omnipotent تا (*tā*)

To use the word تا itself to describe it, we should say it is بی‌همتا (*bi-ham-
tā*), meaning *matchless* and *incomparable*.

- As a noun – yes, a noun too! – it means (among others) a 'match' and
  'a fold' – from which we have the verb تا کردن ('to fold') and the agent
  participle تاشو (*tā-show*, foldable, folding).
- As a numerative, تا is the most common counting word used after numbers,
  which, in certain cases, is indispensable – for example when numbers
  are used as pronouns (see I/3.4):

تو چهار برادر داری ولی من فقط دو تا دارم.

- As a preposition – both temporal and locational – it means *until/up to/as
  far as* (see I/17.1):

تا کنارِ رودخانه دویدم.
باید تاً فردا بمانم.

- In the comparative, it can function as *than* when placed after the verb
  (see 11.6/c):

از تو بیشتر می‌ترسد تا از من.

- Most importantly, as a conjunction (see 12.2.1 also), تا has at least five
  different usages:

a) It means 'in order to' (= برای اینکه) or 'so that' when introducing a
   subsequent clause and will always require the subjunctive:

عینک زدم تا بهتر ببینم.
بیشتر توضیح بدهید تا بفهمم.

b) It also means 'until' when introducing a subsequent clause, with the subjunctive if about future (or future in the past):

صبر می‌کنیم تا بیاید. (We'll wait until he comes.)

صبر کردیم تا بیاید. (We waited for him to come.)

صبر کردیم تا آمد. (We waited until he came.)

c) Introducing the first clause, it can still mean 'until'/'for as long as' with an affirmative verb (see also I/18.5):

تا هوا اینطور است (/باشد) نمی‌توانیم برویم.
تا او در تهران زندگی می‌کرد پدرش زنده بود.

The meaning changes to 'until'/'by the time that' if the verb indicates the completion of an action (and not a state; no progressive tenses; and often a perfect tense in the main clause):

تا این کتاب را تمام کنم موهایم سفید شده است. (By the time I finish this book, my hair will have turned white.)

تا او از سفر برگشت پدرش مرده بود. (By the time he returned from the trip, his father had died.)

d) Introducing the first clause (with the negative), it means 'so long as' – or 'until' if you translate as the affirmative. Use the subjunctive if about the future:

تا غذایت را نخوری بستنی را نمی‌آورم. (I won't bring the ice-cream so long as you don't eat [= until you eat] your food.)

تا غذایم را نخوردم به من بستنی نداد. (She didn't give me ice-cream so long as I hadn't eaten [= until I ate] my food.)

e) Finally, introducing the first clause, it can mean 'as soon as' (= همینکه), with the main stress on tā; see the different tenses and moods below:

تا در را باز کند، همه چیز را خواهد فهمید. (As soon as he opens the door, he will understand everything.)

تا در را باز کرد، همه چیز را فهمید. (As soon as he opened the door, he realized everything.)

تا به خانه می‌آید، می‌رود جلو تلویزیون. (As soon as he comes home, he goes in front of the TV.)

تا دکتر را می‌دید فرار می‌کرد. (He used to run away as soon as he saw the doctor.)

تا دکتر را دید فرار کرد. (He ran away as soon as he saw the doctor.)

12

Correlative
conjunctions

More on
subordinate
clauses

A review of *tā*

12.6 Noun clauses: که vs. اینکه

If you begin a sentence with a noun clause, you would usually need اینکه/این‌که (and not آنکه) at the beginning of the sentence. Such a noun clause may function

- as the subject,
- as direct object (این را که), or
- as indirect object (a preposition + *in-ke*).

See how the conjunction *ke* (in the middle of the sentence) changes to *in-ke* (at the beginning) in the following examples:

Subject:

از اوّل معلوم بود که با او ازدواج نخواهد کرد.) (It was obvious from the beginning that she would not marry him.)

→ اینکه با او ازدواج نخواهد کرد از اوّل معلوم بود.) (That she would not marry him was obvious from the beginning.)

Direct object:

همه می‌دانستند که با او ازدواج نخواهد کرد.) (Everybody knew that she would not marry him.)

→ این را که با او ازدواج نخواهد کرد همه می‌دانستند.) (That she would not marry him [was something that] everybody knew.)

Indirect object:

هیچکس از این خوشش نیامد که او بلند می‌خندید.) (Nobody liked the fact that he laughed loudly.)

→ از اینکه او بلند می‌خندید هیچکس خوشش نیامد.) (That he laughed loudly nobody liked/was not liked by anyone.)

Exercises

Exercise 12.1

Choose the appropriate correlative conjunction (see below) for the blanks, then translate.

چه...چه...(خواه...خواه...)/یا...یا.../نه...نه.../هم...هم.../ نه تنها...بلکه...هم...

Example:

امروز وقت ندارم، ولی .... فردا تو را می‌بینم .... پس فردا

→ ...یا...یا (I don't have time today, but I'll see you either tomorrow or the day after tomorrow.)

١.   چرا آدرسش را از من می‌پرسی؟ من .... او را می‌شناسم .... هرگز در خانه‌اش بوده‌ام.

٢.   من .... از پدرم .... از پسرم هم می‌ترسم.

٣.   او می‌تواند خیلی راحت .... توهین کند .... عذرخواهی.

٤.   من آن خانه را نخواهم خرید، .... پول داشته باشم .... نداشته باشم.

٥.   مردمی که انقلاب کردند در خیابان فریاد می‌زدند: '......... مرگ .... آزادی!'

٦.   یکی از شعارهای انقلاب ایران: '......... شرقی، .... غربی، جمهوریِ اسلامی!'

٧.   بالاخره خبر را خواهد شنید، .... در اینجا باشد .... در ایران.

٨.   گربهٔ ما .... موش می‌خورد .... پرنده‌های کوچک را هم می‌خورد.

٩.   در آن سفر .... به اصفهان رفتیم، به شیراز و مشهد .... رفتیم.

١٠. امشب زیاد اشتها ندارم، .... کمی میوه خواهم خورد .... یک لیوان شیر.

Exercise 12.2

Translate the following sentences into English.

١.   شنیدیم که مریض است، <u>به همین دلیل</u> به خانه‌اش رفتیم.

٢.   حتماً شنیده بودند که استاد مریض است، <u>به خاطرِ آنکه</u> اصلاً به کلاس نیامدند.

٣.   <u>از آنجا که</u> شنیده بودم تو مریض هستی، چند بار به خانه‌ات تلفن زدم.

12

Correlative
conjunctions

More on
subordinate
clauses

A review of *tā*

۴. با عجله رفتم که قبل از شروع جلسه با ناصر حرف بزنم.

۵. زود برگشت، به دلیلِ آنکه پدرش گفته بود نباید دیر برگردد.

۶. زود برگشت تا به پدرش بگوید کار خوبی پیدا کرده.

۷. نتوانست زود کارش را تمام کند، در نتیجه آن شب در اداره خوابید.

۸. به خاطرِ آنکه نمی‌خواست همسرش را بیدار کند، بدونِ صبحانه خانه را
   ترک کرد.

۹. حتّی یک بار هم به موزه نرفته بود، چرا که پول نداشت.

۱۰. به آمریکا رفت با این هدف که آنجا درس بخواند، ولی بعد هنرپیشه شد.

Exercise 12.3

In which of the sentences in the previous exercise could you substitute the
underlined word(s) (without changing the meaning)

a) with چون?
b) with زیرا?
c) with پس?

Exercise 12.4

Connect the two sentences by placing چون (because), اگرچه (although) or
بااینهمه (nevertheless) in the middle, then translate. Example:

سرش درد می‌کرد. در کلاس ماند.

← سرش درد می‌کرد، با اینهمه در کلاس ماند (He had a headache;
nevertheless, he stayed in class.)

۱. می‌داند که من بیمارم. از من برای رانندگی کمک خواسته است.

۲. به او کمک خواهم کرد. او دیروز به من کمک نکرد.

۳. هوا خیلی سرد است. هنوز پائیز شروع نشده است.

۴. نمی‌دانست چطور به آنجا برود. ماشینش را دزدیده بودند.

۵. از همه زودتر آمد. راهش از همه دورتر بود.

۶. خانه‌اش خیلی از آنجا دور بود. زودتر از همه رسید.

۷. خیلی اصرار کرد. می‌دانست نتیجه‌ای ندارد.

۸. می‌دانست نتیجه‌ای ندارد. خیلی اصرار کرد.

۹. زیاد اصرار نکرد. می‌دانست نتیجه‌ای ندارد.

۱۰. می‌دانم او بهترین مرد برای من نیست. خیلی به من علاقه دارد.

Exercise 12.5

In the following sentences, use چنان, همچنان, همچنین, چندان or چند.

۱. عذرخواهی کرده بودم ولی او .... عصبانی بود.

۲. پیرهنم در باران خیس شده بود ولی دیگر .... مهم نبود.

۳. کتاب را به او برگرداندم، .... عکسهای سفرش را.

۴. .... سروصدائی شد که همه بیدار شدند.

۵. این شلوار .... گران نیست و می‌توان خریدش.

۶. باید .... روز دیگر در همان هتل می‌ماندیم.

۷. کار خوبی پیدا کرده بود ولی .... ناراضی بود.

۸. چرا به .... معلم خوبی توهین کردند؟

۹. می‌خواهم دربارهٔ این فیلم بنویسم و .... دربارهٔ فیلمهای قبلی‌اش.

۱۰. دیگر همکار من نیست ولی .... او را می‌بینم.

Exercise 12.6

Change the following *had hardly* structures to *no sooner*. Example:

هنوز از راه نرسیده بود که جلسه شروع شد

تازه از راه رسیده بود که جلسه شروع شد ←

۱. هنوز دو جمله نگفته بودم که گفتند وقتم تمام است.

۲. هنوز روی صندلی ننشسته بودم که برق رفت.

۳. هنوز درسش تمام نشده بود که کار خوبی پیدا کرد.

۴. هنوز پایش خوب نشده بود که سرش هم شکست.

۵. هنوز حرف من تمام نشده بود که سیگاری روشن کرد.

۶. هنوز سوارِ هواپیما نشده بودیم که گفتند موتورش خراب است.

۷. هنوز یک داستان کوتاه ننوشته بود که تصمیم گرفت یک رُمان بلند بنویسد.

۸. هنوز ماشین را ندیده بودم که فریادِ بچه‌ها را شنیدم.

۹. هنوز عینکش را پیدا نکرده بود که اتوبوس ایستاد.

۱۰. هنوز به مدرسه نرسیده بودم که پروین را دیدم.

12

Correlative
conjunctions

More on
subordinate
clauses

A review of *tā*

Exercise 12.7

Translate the following sentences, all of which are using *tā*.

۱. تا نوبت ما برسد، بانک تعطیل شده است.

۲. تا سگ همسایه را دید، به طرفش دوید.

۳. تا سگ همسایه اینجاست، نمی‌شود گربه را تنها گذاشت.

۴. دو تا از پرنده‌ها تا توی اتاق ما آمدند.

۵. در را ببند تا توی اتاق ما نیایند.

۶. تا اسمش را نگوید نمی‌گذارم برود.

۷. او را اینجا نگه می‌دارم تا اسمش را بگوید.

۸. چراغ را روشن کردم تا اتاق تاریک نباشد.

۹. تا پولش را ندهی از اینجا نخواهد رفت.

۱۰. تا پول میز را بدهی من سریع به دستشوئی می‌روم.

آشپز که دوتا شد، آش یا شور می‌شود یا بی‌نمک

When there are two cooks the soup has either too much or
too little salt.

(= Too many cooks spoil the broth.)

UNIT THIRTEEN | فصل ۱۳

How to use digar, hanuz, ham, faghat/tanhā

دربارهٔ: دیگر، هنوز، هم، فقط/تنها

13.1 دیگر (digar) and هنوز (hanuz)

Regardless of how they are translated into English, and regardless of affirmative/negative, the best way to define these two words is this:

- هنوز ('still') is about *continuation*: it shows that something – some situation – still continues;
- دیگر ('other') is about *change*: it shows that something – some situation – has become 'other' or something different.

Table 13.1: *hanuz* vs. *digar*

	AFFIRMATIVE	NEGATIVE
هنوز	هنوز پول دارم I still have money. ['having money' continues]	هنوز پول ندارم I still don't have money./I don't have money yet. ['not having money' continues]
دیگر	دیگر پول دارم *Now* I have money. [Whereas I had none until a while ago.]	دیگر پول ندارم I don't have money any longer. [Whereas I did have some until a while ago.]

See also 12.4 for the use of هنوز in the temporal idiom *had hardly . . . when. . . .*

دیگر is the more problematic of the two and can be used in a variety of senses, or just for emphasis, each time requiring a different translation. See the examples below and the different meanings of دیگر:

- **another:**

    یک کتابِ دیگر خریدم/کتابِ دیگری خریدم (I bought another book.)
    زبانِ دیگری هم بلد هستید؟ (Do you also know another language?)

- **other:**

  در کشورهای دیگر اینطور نیست (It's not so [/'this way'] in other countries.)

  = در دیگرِ کشورها اینطور نیست (same meaning as above; more *form*.)

- **else:**

  دیگر چه می‌دانی؟ (What else do you know?)

  = چه چیز دیگری می‌دانی؟ (What other thing(s) do you know?)

  دیگر با چهَ کسی حرف زدی؟ (Who else did you talk to?)

  = با چه کسِ دیگری حرف زدی؟ (What other person did you talk to?)

- **more:**

  چند روز دیگر اینجا بمان (Stay here for a few more days.)

  باید دو سالِ دیگر درس بخواند (She has to study for two more years.)

  تا دو ساعتِ دیگر خواهد آمد (He will come in two hours [/'after two more hours'].)

- **next:**

  تا هفتهٔ دیگر (/تا هفتهٔ بعد) کارم تمام می‌شود (My work will be finished by next week.)

  قرارِ دیگرت (/بعدی‌ات) با دکتر برای چه روزی است؟ (When is your next appointment with the doctor?)

- **any more:**

  تو را می‌بخشم به شرط آنکه دیگر دروغ نگوئی (I forgive you, provided that you lie no more.)

  بعد از آن عمل، دیگر نمی‌تواند بچه‌دار شود (After that operation, she cannot get pregnant any more.)

- **now (showing change; in this sense often after حالا, but sometimes used alone):**

  (حالا) دیگر در مغازهٔ عمویش کار می‌کند (Now he works at his uncle's store. [He used not to; this is new.])

  (حالا) دیگر وقتی فارسی حرف می‌زنیم می‌فهمد (Now he understands when we talk in Persian.)

- **then:**

  شما که می‌خواستید از هم جدا شوید، چرا دیگر بچه‌دار شدید؟ (You [who] wanted to separate from each other [= get divorced], why then did you parent a child?)

  او از تو بدش می‌آمد، چرا دیگر من را کتک زد؟ (He hated *you*; why then did he beat *me*?)

- **already:**

  اگر آن ساعت بیائی، من دیگر خوابیده‌ام (If you come at that hour, I will already be asleep.)

  تو را دیگر می‌شناسد (He already knows you./He knows you now.)

- **finally (possible change):**

  کی دیگر حالش خوب می‌شود؟ (When will he finally get well?)

  دیگر تمام شد (It's finally over./It's finished now.)

- **also or at least (emphasis/reproach):**

  دیگر نباید به پدرت هم می‌گفتی (You shouldn't have told your father also. [It was already bad enough that you told others!])

  دیگر از من که می‌توانست بپرسد (He could have asked me at least.)

13.1.1 دیگری (digari) *as pronoun*

Here the stress plays an important role:

- **دیگری** (*digári*) (*form.*) – **with unstressed -*i* – means *another [one]* or *someone else*:
  colloquial version: یکی دیگر

  > یک معلم رفت و دیگری (/یکی دیگر) آمد.
  > اگر من این کار را نکنم، دیگری (/یکی دیگر) خواهد کرد.

- **دیگری** (*digarí*) (*form.*) – **with stressed -*i* – means *the other [one]*:
  colloquial version: آن یکی دیگر

  > یکی از دیگری بدتر.
  > از این دو برادر، یکی در تهران است و دیگری (/آن یکی دیگر) در اصفهان.
  > یکی را می‌بینیم ولی دیگری (/آن یکی دیگر) را نمی‌بینیم.

143

13.1.2 یکدیگر *(yek-digar) and* همدیگر *(ham-digar)*

They both mean *each other* or *one another*; both can be used for two or
more. یکدیگر is used only in formal/written Persian, while همدیگر is also
used in colloquial Persian (sometimes shortened as just هم [*ham*]; see 13.2
under هم). Examples:

این دو نفر از یکدیگر (/از همدیگر/از هم) بدشان می‌آید.

چرا مردم باید همیشه به یکدیگر (/به همدیگر/به هم) دروغ بگویند؟

For دیگرگون (*digar-gun*) or دگرگون (*degar-gun*) see 14.3.

13.2 هم *(ham)*

هم (*ham*) usually modifies the word *before* it, which takes the stress, while
هم is often pronounced without stress (except sometimes in (d) below).
This word has a variety of usages and meanings; the following are the most
important of them:

a) You just learned that هم can be short for همدیگر (each other)
    as in:

ما هم را دوست داریم.

b) In the same way, با هم (short for با همدیگر) means 'together':

همیشه آنها را با هم می‌بینم.

با هم به کتابخانه رفتیم.

'Together with . . . ,' however, would be همراه با (*ham-rāh bā*) when it
means accompanying someone (on a way), or just با:

با/همراه با خواهرم به سینما رفتم.

c) The word همراه in (b) is a hint to one of the most productive functions
    of هم – namely, a prefix indicating accompaniment or sharing, having
    in common, etc. You already know words like همکلاسی (*ham-kelāsi*,
    classmate) and همکار (*ham-kār*, colleague, co-worker).

d) And you also know that '. . . هم . . . هم' means 'both . . . and . . .' (see 12.1):
    هم خدا را می‌خواهد هم خُرما را. (He wants both God and the dates. [=
    He wants to have his cake and eat it too.]) – This is the only case
    where هم is not post-positioned and can even be at the beginning of
    a sentence.

e) The first and best known meaning of هم, however, is *also/too* (or *either* in the negative); when used in this sense, هم follows the word that it modifies, and that word takes the main stress:

تو هم، بروتوس؟ (You too, Brutus?) – with stress on *tó*.
از من هم پرسیدند. (They asked me too.) – with stress on *mán*.
گران نیست، ولی خیلی ارزان هم نیست.

f) In the same way, close to our last example about the price, it is used to show some contrast, difference or consequence, like 'as for the other side':

کفشهایم را نمی‌داد، من هم به مادرش گفتم. (She wouldn't give my shoes, so I told her mother.)
آنها حرف می‌زدند، من هم در سکوت گوش می‌کردم. (They were talking, [and] I was listening in silence.)

g) Not quite unrelated to the above meanings, it can mean *moreover*, *additionally* ('what is more') or *but/in contrast*:

تنهائی را دوست نداشت، ازدواج هم نمی‌خواست بکند. (She didn't like being alone, [but] she didn't want to marry either.)
درس نمی‌خوانَد، نمرهٔ خوب هم می‌خواهد. (He is not [/does not care for] studying, [but] he wants good grades ['too'].)
زشت نیست، خیلی هم زیباست. (It's not ugly; [on the contrary,] it's very beautiful.)

h) While it means *also* in the idiom 'not only ... but also ...' (see 12.1), sometimes in the same idiom it can have the meaning of *even* or *in contrast*. Our sentences from (g) above can all be seen as such sentences but with 'not only' deleted. Compare:

نه تنها زشت نیست، خیلی هم زیباست. (Not only is it not ugly, but it is also very beautiful.)

i) It can mean *even* used for emphasis, with or without the word حتّی (*hat.tā*, even) itself. In the following examples, you can use هم or حتّی or both, but as you see they have different positions:

[حتّی] به اندازهٔ الاغ هم نمی‌فهمد. (He doesn't understand even as much as a donkey.)

[حتّی] یک بچّه هم می‌تواند این کار را بکند.

این هفته [حتّی] یک صفحه هم نخوانده‌ام.

از تو هم بهتر بلدم.

After *hanuz* it means *even now/still/yet*:

هنوز هم او را ندیده‌ام. (I haven't seen him even now.)

j) باز هم means *again/anew/still/more* (meanings that باز alone can have,
only with less emphasis):

(still = باز هم here) یک ساعت با او حرف زدم، ولی باز هم قبول نمی‌کرد.

باز هم here =) پنج تا شکلات خورده بود، ولی باز هم می‌خواست.
[some] more)

13.2.1 هم (ham), همچنین (ham-chenin), همینطور (ham-in-towr), نیز (niz)

هم and همینطور، نیز (see 12.3/C, Note 1) can all be synonyms for همچنین
meaning *also*.

One major difference, though: هم is always post-positioned (i.e., placed
after the word that it modifies), and therefore never at the beginning of a
sentence (except in . . . هم . . . هم [both . . . and . . .]; see 13.2/d).

Of these, نیز and همچنین are formal, used in written Persian only, while
همینطور is colloquial (and still more colloquial: همینجور, *ham-in-jur*).

Examples (in which هم is not possible!):

همینطور باید دانست که زیاد وقت نداریم (We [/one] must also know
that we don't have much time.)

علی معلم خواهرم و همچنین از دوستان خوب من بود. (Ali was the
teacher of my sister and [was] also one of my good friends.)

من هم means *me too* as well as *me neither*.

For still more emphasis, sometimes two of these words are used together:

من هم همینطور (me too/same with me)

13.3 فقط (faghat) and تنها (tanhā)

The only meaning of فقط is *only*, and it is more common than تنها in this sense, while تنها means *only*, *lonely*, as well as *alone*.

In the conjunction 'not only ... but also ...,' both *tanhā* and *faghat* can be used in both colloquial and formal Persian.

In the sense of 'the only' (or *my* only, etc.), تنها should be used.

In the following examples, تنها is either the only option or the more formal/literary one:

تنها (/فقط) یک برادر دارم. (I have only one brother.)

او تنها برادرِ من است. (He is my only brother.)

تنها (/فقط) نمی‌دانم او کجاست. (Only, I don't know where he is.)

اینجا تنها هستم. (I am alone here.)

من آدم تنهائی هستم. (I am a lonely person.)

باید تنها (/به تنهائی) غذا بخورم. (I have to eat alone.)

تنهائی مثلِ شکنجه است. (Loneliness is like torture.)

منِ را تنها نگذار. (Don't leave me alone.)

Careful! The way تنها is used to mean 'the only' (or *my* only, etc.) can sometimes leave room for another meaning also, the only difference being the stress and intonation:

A sentence like تنها برادرم را دستگیر کردند means:

a) They arrested my only brother. (*Tanhā* has no stress.)
b) They arrested my brother only. (*Tanhā* pronounced with stress, as well as *barādáram*.)

Also note that if in the same sentence you want to say 'They only arrested *my* brother,' then instead of برادرم you should say برادرِ من because *man* can be pronounced with stress whereas suffixes like *-am* cannot.

Note the difference here also:

تنها سه نفر آمدند. (Only three people came.)

تنها سه نفری که آمدند دوستان برادرم بودند. (The only three people who came were my brother's friends.)

هر سه نفری که آمدند دوستان برادرم بودند. (All three people who came were my brother's friends.)

147

Exercises

Exercise 13.1

Give negative answers to the following questions, using دیگر instead of
هنوز. Example:

هنوز او را می‌بینی؟

نه، دیگر او را نمی‌بینم. ←

۱. هنوز پدرت زنده است؟

۲. هنوز دارند غذا می‌خورند؟

۳. دخترت هنوز من را می‌شناسد؟

۴. هنوز شطرنج بازی می‌کنی؟

۵. هنوز فارسی برایت سخت است؟

۶. هنوز سرت درد می‌کند؟

۷. از پیاز هنوز بدش می‌آید؟

۸ هنوز باید منتظر باشیم؟

۹. هنوز می‌خواهی کتاب بخوانی؟

۱۰. هنوز می‌تواند فارسی حرف بزند؟

Exercise 13.2

Translate the following sentences, all of which are using دیگر.

۱. هنوز خانهٔ دیگرت را به من نشان نداده‌ای.

۲. دیگر باید کم کم برویم.

۳. دیگر از او سؤال نکن.

۴. او امروز در اداره نیست، یک روز دیگر بیائید.

۵. برویم دیگر، انتظار فایده‌ای ندارد.

۶. تو را هنوز نمی‌شناسد، ولی من را دیگر می‌شناسد.

۷. هیچ چیزِ دیگری به تو نگفت؟

۸ اگر دکتر می‌گوید حالش خوب است، چرا دیگر گریه می‌کنی؟

۹. حالا دیگر جوابم را نمی‌دهی؟

۱۰. بسیار خوب، وقت نداشتی بیائی، دیگر چرا تلفن نزدی؟

Exercise 13.3

Choose one of the following to fill in the blanks:

a) دیگر

b) دیگری [with unstressed final -*i*]

c) دیگری [with stressed final -*i*]

d) یکی دیگر

e) یکدیگر

Example:

این دو خواهر خیلی .... را دوست دارند.
یکدیگر ←

۱. این قلم خوب نمی‌نویسد، .... بده.

۲. خیلی خسته‌ام و .... نمی‌توانم بیدار بمانم.

۳. آیا می‌خواهی اشتباهِ قبلی‌ات را یک بار .... تکرار کنی؟

۴. از دیدنش خوشحال شدم چون دو سال بود که ما .... را ندیده بودیم.

۵. اگر به آن نامه جواب نداده است .... بنویس.

۶. یک چشمش نمی‌بیند ولی .... نسبتاً سالم است.

۷. رفت بخوابد چون هیچ کار .... نداشت که بکند.

۸. وقتی زنش از قطار پیاده شد، .... را در آغوش گرفتند و بوسیدند.

۹. باید اوّل این را بخوری تا .... بدهم.

۱۰. آیا او به زبان .... حرف می‌زد؟

Exercise 13.4

Choose one of the following to fill in the blanks, or mention if two are possible:

a) هم (b همینطور (c) نیز

Example:

این موضوع را حتّی من .... نمی‌دانستم.
→ a and c.

۱. پسرم هم ریاضی‌اش خوب است و .... ادبیّاتش.

۲. تازه آمده‌ام هیچ‌کس را .... نمی‌شناسم.

۳. مینا را خوب می‌شناختم، .... به او اعتماد داشتم.

۴. بیرون رفت و در را .... نبست.

۵. خیلی وقت نبود که با .... آشنا شده بودند.

۶. من از آن خوشم نیامد، برادرم هم ....

۷. عصبانی به نظر می‌رسید و سلام .... نکرد.

۸. با پدرم راحت می‌توانستم حرف بزنم، .... با مادرم.

۹. حتّی یک روز .... وقت ندارم.

۱۰. هنوز .... او را می‌بینی؟

Exercise 13.5

In which of the following sentences can you replace تنها with فقط?

۱. تنها هفته‌ای سه ساعت کلاس فارسی دارم.

۲. حتّی پنج دقیقه هم نباید او را تنها بگذاری.

۳. آیا از اینکه تنها به مدرسه برود نمی‌ترسد؟

۴. من تنها یک برادر ولی سه خواهر دارم.

۵. تنها چیزی که از تو می‌خواهد کمی صبر است.

۶. جمعه‌ها نمی‌توانم، شنبه تنها روزی است که می‌توانم.

۷. بالاخره تمام خواهم کرد، تنها نمی‌دانم کی.

۸. صبح تا شب تنها تلویزیون تماشا می‌کند.

۹. چطور توانستی ظرف تنها سه سال هفت کتاب بنویسی؟

۱۰. این تنها روزی بود که او را خوشحال دیدم.

هنوز دهانش بویِ شیر میدهد

His mouth still smells of milk.

(= He is too young and inexperienced yet.)

UNIT FOURTEEN | فصل ۱۴

Remember/forget | یاد/فراموش

Arrange, change, difference | قرار، تغییر، تفاوت

Meaning and 'to mean' | معنی و منظور

14.1 یاد (yād)

Beyond a certain level, what remains to be learned in Persian is the wealth of idioms and phrasal verbs, and how to use them. But we do not intend to turn this book into a dictionary of idioms. In this unit we introduce only a few words with some of the phrasal verbs associated with them, starting with یاد (yād, memory). You already know several of the phrasal verbs using yād.

14.1.1 یاد (and other words) used for learning/teaching

In the following table, only the verbs آموختن (āmukhtan) and فراگرفتن (farā-gereftan) are formal/literary. The nouns آموزش (āmuzesh) and تعلیم (ta'lim) mean *learning* or *education* and can be combined with the verbs گرفتن (kereftan) and دادن (usually for learning or teaching arts and crafts).

Table 14.1: Learning and teaching

LEARNING		TEACHING	
He is learning Persian/is taking Persian lessons (from me).	(از من) فارسی یاد می‌گیرد	He is teaching (me) Persian/is giving Persian lessons (to me).	(به من) فارسی یاد می‌دهد/ فارسی یادم می‌دهد
	(از من) درسِ فارسی می‌گیرد		(به من) درسِ فارسی می‌دهد
	(از من) فارسی می‌آموزد *(form.)*		(به من) فارسی می‌آموزد *(form.)*
	(از من) فارسی فرا می‌گیرد *(form.)*		(به من) فارسی آموزش می‌دهد *(form.)*
He is taking piano lessons (from me).	(از من) تعلیمِ پیانو می‌گیرد	He is giving piano lessons (to me).	(به من) تعلیمِ پیانو می‌دهد

14

Remember/
forget

Arrange,
change,
difference

Meaning and
'to mean'

More examples for learning:

من خیلی چیزها از شما یاد گرفته‌ام.

بچه تازه یاد گرفته است (که) راه برود. (tāze = 'just')

زنم فکر می‌کند هیچوقت رانندگی را یاد نخواهد گرفت.

آموزشگاه جائی است که آدم در آن چیزی بیاموزد.

دانش‌آموز کسی است که در دبستان یا دبیرستان می‌آموزد.

من هم از همین استاد تعلیم آواز گرفتم.

او خوشنویسی را از بهترینَ استادان فراگرفت.

More examples for teaching:

چیزی که به بچّه‌تان یاد نداده‌اید ادب است.

باید به من یاد بدهی غذای ایرانی بپزم.

کسی را می‌شناسید که درس تنبک بدهد؟

معلّم کسی است که تعلیم می‌دهد.

آموزگار کسی است که در دبستان خواندن و نوشتن را به شاگردان آموزش می‌دهد.

14.1.2 یاد (and other words) used for remembering/ forgetting

Some of the phrasal verbs used here for remembering or forgetting will be using quasi-impersonal structures similar to those mentioned under 7.3.

Apart from *yād*, another word that is frequently used here is خاطر (*khāter*, mind; cf. its other usages in 12.2.1); the words حافظه (*hāfeze*, memory) and ذهن (*zehn*, mind) are also used.

In the following table, an asterisk shows where you need the personal/possessive suffixes in the impersonal structures, and in such cases the verb always has to be conjugated for the third person singular.

Table 14.2: Remembering and forgetting

a) to forget/to be forgotten	<div dir="rtl">کسی/چیزی را فراموش کردن کسی/چیزی فراموش شدن کسی/چیزی فراموش* شدن کسی/چیزی را از یاد [/خاطر] بردن کسی/چیزی از یاد [/خاطر] رفتن کسی/چیزی از یادِ [/خاطرِ] کسی رفتن (کسی/چیزی) (از) یاد* [/خاطر*] رفتن</div>

Table 14.2 (*cont'd*)

b)	to cause so. to forget sth.	چیزی را از یادِ [/خاطرِ] کسی بردن
c)	to remember sth. or so./ to remember that . . .	(کسی/چیزی را) به یاد [/خاطر] داشتن کسی/چیزی را به یاد [/خاطر] آوردن به یاد [/خاطر] آوردن که . . . به یادِ کسی/چیزی افتادن کسی/چیزی (به) یاد* آمدن/افتادن (به) یاد* آمدن/افتادن که . . . یاد* [/خاطر*] بودن
d)	to bring sth. to someone's mind/to remind so. of [or that . . .]	چیزی را (به) یادِ [/خاطرِ] کسی آوردن کسی را (به) یادِ چیزی اَنداختن (به) یادِ [/خاطرِ] کسی آوردن که . . . (به) یادِ کسی اَنداختن که . . .
e)	to commit to memory, to memorize	به یاد [/خاطر/حافظه/ذهن] سپردن در یاد [/خاطر/حافظه/ذهن] نگه داشتن از بر کردن/شدن (از) حفظ کردن/شدن
f)	to stay in memory, to have in memory (after memorizing)	به (/در) یاد [/خاطر/حافظه/ذهن] ماندن چیزی را از بر [/از حفظ] بودن/داشتن

Now examples for each of the above:

a) to forget/to be forgotten:

اسم همسایه‌ام را فراموش کرده‌ام.

فراموش نکن که این را من از روز اوّل گفته بودم.

تمام آن مسائل فراموششان شد.

نمی‌توانم رفتار زشتش را از یاد ببرم.

سختی‌های زندگی خیلی زود از یاد می‌رود.

یادم رفت برای پدرم دارو بخرم.

یادت نرود که روز جمعه پولم را می‌خواهم.

تا یادم نرفته (است) بگویم که او هم می‌آید. (. . . Let me say before I forget that)

باید سعی کنی آن را از خاطر ببری.

هنوز اسم آن خیابان (از) خاطرم نرفته است.

14

Remember/
forget

Arrange,
change,
difference

Meaning and
'to mean'

b) to cause someone to forget something:

سعی کردم با گفتنِ یک قصّه، آن اتفاقِ بد را از یادش ببرم.

باید امیدوار بود که این تغییرِ شهر، مرگِ مادرشان را از خاطرشان ببرد.

c) to remember something or someone to remember that ...:

نمی‌دانم چرا ناگهان به یادِ او افتادم.

به یاد می‌آورم که هرروز او را در اتوبوس می‌دیدم.

یادشان افتاد که به گربه غذا نداده‌اند.

یادتان نمی‌آید آن را کجا گذاشته‌اید؟

عجیب خواهد بود اگر یادتان نباشد.

یادت باشد که نامه‌ها را پُست کنی.

خوب به یاد دارم که او دو سال از من بزرگتر بود.

درست به خاطر ندارم چه سالی بود که آن خانه را خریدند.

به خاطر نمی‌آورم کجا با شما آشنا شدم.

متأسّفانه روزِ دقیقش خاطرم نیست.

d) to bring something to someone's mind/to remind someone of [or that ...]:

یک بارِ دیگر تاریخ امتحان را (به) یادِ آنها آوردم.

یادش بیاور که فردا من نخواهم بود.

قولی را که به من داده بود (به) خاطرش بیاور.

(به) خاطرش آوردم که وقت زیادی نداریم.

چشمهای تو مرا (به) یادِ چشمهای مادرت می‌اندازد.

(به) یادش انداختم که امروز جمعه است.

e) to commit to memory, to memorize:

حرفهایش را خوب به یاد [/خاطر/حافظه/ذِهن] سپردم.

امیدوارم اینها را در خاطر [/یاد/حافظه/ذِهن] نگه داری.

تمامِ شعر را از بر کردم.

تمامِ شعر را از بر شدم.

بعد از دو بار خواندن حفظم شد (/حفظش شدم).

اسمِ رودخانه‌ها را حفظ کرده بود.

f) to stay in memory, to have in memory (after memorizing):

مهربانیِ شما در خاطرِ او مانده است.

این شعرِ زیبا همیشه دَر یاد خواهد ماند.

من این شعر را از بر دارم/از برم.

من این شعر را (از) حفظ دارم/(از) حفظم.

Refresh your memory with two related participles that you learned before (see 10.1):

به یاد ماندنی (memorable)

از یاد نرفتنی (unforgettable)

از کسی/چیزی یاد کردن means *to mention so./sth.* or *point out*:

رئیسِ جمهور از دوستیِ میانِ دو کشور یاد کرد.

Another verb that means *to mention* is the compound یادآور شدن (*yād-āvar shodan*):

او همچنین یادآور شد که بزودی به آن کشور سفر خواهد کرد.

یادِ کسی/چیزی (را) کردن is also used or the variant از کسی/چیزی یاد کردن when you are reminded of *so./sth.*, especially when you miss them:

دیروز به آن پارکی رفته بودم که قبلاً با هم می‌رفتیم، خیلی یادش کردم.

هروقت اسمت را می‌شنوند، از آن غذاهای خوشمزه یاد می‌کنند.

When you feel nostalgic about something, you say: یادش به خیر! (*yādash be kheyr*). This can also be used for an absent person:

جوانی، کجائی، که یادت به خیر! (O youth, where are you? I badly miss you.)

یادش به خیر آن سفری که به شیراز رفتیم، چقدر خوش گذشت! (I miss that trip we had to Shiraz – what a good time we had there!)

پدرم، یادش به خیر، همیشه روی آن صندلی می‌نشست. (My father – may his memory be blessed [/I wish he were here] – always used to sit on that chair.)

14

Remember/
forget

Arrange,
change,
difference

Meaning and
'to mean'

14.2 قرار (gharār)

The idioms used with قرار are grouped around its two major meanings:
1) arrangement, and 2) repose/inertia. Those of the second group belong
to formal language; and some related to the first meaning were mentioned
earlier (see 4.4/5). Here is an overview:

قرار بودن means *to be supposed to* and قرار گذاشتن means *to make an arrangement or plan*, both used with subjunctive if a second verb is needed:

قرار است در همانجا خانه‌ای بسازد.

مگر از اوّل قرارِ ما این نبود؟

با دوستم قرار گذاشته‌ام که هر روز برویم شنا.

The verbs قرار داشتن, قرار دادن and قرار گرفتن can each have a different
meaning based on the two basic meanings of قرار mentioned above:

- Related to the first meaning, they mean respectively *to have, to give*
  and *to get an appointment*:

ساعت چهار یک قرار دارم.

دکترم به من برای فردا یک قرار داد.

برای مصاحبه از او یک قرار گرفته‌ام.

- Related to the second meaning, in formal and written language they
  mean respectively *to lie [/be located], to lay [/put]* and *to be placed* –
  used for things, not for people. These are also the verbs often used with
  مورد or تحتِ in quasi-passive structures (mentioned in 9.3):

گلدان در کنارِ پنجره قرار دارد. (The vase is [/lies/is located] beside
the window.)

یک فروشگاه مقابلِ آن خانه قرار داشت. (There was a store opposite
that house.)

آنها چند ماه تحتِ نظر قرار داشتند. (They were under surveillance for
a few months.)

دستش را روی چشمش قرار داد. (She placed her hand on her eye[s].)

بارِ دیگر موضوع را موردِ مطالعه قرار دادند. (They [closely] examined
the subject once more.)

خوابش برد و سرش بر شانهٔ آن خانم قرار گرفت. (He fell asleep and
his head came to rest on that lady's shoulder.)

پیشنهادش خیلی موردِ توجّه قرار گرفت. (His proposal met with a lot
of attention.)

After در اختیار (dar ekhtiyār) or در اختیارِ (~ + -e), these verbs mean *to be, to have* or *to put at someone's disposal*:

سند در اختیارِ وکیل قرار دارد. (The document is at the lawyer's disposal.)

(سند در اختیار وکیل است or وکیل سند را در اختیار دارد=)

چرا سند را در اختیارِ او قرار دادید؟ (Why did you put the document at his disposal?)

(چرا سند را در اختیار او گذاشتید؟=)

با مرگِ پدرتان، ثروتش در اختیارِ شما قرار می‌گیرد. (With your father's death, his wealth will come under your control.)

بیقرار (bi-gharār) means *restless* and *impatient* (+ -i: *restlessness*):

بچّهٔ مریض تا صبح بیقراری کرد. (The sick child was restless until morning.)

بَرقرار کردن/شدن (bar-gharār) means *to establish/to be established*:

بینِ دو کشور صُلح برقرار شد. (Peace was established between the two countries.)

14.3 Change

The only tricky thing about *change* in Persian is that تغییر کردن (tagh.yir ~, *to change*) is *intransitive* – in spite of using کردن – and the *transitive* version is تغییر دادن.

دیگرگون (digar-gun) or دگرگون (degar-gun), both formal and literary, are used with کردن and شدن for respectively the transitive and the intransitive and mostly convey a change in form or color.

عوض کردن/شدن (avaz ~) is also common, with some association with *exchanging* and *trading/swapping*.

تبدیل (tab.dil), مبدّل (mo.bad.dal) and بدل (ba.dal) are also words that are close in meaning and are used with *kardan/shodan*, sometimes with some sense of *altering, transforming* or *converting*. تبدیل is the only word you can use for changing/converting money, and *mobaddal* means *changed*.

In formal Persian, یافتن (yāftan, *to find*) can be used as the verbal part in the compounds تبدیل شدن and تغییر کردن (both *intr.*).

157

14

Remember/
forget

Arrange,
change,
difference

Meaning and
'to mean'

Table 14.3: Changing

TRANSITIVE	INTRANSITIVE
He changed his room. اتاقش را تغییر داد. اتاقش را عوض کرد.	His room changed. اتاقش تغییر کرد. اتاقش عوض شد.
He changed his name to Ali. اسمش را به علی تغییر داد. اسمش را به علی تبدیل کرد.	His name changed to Ali. اسمش به علی تغییر کرد. اسمش به علی تبدیل شد.
He changed his place with Maryam. جایش را با مریم عوض کرد.	His place changed with Maryam['s]. جایش با مریم عوض شد.
He changed the room into a kitchen. اتاق را به یک آشپزخانه تبدیل کرد./ اتاق را تبدیل به یک آشپزخانه کرد.	The room changed into a kitchen. اتاق به یک آشپزخانه تبدیل شد./ اتاق تبدیل به یک آشپزخانه شد.
This event changed his life. این اتّفاق زندگیِ او را تغییر داد. این اتّفاق زندگیِ او را عوض کرد. این اتّفاق زندگیِ او را دگرگون کرد. (form.)	His life changed. زندگیِ او تغییر کرد. زندگیِ او عوض شد. زندگیِ او دگرگون شد. (form.)
He changed his dollars to rials. دلارهایش را به ریال تبدیل کرد.	His dollars [were] changed to rials. دلارهایش به ریال تبدیل شد.

More examples:

او حرف خودش را عوض کرد/تغییر داد. (He changed his word.)

او کتابش را با کتاب من عوض کرد. (He traded his book with mine.)

او خیلی زود لباسش را عوض کرد. (He changed clothes very quickly.)

با رسیدن شب، ناگهان هوا عوض شد/تغییر کرد. (With nightfall, the weather suddenly changed.)

چرا یک موضوع کوچک به چنین مسئلهٔ بزرگی تبدیل شد؟ (Why did a small topic change into such a big problem?)

خبر را که شنید، حالش بکلّی دگرگون شد. (When he heard the news, his mood/condition totally changed.)

14.4 Difference

We seem to know enough about resemblance (see 10.5/D and 11.7); maybe it's time we learned about difference. One thing we learned about difference was the idiom 'with the difference that' when discussing 'except that' (see 5.2.1/c).

The nouns تفاوت (*tafāvot*), اختلاف (*ekhtelāf*) and فرق (*fargh*) and the adjectives متفاوت (*motefāvet*), مختلف (*mokhtalef*) and گوناگون (*gunāgun, form./lit.*) are all used to show difference and dissimilarity.

While *ekhtelāf* can imply some opposition also, *tafāvot* is a more neutral dissimilarity.

As adjectives, it is important to know that *mokhtalef* or *gunāgun* cannot be used for just one different thing: use *motefāvet* if the noun is singular.

Note the differences in meaning and usage:

ایران با آمریکا اختلاف دارد. (Iran has differences [= disputes] with the US)
= ایران و آمریکا اختلاف دارند.

ایران با آمریکا تفاوت (/فرق) دارد. (Iran is different from the US)
= ایران و آمریکا تفاوت (/فرق) دارند.

این دو نسخهٔ خطّی خیلی با هم اختلاف دارند. (These two manuscripts have/show a lot of differences/discrepancies.)

این دو فیلم خیلی با هم تفاوت دارند. (These two films are very different from each other.)

گوناگون or مختلف (a different language) – Don't use یک زبانِ متفاوت here!

کتابهایِ مختلفی خواندم. (I read different books.) = several or many books

کتابهایِ متفاوتی خواندم. (I read a variety of books.) = books that were different

آنها طرحهایِ مختلفی دارند. (They have different plans.) = several or many plans

آنها طرحهایِ متفاوتی دارند. (They have different plans.) = different from each other or from other people's plans

چه فرق (/چه فرقی) می‌کند؟ (What difference does it make?) (Here تفاوت is also possible.)

برای من هیچ فرقی نمی‌کند. (It makes no difference to me.) (Here تفاوت is also possible.)

او رَوشهای گوناگونی را آزمود. (He tried different methods.)

این فرش هم مال ایران است، با این تفاوتَ (/فَرق) که ارزانتر است. (This carpet is also from Iran, except that [= with the difference that] it is cheaper.)

14

Remember/
forget

Arrange,
change,
difference

Meaning and
'to mean'

14.5 Meaning and 'to mean'

معنی (*ma'ni*) or the more formal معنا (*ma'nā*) is *meaning*, while یعنی (*ya'ni*) means *it means* and does not need any verb:

این یعنی چه؟ (What does this mean?)

= معنیِ این چیست؟ (What is the meaning of this?)

عشق یعنی دوستی. (Love means friendship.)

= عشق به معنیِ (/به معنایِ) دوستی است. (Love means friendship.)

= معنیِ عشق، دوستی است. (The meaning of love is friendship.)

When you are talking about *what someone means*, however – and not what *something* means –, then you would normally use words like منظور (*manzur*) and مقصود (*maghsud*) in Persian, words that mean *purpose, aim,* and so on:

منظورت چیست؟ (What do you mean?)

منظورش از آن حرف چه بود؟ (What did he mean by that [/by what he said]?)

ببخشید، منظوری نداشتم. (Sorry, I didn't mean it.)

مطمئنم که منظور بدی نداشته است. (I'm sure he didn't mean anything bad/had no bad intentions.)

مقصودم (/منظورم) این بود که پَس‌فردا دیر است. (I meant that the day after tomorrow would be late.)

For *what is meant/intended* you can usually use موردِ نظر (*mowred-e nazar*):

کتابِ موردِ نظر را پیدا نکردم (I didn't find the intended book/the book I had in mind.)

بالاخره خانهٔ موردِ نظرتان را خریدید؟ (Did you finally buy the house you wanted/had in mind?)

نظر (*nazar*) alone is used in the sense of *view* or *opinion*, or as a synonym for نگاه (*negāh*, look, glance):

در یک نظر (at a glance)

به نظر من (in my opinion)

از نظرِ آموزشی (from an educational point of view)

نظرِ شما کاملاً محترم است. (I fully respect your opinion.)

For به نظر رسیدن/آمدن (*to seem*) see 5.4.1.

Exercises

Exercise 14.1

Decide whether you need یاد دادن or یاد گرفتن and then provide the correct form of the verb. Example:

این معلم می‌تواند زبان فارسی را در شش ماه به شما ....
یاد بدهد ←

۱. هیچ زبانی را نمی‌توان در شش ماه به کسی ....

۲. فرشته هیچوقت سعی نکرد به من فارسی ....

۳. این حرفهای زشت را ممکن است پسرم دیروز از بچهٔ همسایه ....

۴. شاعر شدن را نمی‌توان از استاد دانشگاه ....

۵. اگر نمرهٔ خوب می‌خواهی، باید این پنج درس را خوب ....

۶. استاد بدی نیست، ولی نتوانست این درس را به ما خوب ....

۷. از .... فارسی پشیمان نخواهی شد، حتّی اگر به ایران نروی.

۸. او پارسال از زندانیهای دیگر .... که چطور درِ ماشینها را باز کند.

۹. دیگر برای من دیر است، پیانو زدن را باید وقتی بچّه بودم ....

۱۰. وقتی که بچّه بودم هیچکس به من شنا کردن را ....

Exercise 14.2

Change to the impersonal form (یاد* رفتن), then translate.

Example:

می‌دانم که فراموش نخواهند کرد
(I know that they won't forget.) می‌دانم که یادشان نخواهد رفت ←

۱. فراموش کرده بودی که استاد مریض است؟

۲. فراموش نکن که در خانه اصلاً میوه نداریم.

۳. اگر شماره‌اش را از یاد برده‌ای، در دفتر تلفن نگاه کن.

۴. تمام چیزهائی را که از یاد برده بودم، به یاد آوردم.

۵. برایِ اینکه فراموش نکنی، همین الآن توی کیفت بگذار.

۶. اسم همه را گفت بی آنکه حتّی اسم یک نفر را فراموش کرده باشد.

۷. اگرَ آدرس را فراموش کرده باشی نمی‌توانیم برویم.

۸. این که زبان مادری‌اش را فراموش کرده است باورکردنی نیست.

۹. اگر فراموش نکند به او جایزه می‌دهم.

۱۰. ممکن نیست تمامِ آن حرفها را از یاد برده باشد.

14

Remember/
forget

Arrange,
change,
difference

Meaning and
'to mean'

Exercise 14.3

Translate the following sentences into English and pay attention to the different meanings of *gharār*:

١. امروز سه قرار در سه ادارهٔ مختلف دارم.

٢. اصفهان در جنوب تهران قرار دارد.

٣. با شوهرم قرار گذاشته‌ام که در روزهای چهارشنبه او بچه‌ها را به مدرسه ببرد.

٤. چند زندانیِ دیگر را عفو کردند، ولی او موردِ عفو قرار نگرفت.

٥. آیا قرار نبود مادرتان هم در این سفر با شما باشد؟

٦. بعد از آنکه بچّه‌ها خوابیدند، سکوتِ کامل در خانه برقرار شد.

٧. قبل از آنکه با نیما قراری بگذاری، به بابک زنگ بزن.

٨. سخنرانِ بعدی از جایش بلند شد و پشتِ تریبون قرار گرفت.

٩. اطّلاعاتِ شخصی را نباید در اختیارِ هیچ کسی قرار بدهی.

١٠. برای من هم از دکترت یک قرار بگیر.

Exercise 14.4

Choose the correct form.

١. تو نمیتوانی هر روز حرفت را .... (الف: تغییر کنی/ب: تغییر بدهی/پ: فرق کنی)

٢. میتوانی فردا بیائی، برای من هیچ .... (الف: تغییری نمی‌کند/ب: تغییری نمی‌دهد/پ: فرقی نمی‌کند)

٣. پیشنهادِ من هیچ .... (الف: تغییری/ب: تفاوتی/پ: متفاوتی) با پیشنهادِ شما ندارد.

٤. من هیچ چیزِ .... (الف: تغییری/ب: تفاوتی/پ: متفاوتی) در پیشنهادِ شما نمی‌بینم.

٥. ما هیچ .... (الف: اختلافی/ب: مختلفی/پ: گوناگونی) با شما نداریم.

٦. این عینک در آفتاب رنگش .... (الف: تغییر/ب: عوض/پ: فرق) می‌شود.

٧. برای مهمانها غذاهای .... (الف: اختلافی/ب: تفاوتی/پ: گوناگونی) درست کردیم.

٨. ایران و آمریکا خیلی با هم .... (الف: مختلف/ب: فرق/پ: گوناگون) دارند.

۹. مهمترین .... (الف: تغییر /ب: گوناگون /پ: فرق) میانِ ایران و آمریکا، زبان است.

۱۰. می‌خواهی قلمت را با مالِ من .... (الف: تغییر /ب: عوض /پ: فرق) کنی؟

Exercise 14.5

Choose one of the following to fill in the blanks:

a) معنی (b , یعنی (c) , نظر (d) منظور

۱. چرا امروز اینقدر خسته به .... می‌آئید؟

۲. تا تابستانِ سالِ قبل آنجا بودم، .... بیش از دو سال.

۳. اگر در ایران انگشتِ شستتان را به کسی نشان بدهید فکر می‌کند .... بدی دارید.

۴. ما همه موافقیم ولی ظاهراً پرویز .... دیگری دارد.

۵. آن کلمه را شنیده بودم ولی .... آن را نمی‌دانستم.

۶. نادان .... احمق ولی کمی رسمیتر است.

۷. کارهای عجیبی می‌کرد که هیچکس .... آنها را نمیفهمید.

۸. او تا به حال چند بار .... خودش را عوض کرده.

۹. از دور دستش را تکان می‌داد و من نمی‌فهمیدم .... او چیست.

۱۰. آیا به .... شما او می‌تواند برای این کار مناسب باشد؟

میانِ ماهِ منِ تا ماهِ گَردون   تفاوت از زمین تا آسمان است

The difference between my moon [= beloved] and heaven's is from here to the skies.

(Used to show that there is a lot of difference between two things.)

What is تعارف (ta'ārof)?

The word تعارف (ta'ārof, in colloquial Tehrāni tārof) includes the whole range of social behaviors meant to show courtesy and good manners, most importantly through deference, using words and idioms that have become clichés and should not be taken literally or seriously. When shopping in Tehran, don't be deceived by merchants who verbally *sacrifice themselves for you* (by saying قربانِ شما, *ghorbān-e shomā*) in order to reach deeper into your pocket.

The younger generation is observing these formalities less often; but if you want to use them occasionally, make sure that you are using the correct form in order to avoid embarrassing blunders.

I.i Plural means polite

We know that شما ('you' *pl.*) can be used for a single person also (instead of تو, 'thou' or 'you' *sg.*) to show respect, and we also know that colloquial Persian would sometimes allow using the plural شما with a singular verb for relationships that are halfway between intimate and formal (see I/4.1):

– (?Are you coming with your friend) شما با دوستتان می‌آئید؟
Grammatically correct; consistent in using plural throughout the sentence.
شما با دوستت می‌آئی؟ – Same meaning as above, but used for a relationship which is halfway between intimate and formal.
Note that this inconsistency would be considered bad grammar (as well as impolite) when used mistakenly.

The third person is also treated in the same way in Persian: showing respect to someone *in absentia*, as when you want to talk politely about your friend's parents. In such cases, ایشان (*they*, normally in formal language only) will be used instead of او (*he/she*) in both formal and colloquial Persian:

– آیا آقای رئیس جمهور امروز صحبت خواهند کرد؟ (Note the plural verb.)
– نه، ایشان فردا صحبت می‌کنند.

– 'Will Mr. President talk today?'
– 'No, he will talk tomorrow.'

As was the case with شما, here also colloquial Persian would allow using a singular verb for ایشان (halfway between intimate and formal):

ایشان خودش می‌داند که فقط تا فردا وقت دارد. (He himself knows that he has time only until tomorrow.)

I.ii *We instead of I?*

When speaking polite Persian, sometimes speakers avoid using the pronoun من ('*I*') too often, which, they fear, could convey some attitude of arrogance and pride. As subject of the sentence, of course, it is easy to drop this pronoun (or any other pronoun), since the conjugational ending leaves no room for ambiguity. Another solution is substituting it by other words or pronouns. One such word is بنده (*ban.de*, [your] servant or slave), used frequently in both written and spoken Persian as a substitute for من to show respect. In more colloquial Persian, the plural ما is also used to avoid using من – this is especially common in schools when schoolchildren address their teachers, and using a plural verb is also necessary. Thus, a schoolgirl who has to leave class early would say to the teacher:

خانم، ما امروز باید ده دقیقه زودتر برویم. (Ms, we have to leave ten minutes earlier today.)

By the way, you don't usually hear a child using the word *bande*; children tend to use *mā*. (And using *mā* in this way in colloquial Persian is quite different from the way a monarch might use it or even a sufi in mystic poetry.)
   Examples from colloquial Persian:

A friend saying to another with a touch of humor: چه عجب یادِ ما
کردی! (How nice that you remembered [to call/visit] me!)
A student to the teacher: ببخشید، ما امروز سرمان درد می‌کند (Excuse me, I have a headache today.)

I.iii فرمودن (farmudan)

The original meaning of فرمودن (farmudan) is *to give a farmān* (فرمان, command). In polite language, however, it is used either as (a) an ameliorating/elevating companion of other verbs or (b) a substitute. In the latter case, the context should tell you what verb has been substituted by *farmudan*. These verbs are about activities (especially locomotion), not passive states.

Examples for (a):

بفرمائید جملهٔ بعد را هم بخوانید. (Please [go ahead and] read the next sentence also.)

بفرمائید روی این صندلی بنشینید. – (Please [come and] sit on this chair.) In a sentence like this, بفرمائید could be just making نشستن (to sit) more polite, or – what is more likely – it could have replaced the verb آمدن (to come).

Examples for (b):

از این طرف بفرمائید. (Please come this way.)

بفرمائید تو. (Please come in.) – Here تو (tu) means *inside* in colloquial/Tehrāni.

بفرمائید کی برخواهید گشت؟ (Say, please, when are you going to come back?)

یک چیزی بفرمائید. (Based on the context and situation, this could mean 'Please say something' or – if a guest is being offered something – 'Please help yourself/have something.')

With compound verbs using کردن, the verb کردن can almost always be replaced by فرمودن to make it sound more polite (only if politeness makes sense!):

پنجره را باز کن/کنید. (Open the window [*sg./pl.*].)

→ پنجره را باز بفرمائید. (Please open the window. – Always plural.)

توجّه کنید که زیاد وقت نداریم. (Note that we do not have much time.)

→ توجّه بفرمائید که زیاد وقت نداریم. (Please be aware that we do not have much time.)

However, it is obvious that in certain compounds with کردن that are inglorious in meaning and lack respect, substituting کردن with فرمودن would not be any help: if you say فرار فرمودن instead of فرار کردن (to run away) or ادّعا فرمودن instead of ادّعا کردن (to claim), the effect can only be funny or maliciously ironical.

I.iv عرض کردن vs. فرمودن (arz kardan)

It is very important to remember that when you are using polite expressions – like *farmudan* – you always use them for the addressee, for the other person, not for yourself! Using *farmudan* for oneself would be as embarrassing a blunder as using عرض کردن (arz kardan) for the addressee.

As we saw above, *farmudan* can be used as a substitute for verbs like گفتن (to say) – and when used in this sense, it has a corresponding version for the speaker also: عرض کردن (arz kardan):

شما فرمودید که احتیاجی به آن نیست. (You said that it was not needed.)

(بنده) عرض کرده بودم که امروز بانک تعطیل است. (I had said that the bank is closed today.)

به عرضِ کسی رسیدن (to be informed) and its transitive version به عرضِ کسی رساندن (to inform *so.*) are used respectively for the addressee and the speaker:

همانطور که به عرض شما رسیده است... (As it's been brought to your attention...)

باید به عرضتان برسانم که... (I must let you know that...)

Some of the words used in polite language are as follows (and you will see that even a word like شما has still more respectful substitutes):

من → بنده (*bande*, servant or slave), حقیر (*haghir*, lowly)

تو/شما → سرکار (*sarkār*, overseer), جنابعالی (*jenāb[e]'āli*, your excellency), حضرتعالی (*hazrat[e]'āli*, your eminence) – Don't take the last two very seriously; you can use them for any person to show high respect!

او/آنها → ایشان (*ishān*)

خوردن → میل کردن (*meyl* ~) or میل فرمودن (*meyl* ~)

خواستن → میل داشتن (*meyl* ~)

to be in the presence of a person you respect: در خدمت بودن (*dar khed.mat budan*, to be at service)

167

to go to a person you respect: خدمت رسیدن (*khed.mat residan*, to come to service)

to leave a person you respect: (از خدمت) مرخّص شدن *[az khedmat] mo.rakh.khas shodan*, to take leave from service)

And these are the verbs you use for the addressee:

تشریف داشتن ← بودن (*tashrif dāshtan*)

تشریف آوردن ← آمدن (*tashrif āvardan*)

تشریف بردن ← رفتن (*tashrif bordan*)

استحضار داشتن ← دانستن/اطلاع داشتن (*estehzār dāshtan*) or مستحضر بودن (*mostahzar budan*)

Examples:

کجا میل دارید تشریف ببرید؟ (Where do you want to go?)

تشریف بیاورید غذا میل بفرمائید. (Please come and have food.)

میل دارید آن نامه را برایتان بیاورم؟ (Do you want me to bring you that letter?)

حتماً استحضار دارید (/مستحضر هستید) که آقای سفیر هم تشریف خواهند آورد. (You certainly know that the ambassador will come too.)

حقیر از جنابعالی سؤالی کرده بودم. (I had asked you a question.)

بنده دیروز خدمت رسیدم ولی حضرتعالی تشریف نداشتید. (I came yesterday but you were not there.)

(The last two or three examples are using especially outmoded language, though it is still used by the older generation.)

I.v عرضه (*arze*)

عرضه (*arze*) means 'presentation' (or 'supply' in economics), and عرض کردن is 'to present/supply'; it does not have the usage limitations of عرض and can be used for both the speaker and the addressee:

آیا برنامهٔ جدیدی عرضه خواهید کرد؟ (Will you present a new program?)

اگر تقاضا زیاد باشد، بیشتر عرضه خواهیم کرد. (Should there be more demand, we'll increase the supply.)

APPENDIX II

Colloquial Persian/ Tehrani

پیوستِ ۲

زبان محاوره/ تهرانی

General remarks

Even among the Persian-speaking Iranians, you can find different local dialects and accents in all cities and even villages, but when you talk about colloquial Persian what you have in mind is Tehrani, i.e. Persian as spoken in Tehran, the capital. This is the accent understood all over Iran – and beyond – thanks to the media; the accent that threatens to assimilate all local vernaculars in the course of time.

Here you will learn some of the common changes (from standard to Tehrani), but keep in mind that these changes only occur if the words are common enough at the colloquial level.

Also note that these changes occur in spoken Persian, hardly ever written – except in some modern plays or stories with dialogs, in lyrics of songs, or in more recent times in personal notes of some weblogs on the Internet.

Question: Does one need to learn this Tehrani accent?
Answer: If you want to *talk* (and don't want to be like the only kid in a US school saying 'I am going to be late' when everybody else around you is saying 'I'm gonna be late'), yes!

II.i From standard to Tehrani – some of the changes in pronunciation

(For changes in verbs see II.ii.)

A. Personal pronouns

First and second persons, *sg./pl.*: no change! (من/تو/ما/شما remain unchanged.) There are changes in the third person:

او (he/she) and آن (it/that) both change to اون (*un*, he/she/it/that);

آنها (they/those) changes to اونا (*unā*);

ایشان (he/they in polite language) changes to ایشون (*ishun*).

B. *ān → un* (and occasionally *ām → um*)

As some of the changes in (A) show, *ān* changes to *un* (in آن/آنها/ایشان), something very common in the Tehrani accent, but this change happens only in the most common words.

Examples of words that change:

ایران (*irān*, Iran) → تهرون (*irun*); تهران (*tehrān*, Tehran) → (*tehrun*); خیابان (*khiyābān*, street) → خیابون (*khiyābun*); خانه (*khāne*, house) → خونه (*khune*); تابستان (*tābestān*, summer) → تابستون (*tābestun*).

Examples of words that do not change:

امکان (*emkān*, possibility); داستان (*dāstān*, story); امتحان (*emtehān*, test); سوزان (*suzān*, burning); آلمان (*ālmān*, Germany – foreign names don't change!).

The more formal plural suffix -*ān* (which is not common in colloquial Persian) does not usually change to -*un*; the only exception here might be آقایون because خانوما و آقایون (*khānumā-wo-āghāyun*), the Tehrani version of خانمها و آقایان (ladies and gentlemen), is common at a colloquial level also.

In certain words you can see the change from *ām* to *um*:

تمام (*tamām*, complete) → تموم (*tamum*); کدام (*kodām*, which) → کدوم (*kodum*); بادام (*bādām*, almond) → بادوم (*bādum*); آرام (*ārām*, quiet) → آروم (*ārum*).

C. -*hā → -ā*

As آنها (in A) and خانمها (in B) show, the plural suffix -*hā* is usually reduced to just -*ā*, except after the vowels -*e* and -*ā* (or when some emphasis is needed). Other examples:

میزها (*miz-hā*, tables) → میزا (*mizā*); کتابها (*ketāb-hā*, books) → کتابا (*ketābā*); ایرانیها (*irāni-hā*, Iranians) → ایرونیا (*iruniyā*).

No change in these, however: بچهها (*bach.che-hā*); آقاها (*āghā-hā*).

From
standard to
Tehrani –
some of the
changes in
pronunciation

D. *ham → -am*

The consonant *h* is pronounced softly and often tends to disappear in spoken Persian, unless it is in initial position or when more clarity/emphasis is needed. One good example is هم (*ham*, also) which is usually pronounced *-am* when it immediately follows the word it modifies:

من هم (*man ham*, me too) → منم (*man-am*) (compare with منم = 'I am'!)

E. **Change of *-ar* to *-e* in a few common words**

دیگر (*digar*), اگر (*agar*) and مگر (*magar*) change to دیگه (*dige*), اگه (*age*) and مگه (*mage*). همدیگر (*ham-digar*) also changes to همدیگه (*ham-dige*), but the more formal یکدیگر (*yek-digar*) does not change.

آخر (*ākhar*) changes to آخه (*ākhe*), but only when used as a filler to justify a situation (as *but/because*; see 5.2.1/a), not when it means *last* or *lastly*.

F. **Change of the DDO-marker *rā* to *ro/-o***

را changes to either *-o* (attached to the previous word) or to *ro* (especially after words ending in *-ā* or *-e*, where it cannot be attached as *-o*): کتاب را (*ketāb rā*) becomes *ketāb-o* or *ketāb-ro*, whereas for words like آقا and بچه there is only the *ro* option. (As you remember, the conjunction و [*va*, and] is also pronounced often as *-o* and attached to the previous word, so '*ketābo*' can be both '*ketāb rā*' and '*ketāb va*.')

G. **Revival of the old final *-a* when using enclitics**

The final *-a* sound has almost disappeared from contemporary Persian and changed to *-e* – except for the word نه (*na*, no) and the conjunction و (*va*, and). However, when certain enclitics (like personal suffixes) are added to words ending in *-e*, the old pronunciation may come back to life in the Tehrani accent. If you change بچه را (*bach.che rā*; see F above) to its colloquial/Tehrani form, it is not just *rā* that changes to *ro*: you should say *bach.cha-ro*. Or همه را (*hame rā*) changes to همه رو (*hama-ro*). The same happens with هم (*ham*, also) as well as است (*ast*, is): او بچه است (*u bach.che ast*, He's a child.) → اون بچه س (*un bach.chas*). See H below for a similar change when adding personal suffixes.

171

H. Personal suffixes.

Table II.i will show you the changes in personal suffixes.

Table II.i: How personal suffixes change from standard to Tehrani

Formal/standard	Tehrani		
	AFTER CONSONANTS	AFTER VOWELS (EXCEPT -E)	AFTER THE VOWEL -E (SILENT HÉ)
-am دستم، پایم، گونه‌ام (dástam, páyam, guné'am)	-am دستم (dástam)	-m پام (pām)	(-e → -a +) -m گونه م (gunám)
-at دستت، پایت، گونه‌ات (dástat, páyat, guné'at)	-et دستت (dástem)	-t پات (pāt)	(-e → -a +) -t گونه ت (gunát)
-ash دستش، پایش، گونه‌اش (dástash, páyash, guné'ash)	-esh دستش (dástesh)	-sh پاش (pāsh)	(-e → -a +) -sh گونه ش (gunásh)
-emān دستمان، پایمان، گونه مان (dástemān, páyemān, guné['e]mān)	-emun دستمون (dástemun)	-mun پامون (pāmun)	(-e → -a +) -mun گونه مون (gunámun)
-etān دستتان، پایتان، گونه تان (dástetān, páyetān, guné['e]tān)	-etun دستتون (dástetun)	-tun پاتون (pātun)	(-e → -a +) -tun گونه تون (gunátun)
-eshān دستشان، پایشان، گونه شان (dásteshān, páyeshān, guné['e]shān)	-eshun دستشون (dásteshun)	-shun پاشون (pāshun)	(-e → -a +) -shun گونه شون (gunáshun)

Since this is about spoken Persian and it is usually in less serious texts (as on weblogs) that less careful, ordinary people *write* in Tehrani style, the spelling rules have not been standardized and you might see different styles; for instance, some might drop the *silent hé* (in Table II.i, right column) in writing and join the personal suffixes, which can lead to even more confusion in reading. Moreover, there is also a difference in stress that can help in spoken Persian but cannot be rendered in writing; see the examples below:

Table II.ii: Note the differences in writing and pronunciation when -*ash* is added

	STANDARD/FORMAL	TEHRANI
دست (*dast*, hand)	دستش (*dástash*, his hand)	دستش (*dástesh*, his hand)
دسته (*dasté*, handle)	دسته اش (*dasté-ash*, its handle)	دسته ش (*dastásh*, its handle)
لب (*lab*, lip)	لبش (*lábash*, his lip)	لبش (*lábesh*, his lip)
لبه (*labé*, edge)	لبه اش (*labé-ash*, its edge)	لبه ش (*labásh*, its edge)

As you see here (in the romanization), just a shift in stress can change the formal *his lip* to the Tehrani *its edge*, and keeping that *silent hé* while dropping the *alef* could be some help in reading.

I. Definite marker -*e*

There is a definite marker in colloquial Tehrani which is not considered very polite when used for people; it is the stressed -*e* suffix (-*he* after -*ā*):

مرده هنوزَم اونجا نشسته. (*form.*: آن مرد هم هنوز آنجا نشسته است)
(The man is still sitting there.)

آقاهه خیلی مهربون بود. (*form.*: آن آقا خیلی مهربان بود) (The gentleman was very kind.) – Although we translated آقاهه (*āghāhe*) as 'gentleman' here, you certainly wouldn't want the 'gentleman' himself to overhear you as you refer to him as *āghāhe*!

This -*e* also changes to -*a* when followed by *ro* (= *rā*) or -*am* (= *ham*), etc.

کتابه رو خریدی؟ (Did you buy the book?) – here pronounced *ketābá-ro*, whereas it is normally *ketābé*.

J. Other changes

Changes are usually made in spoken language to make pronunciation easier, and that is why some sounds (vowels and consonants alike) disappear or alter. We will see in II.ii below what happens to verbs; here you see some examples of other changes:

> $n \rightarrow m$ (when before b/m/p): شنبه (*shanbe*, Saturday) pronounced *shambe*.
>
> هیچی ← هیچ چیز/هیچ چیزی (*hich.chi*)
>
> هیشکی ← هیچکس/هیچ کسی (*hish.ki*)
>
> لامذهب (*lā maz.hab*, nonbeliever) → لامصّب (*lā mas.sab*, damned [used as interjection or *adj.* to show anger or disappointment])

II.ii Alterations and contractions in verbs

We should first see what happens to the conjugational suffixes as a general rule, and Table II.iii shows the changes.

Table II.iii: Changes in present tense conjugational suffixes

	STANDARD/FORMAL	TEHRANI
1*sg.*	*-am*	*-am*
	if ending in *-āham* or *-āyam*	*-ām*
2*sg.*	*-i*	*-i*
	if ending in *-āhi* or *-ā'i*	*-āy*
3*sg.*	*-ad* (also *ast* of 'to be', except after *silent hê*)	*-e*
	if ending in *-āhad* or *-āyad*	*-ād*
1*pl.*	*-im*	*-im*
	if ending in *-āhim* or *-ā'im*	*-āym*
2*pl.*	*-id*	*-in*
	if ending in *-āhid* or *-ā'id*	*-āyn*
3*pl.*	*-and*	*-an*
	if ending in *-āhand* or *-āyand*	*-ān*

Here by verbs that end in *-āh-* or *-āy-* we basically mean خواه/خواستن
(*khāstan/khāh*), آ/آمدن (*āmadan/ā*), زا(ی)/زادن (*zādan/zā*, to bear a child)
and maybe a few verbs common in slang Tehrani, but verbs like کاه/کاستن
(*kāstan/kāh*, to decrease) and گشا/گشودن (*goshudan/goshā*, to open) do
not belong to the colloquial level: you neither say می‌گشایه/می‌کاهه nor
می‌گشاد/می‌کاد – you simply don't use them in spoken Persian!

The same is true of all other verbs that do not belong to the colloquial
level. A verb like سترد ن (*setordan*, to eliminate or erase) has no place in
spoken Persian/Tehrani, and you know how to conjugate and use it in
formal/written language – where it belongs.

Apart from changes in conjugational suffixes, there are some changes
also in some of the very common verbs that are most frequently used,
changes that make them shorter and easier to pronounce. The following
are only five of the verbs that undergo such changes (conjugation in Tehrani
given for present and past).

آمدن	**present:** *miyām, miyāy, miyād, miyāym, miyāyn, miyān* (neg.: *nemiyām, . . .*) **past:** *umadam, umadi, umad, umadim, umadin, umadan* (neg.: *nayumadam, . . .*)
رفتن	**present:** *miram, miri, mire, mirim, mirin, miran* (neg.: *nemiram, . . .*) **past:** *raftam, rafti, raf, raftim, raftin, raftan* (neg.: *naraftam, . . .*)
گفتن	**present:** *migam, migi, mige, migim, migin, migan* (neg.: *nemigam, . . .*) **past:** *goftam, gofti, gof, goftim, goftin, goftan* (neg.: *nagoftam, . . .*)
توانستن	**present:** *mitunam, mituni, mitune, mitunim, mitunin, mitunan* (neg.: *nemitunam, . . .*) **past:** *tunestam, tunesti, tunes, tunestim, tunestin, tunestan* (neg.: *natunestam, . . .*)
گذاشتن	**present:** *mi[g]zāram, mi[g]zāri, mi[g]zāre, mi[g]zārim,* *mi[g]zārin, mi[g]zāran* (neg.: *nemi[g]zāram, . . .*) **past:** *gozāshtam, gozāshti, gozāsh, gozāshtim, gozāshtin,* *gozāshtan* (neg.: *na[g]zāshtam, . . .*)

II.iii The special case of the present perfect tense

In the present perfect tense, in its formal version, you have the *-e* of the
past participle followed by the *a-/i-* of the verb *to be*. The Tehrani accent
tries to get rid of one of the two vowels. To make it easier to understand,
we can say that it is the final *-e* which disappears, while its stress is kept
and given to the *-a-/-i-*.

The result is that this Tehrani *present perfect tense* sounds very much like the *simple past tense* except for a shift in stress – and except in the third person singular. Table II.iv compares the two tenses (with Tehrani occupying the two middle columns).

Table II.iv: Present perfect vs. simple past – the verb رفتن

SIMPLE PAST (FORMAL)	SIMPLE PAST (TEHRANI)	PRESENT PERFECT (TEHRANI)	PRESENT PERFECT (FORMAL)
ráftam	*ráftam*	*raftám*	*rafté'am*
ráfti	*ráfti*	*raftí*	*rafté'i*
ráft	*ráf[t]*	*rafté*	*rafté (ast)*
ráftim	*ráftim*	*raftím*	*rafté'im*
ráftid	*ráftin*	*raftín*	*rafté'id*
ráftand	*ráftan*	*raftán*	*rafté'and*

II.iv Prepositions

One preposition that you hear a lot in spoken Persian and don't encounter as often in written Persian is تو/توی (*tu/tuye*) meaning 'inside':

تو خواب راه می‌رود (تو خواب را[ه] میره. = *tu khāb rā[h] mire* = He walks in sleep.)

توپ را در آب (توپو انداخ[ت] تو(ی) آب. = *tup-o andākh[t] tu[-ye] āb* = انداخت = He threw the ball in the water.)

We saw earlier how objective pronouns can be added to some prepositions (see 2.3.3); the Tehrani dialect makes this possible for the prepositions از and به and با also – something not acceptable in formal Persian. (In the case of به and با, a consonantal *h* is added as glide, which is quite unusual.) See how some of these prepositions are pronounced when joined with objective pronouns:

Table II.v: Prepositions + objective pronouns

از	به	با	توىِ	براىِ
ازم *azam/azem*	بهم *behem*	باهام *bāhām*	توم *tum*	برام *barām*
ازت *azat/azet*	بهت *behet*	باهات *bāhāt*	توت *tut*	برات *barāt*
ازش *azash/azesh*	بهش *behesh*	باهاش *bāhāsh*	توش *tush*	براش *barāsh*
ازمون *azamun/azemun*	بهمون *behemun*	باهامون *bāhāmun*	تومون *tumun*	برامون *barāmun*
ازتون *azatun/azetun*	بهتون *behetun*	باهاتون *bāhātun*	توتون *tutun*	براتون *barātun*
ازشون *azashun/azeshun*	بهشون *beheshun*	باهاشون *bāhāshun*	توشون *tushun*	براشون *barāshun*

Examples:

اگه دیدیش ازش بپرس. = اگر او را دیدی از او بپرس.
صندلی کوچیکه رو برام میاره. = آن صندلی کوچک را برایم می‌آورد.

Why does it matter?

You might ask: why should I learn about some usages that are even labeled archaic? Well, because they are not as easily separable from contemporary – even colloquial – Persian as you might think. Iranians like to support or prove their point by citing a line of classical poetry, and certain idioms or proverbs are remnants and carriers of old usages: remember the *optative* mood we mentioned earlier with such everyday expressions as هرچه بادا باد! (Come what may!, see 6.2).

If you asked a person to help you with something while he himself has the same problem and knows no solution, he would cite this proverb (which has the form of a couplet):

کل اگر طبیب بودی/سر خود دوا نمودی (*kal agar tabib budi/sar-e khod davā nomudi*, If the baldhead had been a physician, he would have cured his own head.)

Despite being a very common proverb, some features of early modern Persian – for which you can't find any explanation in a dictionary – are to be found here, like using بودی for the third person singular – and not the second person singular. Here we shall only mention certain archaic features that you might still encounter, just to be familiar with them and not to use them.

III.i The conditional/habitual *-i* suffix

We start with the same بودی in the proverb we just mentioned. This *-i* suffix had the effect of a *mi-* prefix when added to the past tense (usually added to 1*sg.* and 3*sg./pl.* only), used for counter-factual conditionals (where you would use the past progressive now) and for the habitual past ('used to'). Thus, بودی is the same as می‌بود just as نمودی in that couplet is the same as (می‌نمود = می‌نمود). Since this usage was not common for the second person, the same verb (بودی) could also be understood as the second person singular (if no subject was mentioned):

‏اگر بودی = 1) اگر تو می‌بودی؛ (2 اگر او می‌بود.

To simply convey the continuous sense, *mi-* or *hami-* was used: می‌رفت/همی‌رفت (he was going/kept going).

III.ii The prohibitive *ma-* prefix

For the *prohibitive* mood (= negative imperative) early modern Persian used the prefix *ma-* instead of *na-* (still common in poetical language). A couplet by Ḥāfez:

‏سويِ منِ لب چه می‌گزی که: 'مگوی'؟/لبِ لعلی گزیده‌ام که مپرس! (Why are you biting the lip at me, [saying] 'Don't tell'?/I have bitten [= kissed] ruby lips that . . . – don't ask!)

In today's standard Persian, مگوی! (*ma-guy*) and مپرس! (*ma-pors*) would be نگو! (*na-gu*, 'Don't say/tell!') and نپرس! (*na-pors*, 'Don't ask!')
    Apart from poetical language, you can still find this *ma-* in many idioms and proverbs:

‏اسرارِ مگو (*asrār-e magú*, 'unspeakable secrets')

Compare this with اسرار را نگو (*asrār rā nágu*, 'Don't tell the secrets' – with the normal stress on the negative *ná-*).
    Even the common word کشمکش (*kesh-ma-kesh*, 'struggle' or 'scuffle') has this *ma-* in the middle, added to کشیدن (here 'to pull').

III.iii Verbs and the *mi-/be-* prefixes

We are talking now about *poetical* language, so let's make things easier by attributing all that seems to be conflicting with the rules you have learned to *poetic license*. You have learned, for instance, where and how to use the *mi-* and *be-* prefixes with verbs, but these rules do not always apply to past/archaic usage.
    If you want to tell someone, 'You are accusing me of this because that's exactly how you yourself are,' you would normally cite this proverb (again in meters):

‏کافر همه را به کیشِ خود پندارد. (A heretic/nonbeliever thinks that all [other people] are of the same faith as he.)

Here پندارد (which has neither *mi-* nor *be-*) is in fact می‌پندارد (*mi-pendārad*), but the *mi-* is missing.

As for *be-* (in the imperative and subjunctive), you should likewise know that it is sometimes called, very aptly indeed, باءِ زینت (*bā'e zinat*, 'ornamental *be*'), treated in the past like some ornament that could have been worn or left out at will. Sometimes you see that it has been used even for the past tense (او برفت instead of او رفت, 'he went'), and sometimes it is missing where you expect it to be used. Another couplet by Hāfez:

اگر غم لشكر انگیزد که خونِ عاشقان ریزد (If grief moves an army to shed the blood of lovers,/)

من و ساقی بهم سازیم و بنیادش براندازیم (the cup-bearer and I will join forces and uproot it.)

A paraphrased, contemporary version would read:

اگر غم لشكری بیانگیزد که خونِ عاشقان را بریزد
من و ساقی باهم می‌سازیم و بنیادش را بر می‌اندازیم

As you see here, *biyangizad* needs *be-* (because of the conditional *agar*) and *berizad* also needs *be-* (because of the 'final' *ke* [= in order to]), both missing in the original couplet. Similarly, *mi-* is missing in both *mi-sāzim* and *bar-mi-andāzim*.

III.iv The fate of *rā*

In the couplet by Hāfez cited above, the DDO-marker *rā* was missing twice. If you did the same now, it wouldn't be considered a poetic license, but an obvious mistake.

On the other hand, there are cases where you wouldn't normally expect a *rā* now, but it is used in poetical/archaic language:

- Some verbs that need prepositions now (for the indirect object), used to take direct objects + *rā*:

   به او گفتم → او را گفتم (I told him/I said to him) – possible now only in poetry.

- را was even used with the verb بودن to convey possession:

   او مادری دارد → (برایِ او مادری است →) او را مادری است (He has a mother.)

III.v. آنِ (ān-e) or از آنِ (az ān-e) = that of

As possessive pronoun you would normally use مالِ (māl-e) in contemporary Persian:

این مالِ من نیست.

این مالِ میناست؛ آن یکی مالِ کیست؟

In formal/literary language you can still use the older version with آنِ (از):

گرانترین اسبِ جهان از آنِ کیست؟

خوشبختیِ واقعی از آنِ کسی است که ارزشِ زندگی را میشناسد.

III.vi Contractions

Contractions of words used to be very common in classical Persian poetry, but they are generally avoided now – even in contemporary poetry, except when written in traditional styles. The word خاموش (khāmush [scanned long + very long], silent or quenched) could change to خامُش (khāmosh [long + long]), خَموش (khamush [short + very long]) or خَمُش (khamosh [short + long]), depending on the poet's need.

Contraction of اگر (agar, if) could be گر (gar) or just اَر (ar), and it could be combined with other words: thus وَر (var) is اگر + وَ (= 'and if').

Contraction of از (az, from) was زِ (ze, or just z when followed by vowels):

وَز (vaz) = و از (va az),

کَز (kaz) = که از (ke az),

زان (zān) = از آن (az ān),

کزان (kazān) = که از آن (ke az ān), and so on.

III.vii The verb بودن (to be)

If we put together all the different usages of the verb *to be* in early Modern Persian, we have to conclude that this verb had four different infinitives: استن (astan, the '-am, -i, ast...' version), هستن (hastan, the 'hastam, hasti, hast...' version), بودن (budan, 'bovam, bovi, bovad...') and باشیدن (bāshi-dan, 'bāsham, bāshi, bāshad...').

Before the Islamic revolution, the motto of Iran's Ministry of Education, published on the first page of all school books, used to be this line by Ferdowsi:

توانا بُوَد هرکه دانا بُوَد

(tavānā bovad har-ke dānā bovad, 'whoever is wise is strong' or 'knowledge is power')

Here *bovad* is the third person singular of the verb بودن – which means that the verb *to be* could be conjugated as *bovam, bovi, bovad*, etc., although it is mostly the third person singular which can be seen in classical texts of prose and verse.

For the negative also, the shorter or *astan* version had its own shorter negative as:

نَیم (*ni-am* = نیستم)

نِئی (*ne-'i* = نیستی)

نیست (*nist* = نیست)

نِئیم (*ne-'im* = نیستیم)

نِئید (*ne-'id* = نیستید)

نیند (*ni-and* = نیستند)

APPENDIX IV

Good, bad and ugly Persian
Common mistakes

پیوستِ ۴

فارسیِ خوب، بد و زشت

اشتباهات رایج

Do we have *good* and *bad* Persian?

Languages are constantly changing, and there can never be a general consensus on what is good or bad usage in a language like Persian – just as in English some would find the word *general* redundant before *consensus*, and for others it is okay.

In the two volumes of this grammar and workbook, however, you have occasionally seen references to *bad* or *careless* Persian. Here you will see what exactly was meant by that.

IV.i Administrative/journalistic[1] Persian

Careless or bad Persian can be encountered in formal/written Persian only. The way different people speak can differ, based on the social milieu in which they grew up, but you cannot blame anyone for the way he speaks. And don't forget that here we are only talking about the contemporary standard Persian of Iran, not about Persian as it is used in other countries, nor as it used to be in the past – even the quite recent past!

The worst, or ugliest, Persian is what is neither used by ordinary people when they are talking nor by good writers when they are writing. Compare the following:

Formal: این بیماری خطرناک است. (This disease is dangerous.)
Colloquial/Tehrani: این مریضی (/بیماری) خطرناکه. – you note here the change from *ast* to *-e*.
Awkward: این بیماری خطرناک می‌باشد.

---

[1] By 'journalistic Persian' (فارسیِ ژورنالیستی) Iranian writers mean bad or careless Persian.

Appendix IV

Good, bad
and ugly
Persian

Common
mistakes

In the last example, *mi-bāshad* has replaced *ast* (/-*e*) – something that writers of 'good Persian' avoid. Conjugating the verb *to be* as '*mi-bāsham, mi-bāshi*, etc.' is something you will never hear in spoken Persian, and all writers known for their 'good' Persian will avoid it as well, but in the press or in administrative language you will find this on every page by the dozen.

Table IV.i: Substitutes that you had better avoid

USED IN SPOKEN + 'GOOD' PERSIAN	SUBSTITUTES OFTEN USED IN WRITTEN ADMINISTRATIVE/JOURNALISTIC PERSIAN
بودن	باشیدن
کردن	نمودن/ساختن/گرداندن (گردانیدن)
شدن	گشتن/گردیدن

The substitutes for کردن and شدن (on the right column) are especially common with compound verbs. You can find these 'awkward substitutes' in written Persian almost everywhere – except in the writings of those known to be the models of 'good Persian.' Example:

هر نماینده [...] حق دارد در همهٔ مسائل داخلی و خارجی کشور اظهار نظر نماید. (From Iran's Constitution, §84: 'Every representative [...] shall be entitled to express his views on all internal and external matters of the country.') Here نماید has replaced کند.

Careless, journalistic Persian is marked by the bad influence of translations from other languages, using the passive where Persian would normally seek other alternatives (see I/20.1), using the DDO-marker when it is not needed or placing it at the end of a relative clause (see I/19.3), or deleting a verb without justification (see 6.4), etc. An example for deleting a verb:

او در تهران دستگیر و پس از چهارده روز حبس، در زندان درگذشت. (She was arrested in Tehran and passed away in prison after 14 days.) – Here you should say دستگیر شد and the verb cannot be omitted.

IV.ii Persian purists and what they hate most

There has been a Persian purism movement among Iranian intellectuals, writers and linguists since the early twentieth century with ups and downs at different stages – a movement with very little effect on the ordinary people and the way they use the language, no matter to what extent they share the nationalistic sentiments fueling this movement.

Here we won't discuss the more extremist views of those who want to cleanse Persian of all foreign words (which would be like cleansing English of all words of French/Latin origin) and will just mention a few of the objections of the more moderate scholars/linguists. The main point of this group is: if we cannot get rid of all foreign words, we should at least not allow certain grammatical features of foreign languages (read: Arabic) to be used in Persian. Some examples of their recommendations:

- Don't use Arabic broken plurals when you can use Persian plurals, but especially don't use Arabic plurals for Persian words – some of which are rather common, like پیشنهادات (*pishnahādāt* = پیشنهادها = proposals), گزارشات (*gozāreshāt* = گزارشها = reports); and some seem unavoidable, like سبزیجات (*sabzijāt*, the collective noun for 'vegetables').
- Don't use the Arabic *tanvin* for Persian words to make adverbs, like ناچاراً (*nāchār-an*) instead of ناچار/به ناچار (*[be] nāchār*, inevitably or perforce) or گاهاً (*gāh-an*) instead of گاهی (*gāhi*, sometimes).
- Don't use or even make new Arabic compounds like فارغ‌التحصیل (*fāregh-ot-tahsil*, graduate) and use Persian words instead (like دانش‌آموخته, modeled on دانش‌آموز or دانشجو).

IV.iii Common mistakes among learners of Persian

You cannot expect more than a few examples here, but you will certainly find these very helpful. These are some of the most common ones.

- Don't say نمی‌دانم اگر او می‌داند یا نه when you want to say 'I don't know *if* he knows or not.' – yes, *agar* means *if*, but only in conditionals, not in indirect questions! (see 1.4)
  Say instead: نمی‌دانم (که/آیا/که آیا) ...
  Note that you can still say:
  نمی‌دانم اگر او بداند چه خواهد کرد (I don't know what he's going to do if he finds out.) This is the conditional *if*!
- Don't say این یک داستان غمگین است when you want to say 'This is a sad story.' In Persian, only a *person* can be sad, happy, wise, clever, and so on – you need a different word for *things* (see 10.4).
  Say instead: این یک داستان غم‌انگیز است
- Don't say من از آن را جالب پیدا می‌کنم when you want to say 'I find that interesting.' پیدا کردن is only the opposite of گم کردن (to lose). The verb یافتن can be used in both of these senses, but then it is a verb used in formal/literary language only.
  Say instead (*col.*): به نظرم جالب است (/می‌آید) (It seems interesting to me.)
  Or (*form./lit.*): آن را جالب می‌یابم (I find that interesting.)

185

Appendix IV

Good, bad
and ugly
Persian

Common
mistakes

- Don't say باور می‌کنم که آنها می‌دانند when you want to say 'I believe that they know [it].' Use باور کردن only to show that you believe some-one's words (that he is not lying) – as in حرفت را باور می‌کنم.

Say instead: فکر (/تصوّر/گمان) می‌کنم که آنها می‌دانند

- Similarly, don't say من در خدا باور می‌کنم when you want to say 'I believe in God.'

Say instead (*col.*): من به خدا اعتقاد دارم

Or (*form./lit.*): من به خدا باور دارم

When an English word has different meanings or usages, you can be sure that you will need a different word in Persian for each of those meanings/usages. Just take the verb *to take*:

Table IV.ii: The verb *to take*

TO TAKE	PERSIAN EQUIVALENT	OPPOSITE IN PERSIAN
as the opposite of 'to give'	گرفتن	دادن
as the opposite of 'to bring'	بُردن	آوردن
as the opposite of 'to put'	بَرداشتن	گذاشتن

Examples:

او کتاب را داد و من آن را گرفتم. (He gave the book and I took it.)

غذایش را آوردم و او آن را به اتاقش بُرد. (I brought her food and she took it to her room.)

نامه را روی میز گذاشت و من آن را از روی میز برداشتم. (He put the letter on the table and I took it [/picked it up] from the table.)

And finally, to have some fun, compare the verbs used in these short sentences:

۱. گل می‌روید. ۲. شما می‌روید. ۳. فنجان را می‌شویم. ۴. ما عصبانی می‌شویم. ۵. صندلی را به آنجا می‌برم. ۶. پنیر را با کارد می‌برم. ۷. شما چرا می‌خندید؟ ۸. او چرا می‌خندید؟ ۹. شما همیشه می‌رقصید؟ ۱۰. او با من نمی‌رقصید.

فارس – فارسی – ایران – ایرانی   IV.iv

ایران یک کشور است.

فارسی یک زبان است.

فارس یکی از اُستانهای ایران است که شهر مهمّ آن شیراز است.

همچنین **فارس** کسی است که زبان مادری‌اش فارسی است.

ایرانی کسی است که در ایران زندگی می‌کند.

فارسی زبانِ مادریِ همهٔ ایرانیها نیست، حتّی در استانِ فارس.

مثال برای کاربُردِ این کلمه‌ها:

استانِ فارس	زبانِ فارسی	کشورِ ایران	زبانهای ایرانی
مردمِ فارس	ادبیاتِ فارسی	مردمِ ایران	اُسطوره‌های ایرانی
قومِ فارس	شعرِ فارسی	تاریخِ ایران	اقوامِ ایرانی
خلیجِ فارس	کتابِ فارسی	شهرهای ایران	نویسندهٔ ایرانی

KEY TO EXERCISES

Unit 1

Exercise 1.1

١. مینا به من گفت (که) فردا او و مادرش به بیمارستان خواهند رفت.

٢. مادرم به دوستم گفت (که) خانوادهشان را خیلی خوب میشناسد.

٣. حسن به معلم انگلیسی گفت (که) او خیلی تند حرف میزند و حسن
نمیفهمد.

Notes: 1) To show that Hasan is not the subject of the verb حرف زدن, we
have to mention او [see 1.8]; 2) to avoid a confusion of third person pronouns, we mention Hasan's name.

٤. برادر بابک به بابک گفت (که) میداند (که) او درسهایش را خوب
نمیخواند.

Notes: 1) Again we use او to show the change of subject; 2) we are much
more likely here to drop at least one of these *ke* [که]s because they are
so close to each other.

٥. پروین به مادرش گفت (که) دیروز وقت نداشته (است) (که) ظرفها را
بشوید.

٦. ما به پلیس گفتیم (که) آن مرد میخواسته (است) ماشینمان را بدزدد.

٧. پلیس به همسایهمان گفت (که) ماشین او را در شهر دیگری پیدا کردهاند.

٨. مادر به دکتر گفت (که) او تمام روز داشته (است) سرفه میکرده (است).
Note: است dropped in colloquial Persian [see I/13.3]; often in written/
formal Persian too. If you want to keep one of them, keep the one at the
end of the sentence.

٩. معلم به پرویز گفت (که) او دیروز درسش را بهتر یاد گرفته بوده (است).

١٠. پرویز به دارا گفت (که) امروز/آن روز (آنها) دارند به مسافرت میروند.

Exercise 1.2

۱. مینا از من پرسید آیا فردا/روزِ بعد با دوستم به مسافرت نخواهم رفت/.... با دوستمان...نخواهیم...

Note: *Your* in دوستتان could be a real plural or plural used for respect; hence the two versions here.

۲. مادرم از دوستم پرسید آیا دیروز دیر به مدرسه نرسیده (است)/نرسیده‌اند/ .... نرسیده‌ایم

Note: Use نرسیده‌ایم if you are included in that *you*; also note that the mother's use of *pl.* in نرسیدید could be just for respect (hence the *sg.* نرسیده است as one option).

۳. حسن از معلم انگلیسی پرسید چرا آهسته‌تر حرف نمی‌زند که ما بفهمیم./.... آنها بفهمند.

Note: Use ما بفهمیم if you are included in that *we* used by Hasan.

۴. پدر مینا از مینا پرسید از کدام مغازه آن کفشها را خریده (است).

۵. پروین از مادرش پرسید با کی داشته ((است)) دربارهٔ او حرف می‌زده (است).

۶. ما از پلیس پرسیدیم چرا قاتل را زودتر دستگیر نکرده بوده‌اند.

۷. پلیس از همسایه‌مان پرسید آیامطمئن است که او برنگشته (است).

۸. مادر از دکتر پرسید آیا آن قرص‌های زرد را قبل از غذا بخورد یا همراه با غذا.

۹. معلم از پرویز پرسید آیا می‌داند چرا او می‌خواهد پدر و مادرش را ببیند.

Note: There are two shifts of subjects here: the teacher *asks*, Parviz *knows*, the teacher *wants*.... If we repeat او twice (once for the verb می‌داند also), it will be still more confusing. (One solution would be repeating the names, which would not make a beautiful sentence.)

۱۰. پرویز از دارا پرسید آیا نگفته‌اند چرا به او جایزه نمی‌دهند.

Exercise 1.3

۱. مینا از من خواهش کرد (که) آن لباسهای زشت را نپوشم. ۲. مادرم از پدرم خواهش کرد (که) او را در خیابان نبوسد. ۳. حسن ازمعلم انگلیسی خواست (که) کمی دربارهٔ هوای لندن به ما/آنها بگوید. ۴. معلم به من گفت (که) هیچوقت کیفم را آنجا نگذارم. ۵. پروین به مادرش گفت/از مادرش خواست (که) ببیند آیا دامنی

که خریده است قشنگ است. ۶. ما از پلیس خواهش کردیم بگوید چقدر طول
می‌کشد. ۷. پلیس به همسایه‌مان گفت نگران نباشد و همانجا (/همانجا) بماند.
۸. مادر از دکتر خواهش کرد آن قصه‌های تلخ را دیگر به بچه ندهد. ۹. معلم از
پرویز خواست (که) به پدر و مادرش بگوید روزِ بعد به مدرسه بیایند. ۱۰. پرویز
از دارا خواست (که) یک بار دیگر برای او توضیح بدهد.

Exercise 1.4

۱. مینا به من گفت (که) اگر نمی‌توانم، بگذارم او بکند.

۲. مادرم به دوستم گفت (که) کاش (او) موهایش را کوتاه نمی‌کرد.

۳. حسن به معلم انگلیسی گفت (که) اگر او آهسته‌تر حرف بزند، حسن می‌فهمد.

۴. پدر آذر به آذر گفت (که) اگر آن را به مادرش بدهد، او خوشحال می‌شود.

۵. پروین به مادرش گفت (که) کاش آن نامه را اصلاً نخوانده بود.

۶. ما به پلیس گفتیم (که) اگر عجله نکنند، دیگر او را پیدا نخواهند کرد.

۷. پلیس به همسایه‌مان گفت (که) اگر فردا پول را به او نداد، به آنها خبر بدهد.

To reduce ambiguity and risk of confusion, you could also say:

پلیس به همسایه‌مان گفت (که) اگر او فردا پول را نداد، همسایه‌مان
به پلیس خبر بدهد.

۸. مادر به دکتر گفت کاش این دوا را زودتر به او داده بود.

۹. معلم از پرویز پرسید اگر این خط او است، چرا نمی‌تواند بخواند.

۱۰. پرویز به دارا گفت کاش او هم جرئت دارا را می‌داشت.

Exercise 1.5

۱. مینا به من گفت (که) غذا که خوردیم، برویم سینما./....(که) وقتیکه غذا
خوردیم، به سینما برویم. ۲. مادرم به دوستم گفت (که) وقتی آذر به دنیا آمده
(است)، قیافه‌اش عین فرشته بوده (است). ۳. حسن به معلم انگلیسی گفت (که)
معلمی که قبل از او داشته‌ایم/داشته‌اند، نمی‌توانسته (است) اینها را توضیح بدهد.
۴. مادر نیما از نیما پرسید چرا همینکه عمویش آمده (است)، او به اتاقش رفته
(است). ۵. پروین به مادرش گفت (که) داشته (است) تنش را می‌شسته (است)
که آب سرد شده (است). ۶. ما به پلیس گفتیم (که) مردی که ما دیده‌ایم کمی
قدّش بلندتر بوده (است). ۷. پلیس از همسایه‌مان پرسید (که) آیا وقتی برگشته

(است)، تعجب نکرده (است) که چرا در بازست. ۸. مادر به دکتر گفت (که) چشمی که درد می‌کند، چشم راست او است، نه چشم چپش. ۹. معلم از پرویز خواست (که) هرچه را که نمی‌فهمد، بپرسد. ۱۰. پرویز به دارا گفت (که) تا وقتی او زنده بوده (است)، هروقت پرویز را می‌دیده (است) از دارا می‌پرسیده (است).

Exercise 1.6

1. 'Work only six days in the week, because I created the world in six days.'

خدا به موسی گفت (که) فقط شش روز در هفته کار کند، چون او دنیا را در شش روز خلق کرده است.

2. 'The entire day I cried in the mirror.'

فروغ گفت (که) تمام روز در آئینه گریه می‌کرده (است).

3. 'God's benevolence is more than our misdeeds.'

حافظ گفت (که) لطفِ خدا بیشتر از جُرم ما (/آنها) است. (use ما if you consider yourself included.)

4. 'You can listen to/hear this program again at 6:30.'

گویندهٔ رادیو گفت (که) می‌توانیم این برنامه را در ساعت شش و نیم دوباره بشنویم.

5. 'Was I awake in your belly or asleep?'

بچه از مادرش پرسید آیا توی شکم او بیدار بوده (است) یا خواب؟

6. 'I think you had eaten some bad food yesterday.'

دکتر به من گفت (که) فکر می‌کند (که) دیروز/روزِ قبل غذای بدی خورده بوده‌ام.

7. 'Admit (/accept) that you have not understood the meaning of this poem.'

مینا از دوستش خواست (که) قبول کند که معنی آن شعر را نفهمیده (است).

8. 'If you know its meaning (/what it means), tell me!'

دوست مینا به او گفت (که) اگر معنی‌اش را می‌داند، به او بگوید.

9. 'Leave your car here and come with me.'

پلیس به من و دوستم گفت (که) ماشینمان را آنجا بگذاریم و با او برویم. (Note here the change from 'come' to 'go.')

10. 'How would you have carried these alone if I hadn't helped you?'

بابک از پرویز پرسید (که) اگر او کمک نکرده بود، (پرویز) چطور اینها را تنهائی می‌برد؟

(Note that repeating پرویز can help avoid confusion.)

Unit 2

Exercise 2.1

1. *gush-e*, 'I heard with my own ears that he said he wouldn't come.'
2. [no *ezāfe*], 'First I went to the bath (= shower) and washed myself.'
3. *khod-e*, 'I saw his father but did not see Naser himself.'
4. *nazdik-e*, 'Naser himself had gone to a city near Tehran.'
5. *barāye*, 'In that city, Naser bought himself a house.'
6. *khod-e*, 'The windows were small, but the house itself was large.'
7. a) *khāne-ye* [written as خانهٔ], 'He always cooked in his own home and took [it] to the factory.' b) [no *ezāfe*], 'At home, he himself always cooked and....'
8. [no *ezāfe*], 'If you see yourself in the mirror, you'll die from laughing.'
9. *khod-e*, 'I've only seen her picture, but you've seen Mina herself.'
10. *khod-e*, 'Babak's mother herself was born in 1320 [= 1941].

Exercise 2.2

۱. خانهٔ برادر خودم فروخته شد.

۲. دربارهٔ خودِ خانه هیچ نمی‌دانستند.

۳. خودتان را (/خود را) به آن مردهایِ (/مردانِ) جوان نشان ندهید.

۴. نمی‌توانم خودم را (/خود را) زیرِ این میزِ کوچک پنهان کنم.

۵. سگها هرگز صاحبِ خودشان (/صاحبِ خود) را فراموش نمی‌کنند.

۶. من فقط بندِ کفش را می‌خواهم، نه خودِ کفش را.

۷. مرد خودش (/خودِ مرد/مرد خود) خیلی از همسایه‌اش بهتر نبود.

(No *ezāfe* for *mard* here.)

۸ وقتیکه به دبیرستان می‌رفتم (/در دبیرستان بودم) لباسهایم را خودم (/خود) می‌خریدم./... خودم (/خود) لباسهایم را می‌خریدم.

۹. او کتاب را پیدا کرد ولی نتوانست (/نمی‌توانست) عینکِ خودش (/خود) را پیدا کند.

۱۰. او دو روز بعد از خودکشیِ پسرش خودش (/خود) را کشت.

Exercise 2.3

۱. من خودِ مینا را (/من مینا خودش را) خیلی خوب می‌شناختم. ۲. خودِ ما (/ما خودمان/ما خود) چند روز در آن شهر ماندیم و بعد برگشتیم. ۳. ما چند روز

در خودِ آن شهر ماندیم و بعد برگشتیم. ۴. برادر کوچک من خودش (/خودِ برادرِ کوچکِ من/برادر کوچک من خود) آن پرنده را دید. ۵. برادر کوچکِ خودِ من (برادر کوچکِ خودم) آن پرنده را دید. ۶. برادر کوچک من خودِ آن پرنده را دید. ۷. خودِ علی (/علی خودش/علی خود) به من نگفته بود که پدرش مرده است. ۸. علی به خودِ من (/به من خودم) نگفته بود که پدرش مرده است. ۹. علی به من نگفته بود که پدر خودش (/پدرِ خودِ او) مرده است. ۱۰. علی به من نگفته بود که خودِ پدرش مرده است.

Exercise 2.4

1. چرا آن را برایم نیاوردی؟ ('Why didn't you bring it for me?')
2. فیلم طولانی بود و نمی‌توانستم ببینمش ('The movie was long and I couldn't watch it.')
3. بعد از دو هفته به همین کتابخانه پس دادم/پس دادمش ('After two weeks I returned it to this same library.')
4. اگر گرسنه نیستی، نخورش ('Don't eat it if you're not hungry.')
5. خیلی زود پیدایمان کردی/پیدا کردی‌مان ('You found us very fast.')
6. قبل از آنکه به پلیس بگوید کشتندش ('They killed him before he told the police.')
7. همینکه می‌بیندِتان از خوشحالی می‌رقصد ('He dances from joy as soon as he sees you.')
8. اگر تعمیرش کنید (/تعمیر کنیدش)، بهتر می‌خرندش ('If you repair it, they'll buy it better.')
9. می‌توانی نگاهش کنی (/نگاه کنی‌اش)، ولی دستش نزن (/دست نزنش) ('You can see/look at it, but don't touch it.')
10. کاش فراموشش نکرده بودم (/فراموش نکرده بودمش) و می‌گفتمِتان ('I wish I hadn't forgotten it and could have told it to you.')

Exercise 2.5

۱. نامه را پاره نکن، آن را لازم دارم. ۲. قبل از آنکه بخوابی، چراغ را خاموش کن. ۳. من را دوست ندارد و دروغ می‌گوید. ۴. در کتابخانه دوستانم را ندیدم و به خانه برگشتم. ۵. به بچّه غذا دادم و صبر کردم تا بخوابد. ۶. به ما کمک کنید تا این کار را زودتر تمام کنیم. ۷. می‌خواستیم شما را دعوت کنیم ولی شماره تلفنتان را نداشتیم. ۸. آن روز در خانهٔ برادرت تو را دیدم ولی بعد از آن دیگر

تو را ندیدم. ۹. کلید را همانجا گذاشتم تا علی آن را راحت‌تر پیدا کند. ۱۰. ممکن است مالِ همسایه باشد، بسته را باز نکن.

Exercise 2.6

1. Don't tear up the letter, I need it. 2. Turn off the light before you [go to] sleep. 3. He doesn't like me and he's lying. 4. I didn't see my friends in the library and went back home. 5. I fed the child and waited until it fell asleep. 6. Help us finish this job faster. 7. We wanted to invite you but didn't have your phone number. 8. I saw you that day at your brother's home but didn't see you again after that. 9. I put/left the key right there so that Ali would find it more easily. 10. It could be the neighbor's; don't open the package.

Unit 3

Exercise 3.1

1. مناسبی (را)
2. If it is '*the* snow,' then *rā* is necessary, and if it is 'snow shovelling' in general, then you had better use no *rā* at all.
3. Both '*rā*'s are necessary.
4. دانشجوئی (را)
5. You are not a writer and your professor is not a journal, so *rā* is necessary.
6. *Rā* is necessary: intense intellectual involvement with some specific point.
7. چیزهائی (را)
8. Both '*rā*'s are necessary; reason for the first one similar to #6.
9. Both '*rā*'s are necessary; reason for the second one: object of شناختن is usually treated as definite.
10. Both '*rā*'s are necessary; object of نگه داشتن is usually treated as definite, especially when human.

Exercise 3.2

1. After a short while, I picked some appropriate dress [/suit/clothes] and purchased it. 2. Put on some warmer clothes today because you have to shovel the snow. 3. Is it possible for a person to kill another person and forget it? 4. The professor picked a student for that job/for doing that. 5. I wrote my professor a letter and sent him the article. 6. I didn't under-stand some point and asked him/her later. 7. By reading that book I

understood/realized certain things that I didn't know before. 8. I didn't know the meaning of a word and did not understand that sentence. 9. I didn't know the girls but I recognized a boy and went to him. (For the role of *mi-* in the past tense of شناختن see 8.3.3.) 10. The police released the women immediately but kept a man in prison until the next day.

Exercise 3.3

1. a) خمیر دندانها [toothpastes], b) خمیرهای دندان [pastes of tooth].
2. a) توپ بازیها [ball games], b) توپهای بازی [the balls of the game].
3. a) آشپزخانهها [kitchens], b) آشپزهای خانه [the cooks of the house].
4. a) دندانپزشکها [dentists], b) دندانهای پزشک [the teeth of the physician].
5. a) شاگرد اوّلها [best pupils (of classes)], b) شاگردهای اوّل [the first students].
6. a) پدر بزرگها [grandfathers], b) پدرهای بزرگ [big fathers].
7. a) سیب زمینیها [potatoes], b) سیبهای زمینی [apples of the ground].
8. a) خواهر برادرها [siblings], b) خواهرهای برادر [sisters of the brother].
9. a) روزنامهها [newspapers], b) روزهای نامه [the days of the letter].
10. a) دکتر بازیها [doctor games], b) دکترهای بازی [doctors of the game].

Exercise 3.4

۱. نیم ساعتی. ۲. – ۳. سفری. ۴. – ۵. توضیحی. ۶. گریهای. ۷. – ۸ چند دانشجوئی، صحبتی. ۹. چند کتابی. ۱۰. –.

Exercise 3.5

1. It was a beautiful sunset and we watched the sunset at the beach/seashore for about half an hour.
2. Don't tell anybody else the rubbish that he has said.
3. We must take some trip to that city before it is [too] late.
4. I wish he had given a brief explanation before the test so we knew what he wanted from us.
5. [Mr.] Doctor explained about that drug but I've forgotten his words [/what he said].
6. He shed a few tears and begged us to forgive him.
7. She made it up with her friend and invited him to the party.
8. We see a few students each day in class A talk a little bit.
9. I haven't been to Iran but I've read a few books about this country.
10. A Muslim man was asking an American lady about the address of the nearest library.

Exercise 3.6

۱. یک سه چرخه. ۲. یک دست شش انگشتی [here with -i!]. ۳. یک کتاب دو زبانه. ۴. یک برنامهٔ دو ساعته. ۵. یک کالسکهٔ دو اسبه. ۶. یک خداحافظی ده ثانیهای. ۷. یک اتاق سه تخته. ۸ یک خانهٔ هفت اتاقه. ۹. یک خیابان دو طرفه. ۱۰. یک جشن دو روزه.

Unit 4

Exercise 4.1

1. دیروز پیشنهاد کردم نامه را تمام کند (I suggested yesterday that he [should] finish the letter.)
2. This can have different answers:

   دیروز شاید با دوستش به کتابخانه رفته باشد (/رفته است) (Yesterday he may have gone to the library with his friend.).

   The verb can also be می‌رفت ('maybe he was going') or رفت ('maybe he went') or رفته بود ('maybe he had gone').

3. دیروز سعی کردیم غذای خوشمزه‌تری درست کنیم (Yesterday we tried to cook a more delicious meal.)
4. This has two answers, the first of them with two translations:

   دیروز باید چهار صفحهٔ دیگر از آن کتاب را ترجمه می‌کرد (Yesterday she had to translate/she should have translated four more pages of that book.), or:

   دیروز باید چهار صفحهٔ دیگر از آن کتاب را ترجمه کرده باشد (Yesterday she must have translated four more pages of that book.)

5. دیروز ترجیح دادم در خانه بمانم و درس بخوانم (Yesterday I preferred to stay at home and study.)
6. دیروز دوست داشتم چند ساعت در هوای آزاد راه بروم (Yesterday I wished to walk outside ['in free air'] for a few hours.)
7. Two answers:

   دیروز لازم بود از دکترت دربارهٔ قرصها سؤال کنی (Yesterday you needed/had to ask your doctor about the pills.), or:

   دیروز لازم بود از دکترت دربارهٔ قرصها سؤال می‌کردی (Yesterday you should have asked ...)

8. دیروز قرار بود دوستم را به فرودگاه ببرم (Yesterday I was [supposed] to take my friend to the airport.)

9. ‫دیروز می‌ترسیدم پدرم بگوید که پول دانشگاهم را نخواهد داد‬ (Yesterday I feared that my father would say he wouldn't pay my college fees.)

10. ‫دیروز رئیسم قصد داشت ما را دو ساعت زودتر به خانه بفرستد‬ (Yesterday my boss wanted/intended to send us home two hours earlier.)

Exercise 4.2

1. ‫در هفتهٔ اول ممکن نیست در شهر دیگری باشم‬ (I can't be in another city in the first week.)

2. ‫آیا از تو نخواسته‌اند نامه را فقط بیاوری و خودت نخوانی؟‬ (Haven't they asked you to just bring the letter and not read it?)

3. ‫آیا نمی‌دانید دخترم چطور فارسی یاد گرفته است؟‬ (Don't you know how my daughter has learned Persian?)

4. ‫فکر نمی‌کنم روزِ شنبه از ایران برگردند‬ (I don't think they'll return from Iran on Saturday.)

5. ‫فکر نمی‌کرد من هنوز با زنِ اوّلم زندگی کنم‬ (He didn't think I'd still be living with my first wife.)

6. ‫شک نداشتیم که می‌خواهند فقط دو روز بمانند‬ (We had no doubt that they intended to stay for only two days.)

7. ‫آیا قبول ندارید که کارتان اشتباه بوده است؟‬ (Don't you agree that what you did was wrong?)

8. ‫خیلی سعی نکردیم او را قانع کنیم که خودش را نکشد‬ (We didn't try much to convince him not to kill himself.)

9. ‫تردید ندارم که هنوز در آن شهر است‬ (I have no doubt that he is still in that city.)

10. ‫پدرش اوّل اجازه نمی‌داد آن دوستش را ببیند‬ (Her father wouldn't allow her at first to see that friend of hers.)

Exercise 4.3

1. ‫نداشته باشد‬ (No, and I hope she will never have one.)

2. ‫بخورم‬ (No, but I'm supposed to eat with Mina.) – Here ‫بخوریم‬ (pl.) is also possible.

3. ‫می‌خوانم/خواهم خواند‬ (Not yet, but I'll read it next week.)

4. ‫ببینم‬ (Not yet, but I plan to see him tomorrow.)

5. ‫حرف می‌زدم‬ (Not today, but I was talking to him yesterday.)

6. ‫بخرد‬ (No, but perhaps Mina buys it.)

7. است (No, he's certainly home today.)

8. بروم (Not always; in the morning I must take another bus.)

9. Two answers: بفهمد (No, but I'm afraid that my mother will find out.),
or فهمیده باشد (...may have found out.).

10. یاد بگیرد (No, but I must encourage him to learn.)

Exercise 4.4

۱. آمده باشد ۲. می‌آمد ۳. تمام کنی ۴. تمام کرده باشی ۵. تمام می‌کردی ۶. تمام
می‌کردی ۷. شنا کنید ۸ شنا می‌کردیم ۹. شنا کرده باشد ۱۰. صبر کنی ۱۱. صبر
می‌کردی ۱۲. صبر می‌کردی ۱۳. صبر کرده باشی ۱۴. فهمیده باشید ۱۵. می‌فهمیدی.

Exercise 4.5

1. He is smart enough to find a good wife. 2. The weather is cold enough
for you to wear a coat [/an overcoat]. 3. They are close enough to hear
what we are saying. 4. I am hungry enough to eat. 5. You are stupid enough
to repeat this mistake again. 6. She is so weak that she cannot walk [/'weak
enough not to be able to walk']. 7. The child is tired enough to sleep.
8. I have enough money to buy my daughter a car. 9. He talked enough
for us to understand what he meant. 10. I like this house enough not to
sell it. 11. She loves her child enough to buy him new clothes. 12. He is
selfish enough to believe that.

Exercise 4.6

1. بیش از آن زرنگ است که زنِ خوبی پیدا نکند. (He is too smart not to
find a good wife.)

2. هوا بیش از آن سرد است که پالتو نپوشی. (The weather is too cold for
you not to wear a coat [/an overcoat].)

3. بیش از آن نزدیکند که حرفهای ما را نشنوند. (They are too close to not
hear what we are saying.)

4. بیش از آن گرسنه‌ام که غذا نخورم. (I am too hungry not to eat.)

5. بیش از آن احمقی که این اشتباه را باز هم تکرار نکنی. (You are too stupid
to not repeat this mistake again.)

6. بیش از آن ضعیف است که بتواند راه برود. (She is too weak to be able
to walk.)

7. بچّه بیش از آن خسته است که نخوابد. (The child is too tired not to sleep.)

8. من بیش از آن پول دارم که برای دخترم یک ماشین نخرم. (I have too much money to not buy my daughter a car.)

9. بیش از آن حرف زد که منظورش را نفهمیم. (He talked too much for us to not understand what he meant.)

10. بیش از آن این خانه را دوست دارم که آن را بفروشم. (I like this house too much to sell it.)

11. بیش از آن بچه‌اش را دوست دارد که برایش لباس نو نخرد. (She loves her child too much to not buy him new clothes.)

12. بیش از آن خودخواه است که آن را باور نکند. (He is too selfish not to believe that.)

Unit 5

Exercise 5.1

1. فردا بر می‌گردد، مگر اینکه مادرش اجازه ندهد (He'll come back tomorrow, unless his mother doesn't let him.)

2. مادر بزرگ گفت به تو نخواهم گفت، مگر اینکه بگذاری تو را ببوسم (Grandmother said, 'I won't tell you unless you let me kiss you.')

3. او انتخاب می‌شود، مگر اینکه مردم عقل داشته باشند (He will be elected, unless people have good judgment.)

4. این غذا را نمی‌خورم، مگر اینکه خیلی گرسنه باشم (I won't eat this food unless I'm very hungry.)

5. برای او کار نمی‌کنم، مگر اینکه خودش بخواهد (I won't work for him unless he himself asks [me to].)

6. امروز در رستوران غذا می‌خورم، مگر اینکه شوهرم آشپزی کرده باشد (Today I'll eat in the restaurant, unless my husband has cooked.)

7. تو را دوست نخواهد داشت، مگر اینکه هرچیزی که می‌گوید قبول کنی (She wouldn't like you, unless you agree with whatever she says.)

8. در آن خانه زندگی نخواهیم کرد، مگر اینکه مجبور باشیم (We won't live in that house unless we have to.)

9. دیگر با او حرف نخواهم زد، مگر اینکه از من عذرخواهی کند (I won't talk with her anymore unless she apologizes.)

10. به تو احترام خواهند گذاشت، مگر اینکه بدانند که شغلت چیست (They will respect you, unless they know what your job is.)

Exercise 5.2

1. I trust you; otherwise I wouldn't have told you this. 2. My kids are small; otherwise I would have been able to work. 3. He didn't know yesterday; otherwise he wouldn't have laughed so much. 4. You must leave the window open; otherwise the room becomes too warm. 5. You must eat more fruits and vegetables; otherwise your condition won't improve. 6. Iranians are lazy people; otherwise they wouldn't have had so many poets. 7. I want to go to Iran; otherwise I wouldn't have learned Persian. 8. Read that interview; otherwise you won't know him well. 9. He has lied to us; otherwise he would have come himself. 10. People like him; otherwise they wouldn't have voted for him.

Exercise 5.3

1. اگر به تو اعتماد نداشتم، این را به تو نمی‌گفتم. (If I hadn't trusted you, I wouldn't have told you this.)

2. اگر بچّه‌هایم کوچک نبودند، می‌توانستم کار کنم. (If my kids hadn't been small, I would have been able to work.)

3. اگر دیروز خبر داشت، آنقدر نمی‌خندید. (If he had known yesterday, he wouldn't have laughed so much.)

4. اگر پنجره را باز نگذاری، اتاق خیلی گرم می‌شود. (If you don't leave the window open, the room becomes too warm.)

5. اگر میوه و سبزی بیشتر نخوری، حالت بهتر نمی‌شود. (If you don't eat more fruits and vegetables, your condition won't improve.)

6. اگر ایرانیها آدمهای تنبلی نبودند، اینقدر شاعر نداشتند. (If Iranians had not been lazy people, they wouldn't have had so many poets.)

7. اگر نمی‌خواستم به ایران بروم، فارسی یاد نمی‌گرفتم. (If I hadn't wanted to go to Iran, I wouldn't have learned Persian.)

8. اگر آن مصاحبه را نخوانی، او را خوب نخواهی شناخت. (If you don't read that interview, you won't know him well.)

9. اگر به ما دروغ نگفته بود، خودش هم می‌آمد. (If he hadn't lied to us, he would have come himself.)

10. اگر مردم او را دوست نداشتند، به او رأی نمی‌دادند. (If people hadn't liked him, they wouldn't have voted for him.)

Exercise 5.4

1. اگر (I'll say/I'll tell you if you have time.)
2. وگرنه (My car was broken down; otherwise I would have come.)
3. انگار (He was very angry; it looked like he had found out.)
4. مگر اینکه (I will see him too, unless he doesn't come at all.)
5. فقط (I wanted to say; only, I didn't dare.)
6. اگر (If he didn't know, why did he say he did?)
7. Two answers:

   فقط (I too said the same thing as you; only I didn't insult.), or:

   با این تفاوت که (... with the difference that I didn't insult.)
8. فقط (I'll come today also; only, a little later.)
9. وگرنه (I have to help him; otherwise, he won't finish.)
10. انگار (You probably didn't know that she had married?)

Exercise 5.5

1. نخوانده‌ای (If you haven't read that book, you had better not go to class today.)
2. نخواهد فهمید (I hope she calls him; otherwise her brother would never know.)
3. نکند (I can smoke in the yard, unless you don't mind [/unless it makes no difference to you].)
4. کنید (This doesn't look like a party at all, unless you make the music louder.)
5. نمی‌خواست (If she didn't want to buy the book, she should have borrowed it from a [/the] public library.)
6. فکر می‌کردم (If I hadn't seen you, I would have thought something bad had happened.)
7. می‌دانستید (If the house had caught fire, would you have known how to put out the fire?)
8. در نظر دارید (If you intend/plan to marry her, do it in this same year.)
9. اصرار کند (I'll not marry him unless he really insists.)
10. بگیرید (If you divorce tomorrow, won't the child be deprived of having a mother or father?)

Exercise 5.6

۱. اگر اینقدر از من بدت می‌آید، دیگر به من زنگ نزن.

۲. آن نامه را نخواهم نوشت، مگر اینکه التماس کند.

۳. من جرئت نمی‌کنم در این اتاق بخوابم، مگر اینکه شما موفق شوید موش
را پیدا کنید (/...مگر اینکه موفق به پیدا کردنِ موش بشوید).

۴. اگر این آب را قبلاً نجوشانده‌اند، نباید آن را بنوشند.

۵. او آدم خوبی است، وگرنه پولتان را به شما نمی‌داد.

۶. آیا این بد است اگر رنگِ یک چشم با رنگِ چشم دیگر فرق (/تفاوت)
داشته باشد؟

۷. پدر و مادر من خیلی فرق نمی‌کنند (/ندارند)، فقط جوانترند.

۸. اگر زبان را نمی‌دانستی چطور به آنها گفتی چه می‌خواهی؟

۹. اگر نمی‌خواهی همه بفهمند، به او چیزی دربارهٔ آن نگو.

۱۰. به نظر می‌رسد دارند او را تشویق می‌کنند که به ایران برگردد.

Unit 6

Exercise 6.1

1. برگرداند (I didn't want to return, but he made me return against my
will.)

2. خوراند (She fed the child with the same food that she was eating.)

3. ترساند (I'm not usually scared of dogs, but this dog scared me a lot.)

4. خواباند (Before she went to bed herself, she put all the children to bed.)

5. رساندند (They arrived very late, and they finally delivered that letter
to me.)

6. بدواند (This dog must run a lot in order to make you also run a little.)

7. بپوشان (Put on something warm, and also cover yourself well at night.)

8. نشاند (My father sat down and sat my little brother on his knee.)

9. گذراندیم (The first week was very hard, but we had it easier the second
week [/spent the second week more comfortably].)

10. می‌خنداند (He laughed a lot and made everybody laugh.)

Exercise 6.2

1. Yesterday he was reading a book [/books]. (*-ānd*, not causative)
2. Tomorrow she will sing a song in that program. (*-ānad*, not causative)
3. Why did he lay the child on the table? (*-ānd*, causative)
4. He may scare everybody with his loud voice. (*-ānad*, causative)
5. Did she stay longer than 5 hours? (*-ānd*, not causative)
6. He drove very fast in order to arrive early. (*-ānd*, not causative)
7. Should she be the teacher, she will make the students understand the lesson well. (*-ānad*, causative)
8. He says he will be able to, but he can't. (*-ānad*, not causative)
9. I'm glad that he came and delivered the message to you. (*-ānd*, causative)
10. Did my words really scare you? (*-ānd*, causative)

Exercise 6.3

1. بشقاب را برداشتم و به آشپزخانه بردم (I picked up the plate and took it to the kitchen.)

2. کتاب را باز کردم و تا صفحهٔ صد و هفده خواندم (I opened the book and read as far as p. 117.)

3. آن خانم کیست که آنجا نشسته (است) و هیچ نمی‌گوید؟ (Who is that lady who is sitting there and says nothing?)

4. پدر و مادرش به مدرسه رفته‌اند و با معلم صحبت کرده‌اند (Her parents have gone to school and have talked to the teacher.)

5. دیگر او را هرگز نخواهیم دید و با او حرف نخواهیم زد (We will no more see him nor talk to him.)

6. آن ماشین را بفروشید و ماشین بهتری بخرید (Sell that car and buy a better one.)

7. می‌خواهد زبان فارسی را یاد بگیرد و به ایران سفر کند (He wants to learn Persian and travel to Iran.)

8. او هرگز به مدرسه نرفته (است) و حتّی نمی‌تواند اسمش را بنویسد (He has never gone to school and can't even write his own name.)

9. قبلاً به خانهٔ ما آمده بود و با برادرم حرف زده بود (She had previously come to our house and talked to my brother.)

10. باید آب را بجوشانید و چای درست کنید (You must boil the water and make tea.)

Exercise 6.4

1. They got out of the car and went to the hospital. 2. You shouldn't sit in front of the TV without having washed the dishes. 3. She had lost her cat a number of times and found it again. 4. He has finished his food but has not slept yet. 5. In the past days I have met him several times and gone to the movies with him. 6. We passed a few streets and reached that large building. 7. Our car broke down before reaching [/not having yet reached] Tehran. 8. This apple is not quite ripe; give [me] another apple. 9. I got in the taxi and returned home. 10. That bird finally flew off the branch and [flew] away from us.

Exercise 6.5

In numbers 1 (پریده), 9 (شده) and 10 (گذشته) 6 ,(دیده) 5 ,(کرده) 3 ,(شده).

Unit 7

Exercise 7.1

1. گربه‌ها دلشان برايِ (/به حالِ) موشها نمی‌سوزد (Cats don't feel pity for mice.)

2. اگر شب قهوه بخوری دیر خوابت می‌برد (You'll sleep late if you drink coffee at night.)

3. اگر تاکسی نگیریم دیرمان می‌شود (We'll be late if we don't take a taxi.)

4. آیا شما دلتان برای دانشگاه قبلی‌تان تنگ می‌شود (/شده است)؟ (Do you miss your previous university?) – The version with شده است could be preferable in this case, treating the verb as a 'state verb' (see Unit 8).

5. چرا تو اینقدر از غذای ایرانی بدت می‌آید؟ (Why do you hate Persian cuisine so much?)

6. هر وقت شراب می‌خورم گرمم می‌شود (Whenever I drink wine, I feel warm.)

7. چراغ را خاموش کن من خوابم می‌آید (Turn off the light, I want to sleep (/I feel sleepy).)

8. آدم دلش به حالِ (/برايِ) این بچّه‌های گرسنه می‌سوزد (One feels pity for these hungry children.)

9. وقتیکه لباسش را دیدیم ما همه خنده‌مان گرفت (When we saw her dress, we all had to laugh.)

10. اگر هزار بار این فیلم را ببینم باز هم گریه‌ام می‌گیرد (I'll cry again if I see this film a thousand times.)

Exercise 7.2

1. You [= one] can't drink wine in Iran, can you? 2. You [= one] can't talk to a lady in this way. 3. One must write another letter to the university. 4. You [= one] cannot make [so] much noise here. 5. Until last year one could go there without a visa. 6. You [= one] cannot see this film and not laugh. 7. You [= one] shouldn't send the child each year to a new school. 8. I wish one could become young again. 9. In this country you [= one] can marry a ten-year-old girl. 10. Can one like a frog as much as a cat?

Exercise 7.3

1. در ایران مردم نمی‌توانند شراب بخورند، مگر نه؟ (People cannot drink wine in Iran, can they?)

2. تو نمی‌توانی با یک خانم اینطور حرف بزنی (You can't talk to a lady in this way.)

3. باید نامهٔ دیگری برای دانشگاه بنویسیم (We must write another letter to the university.)

4. اینجا نمی‌شود زیاد سروصدا کنید (You cannot make [so] much noise here.)

5. تا پارسال می‌شد (/می‌توانستی) بدونِ ویزا به آنجا بروی (Until last year you could go there without a visa.)

6. آدم نمی‌تواند این فیلم را ببیند و نخندد (One [/you] cannot see this film and not laugh.)

7. نباید بچّه را هر سال به یک مدرسهٔ جدید بفرستیم (We shouldn't send the child each year to a new school.)

8. کاش می‌شد دوباره جوان شوم (I wish I could become young again.)

9. در این کشور مردها می‌توانند با یک دخترِ دَه ساله ازدواج کنند (In this country men can marry a ten-year-old girl.)

10. آیا می‌شود آدم (/آیا آدم می‌تواند) یک قورباغه را به اندازهٔ یک گربه دوست داشته باشد؟ (Can one like a frog as much as a cat?)

Exercise 7.4

1. (نمی‌شود دید) One cannot see from here.

2. (باید...تحقیق کرد) One must first look into their family.

3. (باید...یاد گرفت) Does one [certainly] have to learn this language?

4. (نباید...بود) One shouldn't feel too worried about her new job.

5. (باید دید) It's probably not necessary to see her husband, but one should certainly see her herself.

6. (می‌توان...پرسید) We can ask him himself why he had been following us.

7. (نباید...دست زد) The police have told our neighbor that one should not touch anything.

8. (می‌توان...داشت) Doctor, I must know whether there is (/one can have) hope or not.

9. (*No impersonal structure.*) Couldn't you tell me the truth from the beginning?

10. (بتوان...فهمید) I wish one could understand one day the meaning of these words!

11. (باید...می‌سوخت) The city of Chicago had to burn once in fire in order to be rebuilt.

12. (می‌شد...سوزاند) + (باید دانست) One must know that in the past one could burn scientists in Europe as heretics.

Exercise 7.5

All of them except 2, 6 and 9. By the way, 4 is impersonal only if you read برگرداند as past stem (*bar-gardānd*) and not as subjunctive (*bar-gardānad*).

Unit 8

Exercise 8.1

1. بنشیند (He was standing here for an hour, but now he has gone to sit on that bench.)

2. نشسته (است) (Who's the girl sitting beside you in this photo?)

3. در آغوش گرفت (The mother held the baby in her arms and tried to calm him down.)

4. دراز کشید (He was very tired and immediately lay on the bed.)

5. چمباتمه زده‌ای (Why are you squatting there and doing nothing?)

6. ایستاده (است) (A tall man is standing in the first row and I can't see the singer well.)

7. تکیه کرده‌ای/تکیه کرده بودی (Your shirt has become dirty because you are/you were leaning against that wall.)

8. خیره شده (است) (I'm afraid of this woman who is staring at us.)

9. می‌نشیند (Do you know that boy who is about to sit beside Parviz?)

10. می‌خوابد (Don't make noise, the child/baby must sleep/is about to fall asleep.)

Exercise 8.2

1. در بیاوری (col.)/درآوری (form.) (In Iran when you enter a house/home you must take off your shoes.)
2. چشمش برداشت (He closed the book and took off his glasses.)
3. نمی‌زنی/نمی‌گذاری (If you don't see well, why don't you put on your glasses?)
4. در بیاور (col.)/درآور (form.) (Please take off your pants/trousers so that the doctor can see your knee.)
5. در می‌آوردم (My socks were soaked and I had to take them off.)
6. تن داری (I like what you are wearing right now.)
7. تن داشتم (Do you know why I was wearing black yesterday?)
8. سرت می‌گذاری (I really like the hats you wear.)
9. بپوشی/پایت کنی/به پا کنی (You can't wear these old shoes at a party.)
10. بپوشند/تنشان کنند/به تن کنند (I don't know why men should decide what women should wear.)

Exercise 8.3

1. می‌خواستیم (Yesterday we were waiting for you and wanted to watch a movie with you.)
2. می‌خواستید (Last week you should have asked Nāser to find you a house.)
3. می‌خواهی (Why do you close your eyes every time that you want to talk to me?)
4. بخواهی/خواستی (I'm taking this for now, but I'll bring it for you whenever you want.)
5. خواستم/می‌خواستم (A number of times I was about to answer him, but I changed my mind/decided not to.)
6. می‌خواست (My ex-husband always wanted to teach me swimming, but he was drowned himself in the lake.)
7. خواست (As soon as the child saw her mother, she wanted to run towards her, but she fell down.)
8. می‌خواستی (You could have been the best singer, if you had really wanted it.)
9. بخواهید (If you ask him to, it's unlikely that he will refuse.)
10. خواست (One can ask someone like him to talk to the president.)

Exercise 8.4

1. توانستم (After waiting for a few weeks I was able to see her yesterday.)
2. می‌توان (Can one tell the differences from afar?)
3. می‌توانید (If you see her you can suggest that she should make her article shorter.)
4. توانستیم (Finally we were able to talk to him last Monday at his home.)
5. می‌توانستند (In old times only the rich could travel in coaches.)
6. می‌توان (Can one hope that that law will be passed?)
7. توانست (Do you know how Edison was able to invent electricity?)
8. می‌توانی (Yes, you can climb the tree, but you'll feel giddy.)
9. می‌تواند/می‌توانست (Who can/could have spilled that milk on the table?)
10. توانسته باشد (It's impossible he could have done this yesterday.)

Exercise 8.5

۱. می‌دانم چرا تو را دوست ندارد./می‌دانم چرا از تو خوشش نمی‌آید.
۲. درس جدیدی بود، ولی من همهٔ کلمه‌ها را بلد بودم/می‌دانستم.
۳. آن وقت بود که دانستم کجا می‌رود.
۴. می‌خواهی حقیقت را بدانی؟
۵. می‌دانم کجا بروم.
۶. می‌دانستم کجا می‌رود.
۷. می‌دانم که هنوز برنگشته است.
۸. نمی‌دانم چند عکس از ما گرفته است.
۹. نمی‌دانم چند عکس بگیرم.
۱۰. می‌دانم که گرفتنِ این عکسها کار سختی بوده است.

Exercise 8.6

1. Do you know how to take a picture?
2. I recognized him at once.
3. I saw his car, and I knew that he was coming back.
4. Let him know/tell him that we are waiting for him.
5. Do you know what has happened?
6. We haven't known how he is for a long time.
7. I don't know who has bought that house.
8. We should let him know that his friend's father has died.
9. It's not good to keep him in ignorance.
10. He showed me the picture, and I recognized his father.

Unit 9

Exercise 9.1

No compound verb in this ٢. No compound verb in this sentence. ١.

sentence. ٣. آرام کردن. ۴. کمک کردن. ۵. پس گرفتن. ۶. سعی کردن.

٧. پس فرستادن. ٨ مریض کردن. ٩. علاقه داشتن. ١٠. اصرار کردن.

Exercise 9.2

1. I stayed one day longer in Isfahan to help my mother. 2. After talking to his new boss he did not know what to do. 3. This new drug has made the child much quieter than before. 4. This is part of the aid furnished ['done'] by the Red Cross to the people. 5. Why do you want to take it back so quickly? 6. I must make some more effort to edit that article. 7. They said it was [already] too late and sent us back. 8. This weather will make her still more sick. 9. All my insistence is because of the affection I have for you. 10. His coming was a result of my insistence.

Exercise 9.3

١. می‌دانید چرا او را شکنجه کرده بودند؟

٢. در آن سه روزی که او را شکنجه می‌کردند، اجازه نداشت بخوابد.

٣. به او فشار آوردند که بگوید کجا بوده است.

۴. موضوعی که بررسی می‌کردند احتیاج به دقت زیادی داشت.

۵. می‌دانم که شما هم به این موضوع علاقه دارید.

۶. او را تحتِ هیچ شرایطی عفو نخواهند کرد.

٧. او یکی از آدمهائی است که من به آنها اعتماد دارم.

٨. در موردِ قرارداد باید بگویم که هنوز (دارند) آن را بررسی می‌کنند.

٩. شاگردان کلاس دوّم را تشویق کردند.

١٠. ما با پیشنهادش موافقت نکردیم.

Exercise 9.4

1. Do you know why they had tortured her? 2. In those three days during which they were torturing her, she was not allowed to sleep. 3. They pressed her to say where she had been. 4. The subject they were studying [/considering] required a lot of care. 5. I know that you too are interested in [/like] this subject. 6. Under no circumstances will they pardon him. 7. He

is one of the people that I trust. 8. Regarding the contract I should say
that they are still reviewing it. 9. Second-graders were applauded/praised.
10. We did not agree with his suggestion.

Exercise 9.5

۱. پروین را نمی‌بینم؛ هنوز دارد آشپزی می‌کند؟

۲. نه، دارد یک داستان برای دخترش می‌خواند.

۳. شما خیلی آشپزی را دوست دارید، ولی همیشه چیزی را که پخته‌اید
نمی‌خورید.

۴. اگر می‌خواهید تاریخ معاصر ایران را بخوانید (/در رشتهٔ تاریخ معاصر ایران
درس بخوانید)، باید به دانشگاه دیگری بروید.

۵. می‌دانم که به دانشگاه می‌رود، ولی نمی‌دانم چه می‌خواند.

۶. اگر بهتر درس خوانده بودی (/می‌خواندی) می‌توانستی نمره‌های بهتری
بگیری.

۷. آدم نمی‌تواند غذای ایرانی بخورد و عاشقش نشود.

Or: نمی‌توان غذای ایرانی خورد و عاشقش نشد.

۸ ایرانیها معمولاً با قاشق و چنگال غذا می‌خورند.

۹. از کارد در آشپزخانه یا برای خوردن بعضی میوه‌ها استفاده می‌شود.

Or: کارد در آشپزخانه یا برای خوردن بعضی میوه‌ها موردِ استفاده قرار می‌گیرد.

۱۰. چطور می‌توانی با این موسیقیِ بلند درس بخوانی؟

Unit 10

Exercise 10.1

1. باربَر کسی است که بار می‌بَرَد. (A porter is someone who carries loads.)

2. راننده کسی است که می‌راند. (A driver is someone who drives.)

3. سنگتراش کسی است که سنگ می‌تراشد (A stone carver is someone who
carves stones.)

4. نامه‌رسان کسی است که نامه‌ها را می‌رساند (A mailperson is someone who
delivers the mail ['letters'].)

5. فرماندِه کسی است که فرمان می‌دهد (A commander is someone who gives
commands.)

6. ‫گیرنده کسی (/چیزی) است که می‌گیرد‬ (A receiver is someone who [/something that] receives.)

7. ‫فرستنده کسی (/چیزی) است که می‌فرستد‬ (A sender [/transmitter] is someone who [/something that] sends [/transmits].)

8. ‫بازنده کسی است که می‌بازد‬ (A loser is someone who loses.)

9. ‫سیاه‌پوش کسی است که سیاه می‌پوشد‬ (A black-clad person is someone who is wearing black.)

10. ‫ماهیگیر کسی است که ماهی می‌گیرد‬ (A fisherman is someone who fishes.)

Exercise 10.2

‫۱. دروغگو (دروغ گفتن)، آینده (آمدن)‬

‫۲. رأی‌گیری (رأی گرفتن)، شمارش (شمردن)‬

‫۳. سرباز (سر باختن)، شورش/شورشی (شوریدن)‬

‫۴. راننده (راندن)، کارگردان (کار [را] گرداندن)‬

‫۵. بادآورده (باد آوردن = با باد آورده شدن)‬

‫۶. دستگیری (دست [را] گرفتن)، خبرساز (خبر ساختن)‬

‫۷. سخنران (سخن راندن)‬

‫۸ مشکل‌آفرین (مشکل آفریدن)‬

‫۹. خونخوار (خون خوردن)‬

‫۱۰. کتابخوان (کتاب خواندن)، کتابفروش (کتاب فروختن)‬

Exercise 10.3

1. ‫بچهٔ همسایه در حالیکه گریه می‌کرد به خانه‌شان رفت‬ (The neighbor's child went to their house while he was crying.) Here ‫می‌گریست‬ (instead of ‫گریه می‌کرد‬) is possible, but sounds literary. Also note the position of ‫درحالیکه‬ which we do not place at the beginning of the sentence to avoid a possible confusion about the subject of ‫رفت‬.

2. ‫در حالیکه اشک می‌ریخت از آنجا دور شد و هنوز فریادِ زنان را می‌شنید‬ (He went away from there in tears and he still heard the screams of the women.)

3. ‫در حالیکه فریاد می‌زدند وارد خانه شدند و به دنبالِ مردهای خانه گشتند‬ (They entered the house while they were shouting and searched for the menfolk in the house.)

4. (He در حالیکه می‌لنگید خودش را به من رساند و از حال مادرم پرسید.
approached limping and asked about my mother's well-being.)

5. بچه‌ها در حالیکه شادی می‌کردند به هدایا حمله کردند. (The children attacked
the presents with good cheer.)

6. (We went در حالیکه گردش می‌کردیم تا کنارِ آن دریاچهٔ کوچک رفتیم.
roaming as far as that small lake.)

7. (A few چند نفر نزدیک شدند و در حالیکه تبریک می‌گفتند او را بوسیدند.
people approached and kissed her while congratulating her.)

8. در حالیکه شنا می‌کرد خودش را به قایق نزدیک کرد (Swimming, he came
close to the boat.)

9. (Smiling, در حالیکه لبخند می‌زد گفت: ʼدر عفو لذتی است که در انتقام نیست.ʻ
she said, 'There's a satisfaction in forgiving which is not there in revenge.')

10. در حالیکه می‌دویدم تا خانهٔ عمویم رفتم و خبر را گفتم (Running, I went
to my uncle's home and told the news.)

Exercise 10.4

1. ناامید (Your bag will certainly be found; don't lose hope ['don't be very hopeless'].)

2. استادانه (She is still very young, but she plays the piano very masterfully.)

3. شجاعانه (With these daring words she showed that she was not afraid of anyone.)

4. محترم (How can a respectable man say such an ugly thing?)

5. شجاع (This brave dog did not let that man kidnap my daughter.)

6. احمقانهٔ (I'm ashamed of [/embarrassed by] my own foolish acts.)

7. محترمانه (I got angry because he did not talk to me respectfully.)

8. استاد (He is a master [/expert] in his own field [/work] and is very famous in this city.)

9. ناامیدانه (I guessed he must not be Naser, but still I asked his name hopelessly.)

10. احمق (He may not know everything, but he's not stupid.)

Exercise 10.5

1. Endless. 2. Anti-American. 3. Incorrect. 4. Without an answer; responseless. 5. Having no bath. 6. Thoughtless. 7. Unnecessary. 8. Joyful; full of pleasure. 9. Unkind. 10. Incapable; powerless.

Exercise 10.6

1. بیکار (One who has no job is jobless [/unemployed].)
2. پرخطر (A job that involves a lot of dangers is very dangerous.)
3. پر دردِ سر (Something ['a work'] that has a lot of trouble is troublesome.)
4. کم غلط (A book that does not have many mistakes is a book with few mistakes.)
5. بی‌نتیجه (Something ['a work'] that has no result [/bears no fruit] is pointless/futile.)
6. کم‌سواد (Someone who is not literate enough is only barely literate.)
7. پرکار (Someone who works a lot is hardworking.)
8. بیموقع (Something ['a work'] that is not timely is untimely.)
9. پرحرف (A person who talks a lot is talkative.)
10. کم‌عقل (One who does not have much wisdom is unintelligent.)

Unit 11

Exercise 11.1

1. چه (We shall ultimately see her, whether at her own home in Tehran or in Isfahan.)
2. چه بسا (I used to think he had said this, but I could be wrong.)
3. چه (It was only a short stroll [we had], but you can't imagine how good the weather was!)
4. چه رسد به (This zoo doesn't even have a bear, let alone an elephant.)
5. هرچه (We have to go back home for dinner as soon as possible.)
6. چه بسیار (Don't hurry now; you will have plenty of time for this in Iran.)
7. هرچه (I don't know further [than this] and told you whatever I knew.)
8. چه رسد به اینکه (I don't want to hear his name again, let alone borrow a book from him.)
9. چه (I may not have studied well, but that's none of your business.)
10. هرچه (All these years I have bought her whatever she [has] wanted.)

Exercise 11.2

۱. براحتی. ۲. سریعاً. ۳. سریعاً. ۴. کارَت. ۵. سریع. ۵. وحشی. ۶. وحشیانه‌ای. ۷. نسبتاً.
۸. آرام. ۹. بد. ۱۰. دوستانه.

Exercise 11.3

۱. کمی. ۲. کم. ۳. کمتر. ۴. زیادی. ۵. بیشترِ. ۶. کمتر. ۷. بیشتر. ۸. زیاد. ۹. زیادی.
۱۰. زیادی.

Exercise 11.4

۱. پدرم خیلی بهتر شطرنج بازی می‌کند تا من.

۲. درس دوّم را خیلی زودتر تمام کردیم تا درس اوّل را.

۳. خربزه‌های ایران خیلی بزرگتر و شیرینتر بودند تا خربزه‌های آمریکا.

۴. در مدارس ایران بیشتر به ریاضیات توجه می‌کنند تا در مدارس آمریکا.

۵. او خیلی سریعتر کار می‌کند تا من.

۶. تو بیشتر در خانه می‌مانی تا خواهرت.

۷. شما این مقاله را دقیقتر ترجمه کرده‌اید تا او.

۸. این چیزها را بچّه‌ها بهتر می‌فهمند تا آدم‌بزرگها.

۹. ما خانه‌مان را زودتر خریدیم تا شما.

۱۰. درس تاریخ جالبتر است تا فلسفه.

Exercise 11.5

1. Look, she laughs exactly like her mother! 2. The circumstances of the
country are as bad as before. 3. The speaker referred to the magnitude of
the country's problems. 4. You [/One] can find few poets as great as
Hāfez. 5. I don't like traditional music as much as you do. 6. You must
spend as much time on this child of yours as you did on the previous
one. 7. Had you seen hair as red as this before now? 8. Was she crazy
to marry such a bad man? 9. My days have become as dark as your nights.
10. I'm not as pessimistic as you, but not very optimistic either.

Exercise 11.6

۱. این سگ به بزرگیِ یک اسب است. (/...به اندازهٔ یک اسب بزرگ است.)

۲. این طوطی درست مثلِ آدمها حرف می‌زند.

۳. باور کن، من هم به اندازهٔ تو خسته‌ام (/...به خستگیِ تو هستم).

۴. آیا روزهای تابستان به درازیِ شبهای زمستان هستند؟ (/...به

اندازهٔ...درازند؟)

۵. در این لباس شبیهِ یک گل است.

۶. اگر مثلِ تو تُند (/اگر به تُندیِ تو) بدَوَم می‌میرم.

۷. پیاز تقریباً به اندازهٔ سیر مفید است (/...به مفیدیِ سیر است).

۸. آیا سیر با هر نام دیگری همینقدر بدبو خواهد بود؟ (/...همین اندازه بوی
بد خواهد داشت؟)

۹. این تمرین به اندازهٔ تمرینِ قبلی خسته کننده بود.

۱۰. امیدوارم کارهایش (/رفتارش) به اندازهٔ حرفهایش احمقانه نباشد.

Unit 12

Exercise 12.1

1. ...نه...نه (Why are you asking me about his address? I neither know
   him nor have I ever been to his home.)
2. نه تنها...بلکه (I'm not only afraid of my father, but also of my son.)
3. ...هم...هم (He can very easily both insult and apologize.)
4. ...خواه...خواه or ...چه...چه (I won't buy that house, whether I have
   money or not.)
5. ...یا...یا (The people who made the revolution shouted on the streets:
   '[Either] death or freedom!')
6. ...نه...نه (One of the slogans of the Iranian revolution: 'Neither East[ern],
   nor West[ern] – the Islamic Republic!')
7. ...چه...چه or ...خواه...خواه (She will eventually hear the news,
   whether she is here or in Iran.)
8. نه تنها...بلکه (Our cat eats not only mice but also small birds.)
9. نه تنها...هم (In that trip we not only went to Isfahan, but to Shiraz
   and Mashhad as well.)
10. ...یا...یا (I don't have much appetite tonight; I'll either have some
    fruit or a glass of milk.)

Exercise 12.2

1. We heard that she was sick, therefore (/for this reason) we went to her
house. 2. They had certainly heard that the professor was sick, because
they did not come to class at all. 3. Since I had heard that you were sick,
I called your home several times. 4. I went in a hurry in order to talk to
Nāser before the session started. 5. He returned soon, because his father
had said he was not to return late. 6. She returned soon (/early/fast) to
tell her father that she had found a good job. 7. He was not able to finish
his work quickly; as a result, that night he slept in the office. 8. Since he

did not want to wake up his wife, he left home without breakfast. 9. Not
even once had he visited a museum, because he had no money. 10. She
went to the US with the goal of studying there, but later she became an
actress.

Exercise 12.3

a) 2, 3, 5, 8, 9; b) 2, 5, 9; c) 1, 7.

Exercise 12.4

1. می‌داند که من بیمارم، بااینهمه از من برای رانندگی کمک خواسته است. (He
knows that I'm sick; nevertheless, he has asked me to help as driver.)

2. به او کمک خواهم کرد، اگرچه او دیروز به من کمک نکرد. (I'll help her,
although she didn't help me yesterday.)

3. هوا خیلی سرد است، اگرچه هنوز پائیز شروع نشده است. (The weather is
very cold, although autumn has not started yet.)

4. نمی‌دانست چطور به آنجا برود، چون ماشینش را دزدیده بودند. (She did
not know how to go there, because her car had been stolen ['they had
stolen her car'].)

5. از همه زودتر آمد، اگرچه راهش از همه دورتر بود. (He came earlier than
everybody else, although his way was farther than all of theirs.)

6. خانه‌اش خیلی از آنجا دور بود، بااینهمه زودتر از همه رسید. (Her house
was very far from there; nevertheless, she arrived earlier than everybody else.)

7. خیلی اصرار کرد، اگرچه می‌دانست نتیجه‌ای ندارد. (He insisted a lot,
although he knew that it was useless.)

8. می‌دانست نتیجه‌ای ندارد، بااینهمه خیلی اصرار کرد. (He knew that it was
useless; nevertheless, he insisted a lot.)

9. زیاد اصرار نکرد، چون می‌دانست نتیجه‌ای ندارد. (He did not insist much,
because he knew that it was useless.)

10. می‌دانم او بهترین مرد برای من نیست، اگرچه خیلی به من علاقه دارد. (I
know that he's not the best man for me, although he likes me a lot.)

Exercise 12.5

۱. همچنان. ۲. چندان. ۳. همچنین. ۴. چنان. ۵. چندان. ۶. چند. ۷. همچنان. ۸. چنان.
۹. همچنین. ۱۰. همچنان.

Exercise 12.6

١. تازه دو جمله گفته بودم که گفتند وقتم تمام است.

٢. تازه روی صندلی نشسته بودم که برق رفت.

٣. تازه درسش تمام شده بود که کار خوبی پیدا کرد.

۴. تازه پایش خوب شده بود که سرش هم شکست.

۵. تازه حرف من تمام شده بود که سیگاری روشن کرد.

۶. تازه سوارِ هواپیما شده بودیم که گفتند موتورش خراب است.

٧. تازه یک داستان کوتاه نوشته بود که تصمیم گرفت یک رُمان بلند بنویسد.

٨. تازه ماشین را دیده بودم که فریادِ بچهها را شنیدم.

٩. تازه عینکش را پیدا کرده بود که اتوبوس ایستاد.

١٠. هنوز به مدرسه نرسیده بودم که پروین را دیدم.

Exercise 12.7

1. By the time it is our turn, the bank is closed. 2. As soon as it saw the
neighbor's dog, it ran towards it. 3. So long as the neighbor's dog is here,
we can't ['one cannot'] leave the cat alone. 4. Two of the birds came as
far as inside our room. 5. Close the door, so that they don't come in our
room. 6. I won't let him go until he tells his name. (= So long as he doesn't
tell his name, I . . .) 7. I'll keep him here until he tells his name. 8. I turned
on the light so that the room wouldn't be dark. 9. He won't leave here
until you give him his money. (= So long as you don't give him his money,
he won't leave here.) 10. While you're taking care of the check [= paying
for dinner], I'll quickly go use the bathroom.

Unit 13

Exercise 13.1

١. نه، دیگر پدرم زنده نیست.

٢. نه، دیگر غذا نمیخورند. (.Note the omission of *dārand* in neg!)

٣. نه، دخترم دیگر تو را نمیشناسد.

۴. نه، دیگر شطرنج بازی نمیکنم.

۵. نه، دیگر فارسی برایم سخت نیست.

۶. نه، دیگر سرم درد نمیکند.

۷. نه، از پیاز دیگر بدش نمی‌آید.

۸. نه، دیگر نباید منتظر باشیم.

۹. نه، دیگر نمی‌خواهم کتاب بخوانم.

۱۰. نه، دیگر نمی‌تواند فارسی حرف بزند.

Exercise 13.2

1. You haven't yet shown your other house to me. 2. We must slowly prepare to leave. 3. Don't ask him any more. 4. He is not in the office today, come some other day. 5. Let's go finally, waiting is useless. 6. She doesn't know you yet, but she knows me already. 7. Didn't she tell you anything else? 8. If the doctor says he's okay, why then are you crying? 9. Don't you now answer me (any more)? 10. Okay, you had no time to come, why then didn't you call?

Exercise 13.3

1. *d*; 2. *a*; 3. *a*; 4. *e*; 5. *d*; 6. *c* [*form.*] or *d* [*col.*]; 7. *b*; 8. *e*; 9. *d*; 10. *b*.

Exercise 13.4

1. *a*; 2. *a* and *c* [*form.*]; 3. *b* and *c* [*form.*]; 4. *a* and *c* [*form.*]; 5. *a*; 6. *b*; 7. *a*; 8. *b* and *c* [*form.*]; 9. *a* and *c* [*form.*]; 10. *a*.

Exercise 13.5

In 1, 4, 7, 8, 9.

Unit 14

Exercise 14.1

۱. یاد داد. ۲. یاد بدهد. ۳. یاد گرفته باشد. ۴. یاد گرفت. ۵. یاد بگیری. ۶. یاد بدهد. ۷. یاد گرفتن. ۸ یاد گرفت. ۹. یاد می‌گرفتم. ۱۰. یاد نداد.

Exercise 14.2

1. یادت رفته بود که استاد مریض است؟ (Had you forgotten that the professor was sick?)

2. یادت نرود که در خانه اصلاً میوه نداریم. (Don't forget that we have no fruit at all at home.)

3. ‏اگر شماره‌اش یادت رفته است، در دفتر تلفن نگاه کن.‏ (If you have forgotten his number, check the phone book.)

4. ‏تمام چیزهائی را که یادم رفته بود، به یاد آوردم.‏ (I remembered everything that I had forgotten.)

5. ‏برای اینکه یادت نرود، همین الآن توی کیفت بگذار.‏ (To make sure that you don't forget, put it in your bag right now.)

6. ‏اسم همه را گفت بی آنکه حتّی اسم یک نفر یادش رفته باشد.‏ (He said everybody's names without having forgotten even one person's name.)

7. ‏اگر آدرس یادت رفته باشد نمی‌توانیم برویم.‏ (We can't go if you have forgotten the address.)

8. ‏این که زبان مادری‌اش یادش رفته است باورکردنی نیست.‏ (That he has forgotten his mother tongue is unbelievable.)

9. ‏اگر یادش نرود به او جایزه می‌دهم.‏ (I'll give him a prize if he doesn't forget.)

10. ‏ممکن نیست تمام آن حرفها یادش رفته باشد.‏ (It's not possible that he has forgotten all those words.)

Exercise 14.3

1. Today I have three appointments in three different offices.
2. Isfahan lies to the south of Tehran.
3. I've arranged it with my husband that he takes the children to school on Wednesdays.
4. They pardoned a few other prisoners, but he was not pardoned.
5. Wasn't your mother also supposed to accompany you on this trip?
6. After the kids went to bed, complete silence dominated the house.
7. Call Bābak before you make arrangements with Nimā.
8. The next speaker rose from his place and stood behind the podium.
9. You shouldn't give personal information to anyone.
10. Ask your doctor for an appointment for me also.

Exercise 14.4

‏۱. ب. ۲. پ. ۳. ب. ۴. پ. ۵. الف. ۶. ب. ۷. پ. ۸. ب. ۹. پ. ۱۰. ب.‏

Exercise 14.5

1. c; 2. b; 3. d; 4. c; 5. a; 6. b; 7. a; 8. c; 9. d; 10. c.

219

PERSIAN–ENGLISH GLOSSARY

Including all Persian simple verbs

Though basically a glossary of all the words used in this series in examples and exercises, you will also find here all of the Persian simple verbs (and their present stems), whether mentioned in the series or not. To make it easier for you to find these verbs, we have used bold type for them. Causative forms of verbs (all regular) do not usually have separate entries. When two pronunciations are given for the present stem, the first one is the *official* one, needed for the [singular] imperative, and the second one is what you need for present-tense conjugation.

For compound verbs that use *kardan* or *shodan* as their respectively *transitive* and *intransitive* versions, often the *transitive* version with *kardan* is the only one mentioned here. Most of the compound verbs are to be found under the entry for the non-verbal part.

Parts of speech and similar information (like transitive/intransitive) are given only when found necessary. Arabic broken plurals have been given only if common in Persian, and they appear separately on the list, except for the plurals formed by simply adding -*āt*.

A few proper nouns are also included, for the sake of spelling and pronunciation.

The hyphens used before *ezāfe*s [-*e*] should be disregarded in syllabification, but those used to separate different parts of compound words serve at the same time as markers of syllabic divisions.

An asterisk in impersonal compound verbs shows where you should add the pronoun. A tilde indicates the omission of the entry word (or part of a compound).

For the abbreviations used, see the Introduction. The order of letters in the Persian alphabet (from the right) is:

آ ا ب پ ت ث ج چ ح خ د ذ ر ز ژ س ش ص ض ط ظ ع غ ف ق ک
گ ل م ن و ه ی

آ [ā] → اَمَدَن

آب [āb] water

~ [~ sho.dan] [→ شو ~] to melt, turn to water

آبستن [ā.bes.tan] pregnant

آبی [ā.bi] blue

آپارتمان [ā.pār.te.mān] apartment

آتش [ā.tash] fire

زدن ~ [~ za.dan] [→ زن ~] to set on fire

گرفتن ~ [~ ge.ref.tan] [→ گیر ~] to catch fire

بس ~ [~ bas] ceasefire; truce

سوزی ~ [~ -su.zi] fire accident, incineration

آخر [ā.khar] last (adj.); lastly, finally (adv.)

آخرین [ā.kha.rin] last

آدرس [ād.res] address

آدم [ā.dam] man (impersonal), person, human being; Adam

آدم بزرگ [ā.dam bo.zorg] grown-up person

آدمکش [ā.dam-kosh] murderer

آدمی [ā.da.mi] (impersonal; poet.) man, human being

آذر [ā.zar] Azar (girl's name)

آرا [ā.rā] → آراستن

آراء [ā.rā'] pl. of رأی

آراستن [ā.rās.tan] [آرا, ā.rā] to decorate (lit.)

آرام [ā.rām] [→ آرمیدن] calm; quiet; slow

کردن ~ [~ kar.dan] [→ کن ~] to pacify; to soothe, to calm down

آرزو [ā.re.zu] wish

آرزو داشتن ~ [ā.re.zu dāsh.tan] [→ دار ~] to have (the) wish (no mi- in pres. and progressive tenses)

آرزو کردن [ā.re.zu kar.dan] [~ کن ~] to wish

آرکائیک [ār.kā.'ik] archaic

آرمیدن [ā.ra.mi.dan] [→ آرام, ā.rām] to rest (lit.)

آره [ā.re] yes (col.)

آری [ā.ri] yes [stress on á-] (poet.)

آزاد [ā.zād] free; liberated

کردن ~ [~ kar.dan] [→ کن ~] to free; to release from prison

آزادی [ā.zā.di] freedom

آزار [ā.zār] → آزردن

آزردن [ā.zor.dan] [→ آزار, ā.zār] to torment (form.)

آزما [ā.ze.mā] → آزمودن

آزمودن [ā.ze.mu.dan] [→ آزما, ā.ze.mā] to try, to test (form.)

آسا [ā.sā] → آسودن

آسان [ā.sān] easy

آسمان [ā.se.mān] sky

آسمانی [ā.se.mā.ni] from sky; heavenly; holy

آسودن [ā.su.dan] [→ آسا, ā.sā] to rest (lit.)

آش [āsh] varieties of Persian thick soup

آشام [ā.shām] → آشامیدن

آشامیدن [ā.shā.mi.dan] [→ آشام, ā.shām] to drink (form.)

آبِ آشامیدنی [āb-e ā.shā.mi.da.ni] drinking water

آشپز [āsh.paz] cook [پَز paz → پُختن pokh.tan]

آشپزخانه [āsh.paz-khā.ne] kitchen

آشپزی [āsh.pa.zi] cooking

~ کن [→] ~ کردن [~ kar.dan]
to cook (intr.)

آشتی [āsh.ti] reconciliation

[~ dā.dan (bā)] آشتی دادن (با)
[~ ده →] to reconcile (to or
with) (tr.)

[~ kar.dan (bā)] آشتی کردن (با)
[~ کن →] to reconcile (to or
with) (intr.)

آشفتن [ā.shof.tan] [آشوب →, ā.shub]
to make chaotic (form.)

آشنا [ā.she.nā] acquaintance;
acquainted; familiar

[~ sho.dan (bā)] ~ شدن (با)
to become acquainted (with);
to get to know

آشوب [ā.shub] → آشفتن

آغاز [ā.ghāz] [آغازیدن →] beginning

[~ kar.dan] ~ کردن [→ کن ~] to begin

آغازیدن [ā.ghā.zi.dan] [آغاز →, ā.ghāz]
to begin (lit.)

آغوش [ā.ghush] embrace

در آغوش گرفتن [dar ~ ge.ref.tan]
[~ گیر →] to embrace; to hold in
the arms

آفتاب [āf.tāb] sunshine

آفتابی [āf.tā.bi] sunny

آفریدن [ā.fa.ri.dan] [آفرین →, ā.fa.rin]
to create

آفریقا [āf.ri.ghā] Africa (also افریقا,
ef.ri.ghā)

آفرین [ā.fa.rin] [آفریدن →] bravo!
well done!

آقا [ā.ghā] Mr.; gentleman

آلا [ā.lā] → آلودن

آلمان [āl.mān] Germany

آلمانی [āl.mā.ni] German

آلودن [ā.lu.dan] [→ آلا, ā.lā] to pollute,
to dirty

آلوده کردن [ā.lu.de kar.dan] to make
dirty, to pollute [کردن → کن]

آمدن [ā.ma.dan] [→ آ, ā] to come
For آمدن به نظر see under نظر.

آمرز [ā.morz] → آمرزیدن

آمرزیدن [ā.mor.zi.dan] [→ آمرز,
ā.morz] to absolve

آمریکا [ām.ri.kā] America; the United
States (also امریکا, em.ri.kā)

آمریکائی [ām.ri.kā.'i] American (also
امریکائی, em.ri.kā.'i)

آموختن [ā.mukh.tan] [→ آموز, ā.muz]
to learn [sth. from: از]; to teach
[sth. to: به]

آموز [ā.muz] → آموختن

آموزش [ā.mu.zesh] education;
teaching; learning

[~ dā.dan] ~ دادن [→ ده ~] to
educate; to teach

آموزشگاه [ā.mu.zesh.gāh] educational
institute

آموزگار [ā.muz.gār or ā.mu.ze.gār]
teacher of elementary school

آمیختن [ā.mikh.tan] [→ آمیز, ā.miz] to mix

آمیز [ā.miz] → آمیختن

آن [ān] it; that (adj. and pr.)

از آنِ [az ā.n-e] that of; belonging
to (poet.)

آنان [ā.nān] they, those (pr.; form.; for
people only)

آنجا [ān.jā] there

از آنجا که [az ~ ke] since, because

آنقدر/آنقدر [ān.ghadr] so [much]; as
much; to the extent (that)

آنها [ān.hā] they; those (pr.)

آواز [ā.vāz] traditional singing

آور [ā.var] → آوردن

آوردن [ā.var.dan] [→ آور, ā.var]
to bring

آویختن [ā.vikh.tan] [→ آویز, ā.viz]
to hang

آویز [ā.viz] → آویختن

آه [āh] O!; oh (*interj.*); sigh

آهسته [ā.hes.te] slow/slowly; quiet/quietly

آهن [ā.han] iron

آهنگر [ā.han-gar] ironsmith

آهو [ā.hu] gazelle

آینده [ā.yan.de] future; coming,
approaching, next

آینه [ā.ye.ne] mirror (also, more formal:
آئینه / آیینه, ā.'i.ne)

ابر [abr] cloud

ابرو [ab.ru] eyebrow (*pl.* with both -hā
and -ān)

ابری [ab.ri] cloudy

اتاق [o.tāgh] room

اتّفاق [et.te.fāgh] happening; incident;
event (*pl.* اتفاقات, et.te.fā.ghāt)

[~ of.tā.dan] [→ افت ~] افتادن
to happen

اتّفاقاً [et.te.fā.ghan] incidentally, by
chance

اتوبوس [o.to.bus] bus

اثر [a.sar] 1) effect or influence (*pl.*
اثرات, a.sa.rāt); 2) a work of art
or literature (*pl.* آثار, ā.sār);
3) impression; trace; mark
(*pl.* either آثار or اثرات)

اثر گذاشتن (بر/رویِ) [a.sar go.zāsh.tan
(bar/ru.ye)] [گذار ~ →] to affect
or influence; to impress

اثر گرفتن (از) [a.sar ge.ref.tan (az)]
[گیر ~ →] to be affected,
influenced or impressed (by)

اجازه [e.jā.ze] permission; permit
[~ dā.dan] [→ ده ~] دادن to give
permission; to allow

اجبار [ej.bār] obligation
[~ dāsh.tan] [→ دار ~] داشتن
to be obliged or to have an
obligation; to have to

اجباری [ej.bā.ri] obligatory

احترام [eh.te.rām] respect
(به) گذاشتن ~ [~ go.zāsh.tan (be)]
to respect

احتمال [eh.te.māl] likelihood, probability
(*pl.* احتمالات, eh.te.mā.lāt)
[~ dāsh.tan] [→ دار ~] داشتن to
be likely (no *mi-* in pres. and
progressive tenses)

احتیاج [eh.ti.yāj] need (*pl.* احتیاجات,
eh.ti.yā.jāt)
(به) داشتن ~ [~ dāsh.tan (be)]
[→ دار ~] to have need (of),
to need (no *mi-* in pres. and
progressive tenses)

احمد [ah.mad] Ahmad (boy's name)

احمق [ah.magh] stupid (*adj.*); stupid
person (*n.*)

احمقانه [ah.ma.ghā.ne] foolish;
foolishly

اخبار [akh.bār] news (*pl.* of خبر,
kha.bar)

اختراع [ekh.te.rā'] invention (*pl.*
اختراعات, ekh.te.rā.'āt)
[~ kar.dan] to invent کردن ~
[کن → کردن]

اختلاف [ekh.te.lāf] difference;
discrepancy; dispute (*pl.*
اختلافات, ekh.te.lā.fāt)
(با) داشتن ~ [~ dāsh.tan (bā)]
[→ دار ~] to be different (from);
to have a difference (with)

223

اختیار [ekh.ti.yār] choice; control (pl.
اختیارات, ekh.ti.yā.rāt)

در اختیار [dar ~ -e] at the disposal
of; under the control of

اداره [e.dā.re] office (pl. ادارات, e.dā.rāt)

ادامه [e.dā.me] continuation

ادامه دادن (به) [~ dā.dan (be)]
[→ ده ~] to continue (tr.) (often
with به)

ادب [a.dab] manners; politeness

ادبی [a.da.bi] literary

ادبیّات [a.da.biy.yāt] literature

ادّعا [ed.de.'ā] claim (n.)

کردن ~ [~ kar.dan] to claim
[کن → کردن]

ادویه [ad.vi.ye] spice[s] (originally pl.
of دوا, da.vā)

ادیان [ad.yān] pl. of دین

اذهان [az.hān] pl. of ذهن

اراجیف [a.rā.jif] balderdash, baloney;
nonsense (originally pl. of an
obsolete word)

ارباب [ar.bāb] boss, master, feudal
landowner (originally pl. of
رَبّ, rabb, Lord)

ارز [arz] → ارزیدن

ارزان [ar.zān] cheap

ارزش [ar.zesh] worth; value

ارزشمند [ar.zesh.mand] valuable

ارزیدن [ar.zi.dan] [→ ارز, arz] to be
worth; to cost

اروپا [o.ru.pā] Europe

ارومیّه [o.ru.miy.ye] Lake Urmia in
northwestern Iran

از [az] than; from; of

از بَر [az bar] by heart; by memory

~ بودن/داشتن [~ bu.dan/dāsh.tan]
[→ باش/دار ~] to know by heart

~ کردن/شدن [~ kar.dan/sho.dan]
[→ کن/شو ~] to memorize

ازبکستان [oz.ba.kes.tān] Uzbekistan

ازدواج [ez.de.vāj] marriage

~ کردن (با) [~ kar.dan (bā)]
[~ کن ~→] to marry (with;
no direct object)

از نو [az now] anew; again

اساطیر [a.sā.tir] pl. of اسطوره

اسامی [a.sā.mi] pl. of اِسم

اَسب [asb] horse

استاد [os.tād] professor; master of a craft

استادانه [os.tā.dā.ne] masterful;
masterfully

استان [os.tān] province

استحضار [es.teh.zār] knowledge (form.;
polite language)

استخدام [es.tekh.dām] hiring

~ کردن [~ kar.dan] [→ کُن ~] to
employ, to hire

استخر [es.takhr] pool, pond

استخرِ شنا [~ -e she.nā] swimming
pool

استراحت [es.te.rā.hat] rest

~ کردن [~ kar.dan] [→ کُن ~]
to rest (intr.)

استعداد [es.te'.dād] talent

استفاده [es.te.fā.de] use; benefit

~ کردن (از) [~ kar.dan (az)] [→ کن]
to use; to make use of; to employ

استمراری [es.tem.rā.ri] progressive
(gr.); continuous

اسرار [as.rār] pl. of سِرّ [serr]

اسرع [as.ra'] Arabic comparative form
of سریع, sa.ri', fast used mainly
in expressions like

در اسرع وقت [dar as.ra.'e vaght] as
soon as possible

اسطوره [os.tu.re] myth (pl. اساطیر a.sā.tir)

اسلام [es.lām] Islam

اسلامی [es.lā.mi] Islamic

اِسم [esm] name; noun (gr.) (pl. اسامی, a.sā.mi)

اسم مفعول [es.m-e maf.'ul] past participle (gr.)

اشاره کردن (به) [e.shā.re kar.dan (be)] [← کن ~] to point (out/at), to refer (to)

اسناد [as.nād] pl. of سند

اشتباه [esh.te.bāh] mistake (n.); wrong (adj.) (pl. اشتباهات, esh.te.bā.hāt)

کردن ~ [~ kar.dan] [← کُن ~] to make a mistake; to be mistaken

اشتها [esh.te.hā] appetite

اشخاص [ash.khās] persons, people (pl. of شخص)

اشغال [esh.ghāl] occupation (of land, etc.)

اشک [ashk] tears

ریختن ~ [~ rikh.tan] [← ریز ~] to shed tears

اشکال [ash.kāl] pl. of شکل

اصرار [es.rār] insistence; urging

داشتن (در) ~ or ~ کردن (به) [~ kar.dan (be)/dāsh.tan (dar)] [← دار ~/~ کن] to insist or urge

اصفهان [es.fa.hān] Isfahan (city in Iran)

اصلاً [as.lan] (not) at all

اصلاح [es.lāh] correction; improvement; a haircut (pl. اصلاحات, es.lā.hāt = reforms)

اصلاحات [es.lā.hāt] reforms (pl. of اصلاح, es.lāh correction)

اِضافه [e.zā.fe] addition; the connector '-e' (gr.)

اضطراب [ez.te.rāb] anxiety

اطبّاء [a.teb.bā'] pl. of طبیب

اطراف [at.rāf] around; surroundings (pl. of طرف, ta.raf)

اطّلاع [et.te.lā'] information (pl. اطّلاعات, et.te.lā.'āt)

دادن (به) ~ [~ dā.dan (be)] [← ده ~] to inform; to let know

داشتن (از) ~ [~ dāsh.tan (az)] [← دار ~] to have information (about); to know (of)

اطمینان [et.mi.nān] certainty; trust

دادن (به) ~ [~ dā.dan (be)] [← ده ~] to assure; to reassure

داشتن (به) ~ [~ dāsh.tan (be)] [← دار ~] to have trust (in) (no mi- in pres. and progressive tenses)

کردن (به) ~ [~ kar.dan (be)] [← کن ~] to trust

اظهار کردن [ez.hār kar.dan] [← کن ~] to state; to express

اعتراض [e'.te.rāz] protest (pl. اعتراضات, e'.te.rā.zāt)

کردن (به/علیه) ~ [~ kar.dan (be/a.ley.he)] [← کن ~] to protest (against)

اعتقاد [e'.te.ghād] belief (pl. اعتقادات, e'.te.ghā.dāt)

داشتن (به) ~ [~ dāsh.tan (be)] [← دار ~] to believe (in); to be of the opinion (that: که)

اعتماد [e'.te.mād] trust, confidence

داشتن (به) ~ [~ dāsh.tan (be)] [← دار ~] to trust; to have trust (in)

اعتماد کردن (به) ~ [e'.te.mād kar.dan (be)] [← کن ~] to trust

اعداد [a'.dād] pl. of عدد

اعراب [a'.rāb] pl. of عرب

اغذیه [agh.zi.ye] pl. of غذا

اغلاط [agh.lāt] pl. of غلط

اُفتادن → [oft] افت

افتادن [of.tā.dan] [→ اُفت, oft] to fall

افتان و خیزان [oftān-o-khizān] falling and rising; walking with difficulty (pres. participles of افتادن and خاستن)

افراد [af.rād] persons; individuals (pl. of فرد)

افراز ← افراشتن [af.rāz]

افراشتن [af.rāsh.tan] [→ افراز, af.rāz] to hoist

افروختن [af.rukh.tan] [→ افروز, af.ruz] to kindle (lit.)

افروز ← افروختن [af.ruz]

افزا ← افزودن [af.zā]

افزایش [af.zā.yesh] increase

~ دادن [~ dā.dan] [→ دِه ~] to increase (tr.)

~ یافتن/پیدا کردن [~ yāf.tan/pey.dā kar.dan] [→ یاب/کن ~] to increase (intr.)

افزودن [af.zu.dan] [→ افزا, af.zā] to increase (form.)

افسر ← افسردن [af.sor]

افسردن [af.sor.dan] [→ افسر, af.sor] to freeze; to extinguish (lit.); also فسردن

افسرده [af.sor.de] depressed

افشان ← افشاندن [af.shān]

افشاندن [af.shān.dan] [→ افشان, af.shān] to scatter; to sprinkle

افشردن [af.shor.dan] [→ افشر, af.shor] see فشردن

افعال [af.'āl] pl. of فعل

افغانستان [af.ghā.nes.tān] Afghanistan

افغانی [af.ghā.ni] Afghan; Afghani

افکار [af.kār] pl. of فکر

افکن ← افکندن [af.kan]

افکندن [af.kan.dan] [→ افکن, af.kan] to throw (lit.); see also فکندن

اقلًا [a.ghal.lan] at least

اقلیّت [a.ghal.liy.yat] minority

اقوام [agh.vām] pl. of قوم

اکبر [ak.bar] Akbar; boy's name

اگر [a.gar] if (in conditional; not for indirect questions)

اگرچه [a.gar-che] although

اگر نه [a.gar-ná] if not; if not so, otherwise

الّا [él.lā] except; other than [stress on é-]

و الّا [va el.lā] otherwise [stress on -ā]

الآن [al.'ān] now

الاغ [o.lāgh] donkey

البسه [al.ba.se] pl. of لباس (only form.)

التزامی [el.te.zā.mi] subjunctive (gr.)

التماس [el.te.mās] begging earnestly

~ کردن (به) [~ kar.dan (be)] [→ کن ~] to plead with, to beg earnestly

الزام [el.zām] obligation (pl. الزامات, el.zā.māt)

الفبا [a.lef.bā] alphabet

امتحان [em.te.hān] exam, test (pl. امتحانات, em.te.hā.nāt)

~ دادن [~ dā.dan] [→ دِه ~] to take a test

امر [amr] imperative (gr.); order, command (pl. اوامر, a.vā.mer)

امروز [em.ruz] today

امریکا [em.ri.kā] → آمریکا [ām.ri.kā]

آمریکائی [em.ri.kā.'i] → امریکائی [ām.ri.kā.'i]

امکان [em.kān] possibility (pl. امکانات, em.kā.nāt)

~ داشتن [~ dāsh.tan] [→ دار ~] to be possible or likely (no mi- in pres. and progressive tenses)

اموال [am.vāl] pl. of مال

امید [o.mid] hope

به اُمیدِ [be o.mi.d-e] in the hope of
به اُمیدِ آنکه [be o.mi.d-e ān.ke]
hoping (that)

امیدوار [o.mid.vār] hopeful

~ بودن [~ bu.dan] [→ باش ~] to
hope (lit. 'to be hopeful')

انبار [an.bār] → انباشتن

انباشتن [an.bāsh.tan] [انبار, an.bār] to store

انتخاب [en.te.khāb] selection; choice
(pl. انتخابات, en.te.khā.bāt =
elections)

~ کردن [~ kar.dan] [→ کن ~] to
choose, to pick

انتخابات [en.te.khā.bāt] elections (pl. of
انتخاب, en.te.khāb, selecting)

انتظار [en.te.zār] waiting; expectation

~ داشتن [~ dāsh.tan] [→ دار ~] to
expect; to anticipate

انجام [an.jām] [→ انجامیدن] conclusion;
performance

~ دادن [~ dā.dan] [→ ~ ده] to do
(an assignment)

انجامیدن (به) [an.jā.mi.dan (be)]
[انجام, an.jām →] to lead to;
to result in; to end up

اندا [an.dā] → اندودن

انداختن [an.dākh.tan] [انداز →, an.dāz]
to throw

انداز [an.dāz] → انداختن

اندازه [an.dā.ze] size; extent; amount;
scope

به اندازۀ [be ~ -ye] as much as;
to the extent of

بیش از ~ [bish az ~] too much

اندوختن [an.dukh.tan] [اندوز →,
an.duz] to save; to accumulate

اندودن [an.du.dan] [اندا →, an.dā] to
plaster (lit.)

اندوز [an.duz] → اندوختن

اندیش [an.dish] → اندیشیدن

اندیشیدن [an.di.shi.dan] [اندیش →,
an.dish] to think (form.)

انسان [en.sān] human being; one (pr.)

انسانی [en.sā.ni] human; humane

انعکاس [en.'e.kās] reflection

انعکاسی [en.'e.kā.si] reflexive

انقلاب [en.ghe.lāb] revolution (pl.
انقلابات, en.ghe.lā.bāt)

انگار [en.gār] → انگاشتن

~ (که) [~ (ke)] as if, as though
(col.)

انگاشتن [en.gāsh.tan] [انگار →, en.gār]
to assume; to suppose

انگشت [an.gosht] finger (pl. with both
-hā and -ān)

انگلستان [en.ge.les.tān] England

انگلیسی [en.ge.li.si] English

انگیختن [an.gikh.tan] [انگیز →, an.giz]
to stir, to provoke

انگیز [an.giz] → انگیختن

او [u] he or she

اوامر [a.vā.mer] pl. of امر

اوضاع [ow.zā'] circumstances;
conditions (pl. of وضع)

اوقات [ow.ghāt] pl. of وقت

اوّل [av.val] first

اوّلاً [av.va.lan] firstly

اولاد [ow.lād] children [in relation to
parents]; offspring (originally pl.
of the Arabic ولد [va.lad], son)

اوّلین [av.va.lin] first

اهالی [a.hā.li] residents or inhabitants
(pl. of اهل)

227

اهداف [ah.dāf] pl. of هدف

اهل [ahl] native [of a place] (pl. اهالی,
ahāli, residents or inhabitants)

اهل ... بودن [ah.l-e ... bu.dan]
[→ باش ~] to be from [a city
or country]; to be of [a certain
trait]; to be interested in

ای [ey] oh; O!

ایتالیا [i.tā.li.yā] Italy

ایران [i.rān] Iran

ایرانی [i.rā.ni] Iranian (n.; adj.)

ایست [ist] → ایستادن

ایستادن [is.tā.dan] [ایست ←, ist] to
stand; to stop/pause (causative:
ایستاندن)

ایستگاه [ist.gāh] station

ایشان [i.shān] they (for people only;
more polite than آنها)

ایمیل [i.meyl] email

این [in] this (adj. and pr.)

اینان [i.nān] these (pr.; form.;
for people only)

اینترنت [in.ter.net] Internet

اینجا [in.jā] here

اینطور/این طور [in.towr] in this way;
like this

اینطور/این طور که [in.towr ke] the way
that; as

اینقدر [in-ghadr] so, so much

اینها [in.hā] these (pr.)

این همه/اینهمه [in ha.me] so much;
so many; so

با [bā] with (prep.); also used as prefix

با آنکه [bā ān-ke] even though
(form./wrt.)

با اینکه [bā in-ke] even though

بابک [bā.bak] Babak (boy's name)

بار [bār] 'time' as counting word

بارها [bār-hā] many times

باختن [bākh.tan] [→ باز, bāz] to lose;
to play or gamble

باد [bād] wind

بادآورده [~ ā.var.de] easily gained
('brought with the wind')

بر باد رفتن [bar ~ raftan] [→ رو ~]
to be lost; to go with the wind

بادام [bā.dām] almond

بار [bār] 1) time [counting word];
2) load

بُردن [~ bor.dan] [→ بَر ~] to carry
loads

باریدن [bār] → بار

باران [bā.rān] rain

آمدن [~ ā.ma.dan] [→ آ ~] to rain

بارانی [bā.rā.ni] rainy (adj.); raincoat
(n.)

باریدن [bā.ri.dan] [→ بار, bār] to rain

باز [bāz] 1) → باختن; 2) again; 3) open

باز کردن [~ kar.dan] [→ کن ~] to
open; to unfasten or untie (tr.)

بازار [bā.zār] market, bazaar

بازپسین [bāz.pa.sin] last (lit./poet.)

بازجوئی [bāz-ju.'i] investigation;
interrogation

کردن [~ kar.dan] [→ کن ~] to
investigate; to interrogate

بازگرد [bāz-gard] → بازگشتن

بازگشت [bāz-gasht] return (n.)

بازگشتن [bāz-gash.tan] [بازگرد,
bāz-gard] to return (bāz- is a
prefix) (lit.; see برگشتن)

بازنده [bā.zan.de] loser

باز هم [bāz ham] again, anew; still;
nonetheless

بازی [bā.zi] play; game

بازی کردن [bā.zi kar.dan] [→ کن ~] to play

بازیکن [bā.zi.kon] player [in sports]

باش [bāsh] → بودن

باعث شدن/باعثِ...شدن [bā.'es sho.dan/ bā.'e.s-e ... sho.dan] [→ شو ~] to cause

باغ [bāgh] garden (usually large)

باغچه [bāgh.che] small garden

باغ وحش [bā.gh-e vahsh] zoo

بافتن [bāf.tan] [→ باف, bāf] to knit; to weave; to braid

بافتنی [bāf.ta.ni] product of hand-knitting

باقی [bā.ghi] remaining

بال [bāl] → بالیدن

بالا [bā.lā] (adj./adv.) high, up, above

بالایِ [bā.lā-ye] (prep.) over, above, on

بالا رفتن (از) [bā.lā raf.tan (az)] [→ رو ~] to climb

بالاخره [bel.'a.kha.re] finally

بالیدن [bā.li.dan] [→ بال, bāl] to grow; to boast

بام [bām] roof

بانک [bānk] bank

باور کردن [bā.var kar.dan] [→ کن ~] to believe

~ کردنی [~ kar.da.ni] believable

~ نکردنی [~ na-kar.da.ni] unbelievable

با هم [bā ham] together

~ ساختن [~ sākh.tan] [→ ساز ~] to conspire; to join forces

با همدیگر [bā ham-di.gar] with each other, with one another

باهوش [bā-hush] intelligent

باید [bā.yad] must; should (modal verb; same form for all persons). Other variants sometimes used as synonyms: میباید [mi-bāyad], بایست [bāyest], میبایست [mi-bāyest] or the rather archaic بایستی/میبایستی [bāyesti/mi-bāyesti]

بایست/بایستی [bāyest/bāyesti] (both used also with mi-) → باید

با یکدیگر [bā yek-di.gar] with each other, with one another (form./wrt.)

ببخشید! [be.bakh.shid] (I beg your) pardon!; excuse me! [→ بخشیدن]

بتازگی/به تازگی [be-tā.ze.gi] recently (see تازه)

بجای/(به) جای [be.jā.ye] in place of; instead of

بجز [be-joz] except (see جز)

بچگانه [bach.che.gā.ne] childish, childlike, of children or children's

بچگی [bach.che.gi] childhood; childishness

بچه [bach.che] child (pl. usually with -hā)

بچهدار [bach.che.dār] having child/ children; pregnant

بحث [bahs] argument; dispute

بحثانگیز [bahs-an.giz] controversial

بخت [bakht] fortune; luck

بخش [bakhsh] [→ بخشیدن] section; part

بخشیدن [bakh.shi.dan] [→ بخش, bakhsh] to forgive; to pardon

بخشیدن به [~ be] to bestow upon

229

بَد [bad] bad

بد* آمدن (از) [~* ā.ma.dan (az)]
[آ ~ →] to dislike; to hate

بد گذشتن (به*) [~ go.zash.tan (be*)]
[گذر ~ →] to have a bad time

بدبخت [bad bakht] unfortunate;
ill-fated; unlucky

بدبختانه [bad.bakh.tā.ne] unfortunately,
unluckily

بدبختی [bad bakh.ti] misery;
misfortune; bad luck

بدبو [bad.bu] malodorous; smelly

بدبین [bad.bin] pessimist (from
بد دیدن)

بدل کردن (به) [ba.dal kar.dan (be)]
[کن ~ →] to change (to)

بدونِ [be.du.n-e] without

بَر [bar] [بُردن →] on, over, above (lit.)

برابر [ba.rā.bar] equal; facing; against

در برابرِ [dar ~ -e] in front of;
against

بَرادر [ba.rā.dar] brother

برادری [ba.rā.da.ri] brotherhood;
brotherliness

برانداختن [bar-an.dākh.tan] [→
bar-an.dāz – 'bar-' here is a
prefix] to overthrow

برایِ [ba.rā-ye] for (prep.)

برای این [ba.rā.ye in] for this; for this
reason

برایِ اینکه [ba.rā.ye in-ke] because,
for (conj.)

برخاستن [bar-khās.tan] [→
bar-khiz] to rise; to stand up
(bar- is a prefix)

بر خوردن [bar khor] → بر خور [bar khor]

برخورد [bar-khord] encounter;
approach; clash

بر خوردن (به*) [bar khor.dan (be*)]
[خور ~ →] to be offended
(impersonal in this sense only);
to encounter, to come across

برداشتن [bar.dār] → بردار

برداشتن [bar-dāsh.tan] [بردار,
bar.dār] to pick up (+ mi- in
pres. and progressive tenses)

بُردن [bor.dan] [بَر, bar →] to take
(away), to carry; to win (a prize
or match)

بررسی [bar.ra.si] consideration;
deliberation; examination

کردن ~ [~ kar.dan] [کن ~ →] to
consider; to deliberate; to
examine

برغم/به رغمِ [be ragh.m-e] despite
(form.) (see علیرغم)

برف [barf] snow

برف آمدن [barf ā.ma.dan] [آ ~ →]
to snow

برق [bargh] lightning; electricity

برقرار کردن [bar-gha.rār kar.dan]
[کن ~ →] to set up; to establish

برگ [barg] leaf

برگرد [bar-gard] → برگشتن

برگرداندن [bar.gar.dān] → برگردان

برگرداندن [bar.gar.dān.dan] [برگردان→,
bar.gar.dān] to return sth. or so.
(tr.)

برگشتن [bar-gash.tan] [برگرد →,
bar-gard] to return (bar- is a
prefix)

برنامه [bar.nā.me] program

برنده [ba.ran.de] winner (see بردن,
bor.dan)

بُزُرگ [bo.zorg] big; great; large

بزودی [be-zu.di] soon; before long
(see زود)

بَس [bas] enough

بَس* بودن [bas* bu.dan] [باش* ~ ←]
to have enough of; to be enough
for

بسا [ba.sā] (how) many or (how) much
(poet.; exclamative)

چه بسا [che ~] many a . . . ; maybe;
it could be that

بسانِ/به سانِ [be-sā.n-e] similar to,
like (lit.)

بستن [bas.tan] [بند ←, band] to close,
to shut; to tie, to fasten; to
attach

بستنی [bas.ta.ni] ice-cream

بسته [bas.te] package

بشر [ba.shar] human being, mankind

بسی [ba.si] a lot of (poet.)

بسیار [bes.yār] very; a lot

بسیاری از [bes.yā.ri az] a lot of

بطری [bot.ri] bottle

بعد [ba'd] next (adj., as in 'next week');
afterwards, later, then (conj.)

بعداً [ba'.dan] afterwards, later, then
(adv.)

بعد از [ba'd az] after (prep.)

بعد از ظهر [ba'd az zohr] afternoon

بعدی [ba'.di] next

بعضی [bá'.zi] some (for countables)
(ends in unstressed indefinite -i)

بعید [ba.'id] unlikely; distant

بغیر [be-gheyr] see غیر

بقّال [bagh.ghāl] grocer

بگونۀ/به گونۀ [be-gu.ne.ye] similar to,
like (lit.)

بلبل [bol.bol] nightingale

بَلَد بودن [ba.lad bu.dan] [باش ~ ←] to
know (how to do sth.); to have
learned sth.

بَلَد شدن [ba.lad sho.dan] [شو ~ ←]
to learn (how to do sth.)

بلکه [bal.ke] but rather

بلند [bo.land] high, tall; loud

بله [ba.le] yes [stress on bá-]

بلی [ba.li] yes [stress on bá-] (wrt.)

بلیط/بلیت [be.lit] ticket [from the
French billet]

بموقع [be-mow.ghe'] see موقع

بنابراین [ba.nā-bar-in] therefore ('based
on this')

بَند [band] [بستن ←] rope

بندِ کفش [~ -e kafsh] shoelace

بَندوبَست [ban.d-o-bast] collusion or
a secret deal

بنده [ban.de] slave; servant; bondman

بنیاد [bon.yād] foundation

بو [bu] smell, scent (see خوشبو and
بدبو)

بو دادن [bu dā.dan] [ده ~ ←] to stink
(intr.)

بودن [bu.dan] [باش, bāsh] to be

بوسیدن [bus] → بوس

بوسه [bu.se] kiss

بوسیدن [bu.si.dan] to kiss (pres. stem:
بوس [bus])

بو کردن [bu kar.dan] [کن ~ ←] to
smell; to sniff

به [be] to; also 'in' for languages
(prep.)

بهار [ba.hār] (season of) spring

بهشت [be.hesht] paradise

به مدّتِ [be mod.da.t-e] for (temp.),
for the duration of

به وسیلۀ [be va.si.le.ye] by, by means of

بههیچوجه [be hich-vajh] no way; not
at all

بهتر [beh.tar] better

به‌عنوانِ [be on.vā.n-e] as

بی [bi] without

بیان [ba.yān] statement, expression

~ کردن [~ kar.dan] [→ کن ~] to
state, to express

حوصله see حوصله بی [bi-how.se.le]

بی‌خبر [bi-kha.bar] unaware [of = از];
ignorant; not knowing or not
having heard (of/about)

بیختن [bikh.tan] [→ بیز, biz] to sift

بیخود [bi.khod] in vain; for no reason
(col.)

بیدار [bi.dār] awake

~ شدن [~ sho.dan] [→ شو ~] to
wake up (intr.)

~ کردن [~ kar.dan] [→ کن ~] to
wake up (tr.)

بیرون [bi.run] outside (adv.)

بیرونِ/بیرون از [bi.ru.n-e/bi.run az]
outside (prep.)

~ آوردن [~ ā.var.dan] [→ آور ~] to
take off (clothes); to take out

~ رفتن (از)] [→ رو ~] [~ raf.tan (az)]
to go out; to leave (a place)

بیز [biz] → بیختن

بیست [bist] twenty

بیش [bish] more (lit./wrt.)

بیش از [bish az] more
than (form.)

بیشتر [bish.tar] more; mostly

بیشترِ [~ -e] most of

بی‌صبرانه [bi-sab.rā.ne] impatiently
(see صبر)

بیقرار [bi-gha.rār] restless; impatient

بیقراری [~ -i] restlessness;
impatience

بیکار [bi-kār] jobless; having free
time

بیمار [bi.mār] sick (adj.); sick person,
patient (n.)

بیمارستان [bi.mā.res.tān] hospital

بین [bin] → دیدن

بینا [bi.nā] capable of seeing; not blind
(دیدن →)

بینش [bi.nesh] insight

بینی [bi.ni] nose

پا [pā] 1) → پائیدن; 2) foot

پارتی [pār.ti] party (for amusement)

پارسال [pār.sāl] last year

پارک [pārk] park

پارو [pā.ru] oar, paddle; snow shovel

~ زدن [~ za.dan] [→ زن ~] to row
or paddle

~ کردن [~ kar.dan] [→ کن ~] to
shovel the snow

پاروزنی [pā.ru-za.ni] rowing

پاره [pā.re] torn

~ کردن [~ kar.dan] [→ کن ~] to
tear (up)

پاسخ [pā.sokh] answer (form.)

~ دادن (به)] [→ دِه ~] [~ dā.dan (be)]
to answer; to give an answer
(to) (form.)

پاش [pāsh] → پاشیدن

پاشیدن [pā.shi.dan] [→ پاش, pāsh] to
strew; to sprinkle (causative:
پاشاندن)

پاکستان [pā.kes.tān] Pakistan

پاکستانی [pā.kes.tā.ni] Pakistani

پالا [pā.lā] → پالودن

پالودن [pā.lu.dan] [→ پالا, pā.lā]
to refine

پانزده [pānz.dah] fifteen

پانصد [pān.sad] five hundred

پایان [pā.yān] end

(به) پایان آمدن [be ~ ā.ma.dan]
[~ آ →] to end (intr.)

بی پایان [bi- ~] endless

پائیدن [pā.'i.dan] [→ پا, pā] to last;
to watch or guard

پائیز/پاییز [pā.'iz] autumn

پُختن [pokh.tan] [→ پَز, paz] to cook
(tr./intr.)

پُخت و پَز [pokht-o-paz] cooking
نپخته [na.pokh.te] uncooked

پدَر [pe.dar] father

پدربزرگ [pe.dar-bo.zorg] grandfather

پدر و مادر [pe.da.r-o mā.dar] parents

پذیرفتن → پذیر [pa.zir]

پذیرش [pa.zi.resh] acceptance;
consent; admission;
reception

پذیرفتن [pa.zi.rof.tan] [→ پذیر, pa.zir]
to accept, to agree; to consent
(form./wrt.)

پذیرفتنی [pa.zi.rof.ta.ni] acceptable

پریدن → پَر [par]

پُر (از) [por (az)] full (of); filled
(with)

پراکندن → پراکن [pa.rā.kan]

پراکندن [pa.rā.kan.dan] [→ پراکن,
pa.rā.kan] to scatter (lit.)

پرداخت [par.dākht] payment

پرداختن [par.dākht] [→ پرداز, par.dāz]
to pay

پرداختن → پرداز [par.dāz]

پرسیدن → پرس [pors]

پُرسان پُرسان [por.sān-por.sān]: (while)
asking many times (for
directions)

پرستیدن → پرست [pa.rast]

پرستیدن [pa.ras.ti.dan] [→ پرست,
pa.rast] to worship

پرسش [por.sesh] question (form.)

پرسشی [por.se.shi] interrogative

پرس و جو [por.s-o-ju] inquiry
[~ کردن] [~ kar.dan] [→ ~ کن] to
make a search or inquiry

پرسیدن (از) [por.si.dan (az)]
[→ پُرس, pors] to ask a
question (from)

پَرَندِه [pa.ran.de] bird

پرواز [par.vāz] flight
[~ کردن] [~ kar.dan] [→ ~ کن] to fly

پروانه [par.vā.ne] butterfly; also girl's
name (Parvaneh)

پروردن → پرور [par.var]

پروردن [par.var.dan] [→ پرور, par.var]
to cherish; to rear

پرویز [par.viz] Parviz (boy's name)

پروین [par.vin] Parvin (girl's name)

پرهیز [par.hiz] avoidance
[~ کردن (از)] [~ kar.dan (az)]
[→ ~ کن] to avoid

پری [pa.ri] fairy; Pari (girl's name)

پریدن [pa.ri.dan] [→ پِر, par] to fly
(not used for planes); to jump or
leap (causative: پراندن)

پریروز [pa.ri.ruz] the day before
yesterday

پُختن→[paz] پَز

پزشک [pe.zeshk] doctor

پزشکی [pe.zesh.ki] medicine

پژمردن → پژمر [pazh.mor]

پژمردن [pazh.mor.dan] [→ پژمر,
pazh.mor] to wither (causative:
پژمراندن)

پس [pas] then (in conditional sentences);
therefore; back or behind

پَس دادن (به) [pas dā.dan (be)]
[~ ده ←] to give back (to),
to return (tr.)

پس فرستادن [pas fe.res.tā.dan]
[~ فرست ←] to send back

پس گرفتن [pas ge.ref.tan] [← گیر ~]
to take back

پس از [pas az] after (prep.)

پس فردا [pas-far.dā] the day after
tomorrow

پست [post] post

~ کردن [~ kar.dan] [← کن ~] to mail

پُستچی [post.chi] mailperson

پسر [pe.sar] boy; son

پسرانه [pe.sa.rā.ne] boys', of boys

پشتِ [posht-e] behind (prep.); at the
back of

پشه [pa.she] mosquito

پشیمان [pa.shi.mān] regretful

پشیمان شدن [pa.shi.mān sho.dan]
[← شو ~] to regret; to change
one's mind

پشیمان کردن [pa.shi.mān kar.dan]
[← کن ~] to make so. regret or
change his mind

پلیس [po.lis] police

پنج [panj] five

پنجاه [pan.jāh] fifty

پنجشنبه [panj-sham.be] Thursday

پندار [pen.dār →] پنداشتن

پنداشتن [pen.dāsh.tan] [← پندار, pen.
dār] to assume; to think (form.)

پنهان [pen.hān] hidden

پنهان کردن [pen.hān kar.dan]
[← کن ~] to hide

پنیر [pa.nir] cheese

پوئیدن [pu] → پو

پوست [pust] skin

پوشیدن [push] → پوش

پوشیدن [pu.shi.dan] [پوش ←, push] to
wear; to cover (causative: پوشاندن)

پول [pul] money

پولدار [pul.dār] wealthy

پویان [pu.yān] Puyan; boy's name

پوئیدن [pu.'i.dan] [پو ←, pu] to run in
search of (lit.)

پیاده [pi.yā.de] on foot

~ شدن (از) [~ sho.dan (az)] [← شو ~]
to get off (a vehicle, a horse, etc.)

پیاز [pi.yāz] onion

پیانو [pi.yā.no] piano

پیچ [pich] [پیچیدن ←] turn; screw

پیچیدن [pi.chi.dan] [← پیچ, pich]
to turn or twist (causative:
پیچاندن)

~ کن [pey.dā kar.dan] [← کن ~] پیدا کردن
to find

پیر [pir] old (for animates only)

پیرزن [pir-zan] old woman

پیرمرد [pir-mard] old man

پیراهن [pi.rā.han] shirt (form.);
see پیرهن

پیرو [pey.row] follower

پیرهن [pir.han] shirt (more form.:
پیراهن)

پیش [pish] past, last (as in 'last
week') (adj.)

پیشِ [pi.sh-e] to or with a
person (similar to chez in
French)

پیش از [pish az] before (prep.)

پیش از آنکه [pish az ān-ke] before (conj.)

پیش‌بینی [pish-bi.ni] foresight

پیشرفت [pish.raft] progress
~ کردن [~ kar.dan] [→ کن ~] to make progress

پیش رفتن [pish raf.tan] [→ رو ~] to go forward, to advance

پیشرو [pish-row] forerunner, pioneer, progressive

پیشروی [pish.ra.vi] advance, moving forward (specially of troops)
~ کردن [~ kar.dan] [→ کن ~] to advance (as troops)

پیشنهاد [pish.na.hād] suggestion
~ کردن [~ kar.dan] [→ کن ~] to suggest, to propose

پیغام [pey.ghām] message

پیف! [pif] Eew! (interj.; used for bad smell)

پیما [pey.mā] → پیمودن

پیمودن [pey.mu.dan] [→ پیما, pey.mā] to traverse; to measure

پیوست [pey.vast] appendix; attachment

پیوستن (به) [pey.vas.tan (be)] [→ پیوند, pey.vand] to join

پیوسته [pey.vas.te] connected; joined

پیوند [pey.vand] → پیوستن

تا [tā] until; as soon as; so long as

تا [tā] 'item' as counting word (preferably for non-humans)

تاب [tāb] → تافتن

تا به حال [tā be hāl] until now, so far

تا حالا [tā hā.lā] until now, so far

تابستان [tā.bes.tān] summer

تابستانی [tā.bes.tā.nī] summer's; of summer; summerly

تأثیر [ta'.sir] effect or influence; impression (pl. تأثیرات, ta'.si.rāt)

~ گذاشتن (بر/روی) [~ go.zāsh.tan (bar/ru.ye)] [→ گذار ~] to affect or influence; to impress

~ گرفتن (از) [~ ge.ref.tan (az)] [→ گیر ~] to be affected, influenced or impressed (by)

تاجیک [tā.jik] Tajiki (of people)

تاجیکی [tā.ji.ki] Tajiki (of people or language)

تاجیکستان [tā.ji.kes.tān] Tajikistan

تاختن [tākh.tan] [→ تاز, tāz] to assault; to rush (lit.)

تار [tār] thread; string; a musical instrument

تارزن [tār-zan] tār-player

تاریخ [tā.rikh] history; date (pl. تواریخ, ta.vā.rikh)

تاریخی [tā.ri.khi] historical

تاریک [tā.rik] dark

تاز [tāz] → تاختن

تازه [tā.ze] fresh (adj.); just (adv.)

بتازگی/به تازگی [be-tā.ze.gi] recently

تافتن [tāf.tan] [→ تاب, tāb] to shine (lit.) (causative: تاباندن)

تا کردن [tā kar.dan] [→ کن ~] to fold

تاشو [tā-show] foldable, folding

تاکسی [tāk.si] taxi

تأکید [ta'.kid] emphasis (pl. تأکیدات, ta'.ki.dāt)

~ کردن (روی/بر) [~ kar.dan] [→ کن ~] to emphasize

تأکیدی [ta'.ki.di] emphatic

تبدیل کردن (به) [tab.dil kar.dan (be)] [→ کن ~] to change (to) (tr.); to alter; to convert (currencies) – for intr. use شدن or یافتن (form.) instead of کردن

تبریک [tab.rik] congratulation
(pl. تبریکات, tab.ri.kāt)
[~ gof.tan (be) گفتن (به) ~]
[→ گو ~] to congratulate

تبعی [ta.ba.'i] subordinate (gr.)

تپ [tap] → تپیدن

تپّه [tap.pe] hill

تپیدن [ta.pi.dan] [→ تپ, tap] to beat;
to pulsate

تحتِ [tah.t-e] under; beneath (prep.)
[~ -e . . . قرار گرفتن تحتِ ~ -e . . . gha.rār
ge.ref.tan] [→ گیر ~] to undergo;
to become the object of; to be
subjected to

تحسین [tah.sin] praise; admiration;
applause
[~ kar.dan] [→ کن ~] to کردن ~]
admire; to praise; to applaud

تحصیل [tah.sil] education (pl. always
تحصیلات, tah.si.lāt)

تحقیق [tah.ghigh] research; investigation
(pl. تحقیقات, tah.ghi.ghāt)
[~ kar.dan] [→ کن ~] to کردن ~]
investigate

تخت [takht] bed

تخته [takh.te] board, plank, piece of
flat wood

تخته سیاه [takh.te si.yāh] blackboard

تخفیف [takh.fif] discount

تخم مُرغ [tokh.m-e morgh] egg

تدریس [tad.ris] teaching
[~ kar.dan] [→ کن ~] to کردن ~]
teach (a subject) (form.)

تر [tar] wet (adj.); also: comparative suffix

تراش [ta.rāsh] → تراشیدن

تراشنده [ta.rā.shan.de] carver

تراشیدن [ta.rā.shi.dan] [→ تراش,
ta.rāsh] to carve, to whittle

ترانه [ta.rā.ne] song; also girl's name
(Taraneh)

تراو [ta.rāv] → تراویدن

تراویدن [ta.rā.vi.dan] [→ تراو, ta.rāv]
to trickle; to ooze (lit.)

ترتیب [tar.tib] order; arrangement
ترتیبی دادن [tar.ti.bi dā.dan]
[→ ده ~] to make an
arrangement; to arrange

ترجمه [tar.jo.me] translation
[~ kar.dan] [→ کن ~] to کردن ~]
translate

ترجیح [tar.jih] preference
[~ دادن (به/بر) dā.dan (be/bar)]
[→ ده ~] to prefer (to) (بر in
form./wrt.)

تردید [tar.did] doubt
[~ داشتن (در) dāsh.tan (be)]
[→ دار ~] to doubt; to have
doubts (in)

ترس [tars] [→ ترسیدن] fear

ترسان [tar.sān] fearing

ترسناک [tars.nāk] frightening

ترسیدن (از) [tar.si.dan (az)]
[→ ترس, tars] to be afraid (of);
to fear (causative: ترساندن)

ترش [torsh] [→ ترشیدن] sour

ترشیدن [tor.shi.dan] [→ ترش, torsh] to
become sour

ترک [tark] → ترکیدن

ترک کردن [tark kar.dan] [→ کن ~] to
leave a place (object always
definite)

ترکیدن [tar.ki.dan] [→ ترک, tark]
to explode (causative:
ترکاندن)

تِرم [term] term, semester

تریبون [te.ri.bun] podium; lectern

تشخیص [tash.khis] recognition; distinction; diagnosis

دادن ~ [~ dā.dan] [→ ده ~] to distinguish; to discern

تشریف [tash.rif] honor; honoring (pl. تشریفات, tash.ri.fāt = formalities) (for its usage in polite language see Appendix I)

تشنه [tesh.ne] thirsty

تشویق [tash.vigh] encouragement

کردن ~ [~ kar.dan] [→ کن ~] to encourage; to applaud

تصفیه [tas.fi.ye] purification

کردن ~ [~ kar.dan] [→ کن ~] to purify; to refine; to purge

تصمیم [tas.mim] decision (pl. تصمیمات, tas.mi.māt)

داشتن ~ [~ dāsh.tan] [→ دار ~] to intend; to have the intention (to ...)

گرفتن ~ [~ ge.ref.tan] [→ گیر ~] to decide; to make up one's mind

تصوّر [ta.sav.vor] assumption; imagination (pl. تصوّرات, ta.sav.vo.rāt)

کردن ~ [~ kar.dan] [→ کن ~] to assume or imagine

تصویب [tas.vib] approval; ratification

کردن ~ [~ kar.dan] [→ کن ~] to ratify; to approve

تعارف [ta.'ā.rof, in col. also tā.rof] pleasantries exchanged to show politeness (pl. تعارفات, ta.'ā.ro.fāt)

تعجّب [ta.'aj.job] astonishment

کردن ~ [~ kar.dan] [→ کن ~] to be surprised

تعداد [te.'dād] number

تعدادی از [te.'dā.di az] a number of

تعطیل [ta'.til] closed (a store or office); a holiday (pl. تعطیلات, ta'.ti.lāt = vacations)

تعلیم [ta'.lim] instruction; education (pl. تعلیمات, ta'.li.māt)

تعمیر [ta'.mir] repair, fixing

کردن ~ [~ kar.dan] [→ کن ~] to repair, to fix

تغییر [tagh.yir] change (pl. تغییرات, tagh.yi.rāt)

دادن ~ [~ dā.dan] [→ ده ~] to change (tr.)

کردن/یافتن ~ [~ kar.dan/yāf.tan] [→ کن/یاب ~] to change (intr.) (یافتن more form.)

تفاوت [ta.fā.vot] difference

داشتن (با) ~ [~ dāsh.tan (bā)] [→ دار ~] to be different (from)

تقاضا [ta.ghā.zā] demand; request

کردن ~ [~ kar.dan] [→ کن ~] to demand; to request

تقریباً [tagh.ri.ban] almost; approximately

تکالیف [ta.kā.lif] pl. of تکلیف

تکان [ta.kān] [→ تکاندن] shake; jolt; budging

خوردن ~ [~ khor.dan] [→ خور ~] to shake, budge or move (intr.)

دادن ~ [~ dā.dan] [→ ده ~] to shake, move or rock (tr.)

تکاندن [ta.kān.dan] [→ تکان, ta.kān] to cause to shake

تکرار [tek.rār] repetition

تکرار کردن [tek.rār kar.dan] [→ کن ~] to repeat

تکلیف [tak.lif] homework, assignment (pl. تکالیف, ta.kā.lif)

تکمیل [tak.mil] making complete; supplementing; finishing

تکیه [tek.ye] stress; emphasis; leaning
~ [~ dā.dan/kar.dan دادن/کردن (به)
(be)] [→ ده ~/~ کن ـ] to lean
(against)

~ kar.dan کردن (بر/روی)
(bar/ru.ye)] [→ کن ~] to put
emphasis (on); to emphasize

تلاش [ta.lāsh] effort

~ [~ kar.dan] [→ کن ~] to کردن
make an effort; to attempt; to
try [کن → کردن]

تلخ [talkh] bitter

تلف کردن [ta.laf kar.dan] [→ کن ~] to
waste (tr.)

تلفن [te.le.fon] telephone

تلفن زدن/کردن [te.le.fon za.dan/kar.dan]
[→ زن/~ کن ~] to telephone,
to call

تلفنی [te.le.fo.ni] per phone

تلویزیون [te.le.vi.zi.yon] television

تماشا کردن [ta.mā.shā kar.dan]
[→ کن ~] to watch

تمام [ta.mām] whole, complete; full;
finished

تمام [~ -e] all of

[~ شو → [~ sho.dan] تمام شدن
to get finished

[~ کن → [~ kar.dan] تمام کردن
to finish (tr.)

تمرین [tam.rin] exercise

تمیز [ta.miz] clean

~ [~ kar.dan] [→ کن ~] to کردن
clean

تن [tan] counting word for people
(form. in this sense)

تن [tan] body

تن* بودن [tan* bu.dan] to be
wearing (col.) [→ باش ـ]

تن* کردن [tan* kar.dan] to wear or
put on (col.) [→ کن ـ]

به/بر تن داشتن [be/bar tan dāsh.tan]
[→ دار ~] to be wearing
(clothes) (form.)

به/بر تن کردن [be/bar tan kar.dan]
[→ کن ~] to put on (clothes)
(form.)

تنبک [ton.bak (col.: tom-)] a small
drum common in Iran; also
called ضرب [zarb]

تنبل [tan.bal] lazy

تند [tond] fast (adj./adv.); abrupt; spicy
and hot (taste)

تنگ [tang] tight

تنها [tan.hā] only; alone

نه تنها...بلکه... [na ~ ... bal.ke ...]
not only ... but also ...

تنهائی [tan.hā.'i] solitude

تو [to] you (sg.)

تواریخ [ta.vā.rikh] pl. of تاریخ

توان [ta.vān] → توانستن

توانا [ta.vā.nā] capable; mighty

توانستن [ta.vā.nes.tan] [→ توان, ta.vān]
can, to be able to

توپ [tup] ball

توپبازی [tup-bā.zi] children's play
with a ball

توجّه [ta.vaj.joh] attention

[~ kar.dan (be)] کردن (به)
[→ کن ~] to notice; to pay
attention (to)

توریست [tu.rist] tourist

توسّطِ [ta.vas.sot-e] by (means of),
through (the mediation of)

توصیه [tow.si.ye] recommendation

[~ kar.dan (be)] کردن (به)
[→ کن ~] to recommend

توضیح [tow.zih] explanation

توضیح دادن [tow.zih dā.dan]
[~ دِه ←] to explain

توفیق [tow.figh] success

یافتن/داشتن ~ [~ yāf.tan/dāsh.tan]
[← یاب/دار ~] to find/have
success, to succeed; to be lucky
enough to

توقّع [ta.vagh.gho'] expectation

داشتن ~ [~ dāsh.tan] [← دار ~]
to expect

توقّف [ta.vagh.ghof] stop, halt

کردن ~ [~ kar.dan] [← کن ~] to
stop (intr.), to make a stop

تولد [ta.val.lod] birth

تومان [tu.mān] tuman or toman, a
currency unit (= 10 Iranian rials)

توهین [tow.hin] insult

کردن (به) ~ [~ kar.dan (be)]
[← کن ~] to insult

توی [tu-ye] in; inside (col.)

ثالثاً [sā.le.san] thirdly

ثانیاً [sā.ni.yan] secondly

ثانیه [sā.ni.ye] second (1/60th of a minute)

ثروَت [ser.vat] wealth

ثروَتمند [ser.vat.mand] wealthy

ثلث [sols] one-third (used especially
for quarters/terms in academic
year – excluding summer)

جا [jā] place

جای/(به) جای [(be) jā.ye] in place
of; instead of

جالب [jā.leb] financial

جامعه [jā.me.'e] society

جامعه‌شناس [jā.me.'e-she.nās] sociologist

جامعه‌شناسی [jā.me.'e -she.nā.si]
sociology

جان [jān] life (as opposed to death)

جانب [jā.neb] side, direction (pl.
جوانب, ja.vā.neb)

از جانبِ [az ~ -e] by, through, from

جایزه [jā.ye.ze] award (pl. جوایز, javāyez)

جدا [jo.dā] separate

شدن (از) ~ [~ sho.dan (az)] to be
separated (from); to be divorced

جدید [ja.did] new

جرأت [jor.'at] courage (often written
as جرئت, same pronunciation)

کردن/داشتن ~ [~ kar.dan/dāsh.tan]
[← کن/دار ~] to dare; to have the
courage [دار ← داشتن /کن ← کردن]

جُرم [form] crime; misdeed

جرئت [jor.'at] see جرأت

جز (به/بـ) [(be) joz] except; other than
(prep.)

جز اینکه (به/بـ) [~ in ke] except that
(conj.)

جستجو [jos.to.ju] search

کردن ~ [~ kar.dan] [← کن ~] to
search or look for

جستن [jas.tan] [← جه, jah] to leap; to
jump

جستن [jos.tan] [← جو, ju] to seek; to
[search for sth. and] find (form.)

جست و جو [jos.t-o-ju] see جستجو above

جشن [jashn] celebration

گیر ~ [~ ge.ref.tan] [← گیر ~] to
celebrate

جشن تولد [~ -e ta.val.lod] birthday
party (lit. 'celebration of
birth[day]')

جُفت [joft] pair

یک جُفت [yek ~] a pair of

جلد [jeld] volume (counting word for
books)

جلسه [*ja.la.se*] session; meeting
(*pl.* جلسات, *ja.la.sāt*)

جلو [*je.low*] front; ahead

جلوِ [*je.lo.w-e*] in front of

جمهوری [*ja.mā.hir*] *pl.* of جمهوری

جَمع [*jam'*] plural (*gr.*)

جمعه [*jom.'e*] Friday

جمله [*jom.le*] sentence (*gr.*) (*pl.*
جملات, *jo.me.lāt/jo.ma.lāt*)

جملهٔ موصولی [*jom.le-ye mow.su.li*]
relative clause (*gr.*)

جمهوری [*jom.hu.ri*] republic (*pl.*
جماهیر, *ja.mā.hir*)

جنبیدن [*jonb*] →

جنبیدن [*jon.bi.dan*] [→ جنب, *jonb*] to
move; to wiggle; to hurry
(causative: جنباندن)

جنگ [*jang*] [→ جنگیدن] war

جنگِ جهانی [*jan.g-e ja.hā.ni*] World
War

جنگل [*jan.gal*] forest; woods; jungle

جنگیدن [*jan.gi.dan*] [→ جنگ, *jang*] to
fight

جنوب [*jo.nub*] south

جو [*ju*] → جستن

جواب [*ja.vāb*] answer

جواب دادن (به) [*ja.vāb dā.dan (be)*]
[→ ~ دِه] to answer; to give an
answer (to)

جوان [*ja.vān*] young

جوانب [*ja.vā.neb*] *pl.* of جانب

جوانی [*ja.vā.ni*] youth

جوایز [*ja.vā.yez*] *pl.* of جایزه

جوجه [*ju.je*] chicken

جوش [*jush*] → جوشیدن

جوشیدن [*ju.shi.dan*] [→ جوش, *jush*] to
boil (*intr.*) (causative: جوشاندن)

جَه [*jah*] → جَستن

جهان [*ja.hān*] world

جهانی [*ja.hā.ni*] of the world;
international

جهت [*ja.hat*] reason; direction

به جهتِ [*be ~ -e*] because of

در جهتِ [*dar ~ -e*] in direction of

جهنّم [*ja.han.nam*] hell

جیب [*jib*] pocket

چاپ [*chāp*] 1) → چاپیدن;
2) publication

[→ ~ کن] [~ *kar.dan*] to
~ کردن publish

چاپیدن [*chā.pi.dan*] [→ چاپ, *chāp*] to
plunder

چاره [*chā.re*] remedy; cure; solution;
resort; alternative; choice

~ پذیر [~ *pa.zir*] remediable

چای [*chāy*] tea (also چایی or چائی
chā'i)

چپ [*chap*] 1) → چپیدن; 2) left

چپیدن [*cha.pi.dan*] [→ چپ, *chap*] to
crowd into (causative: چپاندن)

چر [*char*] → چریدن

چرا [*che.rā*] yes (use only to contradict
negative statements/questions;
stress on *ché-*)

چرا؟ [*ché.rā*] why? (stress on *ché-*)

چرا که [*ché.rā ke*] because

چراغ [*che.rāgh*] light, lamp

چرخ [*charkh*] [→ چرخیدن] wheel

چرخیدن [*char.khi.dan*] [→ چرخ,
charkh] to turn (around); to
revolve (causative: چرخاندن)

چریدن [*cha.ri.dan*] [→ چر, *char*] to
graze (causative: چراندن)

چسب [*chasb*] [→ چسبیدن] glue

چسبیدن [chas.bi.dan] [→ چسب, chasb]
to stick; to adhere (causative:
چسباندن)

چش [chesh] → چشیدن

چِشم [cheshm] eye (pl. with both -hā
and -ān)

چشیدن [che.shi.dan] [→چش, chesh] to
taste (causative: چشاندن)

چطور [che-towr] how

چِقدر [che-ghadr] how much (stress
on ché-)

چک [chek] → چکیدن

چکار (or چه‌کار) [che-kār] used to
ask what someone is doing
(see کار کردن)

چِکّه [chek.ke] drop (n.)

~ کردن [~ kar.dan] [→ ~ کن]
to fall in drops, to trickle,
to leak

چکیدن [che.ki.dan] [→ چک, chek] to
trickle (causative: چکاندن)

چگونه [che-gu.ne] how (form./wrt.)

چلان [che.lān] → چلاندن

چلاندن [che.lān.dan] [→ چلان, che.lān]
to squeeze; to wring

چلو [che.low] cooked rice

چلوکباب [che.low-ka.bāb] a Persian
dish: rice and kabab

چم [cham] → چمیدن

چمباتمه (/چنباتمه) زدن [cham.-/
chan.bāt.me za.dan] [→ ~ زن]
to squat

چمدان [cha.me.dān] suitcase

چمیدن [cha.mi.dan] [→ چم, cham]
to strut (poet.)

چنان [che.nān] so; such; in such a way

چنانکه/چنان که [~ ke] as; the way
that

چند [chand] 1) several; 2) how many?

چند بار [chand bār] 1) several
times; 2) how many times?

چند ساله [chand sā.le] how old?

چند وقت [chand vaght] 1) for some
time; 2) for how long?

چندم؟ [chan.dom] (question about
ordinal numbers)

چندان [chan.dān] so, so much, so many
(poet.); that much (col.)

چندین [chan.din] several; more than
just a few

چنین [che.nin] such

چون [chon] because (conj.)

چون [chon] similar to, like (lit.)

چه [che] what

چه... چه... [che ... che ...]
whether ... or ...

چه* بودن [che* bu.dan] [→ ~ باش]
What's wrong with ...? (col.)

چه‌کار [che-kār] see چکار

چه وقت [che vaght] what time? when?

چهار [cha.hār] four

چهارده [cha.hār.dah] fourteen

چهارشنبه [cha.hār-sham.be] Wednesday

چهارصد [cha.hār.sad] four hundred

چهل [che.hel] forty

چی [chi] what (col. of چه)

چیز [chiz] thing

حاضر [hā.zer] ready

حافظ [hā.fez] Hafez or Hafiz (poet, ca.
1326–89)

حافظه [hāfeze] memory

حال [hāl] state (of being); presently;
present (see also زمانِ حال)

در حالِ [dar hā.l-e] during (prep.); while

در حالیکه [dar hā.li-ke] while
(conj.), as; whereas

241

حالا [hā.lā] now

حالت [hā.lat] state; mood (pl. حالات,
hā.lāt)

حبس [habs] imprisonment

[~ kar.dan] [→ کن ~] to
imprison

حتّا [hat.tā] see حتّی

حتماً [hat.man] certainly

حتّی [hat.tā] even (adv.) (sometimes
spelled حتّا)

حدّ [hadd] limit; extent

زیاده از حد [zi.yā.de az ~] too much

حدس [hads] guess

[~ za.dan] [→ زن ~] to guess

حذف [hazf] deletion

[~ kar.dan] [→ کن ~] to delete

¹ حَرف [harf] talk; words (= what
someone says)

[~ za.dan (bā)] [→ زن ~] (با)
to talk (to/with)

پُرحَرف [por-~] gabby; talkative

² حَرف [harf] letter of alphabet (gr.;
pl. حُروف horuf)

حرفِ اضافه [har.f-e e.zā.fe] preposition
(gr.)

حرفِ ربط [har.f-e rabt] conjunction (gr.)

حَرف [ho.ruf] pl. of حُروف

حسن [ha.san] Hasan (also written
Hassan); boy's name

حِفظ [hefz] preservation; protection;
memorization

[~ kar.dan] [→ کن ~] to
preserve; to protect

(از) حفظ کردن/شدن [az ~ kar.dan/
sho.dan] [→ کن/شو ~] to memorize

(از) حفظ بودن/داشتن [(az) ~ bu.dan/
dāsh.tan] [→ باش/دار ~] to have in
memory (what you memorized)

حقّ [haghgh] right (n.) (pl. حقوق,
ho.ghugh)

[~ dāsh.tan] [→ دار ~] to
have the right; to be right

حقوق [ho.ghugh] salary; rights (pl.
of حقّ)

حقوق بشر [ho.ghu.gh-e ba.shar]
human rights

حقیر [ha.ghir] lowly; humble; petty

حکایات [he.kā.yāt] pl. of حکایت

حکایت [he.kā.yat] story; tale
(pl. حکایات, hekāyāt)

حلوا [hal.vā] halva; kind of sweet
Persian confection

حمّام [ham.mām] bath

حمله [ham.le] attack

[~ kar.dan] [→ کن ~] (به)
to attack

حوصله [how.se.le] patience;
forbearance

بی حوصله [bi ~] impatient; in a bad
mood

حیات [ha.yāt] life (form.)

حیاتی [ha.yā.ti] vital

حیاط [ha.yāt] yard

حیرت [hey.rat] surprise

[~ kar.dan] [→ کن ~] to be
amazed

حیرت‌انگیز [hey.rat-an.giz]
astonishing

حیوان [hey.vān] animal (pl. حیوانات,
hey.vā.nāt)

خار [khār] [→ خاریدن] thorn

خارجی [khā.re.ji] external; foreign
(adj.); foreigner (n.)

خاریدن [khā.ri.dan] [→ خار, khār] to
itch; to scratch (causative:
خاراندن)

خاستن [khās.tan] [→ خیز, khiz] to rise (usually with prefix بر, bar)

خاطر [khā.ter] mind

به خاطرِ/بخاطرِ [be- ~ -e] for the sake of

به خاطر آوَردن [be ~ ā.var.dan] [→ آوَر ~] to remember

از خاطر بُردن [az ~ bor.dan] [→ بَر ~] to forget

از خاطر رفتن [az ~ raf.tan] [→ رو ~] to be forgotten

(به) خاطر* آمدن [(be) ~* ā.ma.dan] [→ آ ~] to remember

خاطر* بودن [~* bu.dan] [→ باش ~] to remember

(از) خاطر* رفتن [(az) ~* raf.tan] [→ رو ~] to forget

خامساً [khā.me.san] fifthly

خاموش [khā.mush] extinguished; off (≠ 'on'); silent

~ کردن [~ kar.dan] [→ کن ~] to turn off; to extinguish; to silence

خانُم [khā.nom] Mrs. or Miss, lady (pl. only with -hā)

خانواده [khā.ne.vā.de] family

خانه [khā.ne] house

خانه‌دار [khā.ne.dār] housewife

خبر [kha.bar] news (countable in Persian; pl. also اخبار, akh.bār)

با خبر بودن (از) [bā ~ bu.dan (az)] [→ باش ~] to know (about/of/ from)

خبر دادن (به) [~ dā.dan (be)] [→ ده ~] to let know, to inform

خبر داشتن (از) [~ dāsh.tan (az)] [→ دار ~] to know (about) (no mi- in pres. and progressive tenses)

(با) خبر کردن [(bā) ~ kar.dan] [→ کن ~] to let know, to inform

خبرساز [kha.bar.sāz] newsmaking

خجالت [khe.jā.lat] embarrassment; humiliation; shame

~ کشیدن (از) [~ ke.shi.dan (az)] [→ کش ~] to be embarrassed (about) or feel ashamed (of)

خجالت‌آور [khe.jā.lat-ā.var] embarrassing

خجالتی [khe.jā.la.ti] shy, bashful, coy

خدا [kho.dā] god

خدا حافظ [kho.dā hā.fez] good-bye; adieu (lit., 'may God protect you')

خداحافظی [kho.dā hā.fe.zi] farewell; goodbye; leave-taking

~ کردن (با) [~ kar.dan (bā)] [→ کن ~] to say goodbye (to)

خدایا [kho.dā́.yā] O God!

خدمت [khed.mat] service (pl. خدمات, kha.da.māt) (for its usage in polite language see Appendix I)

خر [khar] 1) → خریدن; 2) donkey; a stupid person; stupid

خراب [kha.rāb] broken [down]; not functioning; in ruins

خراش [kha.rāsh] [→ خراشیدن] scratch

خراشیدن [kha.rā.shi.dan] [→ خراش, kha.rāsh] to scratch (causative: خراشاندن)

خرامیدن [kh.rām] → خرامیدن

خرامیدن [kha.rā.mi.dan] [→ خرام, kh.rām] to strut (poet.)

خربزه [khar.bo.ze] melon

خرج کردن [kharj kar.dan] [→ کن ~] to spend (money)

خرس [khers] bear

خُرما [khor.mā] date (fruit of date palm)

خروش [kho.rush] [→ خروشیدن] cry;
  uproar

خروشیدن [kho.ru.shi.dan] [→
  خروش, kho.ru.sh] to clamour (lit.)

خرید [kha.rid] shopping; purchase

  ~ کردن [→ کن ~] [~ kar.dan] to
  shop, to do shopping

خریدار [kha.ri.dār] purchaser

خریداری [kha.ri.dā.ri] purchase

  ~ کردن [→ کن ~] [~ kar.dan] to
  purchase

خریدن [kha.ri.dan] [→ خر, khar] to
  buy

خز [khaz] → خزیدن

خزیدن [kha.zi.dan] [→ خز, khaz] to
  crawl (causative: خزاندن)

خستن [khas.tan] [only past tense] to
  wound (obsolete)

خسته [khas.te] tired; bored

  ~ کننده [~ -ko.nan.de] tiring; boring

خشک [khoshk] dry

خطّ [khatt] handwriting; line (on a
  page or in geometry)

خطّی [khat.ti] handwritten

خطر [kha.tar] danger

خطرناک [kha.tar.nāk] dangerous

خفتن [khof.tan] [→ خواب, khāb] to
  sleep (lit.; see خوابیدن)

خلق [khalgh] creation

  ~ کردن [→ کن ~] [~ kar.dan] to
  create

خلیج [kha.lij] gulf

خم [kham] [→ خمیدن, kham] bent;
  bend

خمس [khoms] one-fifth; religious tax
  in Islam

خمیدن [kha.mi.dan] [→ خم, kham] to
  bend (causative: خماندن)

خمیر [kha.mir] paste; dough

خمیر دندان [kha.mir dan.dān] toothpaste

خند [khand] → خندیدن

خندان [khan.dān] laughing (from خندیدن)

خندیدن [khan.di.dan] [→ خند, khand]
  to laugh (causative: خنداندن)

خنده [khan.de] laughter

  ~ کردن [~ kar.dan] to laugh

  ~ کنان [~ ko.nān] (while) laughing

  خنده* گرفتن [~* ge.ref.tan]
  [→ گیر ~] to have to laugh

خواب [khāb] [→ خفتن or خوابیدن]
  sleep (n.); asleep (adj.)

  ~* آمدن [→ آ ~*] [~* ā.ma.dan] to
  feel/get sleepy

  ~* بُردن [→ بَر ~] [~* bor.dan] to
  fall asleep

خوابآور [khāb-ā.var] sedative

خوابیدن [khā.bi.dan] [→ خواب, khāb]
  to sleep; to go to bed (causative:
  خواباندن/خوابانیدن)

خواست [khāst] wish

خواستار [khās.tār] one who wants;
  desirous

خواستگار [khāst.gār or khās.te.gār] suitor

خواستن [khās.tan] [→ خواه, khāh] to
  want

  خواستن (از کسی) (که) to ask (so. to)

خواستنی [khāstani] desirable

خواندن [khān] → خواندن

خوانا [khā.nā] legible

خواندن [khān.dan] [→ خوان, khān] to
  read; to study (tr.); to sing; to call

خواندنی [khān.da.ni] readable; worth
  reading

خواننده [khā.nan.de] reader, singer

خواه [khāh] → خواستن

خواه... خواه...‌ [khāh ... khāh ...]
whether ... or ...

خواهان [khā.hān] one who wants;
desirous

خواهَر [khā.har] sister

خواهر و برادر or خواهر برادر [khā.har
ba.rā.dar or khā.ha.r-o ba.rā.dar]
siblings

خواهش [khā.hesh] request (n.)
~ کردن [~ kar.dan] [→ کن ~] to
request

خواه ناخواه [khāh nā-khāh] willy-nilly;
no matter what

خواهی نخواهی [khā.hi na.khā.hi]
willy-nilly

خوب [khub] good

خود [khod] self; one's own
خودت [kho.dat] yourself; your
own (sg.)

خودتان [kho.de.tān] yourselves;
your own (pl.)

خودش [kho.dash] himself/herself/
itself; his/her/its own

خودشان [kho.de.shān] themselves;
their own

خودم [kho.dam] myself; my own

خودمان [kho.de.mān] ourselves;
our own

خودخواه [khod-khāh] selfish;
egocentric

خودکشی [khod.ko.shi] suicide
~ کردن [~ kar.dan] [→ کن ~] to
commit suicide

خوردن [khor] → خور

خوردن [khor.dan] [→ خور, khor]
to eat (also 'to drink' in
colloquial Persian) (causative:
(خوراندن/خورانیدن

خوردنی [khor.da.ni] edible; fit to eat;
food

خوش [khosh] happy, good, nice
خوش* آمدن (از) [~* ā.ma.dan (az)]
[→ آ ~] to like
خوش گذشتن (به*) [~ go.zash.tan
(be*)] [→ گذر ~] to have a good
time

خوشبخت [khosh.bakht] fortunate;
happy (in life); lucky

خوشبختانه [khosh.bakh.tā.ne]
fortunately; luckily

خوشبختی [khosh.bakh.ti] happiness
(in life)

خوشبو [khosh.bu] fragrant;
sweet-smelling

خوشبین [khosh.bin] optimist (from
(خوش دیدن

خوشبینی [khosh.bi.ni] optimism

خوشحال [khosh.hāl] happy, glad
~ شدن [~ sho.dan] [→ شو ~] to
become happy
~ کردن [~ kar.dan] [→ کن ~] to
make happy

خوشحالی [khosh.hā.li] delight;
cheerfulness

خوشگل [khosh.gel] pretty; cute

خوشمزه [khosh-ma.ze] delicious, tasty

خوشنویسی [khosh-ne.vi.si] calligraphy

خون [khun] blood

خونخوار [khun-khār] bloodthirsty;
bloodsucker

خویش [khish] self; one's own [form./
lit.]

خویشتن [khish.tan] self; one's own
[form./lit.]

خیابان [khi.yā.bān] street

خیّاط [khay.yāt] tailor

خیّاطی [khay.yā.ti] sewing; the tailor's
~ کردن [~ kar.dan] [→ کن ~] to sew

خیال [khi.yāl] imagination, fancy

~ داشتن [~ dāsh.tan] [→ دار ~] to intend

~ کردن [~ kar.dan] [→ کن ~] to imagine, to suppose

خیر [kheyr] no (polite/form.)

خیره شدن (به) [khi.re sho.dan (be)] [→ شو ~] to stare (at)

خیز [khiz] → خاستن

خیس [khis] wet

خیسان [khi.sān] → خیساندن

خیساندن [khi.sān.dan] [→ خیس, khis] to soak

خیلی [khéy.li] (stress on khéy-) very; a lot (of, از)

داخل [dā.khe.l-e] in; inside (form.)

داخلی [dā.khe.li] internal

دادن [dā.dan] [→ دِه, deh/دَه, dah] to give

دار [dār] → داشتن

دارا [dā.rā] 1) wealthy; 2) Dara; boy's name

دارای [dā.rā.ye] having; outfitted with

دارو [dā.ru] medication; drug

داستان [dās.tān] story

داشتن [dāsh.tan] [→ دار, dār] to have (no mi- in pres. and progressive tenses)

داغ [dāgh] hot (≠ cold)

دان [dān] → دانستن

دامن [dā.man] skirt

دانا [dā.nā] wise

دانستن [dā.nes.tan] [→ دان, dān] to know (something, not someone: see شناختن)

دانش [dā.nesh] knowledge

دانش‌آموز [dā.nesh-ā.muz] student of elementary or high school

دانشجو [dā.nesh.ju] a college/university student

دانشکده [dā.nesh.ka.de] faculty

دانشگاه [dā.nesh.gāh] university

دانشمند [dā.nesh.mand] scientist

دانه [dā.ne] 'item' as counting word for inanimates

دبستان [da.bes.tān] elementary school

دبیرستان [da.bi.res.tān] high school

دُختَر [dokh.tar] girl; daughter

دخترانه [dokh.ta.rā.ne] girls', of girls

در [dar] 1) → دریدن; 2) door; 3) in (prep.)

دراز [de.rāz] long

~ کش [~ ke-shi.dan] [→ کش ~] to lie down

در آوردن [dar-ā.var.dan] [→ آور ~] to take off (clothes)

دربارهٔ [dar.bā.re-ye] about (prep.)

دَرجه [da.re.je/da.ra.je] degree, grade; rank; thermometer

درَخت [de.rakht] tree (pl. with both -hā and -ān)

درخش [de.rakhsh] → درخشیدن

درخشیدن [de.rakh.shi.dan] [→ درخش, de.rakhsh] to shine

درخور [dar.khor] suitable; appropriate

درخورِ [~ -e] befitting; worthy of

درد [dard] pain (n.)

~ کردن [~ kar.dan] [→ کن ~] to ache, to feel pain

سر* درد کردن [sar* ~ kar.dan] [→ کن ~] to have a headache

دردِ سَر [dar.d-e sar] trouble

دردآور [dar.d-ā.var] causing pain

دردناک [dard.nāk] painful

درس [*dars*] lesson

[~ خوان →] [~ *khān.dan*] ~ خواندن
to study (*intr.*)

[~ دِه →] [~ *dā.dan (be)*] ~ دادن (به)
to teach (*sth.* to *so.*)

درست [*do.rost*] right, correct; fixed

[~ کن →] [~ *kar.dan*] ~ کردن to
correct; to fix; to do or make (as
doing hair, cooking food)

مثل ~ [~ *mes.l-e*] exactly like

درستی [*do.ros.ti*] correctness; accuracy

درگذشتن [*dar-go.zash.tan*] [→ گذر ~]
to pass away

دروغ [*do.rugh*] lie

گفتن ~ [~ *gof.tan*] [→ گو ~] to tell
a lie; to lie

دروغگو [*do.rugh.gu*] liar

درونِ [*da.ru.n-e*] in; inside (*poet.*)

دریا [*dar.yā*] sea

دریاچه [*dar.yā.che*] lake

دریافت [*dar yāft*] receiving, receipt;
perception

[~ کن →] [~ *kar.dan*] ~ کردن to receive

دریافتن [*dar yāf.tan*] [*dar* is a prefix
here; یافتن → یاب] to find out;
to realize

دریدن [*da.ri.dan*] [→ در, *dar*] to tear
(apart) (*lit.*)

دزد [*dozd*] thief

دزد [*dozd*] → دزدیدن

دزدیدن [*doz.di.dan*] [→ دزد, *dozd*] to
steal

دَست [*dast*] hand (*pl.* with both -*hā*
and -*ān*)

[~ دِه →] [~ *dā.dan (bā)*] ~ دادن (با)
to shake hands (with)

[~ زن →] [~ *za.dan (be)*] ~ زدن (به)
to touch; to undertake

دستشوئی [*dast.shu.'i*] lavatory; toilet
(from دست شستن)

دستگاه [*dast.gāh*] apparatus; machine

دستگیر کردن [*dast.gir kar.dan*]
[~ کن →] to arrest

دستگیری [*dast.gi.ri*] arrest

دستور [*das.tur*] order (*n.*)

[~ دِه →] [~ *dā.dan*] ~ دادن to order

دَسته [*das.te*] handle; haft; bunch, bundle

دشمن [*dosh.man*] enemy

دُعا [*do.'ā*] prayer

[~ کن →] [~ *kar.dan*] ~ کردن to pray

دعائی [*do.'ā.'i*] related to prayers;
optative (*gr.*) (also written دعایی)

دَعوَت [*da'.vat*] invitation

دَعوَت کردن (از) [*da'.vat kar.dan*]
[~ کن →] to invite (*so.*)

دفاتر [*da.fā.ter*] *pl.* of دفتر

دَفتَر [*daf.tar*] notebook (*pl.* دفاتر,
da.fā.ter)

دفتر تلفن [*daf.ta.r-e te.le.fon*]
(a private) phone book

دفعه [*daf.'e*] 'time' as counting word
(*pl.* دفعات, *da.fa.'āt*)

دقایق [*da.ghā.yegh*] *pl.* of دقیقه

دقّت [*degh.ghat*] care; precision; attention

دقیق [*da.ghigh*] precise, accurate, exact,
careful

دقیقه [*da.ghi.ghe*] minute (*pl.* دقایق,
da.ghā.yegh)

دُکتُر [*dok.tor*] doctor

بازی ~ [~-*bā.zi*] playing doctor (no
bad associations in Persian)

دگرگون/دیگرگون [*de.gar.gun/di.gar.gun*]
different; transformed

[~ کن →] [~ *kar.dan*] ~ کردن to
change or transform

دِل [del] heart; figuratively 'inside'; also
stomach (col.)

دل* تنگ شدن (برای) [del* tang sho.
dan (ba.rā.ye)] [→ شو ~] to miss

دل* خواستن [del* khās.tan]
[→ خواه ~] to wish, to want

دل* سوختن (برای/به حالِ) [del*
such.tan (ba.rā.ye/be hā.l-e)]
[→ سوز ~] to feel pity for or
take pity on

دلار [do.lār] dollar

دلایل [da.lā.yel] pl. of دلیل

دلسوزی [del-su.zi] pity

دلیل [da.lil] reason (pl. دلایل, da.lā.yel)

دم [dam] [→ دمیدن] breath

دَما [da.mā] temperature (form.)

دمیدن [da.mi.dan] [→ دم, dam] to
blow; to grow (of plants)

دنبال [don.bāl] behind; after

دنبالِ...گشتن [don.bā.l-e ... gash.tan]
[گرد → گشتن] to search for ...

دندان [dan.dān] tooth

دندانپزشک [dan.dān-pe.zeshk] dentist

دنیا [don.yā] world

به دنیا آمدن [be ~ ā.ma.dan] [→ آ ~]
to be born

به دنیا آوردن [be ~ ā.var.dan]
[→ آور ~] to bear, to give
birth to

دو [do] two

هر دو [har do] both

دُو [dow/dav] → دویدن

دوا [da.vā] medicine, medication

دوازده [da.vāz.dah] twelve

دوان دوان [da.vān da.vān] running fast

دوباره [do-bā.re] again

دوچرخه [do char.khe] bicycle

دوختن ¹ [dukh.tan] [→ دوز, duz] to sew

نگاه را دوختن/چشم دوختن (به)
[ne.gāh rā ~/cheshm ~ (be)]
[→ دوز ~] to fix the eyes (on);
gaze (at)

دوختن ² [dukh.tan] [→ دوش, dush] to
milk (more common form:
دوشیدن)

دُور [dow.r-e] around

دور [dur] far, faraway; remote, distant

افتادن ~ [~ of.tā.dan] [→ افت ~] to
be thrown away, to be discarded
(intr.)

انداختن ~ [~ an.dākh.tan] [→ انداز ~]
to throw away, to discard (tr.)

ریختن ~ [~ rikh.tan] [→ ریز ~] to
pour out (tr. only)

دوز [duz] → دوختن¹

دوست [dust] friend

دوستانه [dus.tā.ne] friendly

دوست داشتن [dust dāsh.tan] [→ دار ~]
to like (no mi- in pres. and
progressive tenses)

دوست داشتنی [dust-dāsh.ta.ni]
adorable, lovely

دوش [dush] [→ دوختن² or دوشیدن]
shower

گرفتن ~ [~ ge.ref.tan] [→ گیر ~] to
take a shower

دوشنبه [do-sham.be] Monday

دوشیدن [du.shi.dan] [→ دوش, dush] to
milk (see also: دوختن²)

دو قلو [do-gho.lu] twin

دول [do.val] pl. of دولت

دولت [dow.lat] government (pl. دول,
doval)

دولتی [dow.la.ti] of government or
state; governmental

دوّم [dov.vom] second (2nd)

دوّماً [dov.vo.man] secondly

دوّمین [dov.vo.min] second (2nd)

دویدن [da.vi.dan] [→ دُو, dow → dav] to run (causative: دواندن, da.vān.dan)

دویست [de.vist] two hundred

دَه [dah] ten

ده [deh] village

ده/دَه [deh/dah] → دادن

دَهان [da.hān] mouth (form./wrt.)

دَهَن [da.han] mouth

دید [did] view; opinion

دیدار [di.dār] visit

~ کردن [~ kar.dan] [→ کن] to visit

دیدن [di.dan] [→ بین , bin] to see

دیدنی [di.da.ni] sight; worth seeing; spectacular

دیر [dir] late

دیر* شدن [→ شو ~] [dir sho.dan] to be late

دیروز [di.ruz] yesterday

دیکته [dik.te] dictation, spelling

دیگر [di.gar] other (adj.); else; any longer (adv., in negative sentences); already

دفعهٔ دیگر [daf.'e-ye di.gar] next time [lit. 'other time']

یک ساعتِ دیگر [yek sā.'a.t-e di.gar] within or after (an hour) [lit. 'in another hour']

دیگرگون [di.gar.gun] see دگرگون

دین [din] religion (pl. ادیان, ad.yān)

دیندار [din.dār] believer

دیوار [di.vār] wall

دیوانه [di.vā.ne] crazy; insane

ذهن [zehn] mind (pl. اذهان, az.hān)

به ذهن سپردن [be ~ se.por.dan] to commit to memory

را [rā] 'definite direct object' marker

رابعاً [rā.be.'an] fourthly

راجع به [rā.je'be] about; concerning

راحت [rā.hat] comfortable; easy

براحتی/به‌راحتی [be rā.ha.ti] easily

رادیو [rā.di.yo] radio

راست [rāst] right

راستش [rās.tash] the truth of it; to be honest (col.)

راضی [rā.zi] content; contented; happy, satisfied, pleased

~ کردن [~ kar.dan] [→ کن] to satisfy; to cause to agree

از خود راضی [az khod ~] self-satisfied; self-important; smug

راندن → ران [rān]

راندن [rān.dan] [→ ران ~] to drive

رانندگی [rā.nan.de.gi] driving

~ کردن [~ kar.dan] [→ کن] to drive

راننده [rā.nan.de] driver

راه [rāh] way, road; method

راه رفتن [rāh raf.tan] [→ رو ~] to walk/stroll (at or in some place, not to)

راهرو [rāh.row] corridor

رأی [ra'y] vote; verdict; opinion (pl. آراء, ārā')

رأی دادن [ra'y dā.dan] [→ دِه ~] to vote

رأی‌گیری [ra'y.gi.ri] voting

ربا → ربودن [ro.bā]

ربط [rabt] relation; connection

ربع [rob'] a quarter

ربودن [ro.bu.dan] [→ ربا, ro.bā] to steal (form.)

رد شدن (در/از) [rad sho.dan (dar/az)] [→ شو ~] to fail (in [a test]), to be rejected; also to pass (locational, as on the street)

ردیف [*ra.dif*] row

رزم [*razm*] [→ رزمیدن] battle

رزمیدن [*raz.mi.dan*] [*razm*, رزم →]
to combat (*lit.*)

رس [*res*] → رسیدن

رسا [*re.sā/ra.sā*] far reaching and loud

رسان [*re.sān*] → رساندن

رساندن/رسانیدن [*re.sān.dan/
re.sā.ni.dan*] [*re.sān*, رسان →, *re.sān*]
to cause to reach; to deliver

رَستن [*ras.tan*] [*rah*, ره →] to escape or
be saved

رُستن [*ros.tan*] [→ رو, *ru*] to grow (of
plants) (causative: **رویاندن**)

رستوران [*res.to.rān*] restaurant

رسمی [*ras.mi*] formal

رسید [*re.sid*] receipt (of purchase,
etc.)

رسیدن [*re.si.dan*] [→ رس, *res*] to
reach, arrive

For نظر به نظر رسیدن see under نظر.

چه رسد به [*che re.sad be*]

رسیده [*re.si.de*] ripe (used for fruits)

رشتن [*resh.tan*] [→ ریس, *ris*] to spin

رشته [*reshte*] field (of knowledge or
study); major (in education);
line, thread

رشتۀ تحصیلی [*resh.te-ye tah.si.li*] major
(in education)

رشوه [*resh.ve*] bribe

رضایت [*re.zā.yat*] satisfaction;
agreement

دادن ~ [*~ dā.dan*] [→ ده ~] to
approve; to give consent

رعایت [*re.'ā.yat*] consideration;
observance

کردن ~ [*~ kar.dan*] [→ کن ~] to
observe; to follow

رفتار [*raf.tār*] behavior; conduct;
manners

کردن ~ [*~ kar.dan*] [→ کن ~] to
behave or act

رفتن [*raf.tan*] [→ رو, *row/rav*] to go

رُفتن/روفتن [*rof.tan/ruf.tan*] [→ روب,
rub] to sweep

رفت و آمد [*raf.t-o-ā.mad*] coming and
going; traffic

رقص [*raghs*] [→ رقصیدن] dance

رقصان [*ragh.sān*] dancing

رقصیدن [*ragh.si.dan*] [→ رقص, *raghs*]
to dance (causative: **رقصاندن**)

رم [*ram*] → رمیدن

رُمان [*ro.mān*] novel

رمیدن (از) [*ra.mi.dan*] [→ رم, *ram*] to
shy (away from) (causative:
رماندن)

رنج [*ranj*] [→ رنجیدن] pain; torment

رنجیدن (از) [*ran.ji.dan*] [→ رنج, *ranj*]
to take offence (at)
(causative: **رنجاندن**)

رنگ [*rang*] color

رو [*row/rav*] → رفتن

رو [*ru*] 1) → رُستن or روئیدن 2) face;
3) on

رَوان [*ra.vān*] going; flowing; running;
fluent; soul

روبروی [*ru-be-ru-ye*] in front of; facing

رودخانه [*rud.khā.ne*] river

روز [*ruz*] day

روزانه [*ru.zā.ne*] daily

روز تولد [*ru.z-e ta.val.lod*] birthday

روش [*ra.vesh*] method

روشن [*row.shan*] bright (also 'on' as
light or fire or a device)

کردن ~ [*~ kar.dan*] [→ کن ~] to
turn on; to fire up

روشنی [row.sha.ni] light; brightness

روفتن [ruf.tan] see رُفتن [rof.tan]

روی [ru-ye] on (prep.)

روئیدن [ru.'i.dan] [→ رو, ru] to grow (of plants) (causative: رویاندن)

ره [rah] → رَستن or رَهیدن

رها [ra.hā] free

~ شدن [~ sho.dan] [→ شو ~] to be freed or rescued

رهیدن [ra.hi.dan] [→ ره, rah] to escape or be saved (form./lit.)

ریاضی [ri.yā.zi] mathematical (adj.); mathematics (n.) (pl. ریاضیّات, ri.yā.ziy.yāt);

ریختن [rikh.tan] [→ ریز, riz] to pour; to spill (tr./intr.)

ریخت و پاش [rikh.t-o-pāsh] spillage; squandering

ریز [riz] → ریختن

ریس [ris] → رشتن

ریشه [ri.she] root; stem (gr.)

رئیس [ra.'is] chief; boss; head or director (pl. رؤسا, ro.'a.sā)

رئیس جمهور [ra.'is[-e] jom.hur] president of the republic (ezāfe usually dropped in colloquial Persian)

زا [zā] → زادن and زائیدن

زادن [zā.dan] [→ زا, zā] to bear a child (form.; see زائیدن)

زانو [zā.nu] knee (no -y- glide needed for pl. with -ān)

زائیدن [zā.'i.dan] [→ زا, zā] to bear a child

زَبان [za.bān] tongue; language

زبانِ مادری [za.bā.n-e mā.da.ri] mother tongue

زدا [zo.dā] → زدودن

زدن [za.dan] [→ زن, zan] to hit, to strike; to play an instrument

زدودن [zo.du.dan] [→ زدا, zo.dā] to clean; to rub off

زرنگ [ze.rang] clever

زرنگی [ze.ran.gi] cleverness

زشت [zesht] ugly

زشتی [zesh.ti] ugliness

زمان [za.mān] tense (gr.); time

زمانِ حال [~ -e hāl] present tense (gr.)

زمستان [ze.mes.tān] winter

زمین [za.min] earth; ground; field (in sports); floor

(به) زمین خوردن [(be) za.min khor.dan] [→ خور ~] to fall down; to fall on the ground

زمین‌شناس [za.min-she.nās] geologist

زمین‌شناسی [za.min-she.nā.si] geology

زَن [zan] 1) → زدن; 2) woman; wife

زنانه [za.nā.ne] womanly, feminine, of women or women's

زنبیل [zan.bil] basket

زندان [zen.dān] prison

زندانی [zen.dā.ni] prisoner

زندگی [zen.de.gi] life (= the period from birth to death)

~ کردن [~ kar.dan] [→ کن ~] to live

زنده [zen.de] alive

زنده باد (...)! [zen.de bād] well done!; long live ...!

زنگ [zang] [sound of] ring; bell

زنگ زدن (به) [zang za.dan (be)] [→ زن ~] to call (per phone); to give [so.] a ring

زود [zud] early; fast

بزودی/به‌زودی [be-zu.di] soon; before long

251

زور [zur] force

به زور/بزور [be-zur] forcibly; by
force; against your will; with
too much persistence or
begging

زیستن → [zi] زی

زیاد [zi.yād] much, a lot

زیادی [zi.yā.dí] too much

زیبیدن → [zib] زیب

زیبا [zi.bā] beautiful

زیبائی [zi.bā.'í] beauty

زیبیدن [zi.bi.dan] [→ زیب, zib] to
befit, to become

زیپ [zip] zip, zip fastener, zipper

زیرا [zi.rā] because

زیرک [zi.rak] smart

زیرکانه [zi.ra.kā.ne] smart; smartly

زیستن [zis.tan] [→ زی, zi] to live
(form.)

زینت [zi.nat] ornament

سائیدن → [sā] سا

سابیدن → [sāb] ساب

سابیدن [sā.bi.dan] [→ ساب, sāb] to
grind; to abrade (see also
سائیدن)

ساحل [sā.hel] shore; beach

ساختمان [sākh.te.mān] building

ساختن [sākh.tan] [→ ساز, sāz] to build
(in formal Persian used as a
substitute for کردن, but not
recommended)

ساده [sā.de] simple

ساز [sāz] ← ساختن

ساعات [sā.'āt] pl. of ساعت

ساعت [sā.'at] hour; watch; clock
(pl. ساعات, sā.'āt)

ساقی [sā.ghi] saki; cup-bearer

ساکن [sā.ken] resident (n.; pl. سکنه,
sa.ka.ne); settled (adj.); not
moving

سال [sāl] year

سالانه [sā.lā.ne] yearly; annual (also
سالیانه, sā.li.yā.ne)

سالم [sā.lem] healthy; healthful

سانتیگراد [sān.ti.ge.rād] centigrade

سایه [sā.ye] shadow

سائیدن [sā.'i.dan] [→ سا, sā] to grind;
to abrade (form.; less formal:
سابیدن)

سبب [sa.bab] cause; reason

به سبب [be ~ -e] because of

سبب شدن/سبب ... شدن [~ sho.dan/
~ -e ... sho.dan] [→ شو, sho.dan] to
cause

سببی [sa.ba.bi] causative, factitive (gr.)

سبد [sa.bad] basket

سبز [sabz] green

سبزی [sab.zi] vegetable (pl. sometimes
سبزیجات, sab.zi.jāt)

سبک [sabk] style

سپردن → [se.pār/se.por] سپردن

سپردن [se.por.dan] [→ سپر, se.por, or
سپار, se.pār] to entrust

ستاره [se.tā.re] star

ستودن → [se.tā] ستا

ستاندن → [se.tān] ستان

ستاندن [se.tān.dan] [→ ستان, se.tān]
to take (lit.)

ستایش [se.tā.yesh] praise

ستایش کردن [~ kar.don] [→ کن ~
to praise, to admire

ستردن → [se.tor] ستر

ستردن [se.tor.dan] [→ ستر, se.tor]
to eliminate or erase

سُتودن [so.tu.dan] [← ستا, se.tā]
to praise, to admire

سُتودنی [so.tu.da.ni] admirable,
praiseworthy

سحر [sa.har] dawn

سحرخیز [sa.har-khiz] early riser (from
sleep)

سخت [sakht] hard

[~ گیر ←] [~ ge.ref.tan]
to be strict and harsh

سختگیر [sakht-gir] unyielding,
inflexible, serious

سختگیری [sakht-gi.ri] severity; harsh
treatment

[~ کن ←] [~ kar.dan] to be
strict and harsh

سختی [sakh.ti] difficulty; hardship;
hardness

[be- ~] بسختی/به سختی with
difficulty; hard (adv.)

سخن [so.khan] speech, talk (form.)

[~ gof.tan (bā)] (با)
[~ گو ←] to speak (to) (form.)

سخنران [so.khan.rān] speaker (at a
podium) (from سخن راندن)

سخنگو [so.khan.gu] speaker (n., as a
position); talking (adj.) (from
سخن گفتن)

سَر [sar] head

سُر [sor] → سُریدن

سِرّ [serr] secret (pl. اسرار, as.rār)

سُرا [so.rā] → سُرودن

سرباز [sar.bāz] soldier

سرخ [sorkh] red

سرد [sard] cold

[~* ~ bu.dan] [← باش ~] بودن* to
feel cold

سر* درد کردن [sar* ~ kar.dan]
[~ کن ←] to have a headache

سرزنش [sar-za.nesh] blaming

[~ کردن ←] [~ kar.dan] to
blame

سُرعَت [sor.'at] speed

[be ~] بسرعت/به سرعت speedily;
fast

سرفه [sor.fe] cough (n.)

[~ کردن ←] [~ kar.dan] to
cough

سرگرم کردن [sar-garm kar.dan]
[~ کن ←] to amuse; to entertain

سرگرم کننده [sar-garm ko.nan.de]
amusing

سُرود [so.rud] song; hymn

سُرودن [so.ru.dan] [← سُرا, so.rā] to
compose a poem

سروصدا [sar-o-se.dā] noise

[~ کردن ←] [~ kar.dan] to
make noise

سُریدن [so.ri.dan] [← سُر, sor] to slip

سریع [sa.ri'] fast (adj./adv.)

سریعاً [sa.ri.'an] fast (adv.); speedily

سزاوار [se.zā.vār] deserving; worthy

[~ bu.dan] [← باش ~] to
deserve; to be worthy of

سعدی [sa'.di] Saadi (poet, 13th
century)

سعی [sa'y; y here is a consonant]
effort (pl. مساعی, masā'i)

[~ کردن ←] [~ kar.dan] to try

سفارت/سفارتخانه [se.fā.rat/se.fā.rat-
khā.ne] embassy

سفر [sa.far] travel

[~ kar.dan (be)] کردن (به)
[~ کن ←] to travel (to)

سفید [se.fid] white

سفیدپوست [se.fid-pust] of white
skin/race

سقف [*saghf*] ceiling

ساکن pl. of [*sa.ka.ne*] سکنه

سکوت [*so.kut*] silence

سگ [*sag*] dog

سلام [*sa.lām*] hello, hi

to say [→ کن/گو —] ~ کردن/گفتن
hello

to give [→ رسان —] ~ رساندن (به)
greetings (to)

سلیقه [*sa.li.ghe*] taste; style

سلیقه بی [*bi-* ~] lacking good taste

سلیقگی بی [*bi-sa.li.ghe.gi*] lack good
taste

سنّ [*senn*] age (i.e., years lived)

سنّت [*son.nat*] tradition

سنّتی [*son.na.ti*] traditional

سند [*sa.nad*] document (*pl.* اسناد,
as.nād)

سنگ [*sang*] stone

سنگین [*san.gin*] heavy

سو [*su*] side; direction (*form.*)

سویِ از [*az su-ye*] by, through, from

سویِ (به) [*(be) su-ye*] towards

سواد [*sa.vād*] literacy

باسواد [*bā-* ~] literate

بیسواد/بی سواد [*bi-* ~] illiterate

شدن...سوارِ [*sa.vā.r-e . . . sho.dan*] to
get on or ride in/on (a vehicle/
horse) [شو → شدن]

سؤال [*so.'āl*] question (*pl.* سؤالات,
so.'ā.lāt)

کن → [*~ kar.dan (az)*] کردن (از)
~] to ask (a question *from*)

سوختن [*sukh.tan*] [سوز →, *suz*] to
burn (*tr./intr.*) (causative:
(**سوزاندن**

سوز [*suz*] → سوختن

سوزان [*su.zān*] ablaze; burning; hot;
scorching (from سوختن)

سوزش [*su.zesh*] burning sensation or
twinge

سوّم [*sev.vom*] third (3rd)

سوّماً [*sev.vo.man*] thirdly

سوّمین [*sev.vo.min*] third (3rd)

سه [*se*] three

سه شنبه [*se-sham.be*] Tuesday

سی [*si*] thirty

سیاست [*si.yā.sat*] politics

سیاستمدار [*si.yā.sat-ma.dār*] politician

سیاه [*si.yāh*] black

سیاهپوست [*si.yāh-pust*] of black skin/race

سیب [*sib*] apple

سیب زمینی [*sib za.mi.ni*] potato
('pomme de terre')

سیر [*sir*] full, no more hungry; garlic

سیزده [*siz.dah*] thirteen

سیصد [*si.sad*] three hundred

سیگار [*si.gār*] cigarette

کش → [*~ ke.shi.dan*] کشیدن
to smoke cigarettes

سینما [*si.ne.mā/si.na.mā*] cinema

سینه [*si.ne*] chest; breast

سینه زنی [*si.ne-za.ni*] chest-beating,
a Shiite ritual

شا [*shā*] → شایستن

شاخ [*shākh*] horn

شاخه [*shā.khe*] branch

شاد [*shād*] happy, glad

شادی [*shā.di*] happiness, gladness

کن → [*~ kar.dan*] کردن to
rejoice; to cheer

شاعر [*shā.'er*] poet (*pl.* شعرا, *sho.'a.rā*)

شاعرانه [*shā.'e.rā.ne*] poetical

شاعِره [shā.'e.re] poetess

شاگرد [shā.gerd] pupil

~ اوّل [~ av.val] best student in the class; class winner

شام [shām] supper; dinner

شانزده [shānz.dah] sixteen

شانه [shā.ne] shoulder; comb

شایان [shā.yān] deserving; worthy

شاید [shā.yad] maybe, perhaps; may (modal verb; same form for all persons) (stress on shā-)

شایستگی [shā.yes.te.gi] merit; worthiness

~ داشتن [~ dāsh.tan] [→ دار ~] to deserve; to be worthy of

شایستن [shā.yes.tan] [→ شا, shā] to deserve; to be appropriate (poet.)

شایسته [shā.yes.te] deserving; worthy

~ بودن [~ bu.dan] [→ باش ~] to deserve; to be worthy of

شَب [shab] night

شباهت [she.bā.hat] similarity

~ داشتن (به) [~ dāsh.tan (be)] [→ دار ~] to be similar (to)

شبکار [shab-kār] night shift worker

شبیه [sha.bih] similar

شبیه/شبیه به [~ -e/~ be] similar to

شتاب [she.tāb] [→ شتافتن] hurry

~ کردن [~ kar.dan] [→ کن ~] to hurry

شتافتن [she.tāf.tan] [→ شتاب, she.tāb] to hurry (lit.)

شتر [sho.tor] camel

شترمرغ [sho.tor-morgh] ostrich

شجاع [sho.jā'] brave

شجاعانه [sho.jā.'ā.ne] brave; bravely

شخص [shakhs] person (pl. اشخاص, ash.khās, persons, people)

شخصی [shakh.si] personal

شدن [sho.dan] [→ شو, show/shav] to become

شدنی [sho.da.ni] doable; possible

شراب [sha.rāb] wine

شرایط [sha.rā.yet] treated as pl. of شرط = circumstances; conditions; situation

شرط [shart] condition (pl. شروط, sho.rut)

به شرطی که/به شرطِ اینکه/آنکه [be shar.ti ke/be shar.t-e in ke/ān ke] provided that

شرطی [shar.ti] conditional (gr.)

شرق [shargh] East

شرقی [shar.ghi] Eastern

شرم [sharm] shame

شرمناک [sharm.nāk] ashamed

شروع [sho.ru'] beginning

~ کردن [~ kar.dan] [→ کن ~] to begin (often with به)

شست [shast] thumb; toe

شستشو [shos.to.shu] washing

شستن [shos.tan] [→ شو, shu; in colloquial شور, shur] to wash

شست و شو [shos.t-o-shu] see شستشو above

شش [shesh] six

ششصد [shesh.sad] six hundred

شصت [shast] sixty

شطرنج [shat.ranj] chess

شعار [sho.'ār] slogan; motto

شعر [she'r] poem; poetry (pl. اشعار, ash'ār)

شعرا [sho.'a.rā] pl. of شاعِر

شغل [shoghl] occupation; job (pl. مشاغل, ma.shā.ghel)

شک [shak] doubt

داشتن (به/در) ~] ـ dāsh.tan (be/
dar)] [دار →] to have doubts
(in/about) (no mi- in pres. and
progressive tenses)

کردن (به/در) ~] ـ kar.dan (be/dar)]
[کن ~→] to doubt

شکار [she.kār] hunt

کردن ~] [کن ~→] to hunt ـ kar.dan]

شکارچی [she.kār.chi] hunter

شکر [she.kar] sugar

شکست [she.kast] defeat (n.) [short
infinitive or past stem of the
verb شکستن, she.kas.tan]

خوردن (از) ~] ـ khor.dan (az)]
[خور ~→] to be defeated (by);
to lose

دادن ~] ـ dā.dan] [ده ~→] to defeat

ناپذیر ~] ـ-nā-pa.zir] invincible

شکستن [she.kas.tan] [شکن →, she.kan]
to break (tr. and intr.)
(causative: **شکاندن**)

شکل [shekl] shape; form (pl. اشکال,
ash.kāl)

شکلات [sho.ko.lāt] chocolate

شکم [she.kam] belly

شکن [she.kan] → شکستن

شکنجه [she.kan.je] torture

کردن ~] ـ kar.dan] [کن ~→] to torture

شکننده [she.ka.nan.de] fragile

شما [sho.mā] you (pl.)

شمار [sho.mār] (form.) → شمردن

به) شمار آمدن) [be - ā.ma.dan]
[آ ~→] to be counted or
considered

شمارش [sho.mā.resh] counting

شماره [sho.mā.re] number

شمال [sho.māl] North

شمال غربی [sho.mā.l-e ghar.bi]
Northwest; northwestern

شمر [she.mor; also sho.-] → شمردن

شمردن [she.mor.dan; also sho.-]
[شمر →, she.mor – or (form.)
شمار, sho.mār] to count

شنا [she.nā] swimming

کردن ~] ـ kar.dan] [کن ~→] to swim

شناخت [she.nākht] knowledge;
understanding

شناختن [she.nākh.tan] [شناس →,
shenās] to know (a person), to
be familiar with; to recognize
(causative: **شناساندن**)

شناس [she.nās] → شناختن

شنبه [shan.be/sham.be] Saturday

شنف [she.nof] → شنفتن

شنفتن [she.nof.tan] [شنف →, she.nof,
or شنو, she.now → she.nav] to
hear (see شنیدن)

شنو [she.now → she.nav] → شنیدن

شنوا [she.na.vā] capable of hearing,
not deaf

شنودن [sho.nu.dan] [شنو →, she.now
→ she.nav] (poet.) see شنیدن

شنیدن [she.ni.dan] [شنو →, she.now →
she.nav] to hear

شنیدنی [she.ni.da.ni] worth listening

شو [show/shav] → شدن

شو [shu] → شستن

شور [shur] 1) شستن →; 2)شوریدن;
3) salty; having too much salt

شورش [shu.resh] rebellion

شورشی [shu.re.shi] rebel

شوریدن [shu.ri.dan] [شور →, shur] to
rebel (causative: **شوراندن**)

شوهر [show.har] husband

شَهر [shahr] city

شهردار [shahr.dār] mayor

شهری [shah.ri] urban

شهناز [shah.nāz] Shahnaz (girl's name)

شیاطین [sha.yā.tin] pl. of شیطان

شیر [shir] milk; lion; faucet

شیراز [shi.rāz] Shiraz (city in Iran)

شیرزن [shir-zan] courageous woman, heroine (lit. 'lion-woman' or lioness)

شیرین [shi.rin] sweet
    کردن ~ [~ kar.dan] [→ کن ~] to sweeten; to make or change into sweet

شیطان [shey.tān] Satan (n.); naughty (adj.) (pl. شیاطین, sha.yā.tin)

شیکاگو [shi.kā.go] Chicago

صاحب [sā.heb] owner

صادق هدایت [sā.degh he.dā.yat] Sadegh Hedayat (writer, 1903–51)

صبح [sobh] morning

صبر [sabr] patience
    صبر داشتن [→ دار ~] [sabr dāsh.tan] to have patience [داشتن → دار] (no mi- in pres. and progressive tenses)
    کردن [→ کن ~] [~ kar.dan] to wait
    بی‌صبرانه [bi-sab.rā.ne] impatiently

صحبت [soh.bat] conversation
    کردن ~ [→ کن ~] [~ kar.dan] to speak

صد [sad] hundred

صدا [se.dā] sound; voice
    کردن/زدن ~ [~ kar.dan/za.dan] [→ کن/زن ~] to call so.

صرف کردن [sarf kar.dan] [→ کن ~] to spend, to consume, to have; also to conjugate (gr.)

صفت [se.fat] adjective (gr.) (pl. صفات, se.fāt)

صفت اشاره [se.fa.t-e e.shā.re] demonstrative adjective (gr.)

صفتِ تفضیلی [se.fa.t-e taf.zi.li] comparative adjective

صفتِ عالی [se.fa.t-e ā.li] superlative adjective

صفتِ مفعولی [se.fa.t-e maf.'u.li] 'participial adjective' or past participle = اسم مفعول

صفحه [saf.he] page (pl. صفحات, sa.fa.hāt)

صفر [sefr] zero

صلح [solh] peace

صلیب [sa.lib] cross
    صلیبِ سرخ [~ -e sorkh] red cross

صندلی [san.da.li] chair

صُوَر [so.var] shapes (pl. of صورت)

صورت [su.rat] face; case; shape (pl. in this sense صُوَر, so.var)
    به صورتی که [be su.ra.ti ke] in such a way that
    در صورتی که [dar su.ra.ti ke] in case, in the event that; whereas
    در غیر این صورت [dar ghey.r-e in su.rat] if not so; otherwise

ضدّ [zed.de] used as prefix meaning anti- or counter-; also used after به or بر to mean against
    ضدّ انقلابی [zed-de-en.ghe.lā.bi] counter-revolutionary

ضرورت [za.ru.rat] necessity; need
    داشتن ~ [→ دار ~] [~ dāsh.tan] to be necessary

ضروری [za.ru.ri] necessary (pl. ضروریات, za.ru.riy.yāt, necessities)

ضعفا [zo.'a.fā] pl. of ضعیف

ضعیف [za.'if] weak (pl. ضعفا, zo.'a.fā)

257

ضمائر/ضمایر [za.mā.'er/za.mā.yer] pl.
of ضمیر

ضمیر [za.mir] pronoun (gr.)
(pl. ضمائر, za.mā.'er)

ضمیر اشاره [za.mi.r-e e.shā.re]
demonstrative pronoun (gr.)

طبیب [ta.bib] physician (old-fashioned)
(pl. اطبّاء, a.teb.bā')

طبیعت [ta.bi.'at] nature

طرح [tarh] plan; scheme; design

طرف [ta.raf] direction; side; party
[involved] (pl. اطراف, at.rāf =
around or surroundings)

از طرفِ [az ~ -e] by, through, from

به طرفِ [be ~ -e] towards; in
direction of

طرق [to.rogh] pl. of طریق

طریق [ta.righ] way, road (pl., طرق,
to.rogh)

از طریقِ [az ~ -e] by [way of]

طعم [ta'm] taste (of food); flavor

طلاق [ta.lāgh] divorce

طلب [ta.lab] [طلبیدن →] desire

طلبیدن [ta.la.bi.dan] [→ طلب, ta.lab]
to desire

طور [towr] manner, method

بطوری/به طوری (که) [be ~ -i (ke)]
in such a way (that)

طوطی [tu.ti] parrot

طول [tul] length

کشیدن [~ ke.shi.dan] [→ کش ~]
to continue in time, to go on, to
require or take (time)

طولانی [tu.lā.ni] long

ظاهراً [zā.he.ran] apparently

ظرف [zarf] dish (pl. ظروف, zoruf)

ظرفِ [zar.f-e] within (temp.)

ظروف [zo.ruf] pl. of ظرف

ظهر [zohr] noon

عادت [ā.dat] habit (pl. عادات, ā.dāt)

دادن (به) [~ dā.dan (be)] [→ ده ~]
to make accustomed to, to cause
to get used to (tr.)

داشتن (به) [~ dāsh.tan] [→ دار ~]
to be accustomed (to)

کردن (به) [~ kar.dan (be)]
[→ کن ~] to get accustomed to,
to get used to (intr.)

عاشِق [ā.shegh] lover (pl. عشّاق,
osh.shāgh)

عاشِقِ...بودن [~ -e bu.dan]
[→ باش ~] to love

عاشِقانه [ā.she.ghā.ne] romantic,
amorous; amorously

عاقبت [ā.ghe.bat] conclusion; finally
(pl. عواقب, a.vā.gheb)

عاقل [ā.ghel] wise (used for humans)

عاقلانه [ā.ghe.lā.ne] wise; wisely

عالی [ā.li] excellent

جنابعالی [je.nā.b-e 'ā.li] your
excellency

حضرتعالی [haz.ra.t-e 'ā.li] your
eminence

عجب [a.jab] (how) strange

عجله [a.ja.le] hurry; haste; rush

کردن/داشتن [~ kar.dan/dāsh.tan]
[→ کن/دار ~] to hurry; to
hasten

عجیب [a.jib] strange

عدد [a.dad] number (pl. اعداد, a'.dād)
(gr.)

عذرخواهی [ozr.khā.hi] apology

کردن [~ kar.dan] [→ کن ~] to
apologize

عرب [a.rab] Arab (pl. اعراب, a'.rāb)

عربی [a.ra.bi] Arabic (language)

عرض کردن [arz kar.dan] [→ کن ~] to
say (for use in polite language
see Appendix I)

عرضه [ar.ze] presentation; supply
~ کردن [~ kar.dan] [→ کن ~] to
present; to supply

عروسک [a.ru.sak] doll

عَزیز [a.ziz] dear

عُشّاق [osh.shāgh] pl. of عاشق

عُشر [oshr] one-tenth

عشق [eshgh] love

عصا [a.sā] walking stick, cane

عصبانی [a.sa.bā.ni] angry

عصبانیّت [a.sa.bā.niy.yat] anger

عفو [afv] pardon
~ کردن [~ kar.dan] [→ کن ~] to
pardon

عقل [aghl] wisdom; intellect; reason;
common sense

عقل‌گرا [aghl-ge.rā] rationalist

عقل‌گرائی [aghl-ge.rā.'i] rationalism

عکس [aks] picture; photo
~ گرفتن (از) [~ ge.ref.tan (az)]
[→ گیر ~] to take photos (of)

علاقمند/علاقه‌مند (به) [a.lā.ghe.mand]
interested (in); fond (of)

علاقه [a.lā.ghe] interest; liking; attachment
~ داشتن (به) [~ dāsh.tan (be)] to be
interested in; to like; to be fond
of [داشتن → دار]

علی [a.li] Ali; boy's name

علیرغم/علی‌رغم [a.lā ragh.m-e] in spite
of (more form.: برغم/به رغم)

عمل [a.mal] act; action; practice; [surgical]
operation (pl. اعمال, a'.māl)
~ کردن [~ kar.dan] [→ کن ~] to act;
to perform surgery

عمو [a.mu] uncle (father's side)

عمومی [o.mu.mi] public

عناصر [a.nā.ser] pl. of عنصر

عنصر [on.sor] element (pl. عناصر,
a.nā.ser)

عنوان [on.vān] title (pl. عناوین a.nā.vin)
به‌عنوانِ [be on.vā.n-e] as; in the
position of

عواقب [a.vā.gheb] consequences
(pl. of عاقبت, ā.ghe.bat)

عوض [a.vaz] exchange; substitute
(در) عوضِ [dar ~ -e] in exchange
for; instead of
~ کردن [~ kar.dan] [→ کن ~] to
change; to exchange

عهد [ahd] promise; oath

عهد شکن [ahd-she.kan] promise
breaker; disloyal

عیب [eyb] fault, deficiency (pl. عیوب,
o.yub or معایب, ma.'ā.yeb)

عینِ [ey.n-e] exactly like (col.)

عینک [ey.nak] eyeglasses (in Persian sg.)

عیوب [o.yub] pl. of عیب

غالباً [ghā.le.ban] often

غذا [gha.zā] food (pl. اغذیه, agh.zi.ye)
~ پَز [~ pokh.tan] [→ پَز ~] to
cook (intr.)
~ خوردن [~ khor.dan] [→ خور ~]
to eat (intr.)

غذائی [gha.zā.'i] (of) food; nutritional,
dietary

غرّ [ghorr] → غرّیدن

غرب [gharb] West

غربی [ghar.bi] Western

غرق شدن [ghargh sho.dan] [→ شو ~]
to drown (intr.)

غروب [gho.rub] sunset; dusk; nightfall

غرّیدن [*ghor.ri.dan*] [→ غرّ, *ghorr*] to growl; to rumble

غزل [*gha.zal*] ghazal; a genre in poetry (*pl.* غزلیّات, *gha.za.liy.yāt*)

غصّه [*ghos.se*] grief

غصّه خوردن (برایِ) [*ghos.se khor.dan (ba.rā.ye)*] [→ خور ~] to grieve, to be sad (about)

غلت [*ghalt*] → غلتیدن

غلتیدن [*ghal.ti.dan*] [→ غلت, *ghalt*] to roll (causative: غلتاندن)

غلط [*gha.lat*] wrong; mistake (*pl.* اغلاط, *agh.lāt*)

غلطیدن [*ghal.ti.dan*] [→ غلط, *ghalt*] see غلتیدن

غم [*gham*] grief, sadness

خوردن ~ [*~ khor.dan*] [→ خور ~] to grieve, to be sad

غم‌انگیز [*gham-an.giz*] sad (used for inanimates); causing sadness

غم...داشتن [*gha.m-e ... dāsh.tan*] [→ دار ~] to be sad about, to worry about (no *mi-* in pres. and progressive tenses)

غمگین [*gham.gin*] sad (used for people)

غمگین شدن [*gham.gin sho.dan*] [→ شو ~] to become sad

غمگین کردن [*gham.gin kar.dan*] [→ کن ~] to make sad

غنو [*ghe.now*] → ghe.nav → غنودن

غنودن [*gho.nu.dan*] [→ غنو, *ghe.now* → *ghe.nav*] to repose or sleep (*poet.*)

غیر [*gheyr*] other; also used as negating prefix

(به/بـ) غیر از [*(be) ~ az*] except; other than (*prep.*)

(به/بـ) غیر از اینکه [*(be) ~ az in ke*] except that (*conj.*)

غیر انسانی [*ghey.r-e en.sā.ni*] inhuman; inhumane

غیر شخصی [*ghey.r-e shakh.si*] impersonal (gr.); non-personal

غیر لازم [*ghey.r-e lā.zem*] unnecessary

غیر مستقیم [*ghey.r-e mos.ta.ghim*] indirect

غیر ممکن [*ghey.r-e mom.ken*] impossible

غیر واقعی [*ghey.r-e vā.ghe.'i*] unreal

فارس [*fārs*] 1) Fars: a province in Iran; 2) member of the Persian-speaking ethnicity in Iran

فارسی [*fār.si*] Persian (language)

فارغ التّحصیل [*fā.re.gh-ot-tah.sil*] a graduate student [*lit.*, 'free from studies']

فارغ‌التّحصیل شدن [*fā.re.ghot.tah.sil sho.dan*] [→ شو ~] to graduate (from a college)

فاقد [*fā.ghe.d-e*] lacking

فایده [*fā.ye.de*] use, benefit (*pl.* فوائد, *fa.vā.'ed* or فواید, *fa.vā.yed*)

بی‌فایده [*bi- ~*] in vain; useless

فتادن [*fe.tā.dan* or *fo.-*] [→ فت, *fet* or *fot*] shortened poetical version of افتادن

فرار [*fa.rār*] escape; running away

کردن ~ [*~ kar.dan*] [→ کن ~] to run away

فراگرفتن [*fa.rā-ge.ref.tan*] [*farā-* is a prefix; → گیر ~] to learn (*form.*)

فراموش شدن [*fa.rā.mush sho.dan*] [→ شو ~] to be forgotten

فراموش* شدن [*~*] to forget

فراموش کردن [*fa.rā.mush kar.dan*] [→ کن ~] to forget

فرانسه [*fa.rān.se*] France; French language

فراوان [*fa.rā.vān*] a lot of

فرد [fard] individual (pl. افراد, af.rād, individuals, people)

فردا [far.dā] tomorrow

فرسا [far.sā] → فرسودن/فرسائیدن

فرسائیدن [far.sā.'i.dan] [→ فرسا, far.sā] see فرسودن

فرست [fe.rest] → فرستادن

فرستادن [fe.res.tā.dan] [→ فرست, fe.rest] to send

فرستنده [fe.res.tan.de] sender

فرسودن [far.su.dan] [→ فرسا, far.sā] to erode

فرش [farsh] carpet

فرشته [fe.resh.te] angel; girl's name

فرق [fargh] difference

[~ dāsh.tan (bā) داشتن (با) ~]
[→ دار ~] to be different (from)

[~ kar.dan] [→ کن ~] کردن ~ to be or become different

[~ kar.dan (ba.rā.ye)] کردن (برای) ~
[→ کن ~] to make a difference (to)

فرقی نمی‌کند [far.ghi ne.mi.ko.nad] It makes no difference; it doesn't matter.

فرما [far.mā] → فرمودن

فرمان [far.mān] command

فرمانده [far.mān.deh] commander

فرمودن [far.mu.dan] [→ فرما, far.mā] to give a command; for its usage in polite language see Appendix I

فروختن [fo.rukh.tan] [→ فروش, fo.rush] to sell

فرودگاه [fo.rud.gāh] airport

فروش [fo.rush] → فروختن

فروشگاه [fo.rush.gāh] store, shop

فروشنده [fo.ru.shan.de] seller; cashier

فروغ فرخزاد [fo.rugh far.rokh.zād] Forugh Farrokhzād (poet, 1934–67)

فریاد [far.yād] shout; cry; yelling

[~ za.dan] [→ زن ~] زدن ~ to shout; to cry; to exclaim

فریب [fa.rib] [→ فریفتن] deception; deceit

[~ khor.dan] [→ خور ~] خوردن ~ to be deceived

[~ dā.dan] [→ دِه ~] دادن ~ to deceive

فریبا [fa.ri.bā] charming

فریفتن [fa.rif.tan] [→ فریب, fa.rib] to deceive; to spellbind (form.)

فسردن [fe.sor.dan] [→ فسر, fe.sor] see افسردن

فشار [fe.shār] pressure

[~ ā.var.dan (be)] آوردن (به) ~
[→ آور ~] to put pressure (on)

فشار [fe.shār] [→ فشردن] pressure

[~ ā.var.dan (be)] آوردن (به) ~
[→ آور ~] to put pressure on

فشر [fe.shor] → فشردن

فشردن [fe.shor.dan] [→ فشر/فشار, fe.shor/fe.shār] to press; to squeeze (also افشردن, af.shor.dan)

فَصل [fasl] chapter, unit; season (pl. فصول, fo.sul)

فصول [fo.sul] pl. of فصل

فضول [fo.zul] meddler; nosy person

فعل [fe'l] verb (gr.) (pl. افعال, af.'āl)

فعلاً [fe'.lan] for now, for the time being; presently

فقر [faghr] poverty

فقط [fa.ghat] only

نه فقط...بلکه... [na ~ ... bal.ke ...] not only ... but also ...

فکر [fekr] thought (pl. افکار, afkār)

[~ kar.dan] [→ کن ~] فکر کردن to think

بی فکر [bi- ~] thoughtless; inconsiderate

261

فکن [fe.kan] → فکندن

فکندن [fe.kan.dan] [→ فکن, fe.kan]
to throw (poet.); see also افکندن

فلسفه [fal.sa.fe] philosophy

فوائد/فواید [fa.vā.'ed/fa.vā.yed] pl.
of فایده

فوت [fowt] passing away; death
(form.)

فوت کردن [~ kar.dan] [→ کن ~] to
pass away

فوراً [fow.ran] immediately

فهم [fahm] [→ فهمیدن]
understanding

فهمیدن [fah.mi.dan] [→ فهم, fahm] to
understand; to realize (causative:
فهماندن)

فیل [fil] elephant

فیلسوف [fil.suf] philosopher

فیلم [film] film

قابل [ghābel] capable; qualified; fit

قابلِ [~ -e] fit for; worthy of

غیر قابلِ [ghey.r-e ~ -e] unfit for;
incapable of

قابلمه [ghāb.la.me] [cooking] pot

قاتل [ghā.tel] killer, murderer

قادر [ghā.der] capable; able

شدن ~ [~ sho.dan] [→ شو ~]
to become capable (of doing);
to manage (to do)

کردن ~ [~ kar.dan] [→ کن ~] to
enable

قانع [ghā.ne'] contented; satisfied

کردن ~ [~ kar.dan] [→ کن ~] to
persuade; to convince

قانون [ghā.nun] law (pl. قوانین,
gha.vā.nin)

قایق [ghā.yegh] boat

قبل [ghabl] past, last (as in 'last week')
(adj.)

قبل از [~ az] before (prep.)

قبل از آنکه [~ az ān-ke] before (conj.)

قبلاً [ghab.lan] previously (adv.)

قبلی [ghab.li] former; previous; ex-

قبول [gha.bul] acceptance; consent

شو ~ [~ sho.dan] [→ شو ~] شدن (در/از)
to be accepted (in); to pass (a test)

کردن ~ [~ kar.dan] [→ کن ~] to
accept or admit

قبولاندن [gha.bu.lān.dan] [→ قبولان,
gha.bu.lān] to cause to accept;
to convince

قتل [ghatl] murder

قتل عام [ghat.l-e ām] massacre

قدّ [ghadd] (often a person's) height
or stature

بلند ~ [~ bo.land] tall (person)
[neutral in usage]

دراز ~ [~ derāz] tall (person) [not
very flattering!]

قدر [ghadr] amount; quantity; extent;
value; worth

قدیم [gha.dim] old (used with 'years/
times/ages')

در قدیم = in the past

قدیمی [gha.di.mi] old (for inanimates)

قرار [gha.rār] arrangement; agreement;
appointment

باش ~ [~ bu.dan] [→ باش ~] to be
supposed to

دادن ~ [~ dā.dan] [→ ده ~] to place,
to lay (see also قرارداد as
separate entry)

دارِ ~ [~ dāsh.tan] [→ دارِ ~] 1) to
lie, to be located; 2) to have an
appointment

[→گذار ~] [~ go.zāsh.tan]
to make an arrangement or
appointment

گرفتن ~ [→ گیر ~] [~ ge.ref.tan] to
repose, to settle

قرارداد [gha.rār.dad] contract

قربان [ghor.bān] sacrifice

قربانی [ghor.bā.ni] victim

قرص [ghors] pill

قرض [gharz] debt (pl. قروض, gho.ruz)

دادن ~ [~ dā.dan] [→ ده ~] to
borrow; to take as loan

گرفتن ~ [~ ge.ref.tan] [→ گیر ~] to
borrow; to take as loan

قرمز [gher.mez] red

قرن [gharn] century (pl. قرون, gho.run)

قروض [gho.ruz] pl. of قرض

قرون [gho.run] pl. of قرن

قسم [gha.sam] oath; pledge; swear

(به) خوردن ~ [→ خور ~] [~ khor.dan]
to swear; to take an oath

قشنگ [gha.shang] pretty, beautiful

قصد [ghasd] intention

داشتن ~ [~ dāsh.tan] to intend;
to have the intention to

قصّه [ghes.se] story; tale

قطار [gha.tār] train

قطب [ghotb] pole

قَلَم [gha.lam] pen

قم [ghom] Qom or Ghom (city in Iran)

قوانین [gha.vā.nin] pl. of قانون

قورباغه [ghur.bā.ghe] frog; toad

قوری [ghu.ri] teapot

قول [ghowl] promise

دادن ~ [~ dā.dan] [→ ده ~] to promise

قوم [ghowm] folk; ethnic group;
relative (pl. اقوام, agh.vām)

قهوه [ghah.ve] coffee

قهوه‌ای [ghah.ve.'i] brown

قیافه [ghi.yā.fe] features (mostly the
face); appearance or looks

قیمت [ghi.mat/ghey.mat] price

کار (1 → کاشتن; (2 [kār] work, job

کردن ~ [→ کن ~] [~ kar.dan] to
work (intr.); 'to do' in questions
with چه (see چکار)

کاربرد [kār.bord] usage, function (gr.)

کار خانه [kā.r-e khā.ne] household
chores (pl. کارهای خانه)

کارخانه [kār-khā.ne] factory (pl.
کارخانه‌ها)

کارد [kārd] knife

کارگر [kār-gar] worker; labourer

کارگردان [kār-gar.dān] director (in
cinema and theater) (see گرداندن)

کارگردانی [kār-gar.dā.ni] directing

کردن ~ [→ کن ~] [~ kar.dan] to
direct (in cinema and theater)

کارگزینی [kār-go.zi.ni] recruitment office

کاستن [kās.tan] [→ کاه, kāh] to decrease

کاش/کاشکی [kāsh/kāsh.ki] 'if only' or
'I wish'

کاشتن [kāsh.tan] [→ کار, kār] to plant

کاشکی [kāsh.ki] see کاش

کاغذ [kā.ghaz] paper

کافر [kā.far (originally kāfer)]
unbeliever; infidel; pagan (pl.
كُفّار, kof.fār)

کافی [kā.fi] enough; sufficient (adj.)

کامروا [kām-ra.vā] happy (in life)

کالسکه [kā.les.ke] carriage; coach

کامل [kā.mel] perfect (gr.); complete

کاملاً [kā.me.lan] completely

کاویدن [kāv] → کاو

کاویدن [kā.vi.dan] [کاو ←, kāv] to
excavate; to dig; to search (form.)

کاه [kāh] → کاستن

کاهش [kā.hesh] decrease

~ [~ dā.dan] [دِه ←~] to
decrease (tr.)

~ یافتن/پیدا کردن [~ yāf.tan/pey.dā
kar.dan] [یاب/کن ~ ←] to
decrease (intr.)

کباب [ka.bāb] kabab or kebab,
a grilled meat dish

کبریت [keb.rit] matches

کبوتر [ka.bu.tar] dove; pigeon

کت [kot] jacket

کتاب [ke.tāb] book (pl. کتب, ko.tob –
not used in col.)

کتابخانه [ke.tāb-khā.ne] library

کتابخوان [ke.tāb-khān] a bookworm,
one who loves reading

کتابفروش [ke.tāb-fo.rush] book-seller
کتابفروشی [ke.tāb-fo.ru.shi]
1) bookstore; 2) selling books

کتب [ko.tob] pl. of کتاب – not used in col.

کتک [ko.tak] beating, thrashing

~ [~ khor.dan] [خور ←~] خوردن
to be beaten or thrashed (intr.)

~ [~ za.dan] [زن ←~] زدن to beat
or thrash (tr.)

کثیف [ka.sif] dirty

کج [kaj] slanted or crooked, not straight

کجا [ko.jā] where

کجروی [kaj-ra.vi] deviation, aberration

کچل/کل [ka.chal/kal] baldhead

کدام [ko.dām] which?

کرایه [ke.rā.ye] rent

کرد [kord] Kurd

کردن [kar.dan] [کن ←, kon] to do;
to make

کردی [kor.di] Kurdish

کس [kas] person

کسی [ka.si] someone

کسره [kas.re] the -e vowel (gr.); its
symbol

کش [kesh] → کشیدن

کش [kosh] → کشتن

کشتار [kosh.tār] slaughter; butchery;
massacre

کشتن [kosh.tan] [کُش ←, kosh] to kill

کشتی [kesh.ti] ship

کشمکش [kesh-ma-kesh] struggle or
scuffle

کشنده [ko.shan.de] fatal, lethal

کشو [ke.show] drawer

کشور [kesh.var] country

کشیدن [ke.shi.dan] [کِش ←, kesh] to
draw; to pull; to drag (causative:
(کشاندن

کفش [kafsh] shoe

کل [kal] see کچل

کلاس [ke.lās] class; classroom

کلاه [ko.lāh] hat

کلمه [ka.la.me] word (pl. کلمات,
ka.la.māt)

کم [kam] little; few

کمال [ka.māl] perfection

در/با کمالِ [dar/bā ~ -e] with utmost;
at the height of; extremely

کمتر [kam.tar] less; fewer; less often

کمک [ko.mak] help

~ کمک کردن (به) [~ kar.dan (be)]
[کن ~ ←] to help (sometimes
with direct object and no (به

کمی [ká.mi] a little; a few

کمّی [kam.mi] quantitative

کن [kan] → کندن

کن [kon] → کردن

کنارِ [ke.nā.r-e] beside, at the side of (*prep.*)

کندن [kan.dan] [→ کن, kan] to dig; to pull off

کوب [kub] → کوبیدن or کوفتن

کوبیدن [ku.bi.dan] [→ کوب, kub] to pound or hammer, to mash (causative: کوباندن)

کوبیده [ku.bi.de] kubideh (skewer of ground meat kebab)

کوبیسم [ku.bism] Cubism

کوتاه [ku.tāh] short

کوچک [ku.chek] small

کودک [ku.dak] child (*form.*)

کودکانه [ku.da.kā.ne] childish, childlike (*form.*)

کودکستان [ku.da.kes.tān] kindergarten

کور [kur] blind

کوش [kush] → کوشیدن

کوشش [ku.shesh] effort

~ کردن [→ ~ کن] [~ kar.dan] to make an effort; to try

کوشیدن [ku.shi.dan] [→ کوش, kush] to try, to make an effort

کوفتن [kuf.tan] [→ کوب, kub] to pound, to hammer (*lit.*) (causative: کوباندن)

کوفته [kuf.te] kufta, kofta or köfte (ball of ground meat mixed with other ingredients)

کوه [kuh] mountain

از پُشتِ کوه آمدن [az posh.t-e ~ ā.ma.dan] [→ آ ~] to be a churl or simpleton (*lit.*, 'to come from behind the mountains')

کویر [ka.vir] desert

که [ke] that, which (used in noun clauses)

که؟ [ke] who? (*form./wrt.*) (see کی, ki)

کهنه [koh.ne] worn out, used, old (inanimates)

کِی [key] when?

کی [ki] who? (*col.*)

کیش [kish] faith, religion

کیف [kif] bag

کیفِ پول [ki.f-e pul] purse or wallet

کیلو [ki.lu] kilo

گاو [gāv] cow

گاهی [gā.hi] sometimes

گداختن [go.dākh.tan] [→ گداز, godāz] to melt (*lit.*)

گداز [go.dāz] → گداختن

گذار [go.zār] → گذاشتن

گذاشتن [go.zāsh.tan] [→ گذار, go.zār] to put; to leave behind; to let

گذر [go.zar] → گذشتن

گذرا [go.za.rā] fleeting; transient

گذران [go.za.rān] → گذراندن

گذراندن [go.za.rān.dan] [→ گذران, go.za.rān] to spend (time)

گذشتن [go.zash.tan] [→ گذر, go.zar] to pass (causative: گذراندن)

گذشته [go.zash.te] past (*adj.; n.; gr.*)

گرا [ge.rā] → گرویدن or گرائیدن

گرامر [ge.rā.mer] grammar

گران [ge.rān] expensive

گرایش [ge.rā.yesh] inclination

~ داشتن/یافتن (به) [~ dāsh.tan/ yāf.tan (be)] [→ ~ دار/یاب] to be inclined (to)

گرائیدن [ge.rā.'i.dan] [→ گرا, ge.rā] to incline

گربه [gor.be] cat

گرد [gard] → گردیدن or گشتن

گردان [gar.dān] → گرداندن

265

گرداندن/گردانیدن [gar.dān.dan/gar.dā.ni.dan] [→ گردان, gar.dān] to cause to turn; to manage and run an enterprise

گردش [gar.desh] a stroll; a leisurely walk

~ کردن [~ kar.dan] [→ کن ~] to stroll

گردون [gar.dun] firmament; heaven

گردیدن [gar.di.dan] [→ گرد, gard] to turn (= گشتن) (causative: گرداندن)

گرسنگی [go.res.ne.gi] hunger

گرسنه [go.res.ne] hungry

گرفتار [ge.ref.tār] captive, occupied, busy

~ کردن [~ kar.dan] [→ کن ~] to catch or arrest, to entangle, to preoccupy

گرفتاری [ge.ref.tā.ri] captivity, entanglement, trouble

گرفتن [ge.ref.tan] [→ گیر, gir] to take (≠ 'give')

گرم [garm] warm

~ بودن [~* bu.dan] [→ باش ~] to feel warm

گرویدن [ge.ra.vi.dan] [→ گرا, ge.rā] to incline

گره [ge.reh] knot, tie (n.)

گری [ge.ri] → گریستن

گریان [ger.yān] crying, weeping

گریختن [go.rikh.tan] [→ گریز, go.riz] to flee (lit.) (causative: گریزاندن)

گریز [go.riz] → گریختن

گریستن [ge.ris.tan] [→ گری, ge.ri] to cry, to weep (lit.) (causative: گریاندن, ger.yān.dan)

گریه [ger.ye] crying

~ کردن [~ kar.dan] [→ کن ~] to cry, to weep

~ کنان [~ ko.nān] (while) crying

~* گرفتن [~* ge.ref.tan] [→ گیر ~] to have to cry

گز [gaz] → گزیدن [ga.zi.dan]

گزار [go.zār] → گزاردن

گزاردن [go.zār.dan] [→ گزار, gozār] to perform; to carry out (form.)

گزارش [go.zā.resh] report

گزیدن [ga.zi.dan] [→ گز, gaz] to bite; to sting (form./lit.)

گزیدن [go.zi.dan] [→ گزین, go.zin] to choose, to select

گزین [go.zin] → گزیدن

گزینش [go.zi.nesh] selection; choice

گسستن [go.sas.tan] [→ گسل, go.sal] to sever; to disconnect (lit.) (causative: گسلاندن)

گسیختن and گستن → گسل [go.sal]

گسیختن [go.sikh.tan] [→ گسل, go.sal] to sever; to rupture (lit.) (causative: گسلاندن)

گشا [go.shā] → گشودن

گشتن [gash.tan] [→ گرد, gard] to turn; to stroll

دنبال ...گشتن [don.bā.l-e ... ~] to search (for) (causative: گرداندن)

گشودن [go.shu.dan] [→ گشا, go.shā] to open (form.)

گفتار [gof.tār] saying; speech

گفتگو [gof.to.gu] conversation (originally گفت‌وگو)

~ کردن [~ kar.dan] [→ کن ~] to talk (with/about: با/درباره)

گفتن [gof.tan] [→ گو, gu] to say (to = به)

گفتنی [gof.ta.ni] worth saying or
mentioning

گفت و گو [gof.t-o-gu] see گفتگو above

گل [gol] flower

گلدان [gol.dān] vase

گلزار [gol.zār] rose garden

گلِ سرخ [go.l-e sorkh] red rose

گلگون [gol.gun] rosy; rose-like

گم [gom] lost

گم شدن [~ sho.dan] [→ شو ~] to be
lost

گم کردن [~ kar.dan] [→ کن ~] to
lose (sth.)

گمار [go.mār] → گماردن/گماشتن

گماردن/گماشتن [go.mār.dan/go.māsh.tan]
[→ گمار, go.mār] to appoint
(form.)

گمان [ga.mān (form.: go.mān)]
assumption

کردن ~ [~ kar.dan] [→ کن ~] to
assume; to suppose; to guess

گنج [gonj] → گنجیدن

گنجیدن [gon.ji.dan] [→ گنج, gonj] to
fit in; to be contained (causative:
گنجاندن) (form.)

گند [gand] → گندیدن

گندیدن [gan.di.dan] [→ گند, gand] to rot

گو [gu] → گفتن

گوار [go.vār] → گواردن/گواریدن

گواردن/گواریدن [go.vār.dan/
go.vā.ri.dan] [→ گوار, go.vār]
to digest

گوسفند [gus.fand] sheep

گوش [gush] ear

(به) کردن ~ [~ kar.dan (be)]
[→ کن ~] to listen to (used with
direct or indirect object)

گوشت [gusht] meat

گوشی [gu.shi] receiver (of a phone)

گوناگون [gu.nā.gun] diverse; different
(form.)

گونه [gu.ne] kind, type (form.); cheek

گوینده [gu.yan.de] announcer; speaker
or sayer of sth.

گوئی/گویی (که) [gu.'i (ke)] as if, as
though (form.)

گیج [gij] giddy or dizzy; confused; silly

سر* گیج رفتن [sar* gij raf.tan]
[→ رو ~] to feel dizzy or giddy

گیر [gir] → گرفتن

گیرا [gi.rā] attractive; catching

گیرنده [gi.ran.de] receiver

لازم [lā.zem] necessary; intransitive (gr.)

داشتن ~ [~ dāsh.tan] [→ دار ~] to need

لاغر [lā.ghar] thin, slim

لاغر شدن ~ [lā.ghar sho.dan] [→ شو ~]
to lose weight

لایق [lā.yegh] deserving; worthy; capable

بودن ~ [~ bu.dan] [→ باش ~] to
deserve; to be worthy of

لب [lab] lip (pl. with both -hā and -ān)

لباس [le.bās] clothes (in general); dress
(pl. البسه, al.ba.se; only form.)

لباسِ شنا ~ [~ -e she.nā] swimsuit

لبخند [lab.khand] smile

زدن ~ [~ za.dan] [→ زن ~] to smile

لبه [la.be] edge

لذّت [lez.zat/laz.zat] enjoyment,
pleasure (pl. لذّات, laz.zāt)

بَردن (از) ~ [~ bor.dan (az)] [→ بَر ~]
to enjoy ['get pleasure from']

لرز [larz] → لرزیدن

لرزان [lar.zān] trembling

لرزیدن [lar.zi.dan] [→ لرز, larz] to
tremble (causative: لرزاندن)

لزوم [lo.zum] necessity

لشکر [lash.kar] army

لطف [lotf] benevolence

لطفاً [lot.fan] please (adv., used with imperative)

لعل [la'l] ruby

لغز [laghz] → لغزیدن

لغزیدن [lagh.zi.dan] [→ لغز, laghz] to slip or slide (causative: لغزاندن)

لم [lam] → لمیدن

لمیدن [la.mi.dan] [→ لم, lam] to recline

لندن [lan.dan] London

لنگ [lang] [→ لنگیدن] lame

لنگان [langān] limping (also لنگ لنگان [lang-langān] or لنگان لنگان)

لنگیدن [lan.gi.dan] [→ لنگ, lang] to limp

لهجه [lah.je] accent, dialect

لیاقت [li.yā.ghat] merit; worthiness; capability

[→ دار ~, dāsh.tan] [~ داشتن] to deserve; to be worthy of

لیوان [li.vān] glass (for drinks); mug

ما [mā] we

مادَر [mā.dar] mother

مادربزرگ [mā.dar-bo.zorg] grandmother

مار [mār] snake

ماست [māst] yoghurt

ماشین [mā.shin] car; machine

ماضی [mā.zi] past (gr.)

ماضی بعید [~ -ye ba.'id] past perfect tense ('remote past')

ماضی مطلق [~ -ye mot.lagh] simple past tense ('absolute past')

ماضی نقلی [~ -ye nagh.li] present perfect tense ('narrative past')

مالیدن → مال

مال [māl] property, wealth (pl. اموال, am.vāl)

مالِ [~ -e] property of, belonging to

مالِ کی؟ [mā.l-e ki] whose?

مالی [mā.li] financial

مالیدن [mā.li.dan] [→ مال, māl] to rub (causative: مالاندن)

مأمورِ پلیس [ma'.mu.r-e po.lis] policeman

مان [mān] → ماندن ; also → مانستن

ماندن [mān.dan] [→ مان, mān] to stay, to remain

ماندنی [mān.da.ni] lasting

مانستن (به) [mā.nes.tan (be)] [→ مان, mān] to be similar to; to resemble

مانندِ [mā.nan.d-e] like; similar to (form.)

ماه [māh] month; moon

ماهانه [mā.hā.ne] monthly (also ماهیانه, mā.hi.yā.ne)

ماهر [mā.her] skilled

ماهی [mā.hi] fish

ماهیگیر [mā.hi.gir] fisher

مبدّل [mo.bad.dal] changed

متأسّف [mo.te.'as.sef] sorry, regretful

متأسفانه [mo.te.'as.se.fā.ne] regrettably, unfortunately

متر [metr] meter

متعدی [mo.te.'ad.di] transitive (gr.)

متفاوت [mo.te.fā.vet] different

متوجّه شدن [mo.te.vaj.jeh sho.dan] [~ شو →] to notice

مثال [me.sāl] example

مثلِ [mes.l-e] like, similar to

مثل هم [mes.l-e ham] alike; in the same way

درست مثلِ [do.rost mes.l-e] exactly like

مُجاز [mo.jāz] permissible; officially
authorized

~ کردن [~ kar.dan] [→ ~ کن] to
authorize [officially]; to legalize

مجبور [maj.bur] compelled; forced

~ بودن [~ bu.dan] [→ ~ باش] to be
compelled to; to have to

~ شدن [~ sho.dan] [→ ~ شو] to be
compelled or forced

~ مجبور کردن [~ kar.dan] [کن ~ →]
to force; to compel

مجلس [maj.les] parliament (pl. مجالس,
ma.jā.les)

مجهول [maj.hul] passive (gr.);
unknown

محاوره [mo.hā.ve.re] conversation

محترم [moh.ta.ram] respected; respectful

محترمانه [moh.ta.ra.mā.ne] respectfully

محروم [mah.rum] deprived

(از) ~ کردن [~ kar.dan (be)]
[→ ~ کن] to deprive

محله [ma.hal.le] neighborhood (pl.
محلات , ma.hal.lāt)

محمّد [mo.ham.mad] prophet of Islam;
boy's name

مختلف [mokh.ta.lef] different

مخصوصاً [makh.su.san] especially

مِداد [me.dād] pencil

مداد تراش [me.dād ta.rāsh]
pencil sharpener

مدارس [ma.dā.res] pl. of مدرسه

مدافع [mo.dā.fe'] defending; defensive

مدّت [mod.dat] duration; period

مدرسه [mad.re.se] school (below a
college) (pl. مدارس , ma.dā.res)

مراتب [ma.rā.teb] pl. of مرتبه

مراسم [ma.rā.sem] ceremony
(originally pl. of مرسوم , marsum)

مربوط [mar.but] related

مرتبه [mar.te.be/mar.ta.be] 'time' as
counting word (pl. مراتب,
ma.rā.teb)

مرخّص [mo.rakh.khas] released (for
its usage in polite language see
Appendix I)

مرد [mard] man

مَردانه [mar.dā.ne] manly, masculine, of
men or men's

مردم [mar.dom] people

مردن [mor.dan] [→ میر , mir] to die

مردنی [mor.da.ni] feeble, weak; about
to die

مرده [mor.de] dead

مرسوم [mar.sum] custom or customary
(adj.) (pl. مراسم , ma.rā.sem =
ceremony)

مرغ [morgh] hen; chicken (as food);
bird

مرغابی [mor.ghā.bi] duck

مرکّب [mo.rak.kab] complex (gr.);
compound, multipart; ink

مرگ [marg] death

مرور [mo.rur] review

~ کردن [~ kar.dan] [→ ~ کن] to
review

مریض [ma.riz] sick (adj.); sick person,
patient (n.)

مریم [mar.yam] Maryam (= Miriam,
Mary)

مسائل [ma.sā.'el] pl. of مسئله

مساعی [ma.sā.'i] pl. of سعی

مسافرت [mo.sā.fe.rat] travel, journey (n.)

به مسافرت رفتن [be ~ raf.tan]
[→ ~ رو] to go on a trip

~ کردن (به) [~ kar.dan (be)]
[→ ~ کن] to travel (to)

مستحضر [mos.tah.zar] aware; informed (form., polite language)

مستقیم [mos.ta.ghim] direct, straight

مسلمان [mo.sal.mān] Muslim, Moslem

مسواک [mes.vāk] toothbrush

مسواک زدن [mes.vāk za.dan] [← زن ~] to brush (the teeth)

مسئله [mas.'a.le] problem (pl. مسائل, ma.sā.'el)

مسئول [mas.'ul] responsible; in charge

مسئولانه [mas'ulāne] responsible, responsibly

غیرِ مسئولانه [gheyr-e- ~] irresponsible, irresponsibly

مسئولیّت [mas.'u.liy.yat] responsibility

مشابه [mo.shā.beh] alike; similar (add ezāfe for 'similar to')

مشابهت [mo.shā.be.hat] similarity

مشاغل [ma.shā.ghel] pl. of شغل

مشاهیر [ma.shā.hir] pl. of مشهور

مشروط [mash.rut] conditioned

به آنکه/بر آنکه ~ [~ be ān ke/bar ān ke] on the condition that; provided that

مشکل [mosh.kel] difficult (adj.); problem (n., pl. مشکلات, mosh.ke.lāt)

مشکل‌آفرین [mosh.kel-ā.fa.rin] problematic; creating problems

مشهد [mash.had] Mashhad (city in Iran)

مشهور [mash.hur] famous (pl. مشاهیر, ma.shā.hir)

مصاحبه [mo.sā.he.be] interview

مَصدَر [mas.dar] infinitive (gr.)

مصدّق [mo.sad.degh] (Mohammad) Mosaddegh, PM of Iran (1951–53)

مصر [mesr] Egypt

مضارع [mo.zā.re'] present tense (gr.)

مضاعف [mo.zā.'af] double

مطالعه [mo.tā.le.'e] studying; consideration; reading (pl. مطالعات, mo.tā.le.'āt)

مطبوع [mat.bu'] pleasant (an obsolete meaning is 'printed matter')

مطبوعات [mat.bu.'āt] the press (pl. of مطبوع, mat.bu')

مطّلع [mot.ta.le'] well-informed; knowledgeable; up-to-date

بودن (از) ~ [~ bu.dan (az)] [← باش ~] to know (about/of)

کردن ~ [~ kar.dan] [← کن ~] to inform; to let know

مطمئن [mot.ma.'en] sure, certain

معادل [mo.'ā.del] equivalent

معاصر [mo.'ā.ser] contemporary

معالجه [mo.'ā.le.je] cure; treatment; healing (pl. معالجات, mo.'ā.le.jāt)

کردن ~ [~ kar.dan] [← کن ~] to cure; to treat; to heal

معانی [ma.'ā.ni] pl. of معنی

معایب [ma.'ā.yeb] pl. of عیب

معدنکار [ma'.dan-kār] miner, mine worker

معذلک [ma.'a.zā.lek] nonetheless

معهذا [ma.'a.hā.zā] nonetheless

معرفه [ma'.re.fe] definite (gr.)

معرّفی [mo.'ar.re.fi] introducing

کردن (به) ~ [~ kar.dan (be)] [← کن ~] to introduce (to)

معروف [ma'.ruf] famous

معشوق [ma'.shugh] beloved (masc.)

معشوقه [ma'.shu.ghe] mistress; beloved (fem.)

معلّم [mo.'al.lem] teacher

معلوم [ma'.lum] obvious, clear, known

معمولاً [ma'.mu.lan] usually

معنی [ma'.ni] meaning; also معنا [ma'.nā] (pl. معانی ma.'ā.ni)

مفعول [maf.'ul] object (gr.)

مفعولی [maf.'u.li] objective (gr.)

مغازه [ma.ghā.ze] shop, store

مُفرَد [mof.rad] singular (gr.)

مفعول [maf.'ul] object (gr.)

مفید [mo.fid] useful

مقابلِ [mo.ghā.be.l-e] in front of; opposite

مقادیر [ma.ghā.dir] pl. of مقدار

مقاله [ma.ghā.le] article (pl. مقالات, ma.ghā.lāt)

مقام [ma.ghām] status; position

در مقام [dar ~ -e] as; in the position of

مقایَسه [mo.ghā.ye.se] comparison

مقدار [megh.dār] amount (pl. مقادیر, ma.ghā.dir)

مقداری [megh.dā.ri] some amount of

مقصود [magh.sud] purpose; intention

مک [mek or mak] → مکیدن

مکیدن [me.ki.dan (form.: ma.-)] [→ مک, mek or mak] to suck

مگر [má.gar] unless; except that (conj.); except (prep.)

ملّا [mol.lā] mullah

ملاقات [mo.lā.ghāt] visit; meeting
(با) کردن ~ [~ kar.dan (bā)] [→ کن ~] to visit; to meet

مِلک [melk] property

مِلکی [mel.ki] possessive

ممکن [mom.ken] possible; likely

ممنوع [mam.nu'] forbidden
کردن ~ [~ kar.dan (be)] [→ کن ~] to forbid

من [man] I (pr., 1sg.)

مناسب [mo.nā.seb] appropriate, suitable

منتظر [mon.ta.zer] waiting
منتظرِ [~ -e] waiting for

منجر شدن (به) [mon.jar sho.dan (be)] [→ شو ~] to lead to; to result in

منظور [man.zur] purpose; aim

منع [man'] prohibition
(از) کردن ~ [~ kar.dan (az)] [→ کن ~] to prohibit; to bar

موارد [ma.vā.red] pl. of مورد

مواظب [mo.vā.zeb] watchful, alert
بودن ~ [~ bu.dan] [→ باش ~] to be careful (intr.)

مواظبِ...بودن [~ -e ... bu.dan] [→ باش ~] to watch over, to look after; keep an eye on

موافق [mo.vā.fegh] in agreement; of one mind; in accord

موافقت [mo.vā.fe.ghat] agreement; consent
کردن ~ [~ kar.dan] [→ کن ~] to agree; to consent

مواقع [ma.vā.ghe'] pl. of موقع

موتور [mo.tor] engine; motor

موجب [mow.jeb] causing, necessitating
موجب شدن/موجبِ...شدن (e-) ~ [sho.dan] [→ شو ~] to cause

مورد [mow.red] case; instance (pl. موارد, ma.vā.red)

در موردِ [dar ~ -e] about; concerning; in the case of

موردِ [~ -e] object of; subjected to

موردِ ...قرار گرفتن/واقع شدن ...e- ~ [gha.rār ge.ref.tan/vā.ghe' sho.dan] [→ گیر/شو ~] to undergo; to become the object of; to be subjected to

موزه [mu.ze] museum

موسی [mu.sā] Moses

موسیقی [mu.si.ghi] music

موش [mush] mouse

موضوع [mow.zu'] subject; issue;
matter; topic (pl. موضوعات,
mow.zu.'āt)

موفّق [mo.vaf.fagh] successful

شدن [~ sho.dan] [→ شو ~] to
succeed; to manage to

موقع [mow.ghe'] time (pl. مواقع,
ma.vā.ghe')

بموقع/به موقع [be-mow.ghe'] on time

موقعی که [mow.ghe.'i ke] when
(conj.); also written joined:
موقعیکه

مولوی [mow.la.vi] Rumi (poet, 1207–73)

مهربان [meh.ra.bān] kind (adj.)

مهربانی [meh.ra.bā.ni] kindness

مهمّ [mo.hemm] important

مهمان [meh.mān] guest

مهمانی [meh.mā.ni] party

میانِ [mi.yā.n-e] in the middle of; inside

می‌باید/می‌بایست/می‌بایستی [mi-bāyad/
mi-bāyest/mi-bāyesti]
باید →

میر [mir] → مردن

میز [miz] table

میل [meyl] wish; inclination (for its
usage in polite language see
Appendix I)

میلیون [mil.yon] million

مینا [mi.nā] Mina (girl's name)

میوه [mi.ve] fruit

ناامید [nā-o.mid] hopeless

ناامیدانه [nā-o.mi.dā.ne] hopeless;
hopelessly

نابود کردن [nā.bud kar.dan] [→ کن ~]
to annihilate, to destroy; to cause
to become extinct or nonexistent

ناتوان [nā.ta.vān] incapable

ناچار [nā.chār] inevitable; unavoidable

ناچیز [nā.chiz] insignificant, worthless

نادان [nā-dān] ignorant; stupid

نادرست [nā.do.rost] incorrect

ناراحت [nā.rā.hat] uncomfortable;
upset; sad

ناسالم [nā-sā.lem] unhealthy; harmful

ناصر [nā.ser] Naser; boy's name

ناقص [nā.ghes] incomplete; not whole;
deficient or defective

ناگهان [nā.ga.hān] suddenly

نال [nāl] → نالیدن

نالیدن [nā.li.dan] [→ نال, nāl] to moan;
to lament

نام [nām] [→ نامیدن] name (more
formal than اسم, esm)

نامعلوم [nā-ma'.lum] unclear, unknown
(see معلوم)

ناممکن [nā-mom.ken] impossible (form.)

نامه [nā.me] letter

نامه‌رسان [nā.me-re.sān] mailperson

نامهربان [nā.meh.ra.bān] unkind

نامیدن [nā.mi.dan] [→ نام, nām] to name

نپخته [na.pokh.te] → پختن

نتایج [na.tā.yej] pl. of نتیجه

نتیجه [na.ti.je] result (pl. نتایج, na.tā.yej)

در نتیجه [dar ~] as a result

نترس [na-tars] fearless (see ترس)

نجات [ne.jāt] rescue

دادن ~ [~ dā.dan] [→ دِه ~] to
rescue; to save

پیدا کردن/یافتن ~ [~ pey.dā kar.dan/
yāf.tan] [→ کن/یاب ~] to be
rescued

نجوم [no.jum] astrology (originally
pl. of the Arabic نجم [najm],
star)

نجیب [na.jib] noble; gentle; honest

نخست [no.khost] first (1st)

نخستین [no.khos.tin] first (1st)

نخود [no.khod] chickpea

نخیر [na.kheyr] no (polite)

ندا [ne.dā] call

ندائی [ne.dā.'i] vocative (gr.) (also
written ندایی)

نَزدیک [naz.dik] near (adj.)

نَزدیکِ [~ -e] near (prep.)

[→ باش ~] [~ bu.dan ke] بودن که ~
to be about to

[→ شو ~] [~ sho.dan] شدن ~ to
approach, to come near

نسبتاً [nes.ba.tan] relatively

نسخه [nos.khe] copy; manuscript;
a doctor's prescription

نشان [ne.shān] → نشاندن

نشان دادن (به) [ne.shān dā.dan (be)]
[→ ده ~] to show (sth. to so.)

نشاندن [ne.shān.dan] [→ نشان, ne.shān]
to cause to sit

نشانه [ne.shā.ne] sign

نشست [ne.shast] session

نشستن [ne.shas.tan] [→ نشین, ne.shin]
to sit (causative: نشاندن)

نشین [ne.shin] → نشستن

نصایح [na.sā.yeh] pl. of نصیحت

نصف [nesf] half

نصیحت [na.si.hat] advice (pl. نصایح,
na.sā.yeh)

[→ کن ~] [~ kar.dan] کردن ~ to
advise (with direct object or
with به)

نظر [na.zar] view, opinion (pl. نظرات,
na.za.rāt)

[be ~] به نظر آمدن/به نظر رسیدن
ā.ma.dan/re.si.dan] [→ آ/رس ~]
to look, to appear, to seem

در نظر داشتن [dar na.zar dāsh.tan]
[→ دار ~] to be set to; to have it
in mind; to intend

تحتِ نظر [tah.t-e ~] under surveillance

موردِ نظر [mow.re.d-e ~] intended

اظهارِ نظر کردن [ez.hā.r-e ~ kar.dan]
[→ کن ~] to express one's view

نفر [na.far] person (only as counting
word) (pl. نفرات, na.fa.rāt)

نفرت [nef.rat] hatred

[~ داشتن (از)] [~ dāsh.tan (az)]
[→ دار ~] to hate

نفرت‌انگیز [nef.rat-an.giz] hateful;
revolting

نفس [na.fas] breath

[→ کش ~] [~ ke.shi.dan] کشیدن ~
to breathe

نفهم [na-fahm] stupid,
uncomprehending (see فهم)

نفی [nafy; y here is a consonant]
negation

نقل [naghl] conveying; transfer;
narrating; quotation

نقلِ قول [naghl-e ghowl] indirect (or
reported) speech (gr.); citation,
quotation

نکته [nok.te] point (as 'a point made');
epigram (pl. نکات, no.kāt/ne.kāt)

نکره [na.ka.re] indefinite (gr.)

نکوه [ne.kuh] → نکوهیدن

نکوهش [ne.ku.hesh] blame; reproach
[→ کن ~] [~ kar.dan] کردن ~ to
blame; to reproach

نکوهیدن [ne.ku.hi.dan] [→ نکوه,
ne.kuh] to blame; to reproach
(form.)

نگاشتن ← [ne.gār] نگار

نگاشتن [ne.gāsh.tan] [→ نگار, ne.gār]
to paint; to write (lit.)

نگاه [ne.gāh] look; gaze

~ کردن [~ kar.dan] [→ کن ~] to
watch

~ کردن به [~ kar.dan be] [→ کن ~]
to look at

نگران [ne.ga.rān] worried, concerned,
anxious

~ بودن [~ bu.dan] [→ باش ~] to
worry

نگریستن [ne.ga.ris.tan] [→ نگر, ne.gar]
to look

نگه داشتن [ne.gah dāsh.tan] [→ دار ~]
to keep (+ mi- in pres. and
progressive tenses)

نما ← [no.mā] نمودن

نمایش [na.mā.yesh/no.-] a play;
showing or presenting

~ دادن [~ dā.dan] [→ دِه ~] to show;
to present

نماینده [na.mā.yan.de/no.-]
representative

نمره [nom.re] grade (at school);
number

نمودن [no.mu.dan] [→ نما, no.mā] to
show; to appear; used also as a
weak substitute for کردن in wrt.
(not recommended)

نو [now] new

از نو [az now] anew; again

نواختن ← [na.vāz] نواز

نواختن [na.vākh.tan] [→ نواز, na.vāz]
to play an instrument; to strike
(form.)

نود [na.vad] ninety

نوزده [nuz.dah] nineteen

نوشیدن ← [nush] نوش

نوشتن [ne.vesh.tan] [→ نویس, nevis]
to write

نوشیدن [nu.shi.dan] [→ نوش, nush]
to drink

نوشیدنی [nu.shi.da.ni] drink

نوه [na.ve] grandchild

نوشتن ← [ne.vis] نویس

نویسنده [ne.vi.san.de] writer

نه [noh] nine (9)

نه [na] no

نه...نه... [na...na...] neither...nor...

نهادن ← [nah] نه

نهادن [na.hā.dan] [→ نه, nah] to lay;
to put (form.)

نهایت [nahāyat] end; extremity

در/با نهایتِ [dar/bā ~ -e] with
utmost; at the height of

نهصد [noh.sad] nine hundred

نهفتن [na.hof.tan] [only past tense; lit.]
to hide

نهفته [na.hof.te] hidden (lit.)

نی [ney] reed; traditional Iranian flute

نیّت [niy.yat] desire; objective

نیرو [ni.ru] power

نیرومند [ni.ru.mand] powerful

نیز [niz] also (form.)

نیش زدن [nish za.dan] [→ نیش ~] to
sting or bite (used for insects or
snakes)

نیک [nik] good (form.)

نیم [nim] half (used especially for
half-hours)

نیما [ni.mā] Nima; boy's name

نیمکت [nim.kat] bench

نیمه [ni.me] half

نیویورک [ni.yo.york] New York

وَ [va/-o] and

واپسین [vā.pa.sin] last (adj.; lit.)

وارد شدن [→ شو] [vā.red sho.dan] to enter

واقع [vā.ghe'] real; reality (seldom used alone; واقعیت and واقعی are more common)

در ~ [dar ~] in fact; as a matter of fact

بودن ~ [~ bu.dan] [→ باش ~] to be located (form.)

شدن ~ [~ sho.dan] [→ شو ~] to happen; to be subjected to (form.)

واقعاً [vā.ghe.'an] really

واقعگرا [vā.ghe'-ge.rā] realist

واقعگرائی [vā.ghe'-ge.rā.'i] realism

واقعی [vā.ghe.'i] real

واقعیّت [vā.ghe.'iy.yat] reality (pl. واقعیّات, vā.ghe.'iy.yāt)

والدین [vā.le.deyn] parents

وجود [vo.jud] existence

داشتن ~ [~ dāsh.tan] [→ دار, ~] to exist

با وجودِ [bā ~ -e] in spite of

وجه [vajh] mode (gr.)

وحشی [vah.shi] wild; barbarous

وحشیانه [vah.shi.yā.ne] savagely; brutally; wildly

ورز [varz] → ورزیدن

ورزش [var.zesh] sport, exercise

کردن ~ [~ kar.dan] [→ کن ~] to exercise [sports] (intr.)

ورزیدن [var.zi.dan] [→ ورز, varz] to exercise; to cherish (form.)

ورود [vo.rud] arrival

وسائل/وسایل [vA.sā.'el/va.sā.yel] pl. of وسیله

وسیله [va.si.le] means; instrument (pl. وسائل, va.sā.'el, or وسایل, va.sā.yel)

نقلیّه ~ -ye [~ -ye nagh.liy.ye] means of transport; vehicle

وضع [vaz'] situation (pl. اوضاع, ow.zā')

وطن [va.tan] homeland

وطن‌فروش [va.tan-fo.rush] traitor [to one's country]

وقت [vaght] time (pl. اوقات, ow.ghāt)

وقتی (که) [vagh.ti (ke)] when (conj.); also written joined: وقتیکه

وکلا [vo.ka.lā] pl. of وکیل

وکیل [va.kil] lawyer, attorney; deputy (pl. وکلا, vo.ka.lā)

مجلس e ~ [~ -e maj.les] member of parliament

مدافع ~ [~ mo.dā.fe'] lawyer, defending attorney

وگرنه [va gar ná] otherwise, if not so

ولی [va.li] but (conj.)

ویرایش [vi.rā.yesh] editing

کردن ~ [~ kar.dan] [→ کن ~] to edit

ویزا گرفتن [vi.zā ge.ref.tan] [→ گیر ~] to get a visa

هاروارد [hār.vārd] Harvard

های و هو [hā.y-o-hu] fuss; hubbub; ranting; ado

هتل [ho.tel] hotel

هجده [hej.dah] eighteen

هدف [ha.daf] goal; target; objective; cause (pl. اهداف, ah.dāf)

هدایا [ha.dā.yā] pl. of هدیه

هدیه [hed.ye] gift, present (pl. هدایا, ha.dā.yā)

هر [har] every

هراس [ha.rās] → هراسیدن fear

هراسیدن [ha.rā.si.dan] [→ هراس, ha.rās] to fear (causative: هراساندن)

هر چقدر [*har che.ghadr*] however much

هرچه [*har-che*] whatever; however much

هرچه بادا باد! [*har.che bā.dā bād*]
Come what may! Whatever will
be, will be!

[~ *zud.tar*] هرچه زودتر as soon as
possible

هر دو [*har do*] both

هر روز [*har ruz*] everyday

هر قدر [*har ghadr*] however much

هرگز [*har.gez*] never (*form.*)

هزار [*he.zār*] thousand

هزاران [*he.zā.rān*] thousands of

هشت [*hasht*] eight (8)

هشتاد [*hash.tād*] eighty

هشتصد [*hasht.sad*] eight hundred

هفت [*haft*] seven (7)

هفتاد [*haf.tād*] seventy

هفتصد [*haft.sad*] seven hundred

هفته [*haf.te*] week

هفده [*hef.dah*] seventeen

هم [*ham*] too; also

هم... هم... [*ham . . . ham . . .*]
both . . . and . . .

همان [*ha.mān*] the same; that same

همانجا [*ha.mān.jā*] right there

همانطور/همان‌طور [*ha.mān towr*] in the
same way

همانطور که [~ *ke*] as; while

همانند [*ha.mā.nand*] alike; the same
(*form./lit.*)

همانندِ [~ -*e*] like; similar to

همچنان [*ham.che.nān*] still (*lit.*)

همچنانکه/همچنان که [~ *ke*] as; while
(*form.*)

همچنین [*ham.che.nin*] also (*form.*)

همچون [*ham-chon*] similar to, like (*lit.*)

همدیگر [*ham-di.gar*] each other

همراه با [*ham.rāh bā*] together with

همسان [*ham.sān*] alike; similar
(*form./lit.*)

همسایه [*ham.sā.ye*] neighbor

همسر [*ham.sar*] spouse; wife or
husband [polite language]

همکار [*ham.kār*] colleague; co-worker

همکلاسی [*ham-ke.lā.si*] classmate

همگان [*ha.me.gān*] everybody (*poet.*)

همه [*ha.me*] all; everybody

همه جا [*ha.me jā*] everywhere

همه چیز [*ha.me chiz*] everything

همه کس [*ha.me kas*] everyone

همیشه [*ha.mi.she*] always

همین [*ha.min*] this same

همین که [~ *ke*] as soon as

همینطور/همین‌طور [*ha.min towr*] in the
same way; also

همینطور که [~ *ke*] as; while

همینجا [*ha.min.jā*] right here

همینکه [*ha.min-ke*] as soon as

هند [*hend*] India (also هندوستان,
hendustān)

هندوانه [*hen.de.vā.ne*] watermelon

هندوستان [*hendustān*] → هند

هندی [*hen.di*] Indian

هنر [*ho.nar*] art; craft; skill

هنرپیشه [*ho.nar-pi.she*] actor or actress

هنگام [*hen.gām/han.gām*] time (*lit.*)

هنگامی که [*hen.gā.mi/han.gā.mi ke*]
(*lit.*) when (*conj.*); also written
joined: هنگامیکه

هنوز [*ha.nuz*] still [*adv.*]; yet (in *neg.*)

هوا [*ha.vā*] weather; air

هواپیما [*ha.vā-pey.mā*] airplane

هوش [hush] intelligence

باهوش [bā- ~] intelligent

هیچ [hich] none; nothing; at all

هیچ‌چیز [hich-chiz] nothing

هیچ‌جا [hich-jā] nowhere

هیچ‌کجا [hich-ko.jā] nowhere

هیچ‌کدام [hich-ko.dām] none (of)/ neither (of)

هیچ‌کس [hich-kas] no one, nobody

هیچ‌گاه [hich-gāh] never (form./lit.)

هیچ‌گونه [hich-gu.ne] not of any sort/at all (form./lit.)

هیچ‌وقت [hich-vaght] never

هیچیک [hich-yek] none (of)/neither (of)

یا [yā] or (conj.)

یا ... یا ... [yā ... yā ...] either ... or ...

یاء نسبت [yā.'e nes.bat] attributive 'ی' or stressed -i suffix

یاب [yāb] → یافتن

یاد [yād] memory

به یاد ماندنی [be yād mān.da.ni] memorable

(به) یاد* آمدن [(be) yād* ā.ma.dan] [~ آ ~ →] to occur to, to come to mind, to remember

(به) یاد آوردن [be yād ā.var.dan] [~ آور →] to remember, to bring (back) to mind

یادآور شدن [yād-ā.var sho.dan] [~ شو →] to mention

(به) یادِ ... افتادن [(be) yā.d-e ... of.tā.dan] [~ افت →] to be reminded (of)

(به) یاد* افتادن [(be) yād* of.tā.dan] [~ افت →] to occur to, to come to mind

(به) یادِ ... انداختن [(be) yā.d-e ... an.dākh.tan] [~ انداز →] to remind (of)

(از) یاد بُردن [az yād bor.dan] [~ بَر →] to forget

(به) یاد* بودن [(be) yād* bu.dan] [~ باش →] to remember

یاد دادن (به) [yād dā.dan (be)] [~ ده →] to teach (sth. to so.)

(از) یاد رفتن [az yād raf.tan] [~ رو →] to be forgotten

(از) یاد* رفتن [~] to forget

از یاد نرفتنی [az yād na-raf.ta.ni] unforgettable

(به) یاد سپردن [be yād se.por.dan] [~ سپر/سپار →] to commit to memory

یاد کردن (از) [yād kar.dan (az)] [~ کن →] to mention

یاد گرفتن (از) [yād ge.ref.tan (az)] [~ گیر →] to learn (sth. from so.)

یازده [yāz.dah] eleven

یافتن [yāf.tan] [یاب →, yāb] to find

یخ [yakh] ice

یخچال [yakh.chāl] refrigerator, fridge

یعنی [ya'.ni] meaning; it means; i.e.

یک [yek] one (1)

یکی [ye.ki] someone; one

یکی از [ye.ki az] one of

یکدیگر [yek-di.gar] one another; each other

یکسان [yek.sān] alike; similar (form.)

یکشنبه [yek-sham.be] Sunday

INDEX